The Fujifilm X-T5

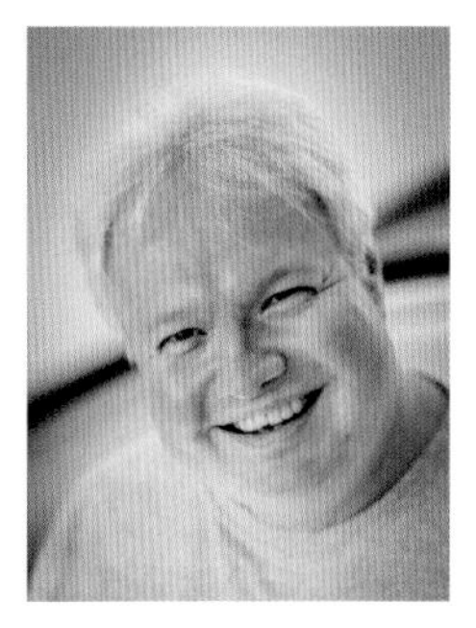

Rico Pfirstinger studied communications and has been working as a journalist, publicist, and photographer since the mid-'80s. He has written numerous books on a diverse range of topics, from computing technology to digital desktop publishing to sled dog racing. He worked as the department head of special assignments for Hubert Burda Media in Munich, Germany, and he also served as chief editor for a winter sports website.

After eight years as a freelance film critic in Los Angeles, Rico now lives in Germany and devotes his time to digital photography and compact camera systems.

Rico writes the popular X-Pert Corner blog and leads workshops called Fuji X Secrets where he offers insights, tips, and tricks on using the Fujifilm X-series cameras. He is also a regular contributor in the Gear Talk section of *FUJI-LOVE* magazine.

Rico Pfirstinger

The Fujifilm X-T5

134 X-Pert Tips to Get the Most
Out of Your Camera

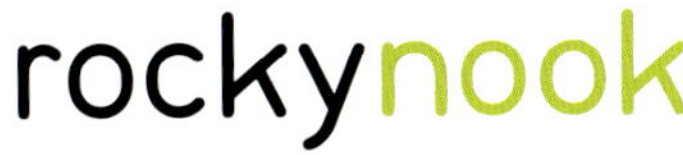

The Fujifilm X-T5
134 Tips to Get the Most Out of Your Camera
Rico Pfirstinger

Project editor: Maggie Yates
Project manager: Lisa Brazieal
Marketing coordinator: Katie Walker
Layout and type: Petra Strauch

ISBN: 979-8-88814-021-5
1st Edition (1st printing, November 2023)
©2024 Rico Pfirstinger
All images ©Rico Pfirstinger unless otherwise noted

Rocky Nook Inc.
1010 B Street, Suite 350
San Rafael, CA 94901
USA

www.rockynook.com

Distributed in the UK and Europe by Publishers Group UK
Distributed in the U.S. and all other territories by Publishers Group West

Library of Congress Control Number: 2023933372

Printed in Korea

Table of Contents

1. YOUR X-T5 SYSTEM

To start off, here's a brief overview of the buttons and controls on your Fujifilm X-T5:

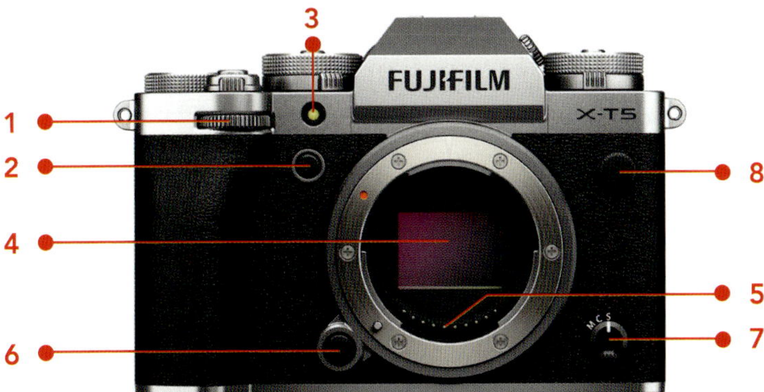

Fig. 1: X-T5 front view: front command dial with integrated button (1), Fn button (2), AF assist lamp/self-timer indicator lamp (3), X-Trans sensor (4), electronic lens contacts (5), lens release button (6), focus selector (7), flash sync connector (8)

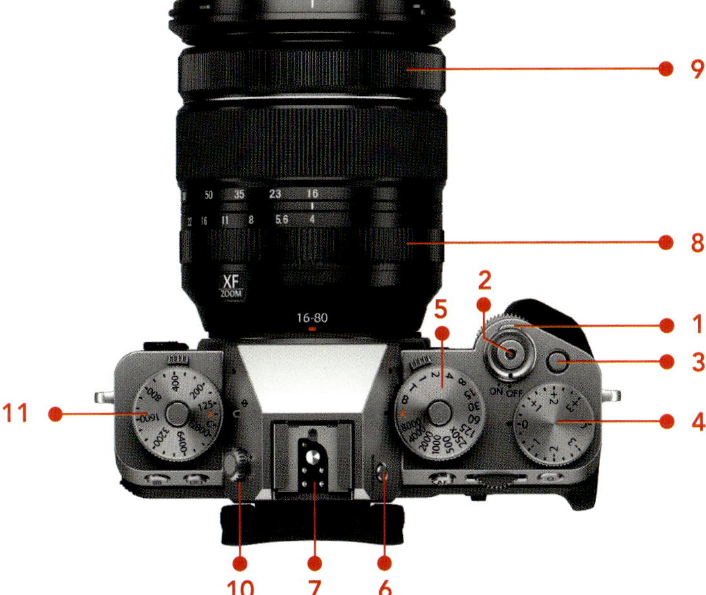

Fig. 2: X-T5 top view (with XF16–80mmF4 R OIS WR lens): on/off switch (1), shutter release button (2), Fn button (3), exposure compensation dial (4), shutter speed dial with stacked STILL/MOVIE mode selection dial (5), view mode button (6), hot shoe (7), aperture ring (8), focus ring (9), diopter adjustment dial (10), ISO dial with stacked DRIVE mode dial (11)

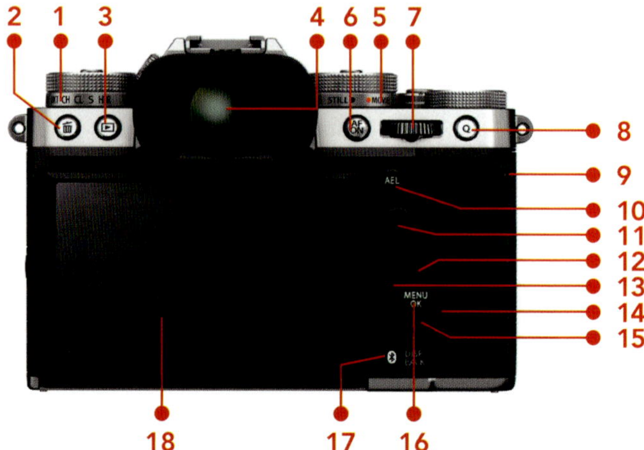

Fig. 3: X-T5 rear view: DRIVE mode dial (1), delete ("trash") button (2), playback button (3), viewfinder (4), STILL/MOVIE mode selection dial (5), AF-ON button/Fn button (6), rear command dial with integrated Fn button (7), Q button/Fn button (8), status indicator lamp (9), AE-L button/Fn button (10), focus stick with integrated button (11), upper selector/Fn button (12), left selector/Fn button (13), right selector/Fn button (14), lower selector/Fn button (15), MENU/OK button (16), DISP/BACK button (17), LCD monitor (18)

1.1 THE BASICS (1): THINGS YOU SHOULD KNOW ABOUT YOUR CAMERA

RTFM! Read the Fuji Manual!	TIP 1

In case you have misplaced your user manual, or if you want the most recent edition, you can obtain downloadable PDF versions [1] in various supported languages from Fujifilm. You will also find updates and supplementary material that cover new features and changes based on firmware updates.

Please do yourself a big favor and thoroughly study the manual to get acquainted with the functions of your camera, and don't forget that your lenses come with user manuals, as well. This book doesn't replace the camera manual; it serves as an *enhancement* to the manual and offers valuable tips and background information about how to use the various features and functions to get the most out of your equipment.

Please note that this book is exclusively about using the X-T5 for photography and doesn't include content about the camera's video features.

Spare batteries and third-party knockoffs	TIP 2

The X-T5 is a small, portable camera. It's running on modern NP-W235 batteries with a capacity of 2200 mAh. Depending on how you use the camera, a fully charged battery will typically last for 500 to 700 shots.

I recommend setting the camera to one of its three Boost Modes (SET UP > POWER MANAGEMENT > PERFORMANCE > BOOST) for maximum autofocus speed and the best over-all performance.

Please note:

- The X-T5 features an accurate battery indicator with five bars and a percentage display. However, the display's accuracy may depend on using original NP-W235 batteries from Fujifilm.

- In shooting mode, the percentage display is available only in the INFO display. To activate the INFO display, (repeatedly) press the DISP/BACK button until the INFO display appears on the rear LCD monitor. In playback mode, the percentage indicator is also available in the INFO display, which can be accessed with the DISP/BACK button *or* by pressing the upper selector key (or moving the focus stick upward) to cycle through two extended image information pages.

- When the battery indicator shows one remaining red bar, it's almost time to replace/recharge the battery.

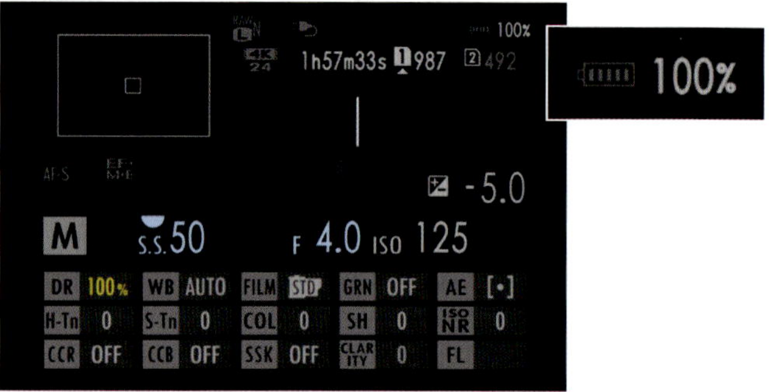

Fig. 4: The **INFO display** features an accurate battery life indicator with a percentage display. You can access the INFO display with the DISP/BACK button.

Since your X-T5 uses NP-W235 batteries, you cannot interchange batteries between the X-T5 and older X-camera models like the X-T3 or X-Pro3. There is also no adapter that would allow using the smaller NP-W126S batteries from older cameras in the new X-T5.

You can obtain NP-W235 batteries from Fujifilm, or you can use compatible products from third-party vendors.

Aftermarket batteries usually don't offer the same quality and performance as the more expensive Fujifilm originals. The NP-W235 is a smart battery that communicates with the camera and transmits data about its health status and the number of charging cycles (SET UP > USER SETTING > BATTERY AGE). In all the aftermarket batteries I tested, this health status information was incorrect. Some brands also didn't transmit internal temperature information to the charger.

Your mileage may vary: You may experience inaccurate battery life displays with third-party offerings, and the camera may unexpectedly switch off due to a depleted battery even though the indicator showed there was still power left. On the other hand, third-party offerings are usually more affordable: You sometimes get two knockoffs for the price of one original NP-W235 from Fujifilm.

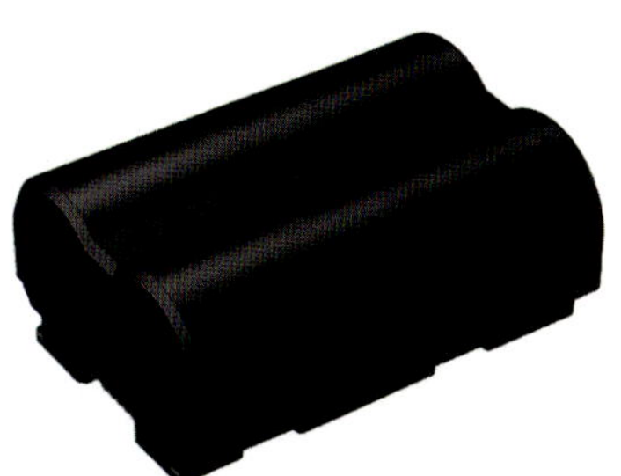

Fig. 5: Fujifilm's original **NP-W235** battery is without doubt the benchmark, but it's also more expensive than third-party knockoffs.

If you store your camera for several days (or longer) without a charged battery, the X-T5's built-in emergency power source may run out of juice, and all camera and user settings will reset to factory conditions.

<table><tr><td>Battery chargers and power banks</td><td>TIP 3</td></tr></table>

Along with spare batteries, the aftermarket also offers external chargers. A high-quality external Power Delivery charger for the new NP-W235 battery is Fujifilm's optional BC-W235 dual charger. This charger requires a USB-C input with at least 15W (better to use 30W) and Power Delivery (PD), and since it doesn't come with a power supply or USB charging cable, you are supposed to use the 15W power supply and the USB-C data/charging cable that came bundled with your X-T5. This means that if you want to charge batteries in the camera and in the BC-W235 *at the same time,* you need a different (or second) power supply and an additional USB-C charging cable with Power Delivery.

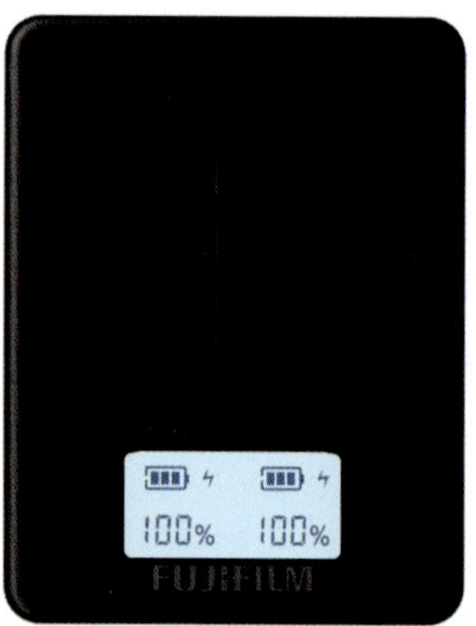

Fig. 6: If you don't want to charge your batteries inside the camera, you can use Fujifilm's optional **BC-W235 dual battery charger** with Power Delivery. For optimal performance, you should connect it to a USB-C power supply with an output of at least 30W.

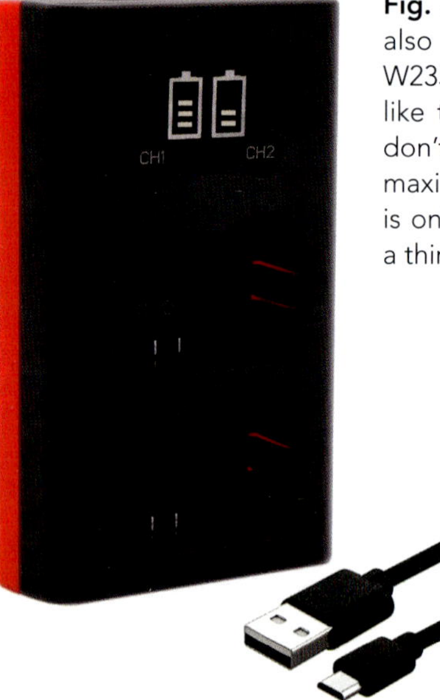

Fig. 7: **Third-party suppliers** are also offering chargers for the NP-W235. Be careful, though: models like this dual charger from Baxxtar don't support Power Delivery. Its maximum available charging power is only 10.5W for both slots—about a third of the BC-W235's capability.

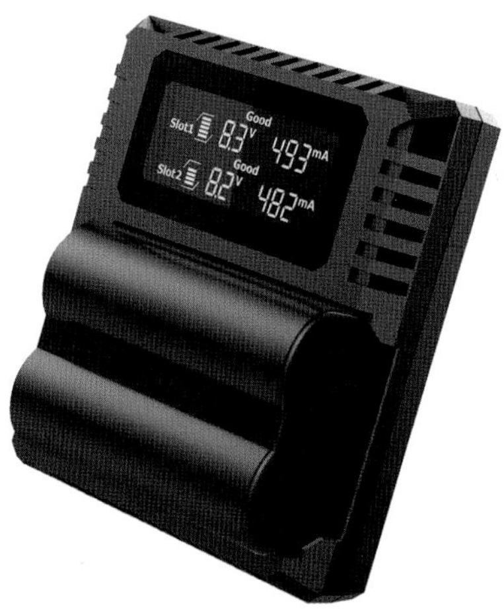

Fig. 8: A better, yet still affordable third-party charger for the NP-W235 is the **FX3 from Nitecore**. This dual battery charger still doesn't support Power Delivery (PD) but it supports Quick Charge (QC) with a 9V input (18W for both slots) and features battery temperature and health indicators.

Let's be clear: The 15W USB-C power supply that came with your X-T5 is the bare minimum. To get more bang, I recommend a USB-C power supply with a minimum of 30W or 45W. With 30W, you can quick-charge two depleted NP-W235 batteries in the BC-W235 in 2.5 hours or less.

My recommendation is to use small but powerful USB-C multiport power supplies with state-of-the-art GaN (gallium nitride) technology. Since the X-T5 supports USB-C with Power Delivery, you can speed-up charging by using a USB-C power supply with at least 30W, and a USB-C to USB-C cable that supports Power Delivery.

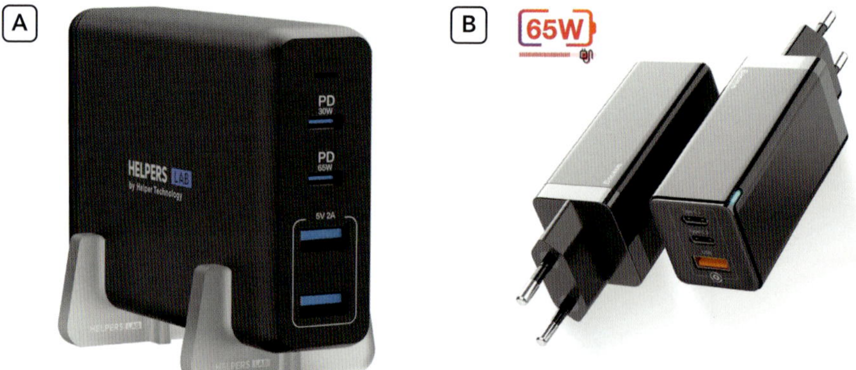

Fig. 9: Powerful **USB-C multi-port power supplies** come in many shapes (**A**) and sizes (**B**). For state-of-the-art technology and performance, look out for small and lightweight offerings using GaN technology. Depending on how many devices you need to charge within a given timeframe, make sure to select a power supply with enough juice to charge several batteries at the same time. Multiport power supplies are also convenient for traveling or on-location charging. Make sure to use USB-C cables that support Power Delivery (PD). Most PD cables support up to 60W, but there are also premium offerings with up to 100W. This means that you can also use these cables to supply power to higher-end laptops.

When traveling, don't forget that different countries use different formats for power outlets, so you may want to carry a suitable travel adapter.

As an alternative to external battery chargers, your batteries can also be charged inside the camera via the built-in USB-C port. In addition to dedicated USB-C power supplies, you can use a USB-A to USB-C or a USB-C to USB-C cable to connect the camera to pretty much *any* power source with a USB outlet, such as your laptop, phone charger, or a regular power bank. Be careful, though: With a weak phone charger, it could take all night to refill a depleted battery.

USB chargers and mobile power banks not only charge your X-T5, they can also power your camera while it is switched on and in use. Fujifilm recommends power banks from Anker, but there are many innovative alternatives from other brands. Just make sure that the power supply or power bank in question offers USB-C Power Delivery and enough wattage to quick-charge your device(s). For example, to quickly charge three batteries (one in your camera and two in an attached dual battery charger) as fast as possible, you need at least 45W (15W + 30W). Please note that even when you power the X-T5 externally, an NP-W235 battery must be inserted in the camera.

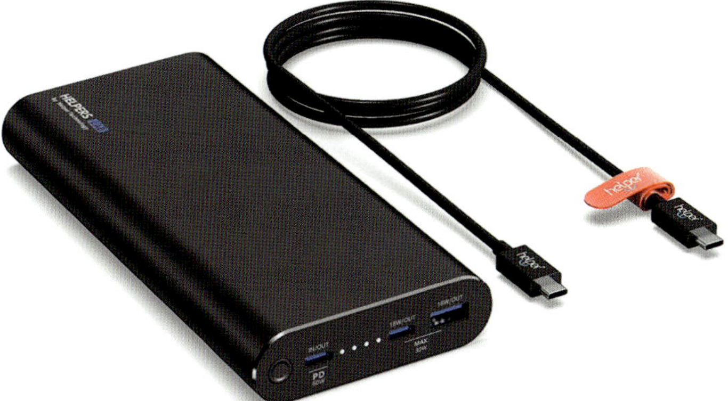

Fig. 10: USB-C power banks are useful accessories for users who want to power the camera in the field for long exposures, extended video recording, time-lapse photography, or interval shooting. Once again, look out for models that support Power Delivery with at least 30W. Personally, I use small and powerful units like this sleek 90W battery.

As a road warrior, you might also be interested in car charging options for your X-T5 or the BC-W235. Once again, Power Delivery is your friend, as there's a wide choice of cigarette-lighter chargers with USB-C PD outputs.

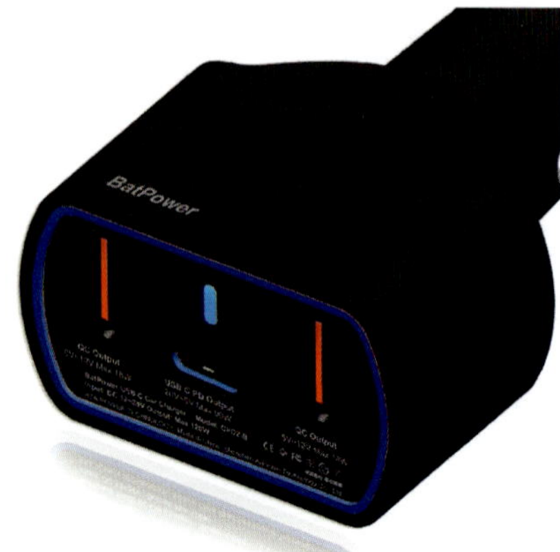

Fig. 11: Most **USB-C car chargers** with Power Delivery feature a modest output somewhere between 18W and 45W, but there are notable exceptions like this 120W monster that won't just power and charge your X-T5 but also power-hungry high-performance laptops like the 16" Apple MacBook Pro.

| TIP 4 | Where to find the latest firmware |

Fujifilm keeps improving the firmware of your cameras and lenses.

- To check which firmware version is installed in your camera and lens, switch the camera on while pressing and holding the DISP/BACK button.

- You can and should download the latest firmware versions for your cameras and lenses online from Fujifilm [2]. While you are there, you can also download current versions of Fuji's application software, such as RAW File Converter EX, Fujifilm X RAW Studio, and Fujifilm X Acquire.

- A step-by-step video guide illustrating the firmware upgrade process [3] is available online [4]. At Fujifilm's support website, macOS [5] and Windows [6] users can also find detailed firmware download instructions for their operating systems.

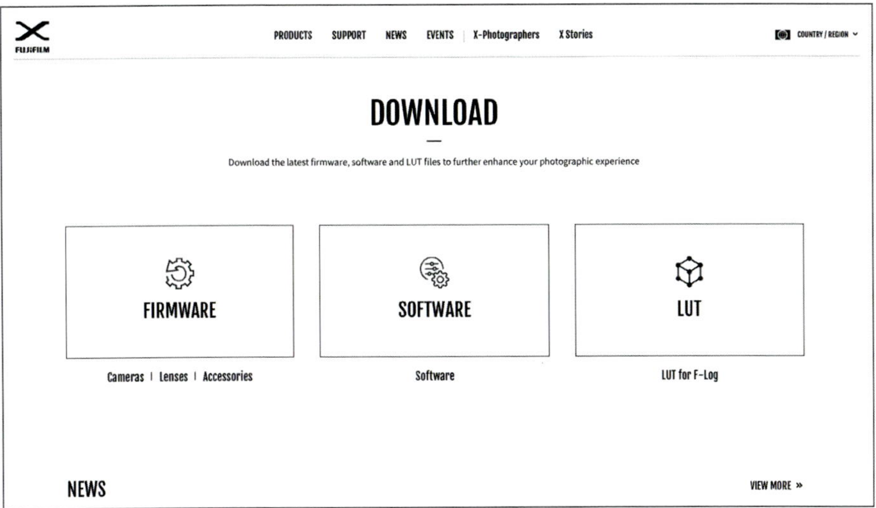

Fig. 12: Fujifilm's **Download Software & Firmware** webpage is your hub to obtain firmware updates for your X-T5 and lenses as well as current versions of supplementary software such as X RAW Studio and RAW File Converter EX.

Updating your firmware	TIP 5

- If you can't find a new firmware version on Fuji's firmware update page, there's a chance your web browser is still caching an older version of this page. In this case, either delete your browser cache or force your browser to reload the webpage from the server.

- Make sure your computer doesn't change the name of the new firmware files you download due to naming conflicts caused by previous firmware versions that are still residing in your download folder. The correct file name of the camera firmware for your X-T5 is always FWUP0030.DAT, irrespectively of the firmware version.

- Make sure the battery is fully charged when updating your firmware.

- Always copy new firmware files for your camera or lenses into the top directory of your SD memory card, and always use cards that have been freshly formatted in your camera. After you have copied the firmware to the card, make sure to properly unmount the card from your computer before removing it.

- If you want to update the firmware for a specific lens or accessory, make sure that lens or accessory is attached to the camera when you initiate the update process.

- To start the update process for your camera or a lens, switch on the camera while pressing and holding the DISP/BACK button and follow the instructions on the screen.

- Never switch the camera off during the update process. The camera will tell you when the update is complete. Only then can you safely switch it off.

If the firmware in your camera or lens needs to be updated due to compatibility issues, the camera may alert you of this problem when you switch it on. If that's the case, download the new firmware from the website links provided in tip 4 and update your camera and/or lens.

TIP 6	Wireless firmware updates using Bluetooth and Wi-Fi

Since your camera supports Bluetooth, you can perform wireless firmware updates using your smartphone or tablet and Fujifilm's free Camera Remote app or the newer XApp, which are available for iOS and Android. You can find a useful manual explaining the app's various functions online [7]. As of June 2023, wireless updates are available for only the camera body's firmware, not for lenses or accessories.

When your X-T5 is paired with your wireless device, the app will announce the availability of new camera firmware and offer to download it to your smartphone or tablet. From there, the firmware file is transferred to the camera via the camera's Wi-Fi hotspot.

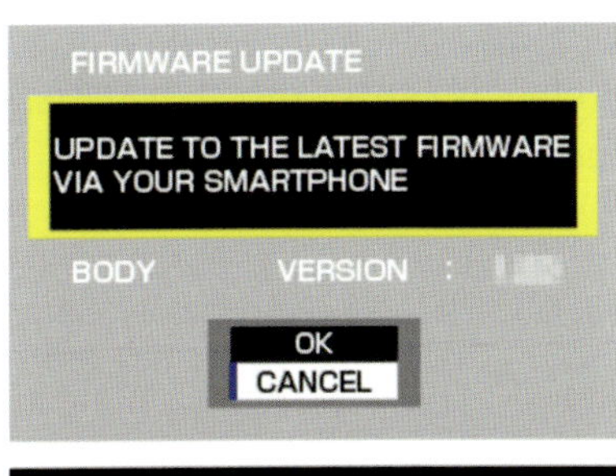

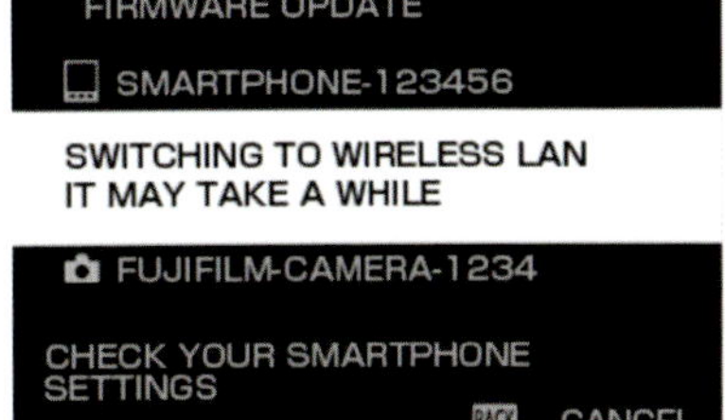

Fig. 13: Wireless firmware update: After the app on your smartphone or tablet has finished downloading new camera firmware, its Wi-Fi network is switched to the camera's own hotspot to transfer the firmware file to the camera.

Using an app is a good option for users who want to install new firmware without accessing a personal computer. You can find step-by-step instructions for wireless firmware updates online [8].

<table>
<tr><td>Which memory cards to use</td><td>TIP 7</td></tr>
</table>

Turbo-charge your camera and its built-in buffer memory by using the fastest and most reliable UHS-I and UHS-II memory cards as follows:

- Since your X-T5 offers two fast UHS-II slots with transmission speeds of up to 300 MB/s, I highly recommend **Sony SF-G** or **Sony SF-G Tough** cards with write speeds up to 299 MB/s. These cards are also known to be particularly reliable and hang-up resistant when used with high-performance cameras like the X-T5.

- If the speed and performance of your X-T5 doesn't concern you, you can also use cards with the slower UHS-I standard and transfer rates of 95 MB/s or less. In this category, I recommend **SanDisk Extreme Pro 95 MB/s** cards, which are now also marketed as cards with "170 MB/s." However, this doesn't affect the write speed.

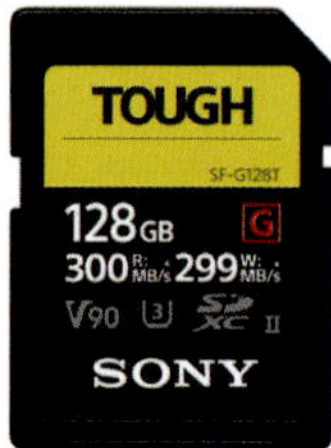

Fig. 14: For maximum UHS-II performance and compatibility, I recommend superfast **Sony SF-G** cards (Sony Tough with up to 299 MB/s write speed).

Look out for fakes! Sadly, there's a fair share of fake SD cards on the market. High-end brands and models are particularly affected, so make sure to buy your fast UHS-I and UHS-II cards from reputable sources. Fake cards aren't just slower and less reliable than the originals, they also tend to lie about their actual capacity. A fake 64 GB card could contain a cheap 8 GB chip with a manipulated controller that simulates 64 GB to the camera, resulting in severe data loss.

Fujifilm has also set up a website [9] listing memory cards and accessories that have been tested with the X-T5.

TIP 8	Working with dual card slots

Your X-T5 offers two SD card slots numbered 1 and 2. This means you can use two SD cards at the same time.

Please note:

- The primary SD card slot of your X-T5 is slot 1. If you are only working with a single SD card, always put it in this slot.

- Both slots support UHS-II, making them suitable for very fast memory cards like the Sony SF-G series.

Using two memory cards at the same time gives you three options to configure how image data is transferred to your SD cards. To do so, select SET UP > SAVE DATA SET-UP > CARD

SLOT SETTING (there are separate selections for either still image or movie mode) and pick one of the following options:

- **SEQUENTIAL**: In this default mode, the camera saves all image data (RAW and JPEG/HEIF) to a manually selected card slot. To change the slot, choose SET UP > SAVE DATA SET-UP > SELECT SLOT (SEQUENTIAL).

- **BACKUP**: In this mode, the X-T5 is sending all image data (RAW and JPEG/HEIF) to both slots at the same time, creating a backup copy that can be useful when one of the cards gets lost or suffers data loss. In this mode, the overall data transfer rate is limited by the slower of the two cards that are in use. This can become a performance issue in situations that require many images being taken with high burst rates while shooting FINE+RAW, so make sure the cards in both slots are equally fast.

- **SEPARATE**: This setting splits the image data up by saving RAW files to slot 1 and JPEGs or HEIFs to slot 2, so it is useful only when you are shooting FINE+RAW or NOR-MAL+RAW. If you shoot RAW-only or JPEG/HEIF-only, SEPARATE mode becomes BACKUP mode, saving your RAW or JPEG/HEIF data to both cards at the same time.

I always recommend shooting FINE+RAW or NORMAL+RAW. If you follow this advice, selecting SEPARATE mode (and using the fastest UHS-II cards available in slots 1 and 2, respectively) will give you the best camera performance in terms of continuous burst rates.

However, SEPARATE mode also has its quirks:

- Splitting up RAW and JPEG/HEIF image data to slots 1 and 2 only works in regular shooting mode (i.e., when you take a new picture), not when you are using the camera's built-in RAW converter to create a JPEG/HEIF/TIFF from a RAW file on card 1. JPEGs, HEIFs and TIFFs generated from RAWs on card 1 are also saved on card 1 (the RAW card) instead of card 2 (the JPEG/HEIF card).

- In playback mode, the X-T5 will display smaller-sized JPEG images that are embedded in the RAW files on card 1 instead of showing the full-resolution JPEGs or HEIFs on card 2. To access the full-resolution JPEGs or HEIFs (e.g., to zoom in and check critical focus), you must manually switch slots in playback mode by pressing and holding the playback button until the camera confirms the switch. Sadly, the camera will revert to the previous card as soon as you take another picture, so you'll have to go through the motions of switching slots in playback mode after each shot.

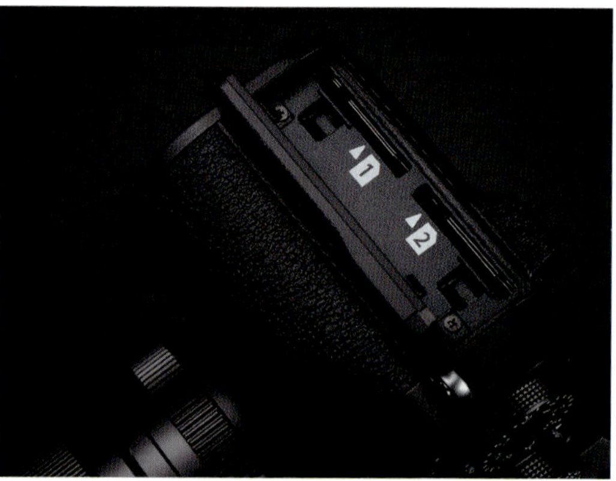

Fig. 15: Your X-T5 can work with **two SD memory cards at the same time**. For maximum performance, you should use fast UHS-II cards.

TIP 9	Resetting the frame counter and assigning a new image starting number

Make sure you only use a single SD card in slot 1 and then follow these steps to reset the image counter to zero:

- First select SET UP > SAVE DATA SET-UP > FRAME NO. > RENEW, then format the SD card with SET UP > USER SET-TING > FORMAT > SLOT 1 and take a picture. The frame counter will start from zero.

- To avoid another automatic image counter reset when you are reformatting an SD card, select SET UP > SAVE DATA SET-UP > FRAME NO. > CONTINUOUS.

If you like, you can assign pretty much *any* number as the camera's frame-counter starting number. The method is like the above but involves an extra step in your computer. Again, only use a single SD card in slot 1:

- Select SET UP > SAVE DATA SET-UP > FRAME NO. > RE-NEW, and then format the SD card with SET UP > USER SETTING > FORMAT > SLOT 1. The frame counter will start from zero.

- Take one image, then remove the SD card from your camera and insert it in your computer. Locate your image (for example DSCF0001.JPG or DSCF0001.RAF) in the DCIM folder and change the frame-number portion of the file name (0001) to the number you'd like to use as your new starting point. For example, you can change the file name to DSCF2000.JPG.

- Properly unmount and remove the SD card from your computer and put the card back into your camera. Now take another picture. The camera will use the modified frame number as a starting point. In our example, the next image's name would be DSCF2001.

- To avoid another automatic frame-counter reset when you are reformatting an SD card, select SET UP > SAVE DATA SET-UP > FRAME NO. > CONTINUOUS.

<table>
<tr><td>Use Boost mode!</td><td>TIP 10</td></tr>
</table>

In its default NORMAL performance setting, the X-T5 operates with limited performance to conserve power. To enjoy the camera's full capabilities, it's necessary to select SET UP > POWER MANAGEMENT > PERFORMANCE > BOOST or assign Boost mode to one of the camera's Fn or Touch-Fn buttons. Since the X-T5 consumes more power in Boost mode, it's smart to always have replacement batteries at hand.

Boost mode offers better autofocus performance and a higher frame rate in the electronic real-time live view. In the X-T5, there are four different Boost mode options:

- EVF/LCD LOW LIGHT PRIORITY is a new setting that optimizes the live view for very dark scenes by reducing the frame rate. In situations that require long exposure times or very high ISO settings, this results in a clearer and more realistic live view image with less noise. In situations like this, the live view image can easily start to blur due to a massively decreased frame rate, so using the camera on a tripod is advisable.

- EVF/LCD RESOLUTION PRIORITY optimizes the resolution of the live view image. The frame rate is capped at 60 fps. This mode is ideal for landscapes, portraits, etc. – pretty much everything that isn't very dark or involves high-speed action.

- EVF FRAME RATE PRIORITY (100P) increases the frame rate of the EVF to 100 fps. This can be useful for action scenes with moving subjects and/or panning shots.

- EVF FRAME RATE PRIORITY (200P EQUIV.) further increases the perceived frame rate at the possible cost of losing image brightness in the live view. I generally do not recommend this setting.

Important: When the camera is set to ECONOMY mode, it will enter an energy saving mode after several seconds of user inactivity. This results in a dramatic reduction of the live view's frame rate. As soon as a button is pressed or a dial is turned, the live view goes back to normal. Also note that the frame rate reduction in ECONOMY mode doesn't occur when the camera is connected to an external USB-C power source.

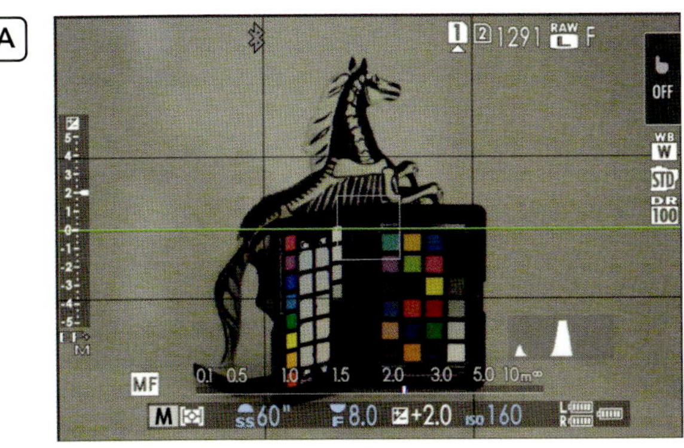

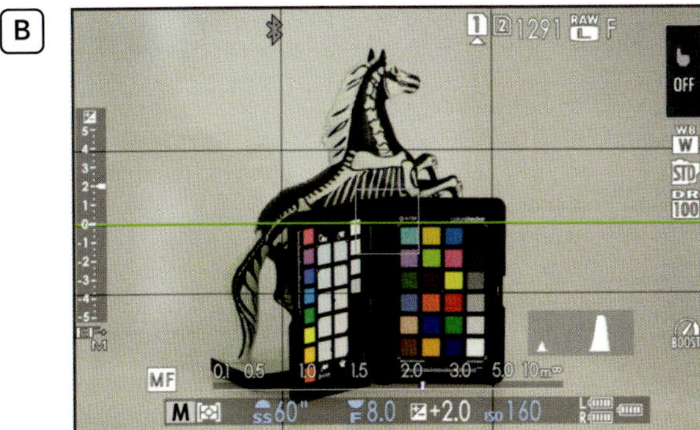

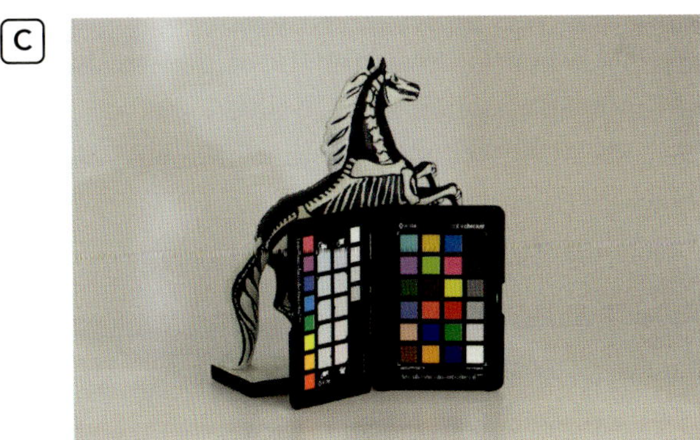

Fig. 16: This example illustrates the **difference between NORMAL and EVF/LCD LOW LIGHT PRIORITY BOOST** performance settings. I was pointing the camera at a dimly lit scene with a manual exposure setting of 60 sec. In NORMAL mode (**A**), the live view appears very noisy. It's also underexposed and doesn't correctly simulate the set exposure. In EVF/LCD LOW LIGHT PRIORITY BOOST mode (**B**), the live view looks much clearer, and this time, the exposure simulation is quite realistic. The final image (**C**) is the actual straight-out-of-camera JPEG that the camera produced after taking the shot.

Obviously, EVF/LCD LOW LIGHT PRIORITY BOOST mode is preferable in extreme low-light situations. However, we should still be careful: If you reduce the incoming light a few additional stops and further increase the exposure time to compensate, even EVF/LCD LOW LIGHT PRIORITY BOOST mode won't be capable of correctly simulating the resulting image brightness in the live view. Of course, this also applies to long daytime exposure shots that are taken with very strong neutral density (ND) filters.

TIP 11	Keeping the camera sensor clean

Sooner or later, all cameras with interchangeable lenses accumulate dust or dirt on the sensor. This manifests as spots on your image, especially in photos taken at small apertures. You can prevent this from happening by taking measures to avoid sensor dust as much as possible. You can also remove dust by using your camera's built-in cleaning mechanism:

- Select SET UP > USER SETTING > SENSOR CLEANING > OK to momentarily activate the built-in cleaning mechanism that helps loosen dust particles. By default, this mechanism will be employed when you switch *off* the camera. I recommend setting the camera to also activate this mechanism when the X-T5 is switched *on*: to do this, select SET UP > USER SETTING > SENSOR CLEANING > WHEN SWITCHED ON > ON.

In addition, it's sensible to adhere to a regimen that avoids exposing the camera to dust and dirt:

- Never leave the camera without a lens mounted or without its protective body cap in place.

- Don't change lenses in dusty/windy/rainy environments.

- When changing lenses, always hold the camera with the open lens mount pointed downward—never upward.

- When you attach a new lens, make sure the rear glass of the lens is clean and free of dust particles. Otherwise, dust from the lens could travel to the sensor.

- Never touch the sensor!

Fig. 17: Dust spots on the sensor made visible. This sensor badly needs cleaning.

Do-it-yourself sensor cleaning	TIP 12

When the built-in sensor-cleaning function doesn't do a proper job, you have three basic options for cleaning the sensor by yourself:

- Touchless cleaning
- Dry cleaning
- Wet cleaning

Touchless cleaning involves using a blower, like the *Giottos Rocket Air Blaster*, to rid the sensor of dust particles. An important feature of such devices is a filter in the intake valve that prevents contaminated (dusty) air from being blown against the sensor.

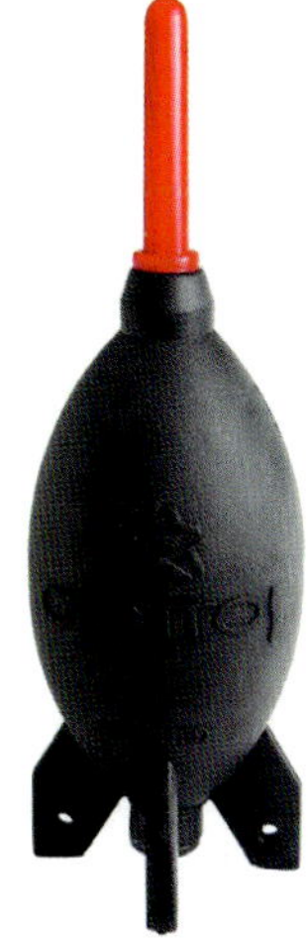

Fig. 18: Touchless sensor cleaning: **Giottos Rocket Air Blaster**.

Important: Don't use compressed air from aerosol cans that contain propellants. Particles could hit the sensor like tiny projectiles and damage the protective surface!

A popular means to **dry clean** the sensor is to use the *Pentax Sensor Cleaning Kit*. The sticky head of this funny-looking cleaning device picks up dust and dirt from the sensor surface and transfers it to sticky paper sheets that are included with the product.

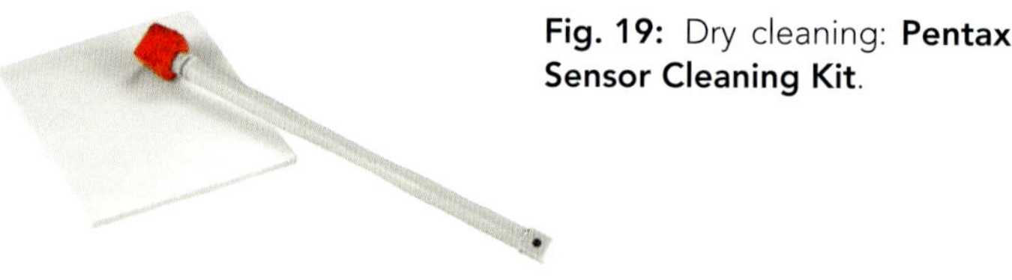

Fig. 19: Dry cleaning: **Pentax Sensor Cleaning Kit**.

Tough sensor dirt (like water or oil stains) requires **wet cleaning** with a *sensor swab*. Suitable but expensive products are offered by companies likes Photographic Solutions and Visible Dust. They consist of wipers that are wetted with special cleaning fluids (such as Eclipse). Wipe one side of the swab from left to right over the full width of the sensor, and then from right to left with the other side of the swab. Your X-T5 requires swabs that match APS-C-sized sensors. At Photographic Solutions, this translates into product size number 2.

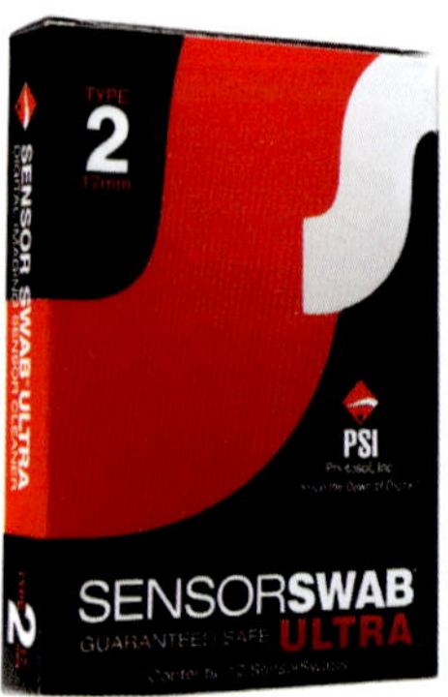

Fig. 20: Wet cleaning: **sensor swabs** from Photographic Solutions.

Inexpensive and effective alternatives to products from Visible Dust or Photographic Solutions are APS-C-sized swabs from the brand VSGO.

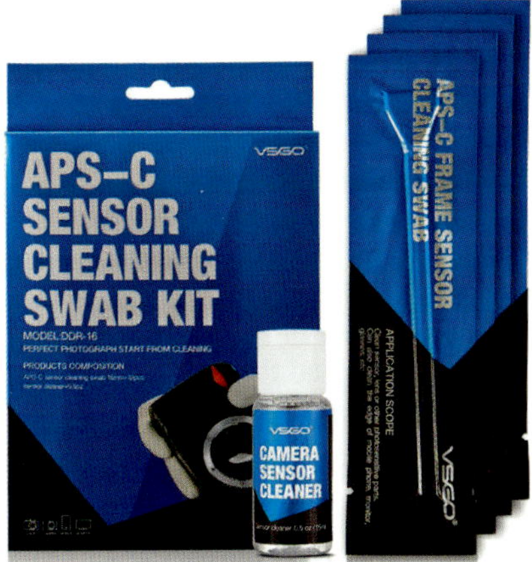

Fig. 21: My personal sensor cleaning choice for X-mount cameras: **VSGO** swabs and cleaning fluid.

Since your X-T5 features in-body image stabilization (IBIS), DIY sensor cleaning is a little bit trickier. Here are step-by-step instructions on how to prepare your X-T5 for wet and dry sensor cleaning:

- Press and hold down the DISP/BACK button while you turn on your camera, just like you would to update the firmware. Doing so disables the IBIS and keeps the sensor in place.

- Remove the lens or body cap and clean the sensor as usual. Make sure that the camera remains switched ON during the cleaning process.

- After you are finished cleaning the sensor, switch off the camera.

Please note that keeping the camera turned on during sensor cleaning is an exception that we only make for cameras with IBIS. All other cameras should always be powered off during sensor cleaning.

***Important:** There's a small chance that sensor spots are caused by dust particles enclosed **behind** the protective surface of the sensor. If some spots simply won't go away, the camera needs to be serviced by Fujifilm.*

<table><tr><td>TIP 13</td><td>Pixel mapping</td></tr></table>

Your X-T5 includes an automatic pixel-mapping feature. To use it, select IMAGE QUALITY SETTING > PIXEL MAPPING. Pixel mapping detects defective pixels on your sensor and maps them out, meaning they are interpolated with the information of surrounding pixels. Since the number of hot pixels increases with sensor temperature, pixel mapping is only available when the camera hasn't already heated up.

Please note that a few defective pixels are perfectly normal in every digital camera. As the sensor ages (even when the camera is not in use), the number of dead pixels increases. In addition to the manufacturing process, defective pixels are also caused by cosmic radiation. For example, frequently taking your camera on long-haul flights will increase the risk.

Knowing all this, it's a good idea to regularly use the pixel-mapping function to keep the defective pixel map inside your camera up to date. It takes just a few seconds.

1.2 THE BASICS (2): THINGS YOU SHOULD KNOW ABOUT YOUR LENSES

Your camera is compatible with the following native X-mount lenses:

- Fujinon XF lenses (prime and zoom lenses).

- Fujinon XC lenses (compact and affordable lenses).

- Zeiss Touit X-mount lenses (primes).

- Third-party lenses from companies like Sigma, Tamron, Tokina, Viltrox, or Samyang.

Native autofocus lenses from Fujinon and Zeiss are fully compatible with all X-series cameras. With autofocus lenses from third-party manufacturers, your mileage may vary. There may be issues with performance and compatibility, and firmware upgrades may require different procedures and additional equipment. That said, Fujifilm opening the X-mount to third-party vendors and their broad selection of APS-C lenses is certainly a bonus.

Decoding XF18–135mmF3.5–5.6 R LM OIS WR	TIP 14

This tip is of the "what you always wanted to know but never dared to ask" variety:

- **XF:** "X" means X-mount or X series; "F" means Fine, designating Fuji's premium line of lenses. There's also the smaller, more affordable XC line ("C" stands for Compact or Casual). And let's not forget GF lenses for GFX medium format cameras (G-mount).

- **18–135mm:** This is the focal length range of the zoom lens. To translate the numbers to their full-frame equivalents, you must multiply them by the APS-C crop factor [10] of 1.5. Hence, the field of view (FOV) of an 18–135mm zoom on your X-mount camera is identical to the FOV of a 27–202mm zoom lens on a full-frame (35mm format) camera. By the way: Lenses with zoom motors add "PZ" to their name, meaning "power zoom." An example would be the XF18–120mmF4 LM PZ WR.

- **F3.5–5.6:** This range describes the maximum aperture opening at the low and high ends of the focal length range. In this case, the lens offers a maximum aperture of f/3.5 at 18 mm and f/5.6 at 135 mm.

- **R:** This stands for Ring and indicates that the lens features an aperture ring. This is a standard feature of almost all Fujinon XF lenses. XC lenses don't offer an aperture ring. With ringless lenses, the aperture setting is always controlled with the command dial in exposure modes **A** or **M**.

- **LM:** This stands for Linear Motor, which ensures quick and silent autofocus operation.

- **OIS:** This is the Optical Image Stabilizer [11]. In concert with the IBIS of your X-T5, this feature allows you to perform handheld shots with this lens at shutter speeds that are much slower than you would usually need to eliminate camera shake. For example, in situations that would normally require a shutter speed of 1/160 sec. to ensure a clear image, you could shoot with 1/8 sec. and still get usable results. It's important to remember that motion blur often plays a role at slower shutter speeds since many subjects tend to move. Obviously, the OIS cannot reduce motion blur [12]—only blurring that occurs due to camera shake (i.e., the shaky hands of the photographer).

- **WR** denotes weather resistant lenses.

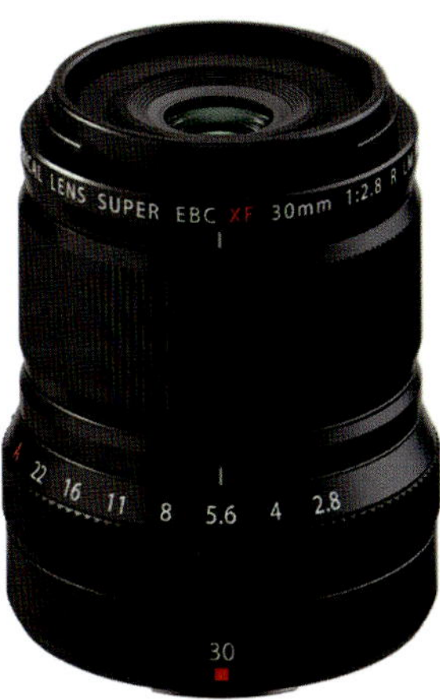

Fig. 22: Along with the XF35mmF2 R WR, XF23mmF2 R WR, XF50mmF2 R WR, and XF16mmF2.8 R WR, the **XF30mmF2.8 R LM WR Macro** is one of Fujifilm's popular compact prime lenses for the X series. These lenses are weather resistant, and their lean design doesn't obscure the optical viewfinder of the X-Pro1, X-Pro2, and X-Pro3.

OIS and IBIS	TIP 15

Many XF and XC lenses feature built-in Optical Image Stabilization (OIS). In addition to that, the X-T5 offers In Body Image Stabilization (IBIS), which works with all lenses, even manually adapted third-party lenses.

OIS and IBIS perform the same task: they prevent camera shake and blurry images in situations that require you to take handheld shots at a slower-than-usual shutter speed.

To control the OIS/IBIS, many XF lenses offer a dedicated OIS on/off switch on the lens barrel. The OIS in XC lenses and newer XF lenses like the XF16–80mmF4 is controlled through the camera menu. The latter also applies to the IBIS of the X-T5 with lenses (native or adapted) that don't have built-in OIS.

For handheld shots, an old rule of thumb recommends using shutter speeds that are at least as fast as the reciprocal of the full-frame-equivalent focal length that is in use. Wait, what? Here's an example: With a 50 mm lens and an APS-C crop factor of 1.5, the minimum safe shutter speed for handheld shooting would be *[1 / (50 × 1.5)] sec. = 1/75 sec.* In other words, when you are shooting handheld with a 50 mm lens and don't want shaky images, you should use shutter speeds at least as fast as 1/75 sec. Or you can use the IBIS/OIS to add a few more stops of leeway.

Of course, rules of thumb don't apply to everybody. Some users have quite steady hands, while others have a shaky grip. The settings and equipment that work for me may not work for you. However, the OIS will always give you a few extra stops of shutter-speed headroom.

In SHOOTING SETTING > IS MODE, you can choose between two basic IBIS/OIS modes:

- **OIS mode 1** (CONTINUOUS) is the default setting. It's always stabilizing the image, even when you are just looking through the viewfinder before you press the shutter button.

- **OIS mode 2** (SHOOTING ONLY) engages only when you fully depress the shutter button to take an image (or half-press the button in AF-C mode).

Please note that the IBIS/OIS can potentially also *introduce* camera shake, especially at faster shutter speeds. This adverse effect is more likely to occur in OIS mode 1 than in mode 2. However, OIS mode 1 is more effective when used at very slow shutter speeds, such as 1/15 sec., 1/8 sec., or even 1/4 sec.

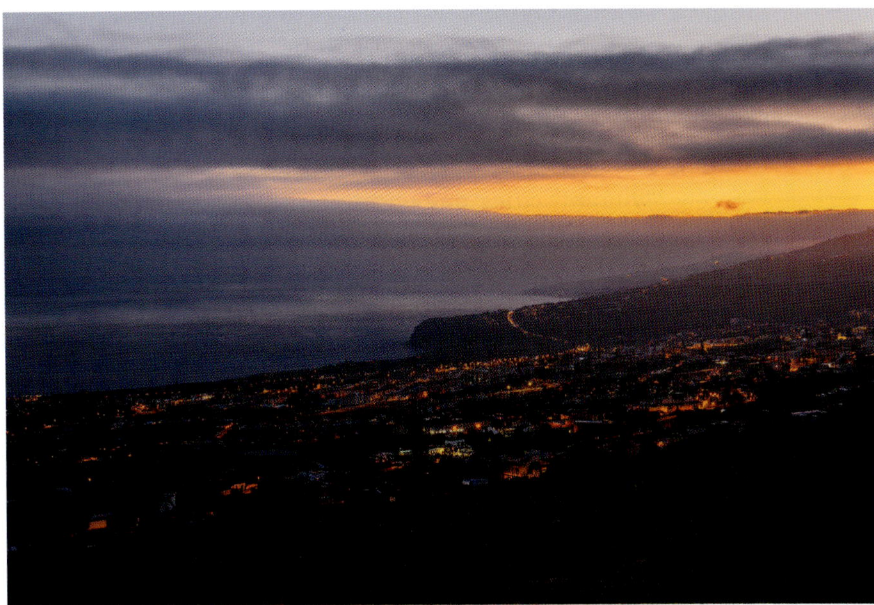

Fig. 23: The **optical image stabilizer** of the XF16–80mmF4 R OIS WR in action: Thanks to image stabilization, I could use a shutter speed of 1/2 sec. for this handheld sunrise shot. The combination of OIS and IBIS was able to successfully compensate for camera shake caused by my hands and body.

These are my recommendations for using OIS and IBIS:

- Only use (switch on) OIS/IBIS when necessary. When you are using fast shutter speeds that don't require image stabilization, you can safely turn the OIS off to eliminate it as a potential interference. That said, I once found the OIS useful even at shutter speed of 1/2000 sec. and 1/4000 sec. when I was shooting with an XF18–55mm lens from a small helicopter with extreme high-frequency vibration.

- I generally prefer to use the OIS in mode 2 ("shooting only"). However, mode 1 is more useful at very slow shutter speeds and when you are using telephoto lenses, because in mode 1, the OIS and IBIS will also stabilize the live view image, making it easier to compose and focus a shot.

- Consider turning off the OIS/IBIS when you are working from a good tripod or with shutter speeds that are slower than a second. Of course, this decision very much depends on the sturdiness of the tripod, prevailing wind conditions, and vibrations caused by traffic. Shooting in "vibrant" cities, one encounters many situations where leaving OIS/IBIS on is a good idea even with the sturdiest of tripods.

- Depending on the lens, you might also want to switch OIS/IBIS off for panning [13] shots in case you find it difficult to smoothly track your subject with the OIS turned on.

- OIS/IBIS mode 2 is known to interfere with long time exposures on tripods. Until this bug has been fixed, I strongly recommend using mode 1 or turning it off for long exposures of more than a second.

By the way, OIS and IBIS both emit a soft humming sound, even when the function is turned off. Don't worry about the noise—it's perfectly normal.

Important: If you are using a manually adapted third-party lens on an X-T5, the IBIS can only perform correctly if you have entered and selected the focal length of the attached lens in SHOOTING SETTING > MOUNT ADAPTOR SETTING.

TIP 16	How the XF23mmF1.4 R, XF16mmF1.4 R WR, and XF14mmF2.8 R differ

Unlike standard X-mount lenses, the older wide-angle primes XF14mmF2.8 R, XF16mmF1.4 R WR, and XF23mmF1.4 R feature a more traditional manual focus ring with a clutch mechanism.

- Pull the focus ring toward the camera to set the lens to manual focus.

- Push the focus ring away from the camera to set the lens to autofocus.

- Alternatively, you can use the camera's own focus mode selector to set it to manual focus mode. In this case, the lens remains in autofocus mode, and you can only use Instant AF (usually assigned to the AF-ON button) to change the focus. This also means you cannot manually adjust focus on the lens after focusing with Instant AF.

- You cannot use Instant AF (AF-ON button) to focus when the focus ring of the lens is set to manual focus. In this case, you can only use the manual focus ring to change or adjust focus.

- The analog depth-of-field (DOF) [14] markers on the lens barrel are less conservative (and in my opinion less useful) than the camera's pixel-based scale. This is because the pixel-based scale is using a much smaller circle of confusion [15] to display DOF ranges for pixel-sharp results at 100% magnification, whereas the engraved scale on the lens uses a value that's based on looking at typically sized prints from a typical distance with typical eyesight. Some photographers regard the engraved scale (which equals your camera's electronic film format-based scale) as more practical. Personally, I prefer the pixel-based scale.

- It's not possible to reverse the focusing direction of the manual focus ring with these three lenses.

- If you set your camera to AF+MF mode (AF/MF SETTING > AF+MF > ON), you can use this feature only when the lens clutch is set to MF and the camera is set to AF-S. In this configuration, you can autofocus by half-pressing the shutter button, and then manually adjust the focus with the focus ring (while keeping the shutter button half-pressed).

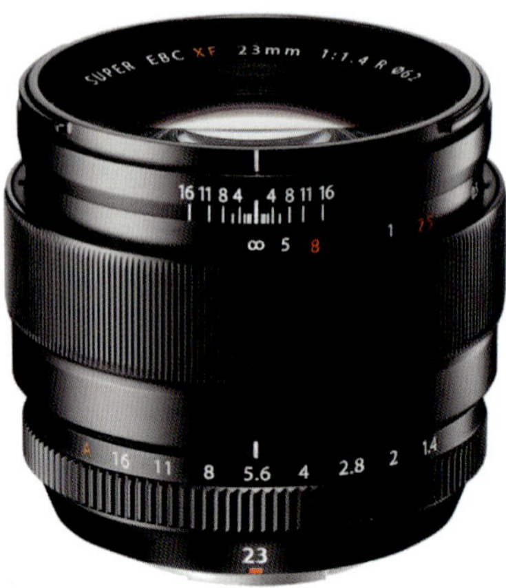

Fig. 24: Fujinon XF23mmF1.4 R with engraved distance and DOF markers. It's a nice retro touch, but you lose some state-of-the-art digital functionality.

| TIP 17 | Using the Lens Modulation Optimizer (LMO) |

The X-T5 supports the Lens Modulation Optimizer or LMO. This feature premiered in the X100S and X20 fixed-lens cameras (where it can't be switched off). It counteracts common optical phenomena (like diffraction [16] and corner softness) when the camera converts the RAW data into JPEG images. To make it work, the firmware of the attached lens sends its LMO correction data to the camera as hidden metadata with every image.

- Fujinon XC zoom lenses and Zeiss Touit lenses don't support the LMO. However, some third-party lenses (like the Viltrox XF13mmF1.4) do support the LMO.

- LMO data is proprietary and not available to external RAW converters.

If your lens supports the LMO (all Fujinon XF lenses do), you should enable the function by selecting IMAGE QUALITY SETTING > LENS MODULATION OPTIMIZER > ON. You can also use the built-in RAW converter of your camera (PLAY-BACK MENU > RAW CONVERSION) to enable or disable the LMO for a specific JPEG result. With this method, it's easy to create and compare versions of a shot with and without LMO enhancements.

The LMO mitigates the following optical effects:

- **Diffraction softness:** This effect increasingly occurs when the lens is stopped down beyond a certain point. APS-C cameras with 40 MP typically exhibit visible diffraction at apertures of 8 and smaller. While stopping down in-creases the overall depth of field (DOF), it also reduces the maximum resolution of the lens/camera combination. The LMO counteracts this effect and reconstructs some of the lost detail.

- **Corner softness:** Even the best lenses aren't as sharp in the corners as they are in the center. The LMO can digi-tally compensate for that loss of quality.

LMO corrections are currently supported only in-camera with the built-in RAW converter. External converters such as Adobe Lightroom or Capture One Pro can't process LMO data. This means LMO corrections are visible only in JPEGs that have been generated by the camera.

That said, Capture One Pro offers specific Fujifilm lens profiles that not only replace Fujifilm's built-in digital lens corrections but can also reduce diffraction blur and enhance corner sharpness. The same applies to DxO PhotoLab and PureRAW.

<table>
<tr><td>Things you should know about digital lens corrections</td><td>TIP 18</td></tr>
</table>

Most modern lenses achieve their optimal image quality through a combination of optical and digital corrections. Corrections are mostly applied to the three following phe-nomena:

- **Vignetting:** This effect results in a loss of brightness from center to corner. Vignetting [17] is more pronounced at large (open) apertures.

- **Distortion:** There are pincushion- and barrel-type distortions [18], both of which make straight lines seem curved. Some primes like the XF14mm, XF23mmF2, XF35mmF1.4, XF56mm (old and new), and XF90mm are fully optically corrected for distortion. Others (such as the Zeiss Touit range, compact pancake lenses, the XF35mmF2 and XF16mmF2.8, or zoom lenses) require a combination of optical and digital distortion correction.

- **Chromatic aberration:** Chromatic aberration [19] results in color fringing. This effect can be corrected (or mitigated) with apochromatic lenses, or digitally corrected during RAW conversion.

Some camera makers rely on dedicated correction profiles that must be provided by each RAW converter maker. Fujifilm isn't one of these companies. Instead, all current Fujifilm cameras store digital corrections as metadata in the RAW file. RAW converters can access this lens-specific metadata and use it to apply appropriate corrections. This way, the built-in RAW converter and external RAW conversion software, such as Adobe Lightroom or Capture One, can use the metadata in the RAW file to correct or mitigate vignetting, distortion, and chromatic aberration.

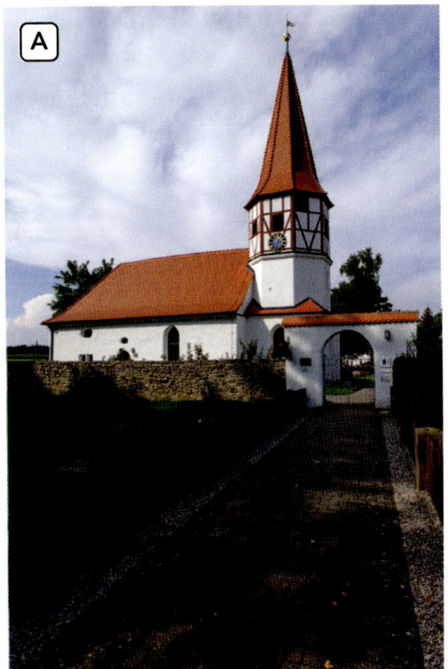 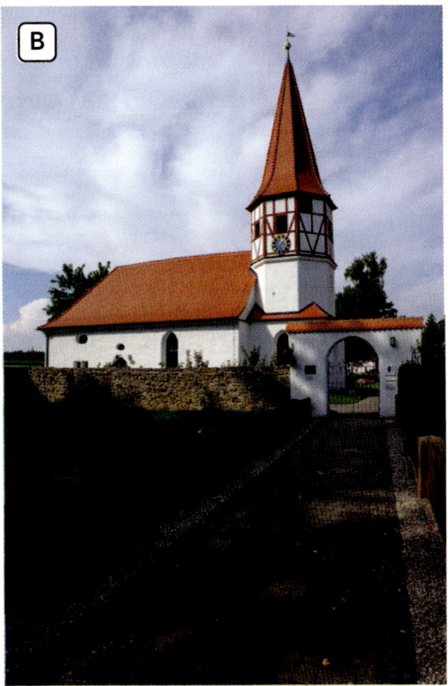

Fig. 25: This XF16–80mmF4 R OIS WR example shows the same image with (**A**) and without (**B**) digital lens corrections for distortion, vignetting, and chromatic aberration. It was shot at f/8 with a focal length of 16 mm.

A major benefit of this method is that many RAW converters automatically support new lenses since Fujifilm delivers the correction data via the RAW metadata. Obviously, not all subjects or images require the same amount of digital correction (it can also be a simple matter of taste), so full user control over the application of digital lens corrections is a very nice feature.

Luckily, software like Adobe Lightroom and Capture One offer control over how much digital metadata distortion (or vignetting) correction should be applied. Other programs simply ignore lens-correction metadata. With such programs, all corrections must be applied either manually or by using a dedicated profile.

Capture One Pro even supports both options: it can apply RAW metadata-based lens corrections, and it offers a set of dedicated lens correction profiles for many X-mount lenses. It's up to you to choose the digital lens correction option that suits you best.

| TIP 19 | Analog and digital teleconverters |

A teleconverter is installed between the camera body and a compatible XF lens, where it extends the effective focal length of the lens by a factor of either 1.4 or 2. This leads to losing either one or two aperture stops of brightness, and it puts a toll on image resolution. Hence, teleconverters should be used in concert with premium lenses that offer a resolution reserve robust enough to make the toll on image quality negligible.

As of the writing of this book, the following teleconverters are available from Fujifilm:

- The **XF1.4x TC WR** and **XF2x TC WR** for X-mount are mechanically compatible with the XF50–140mmF2.8 R LM OIS WR, XF100–400mmF4.5–5.6 R LM OIS WR, XF150–600mmF5.6–8 R LM OIS WR, XF70–300mmF4–5.6 R LM OIS WR, and the XF80mmF2.8 R LM OIS WR Macro. It is *not* recommended to use them with the XF200mmF2 R LM OIS WR.

- The **XF1.4x TC F2 WR** is compatible and included with the XF200mmF2 R LM OIS WR high-end telephoto prime and can also be used in concert with the other lenses mentioned above.

Unlike screw-on conversion lenses for the X70 and X100 series cameras, XF teleconverters have an impact on the speed (maximum brightness) of the resulting lens combination. To give you an example, the XF2x TC WR effectively turns the ultra-sharp XF80mmF2.8 R LM OIS WR Macro lens into an XF160mmF5.6 R LM OIS WR Macro. Setting the aperture of this combo to f/2.8 means setting an effective aperture of f/5.6. Using a 2x teleconverter, the light loss comprises two stops, whereas 1.4x converters take away one stop of light.

Luckily, these issues are recognized and handled by the camera and lens firmware (if you have kept them up to date). The firmware will automatically adjust the on-screen info displays and the EXIF [20] data to reflect the *effective* aperture values. It will also change the lens-correction meta-data (factoring in updated values for distortion, vignetting, and chromatic aberration) and include the presence of the teleconverter in the EXIF lens description.

Don't confuse optical teleconverter lenses with the built-in **digital teleconverter** of your X-T5. The digital teleconverter is available in SHOOTING SETTING > DIGITAL TELE-CONV. with 1.4x and 2x options. However, this is just a cropping tool that delivers a crop of the camera's full 40 MP image. It only affects the JPEG or HEIF files, not the RAW data. The full (uncropped) image is still recorded in the RAW data and can be restored with the camera's internal RAW converter or by processing it in an external converter like Adobe Lightroom.

SHOOTING SETTING > SPORTS FINDER MODE is another cropping tool that behaves like a digital teleconverter. The idea behind this mode is simulating the OVF of the X100 and X-Pro series and their ability to spot and track a moving subject before it enters the actual frame. It results in a 1.29x digital crop that not only affects the JPEGs and HEIFs, but also the RAW data. In RAW converters like Lightroom, you may even experience an erroneous digital distortion and vignetting correction, as the software is treating the cropped RAW data like an uncropped image, resulting in overcorrection. In any case, Sports Finder Mode effectively transforms your APS-C camera into a Micro Four Thirds (MFT) camera with a 3:2 aspect ratio. I strongly recommend leaving this feature in the OFF position.

| TIP 20 | Use the included lens hood! |

Fujifilm XF and some XC lenses come with a fitted lens hood, which should be used whenever possible. In addition to its optical benefits, the hood protects the lens and the front glass element from damage.

Lens hoods can pose problems too. They make the lens bigger than it is, and they can block the camera flash or the autofocus assist light. They also use up extra space in your bag, although most hoods can be reverse-mounted on the lens for transport purposes.

When you shoot with a small shoe-mounted flash, or when you depend on using the AF assist lamp, it's best to remove the lens hood.

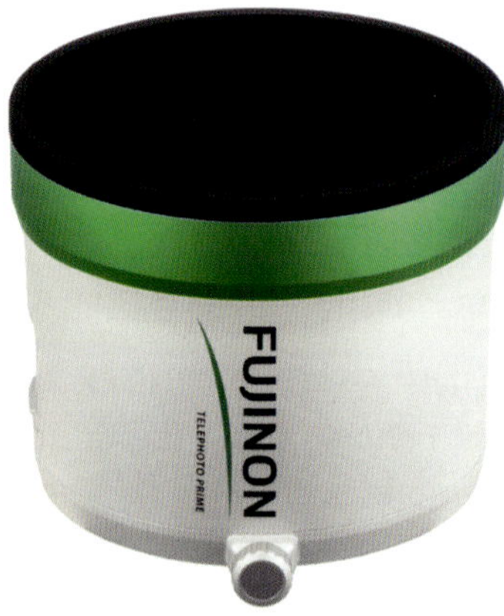

Fig. 26: Lens hoods like this large attachment for the **XF200mmF2 R LM OIS WR** offer optical benefits and robust lens protection.

Important: Don't use screw-on lens hoods with lenses that feature a retractable inner tube, such as the XF60mmF2.4 R Macro, or the XF35mmF1.4 R. The inner tube of these lenses doesn't respond well to shocks and pressure. By using a screw-on hood, you'd directly transfer pressure or shocks from the lens hood to the delicate inner lens tube. It's a recipe for disaster.

Lens protection filters—yes or no?   **TIP 21**

Digital cameras like the X-T5 don't require the UV or sky-light filters that were popular in the days of analog film photography. This means that a permanently affixed UV filter has no optical purpose, and only serves as protective glass. This additional glass can have a negative effect on image quality, especially at night or when you shoot against a bright light source. Filters increase the risks of ghosting, unwanted reflections, and a loss of contrast.

I recommend using protective glass only in situations that require this additional protective layer. In most situations, the lens hood should provide sufficient protection. If you still decide to use a filter, make sure to choose a high-quality product. Fujifilm offers suitable protective filters that feature the same Super EBC coating used on their XF and XC lenses. Be prepared to pay a premium, though.

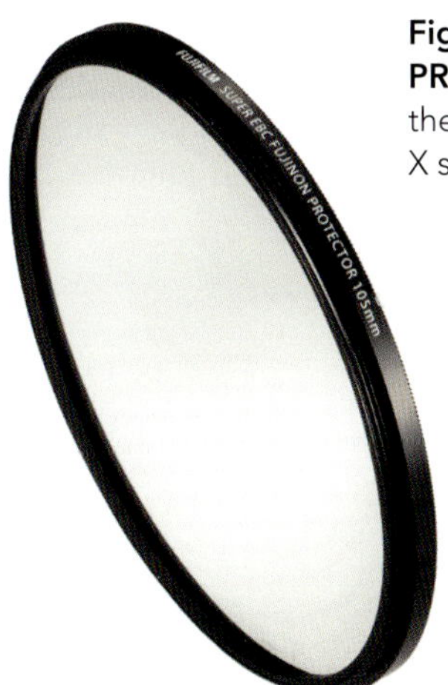

Fig. 27: With a diameter of 105 mm, the **PRF-105** for the XF200mmF2 is (so far) the largest lens protection filter for the X series.

<table><tr><td>**TIP 22**</td><td>39 mm filters can be tricky!</td></tr></table>

The XF60mmF2.4 R Macro and XF27mmF2.8 (R WR) lenses require filters with a 39 mm thread. These filters are designed to allow the inner lens barrel to freely retract into the outer barrel while the filter is attached. If this isn't possible (for example, because a thin step-up ring is directly attached to the lens or because the filter's overall diameter is too large), the lens can be damaged when the filter or step-up ring collides with the outer barrel of the lens.

A typical indicator for this and other mechanical lens problems is a message alerting you that the camera needs to be switched off and on again. A possible solution is putting a spacer (a fitting 39 mm filter, for example) between the lens and the step-up ring. You should remove the glass from the spacer. You can refit a cheap, old, or unused 39 mm filter to do the job if it doesn't interfere with the outer lens barrel when the inner barrel is retracting.

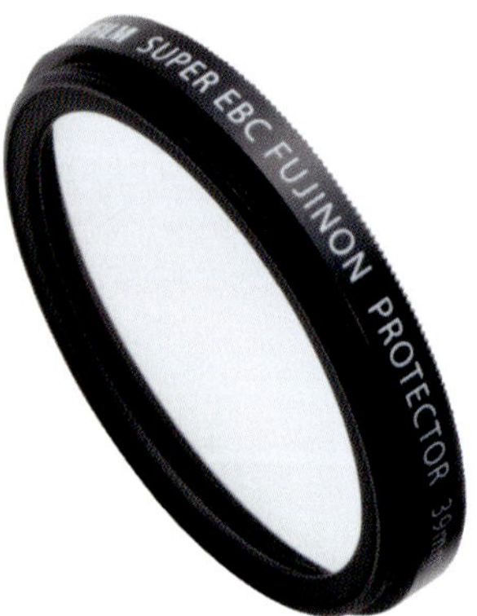

Fig. 28: A **39 mm protection filter** by Fujifilm. A filter like this can also be used as a spacer between the lens (XF60mm or XF27mm) and a step-up ring.

<table><tr><td>**TIP 23**</td><td>Switch off the camera when changing lenses!</td></tr></table>

The user manual of your camera tells you to switch off the camera before changing lenses. Then again, who cares, right? In the heat of the moment, many of us forget (or simply don't have the time) to follow this advice, and so far, nothing terrible has happened.

However, instead of getting into a bad habit, we should consider why Fujifilm is telling us to change lenses only when the camera is turned off:

- Several lenses (like the XF60mmF2.4 R Macro or the XF27mmF2.8) have moving inner barrels. During focusing, the inner barrel can protrude beyond the protective edge of the outer barrel. The secure storage and transport state for these lenses is always with a fully retracted inner barrel, and this secure state is automatically entered when you turn off the camera *before* you remove the lens.

- The same applies to lenses like the XC15-45mmF3.5–5.6 OIS PZ power zoom. Switch off the camera while the lens is still attached, and the power zoom will safely retract to its compact transport and storage position. If you remove the lens before turning off the camera, your lens may end up in a less compact and more vulnerable state.

- When the camera/lens is powering off, a lock mechanism holds the linear motor driven inner-focusing element of some lenses (like the XF200mmF2 R LM OIS WR) in place. This suppresses clacking noises (caused by the loose lens group) when you carry the lens around off-camera. If you remove the lens while the camera is still powered on, this locking mechanism will not be activated. By the way, clacking sounds are perfectly normal for other lenses with inner-focusing mechanisms, such as the XF90mmF2 R LM or XF50–140mmF2.8 R LM OIS WR, so don't worry, nothing is broken. Off-camera, there's simply no camera-powered magnetic field to hold the rear element in place, so it will loosely move in the barrel when you shake the lens.

<table>
<tr><td>TIP 24</td><td>Confusion about lens support for 40 megapixels</td></tr>
</table>

With the announcement of the X-H2, Fujifilm published a list of lenses "to get the maximum benefit" from the new 40.2-megapixel sensor that is also working in your X-T5. The list encompasses a variety of XF prime and zoom lenses, most of them recent models that are still actively sold and promoted. This guideline was quickly misinterpreted as a compatibility chart, implying that lenses not on the list weren't fully compatible with 40 MP bodies like the X-H2 and X-T5.

Use the following lenses to get the maximum benefit from X-H2's 40.2 megapixel sensor

XF16mmF2.8 R WR / XF18mmF1.4 R LM WR / XF23mmF1.4 R LM WR / XF23mmF2 R WR / XF27mmF2.8 R WR / XF33mmF1.4 R LM WR / XF35mmF2 R WR / XF50mmF1.0 R WR / XF50mmF2 R WR / XF56mmF1.2 R WR / XF80mmF2.8 R LM OIS MACRO / XF90mmF2 R LM WR / XF200mmF2 R LM OIS WR / XF8-16mmF2.8 R LM WR / XF16-55mmF2.8 R LM WR / XF18-120mmF4 LM PZ WR / XF50-140mmF2.8 R LM OIS WR / XF70-300mmF4-5.6 R LM OIS WR / XF100-400mmF4.5-5.6 R LM OIS WR / XF150-600mmF5.6-8 R LM OIS WR

Fig. 29: Fujifilm's infamous list of lenses for the new 40 MP sensor quickly developed a life of its own, leading to rumors and misinformation.

Misinformation tends to spread fast, so here's the real deal about lenses (old and new) and the high-resolution 40 MP sensor:

- No lens suddenly turns worse when it is mounted on a high-resolution sensor—not even manually adapted legacy glass with soft resolution and corner issues. If you keep your established workflow, using older lenses with a 40 MP sensor won't negatively impact your results. Of course, more sensor resolution means that you can spot deficiencies more clearly at the highest magnification level (a.k.a. pixel peeping), but that's inconsequential for real-world applications where you print or display your work in the same size and resolution as ever.

- A higher sensor resolution means better oversampling. In the real world, you will rarely have to export images with your camera's full 40 MP resolution. Most digital images end up on social media, on sites like Flickr, or on 4K displays, so your required export resolution will rarely exceed 10 megapixels. Since cameras with Bayer or X-Trans sensors record only one third of the actual RGB image information in the RAW file (the missing two thirds are interpolated during RAW conversion), it's beneficial to "oversample." Tests have shown that four-times oversampling renders great results. Wait, what? Four-times oversampling means that your *recording resolution* is four times as high as the *export resolution* of your files. This is why GFX cameras record 100 megapix-els—they produce amazing 25 MP images! So, with the 40 MP sensor in your X-T5, you'll get awesome 10 MP files, which is perfect for 4K displays. Simply select a size percentage of 50% when you export a JPEG in Lightroom or Capture One. Or select size "S" when creating files using your camera's built-in RAW converter. By merging four native *recording pixels* into one high-quality *export pixel*, 50% downsampling gets rid of most demosaicing artifacts. The resulting 10 MP files look cleaner and more detailed than files that were natively recorded with a 10 MP camera.

- Fujifilm's list omits lenses that are optically identical with lenses that are on it. For example, the XC35mmF2 houses the same optics as the XF35mmF2 R WR. The same ap-plies to the XF27mm2.8 and the new XF27mmF2.8 R WR. And yet, the XF35mmF2 R WR and the older XF27mm2.8 didn't make the list. Huh!

- By ignoring older lenses like the wonderful XF60mmF2.4 R Macro, Fujifilm's lens list appears to be marketing-driven. And don't forget that lenses behave differently at different aperture settings. For example, the discontinued XF56mmF1.2 R didn't make the list, probably because it doesn't deliver perfect corner sharpness at f/1.2. However, stop down to f/5.6, and it will render results that were good enough for dpreview.com to use it as their reference lens for their Fujifilm camera tests, including those with 40 MP sensors.

- Pixel peeping is *not* your friend. With increasing sensor resolution, reviewing images at 100%+ magnification on your PC becomes more and more like looking through a microscope. You'll see things and issues that are invisible when you are looking at the "big picture" that is hanging on a wall, shown on a 4K monitor, or displayed on Flickr.

Upgrading to 40 MP doesn't mean that you must also upgrade your lenses. If you were happy with your existing set of lenses and don't change your workflow, everything will be just fine, and you can still benefit from better oversampling. However, if you modify your workflow by suddenly exporting larger files or printing larger than before, your mileage may vary. The same applies if you cannot resist the urge to inspect your shots at screen magnification levels of 100% or more.

At maximum magnification, the 40 MP sensor in your X-T5 reveals and amplifies the qualities and weaknesses of every lens, so issues that have always been there become more visible. However, these amplified issues disappear in the real world when you apply established workflows and look at the big picture.

1.3 THE BASICS (3): USEFUL ACCESSORIES

There is a rich selection of accessories for your X-T5. Whether or not you believe such add-ons are useful, I'll cover a few select items that can, in my opinion and experience, improve the functionality of your camera.

<table><tr><td>Optional handgrips</td><td>TIP 25</td></tr></table>

An optional handgrip can improve the ergonomics of the X-T5 when you are using large, heavy lenses or if you have large hands.

The Metal Hand Grip MHG-XT3 for the X-T3 doesn't fit on the X-T5, and Fujifilm never offered an "MHG-XT4" for the X-T4. Luckily, there's now an MHG-XT5 with a built-in Arca-Swiss-style tripod rail. However, this grip is rather expensive.

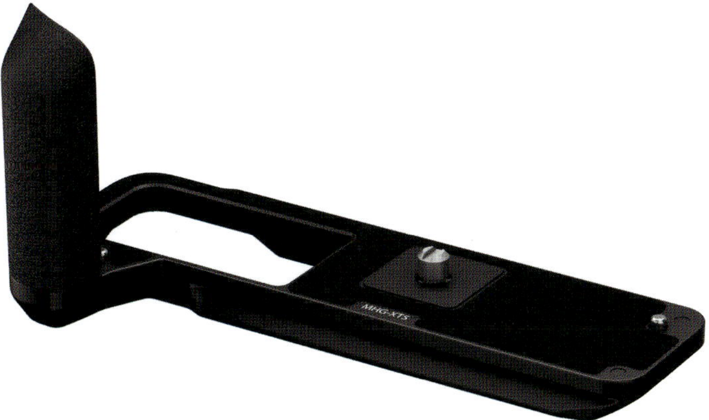

Fig. 30: Fujifilm's **MHG-XT5** is a premium metal handgrip for the X-T5 with built-in Arca Swiss tripod support.

More affordable alternatives from SmallRig still provide full access to the battery compartment and are also compatible with Arca-Swiss-type tripod heads. SmallRig offers at least two different handgrips for the X-T5: a regular metal grip in silver (product number 4136) or black (product number 4260), and an L bracket (product number 4137) to facilitate vertical shooting from a tripod.

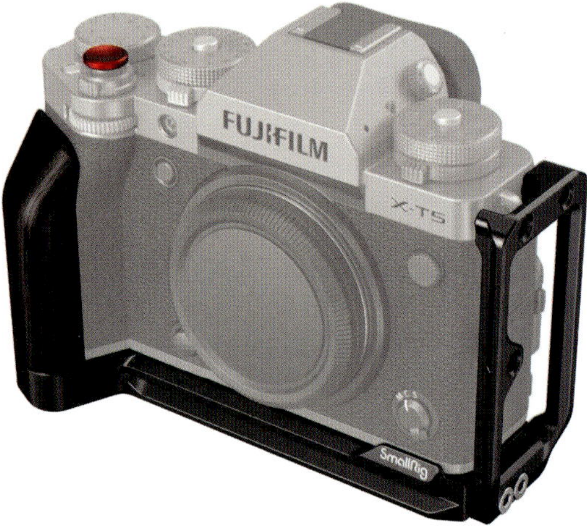

Fig. 31: The **SmallRig 4137 L bracket** makes upright shooting from a tripod easy.

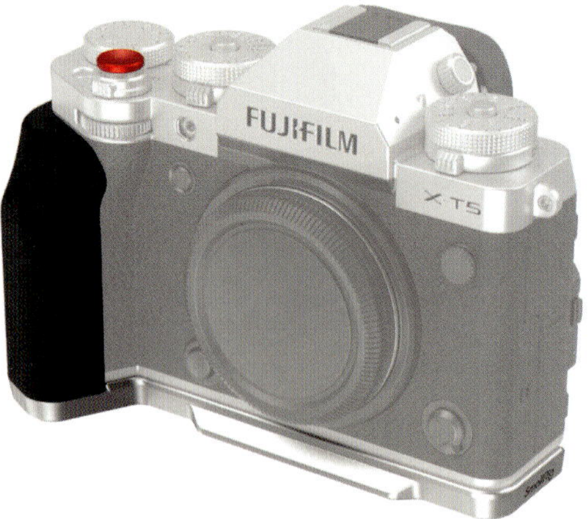

Fig. 32: The **SmallRig 4136 grip** comes in silver and is a less expensive alternative to Fujifilm's MHG-XT5 grip.

Even though the SmallRig 4136 is a little bit larger than Fujifilm's MHG-XT5, it weighs approx. 20 grams less (I measured 74 g vs. 95 g). It's also considerably cheaper but at the same time not as robust as the very well-made Fuji grip, especially considering the quality and durability of the attachment screw. On the other hand, the SmallRig grip allows you to attach a hand strap, and the package even includes a red "soft release button" that you can screw into the X-T5's mechanical shutter button remote release thread.

Another accessory for Fujifilm cameras is the Bluetooth-enabled tripod grip TG-BT1. Used as a grip, it can stabilize the camera during shooting, so you can achieve slower shutter speeds without camera shake. Used as a tripod, it can help you make steady long exposures by placing it on a table or a wall.

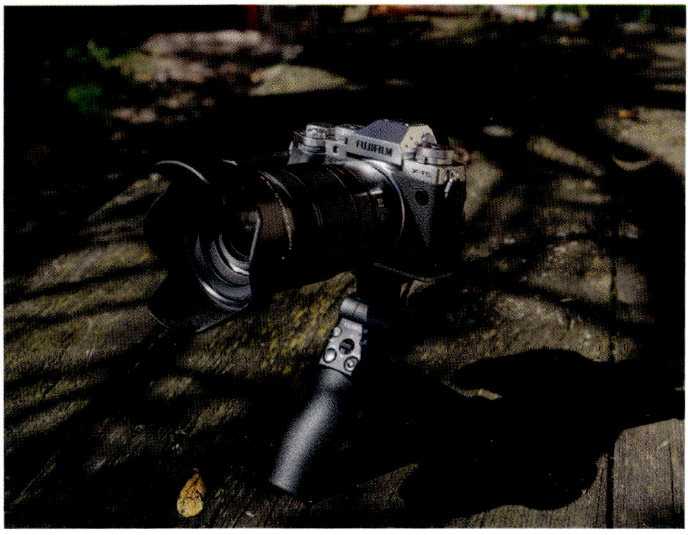

Fig. 33: My X-T5 with an attached XF18–120mmF4 LM PZ WR on a **TG-BT1 tripod grip**.

The TG-BT1 features a few buttons and levers and talks to the camera via Bluetooth, so you can also use it as a wireless remote release for stills and video. Combined with a power zoom lens like the XF18–120mmF4 LM PZ WR, you can also remotely control the zoom function. Finally, the TG-BT1 can serve as a selfie stick to record images or "walk and talk" videos.

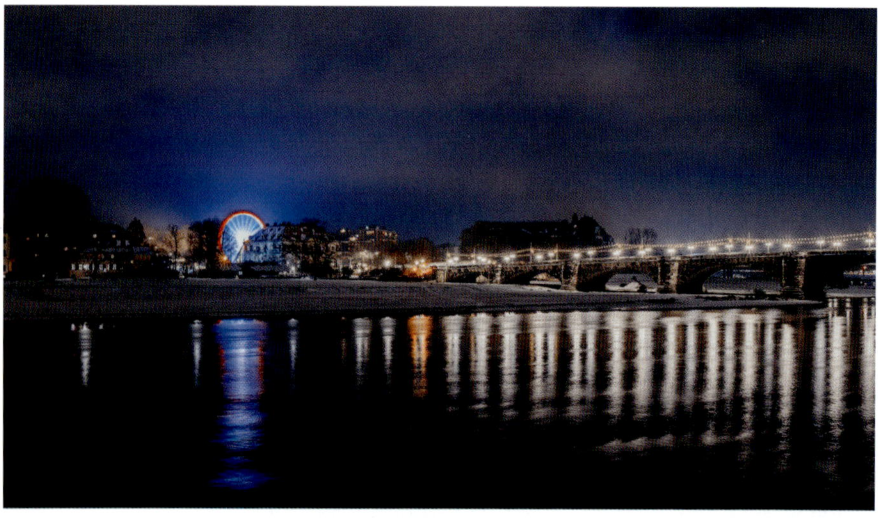

Fig. 34: This long exposure was taken with the **X-T5 and TG-BT1** sitting on a wall.

Please note that there's no vertical battery grip for the X-T5. If you need more power than the single battery in the camera can provide, you can connect an external power source via the USB-C port.

TIP 26	Remote shutter release options

From time to time you may encounter situations that require you to remotely release the shutter without vibration. A quick-and-dirty method is to use the camera's self-timer with a delay of either two or ten seconds, although a better way is to use a remote shutter release.

Your X-T5 offers three remote shutter release options:

- A **mechanical thread** in the shutter release button allows you to connect a traditional screw-in cable release.

- You can connect electronic remote shutter releases to the camera's **RR-100 remote release port** (a 2.5 mm input on the left side of the body).

- You can trigger the shutter via **Bluetooth** using Fujifilm's free Camera Remote app [21], the new XApp, or a TG-BT1 tripod grip.

Electronic shutter releases are available in tethered and wireless versions. Wireless options always consist of a transmitter and a receiver. The transmitter sends a trigger signal that is picked up by the receiver, which triggers the camera with an electronic cable that's connected to the RR-100 remote release port.

Fujifilm offers a simple RR-100-compatible remote shutter release cable, but there are more sophisticated (both tethered and wireless) solutions available from third parties, such as programmable intervalometers.

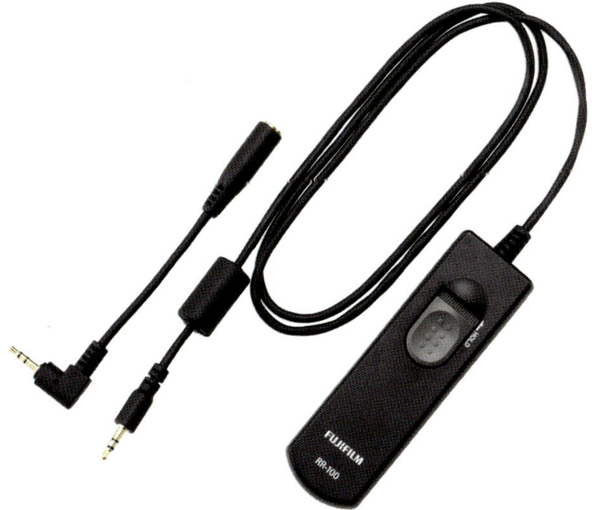

Fig. 35: Fujifilm's **RR-100** is a simple and reliable remote release for your X-T5.

The RR-100 remote release port of the X-T5 is compatible with a widely used Canon remote shutter release standard. Personally, I'm a big fan of Canon's simple yet effective **RS-60E3** electronic remote shutter release. It's small and affordable, and it shines with a nice attention to detail.

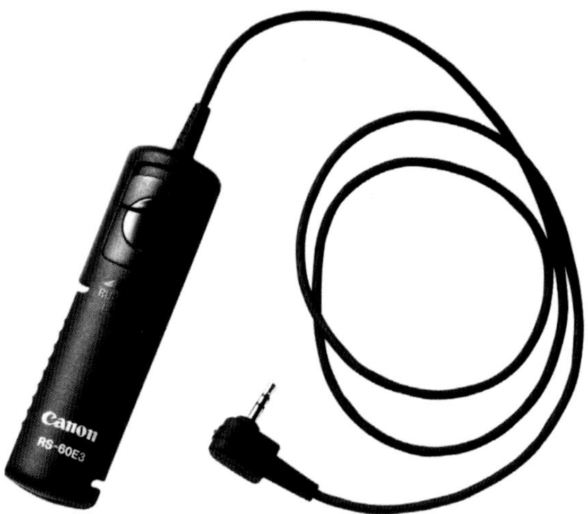

Fig. 36: The **Canon RS-60E3** is my favorite electronic cable release for Fujifilm X cameras—thanks to its attention to detail. Two notches make it easy to neatly spool the cable around the release after shooting. There is also a built-in socket for the 2.5 mm plug that prevents the cable from unspooling in the bag.

Since your X-T5 supports Bluetooth, you can use a semi-permanent wireless connection to your smartphone or tablet to release the shutter with the Camera Remote app [22], the newer XApp, or with a Fujifilm **TG-BT1** tripod grip. Alternatively, you can remotely control your X-T5 via a Wi-Fi connection. Step-by-step instructions are available online [23].

2. USING THE FUJIFILM X-T5

2.1 READY, SET, GO!

New users often ask about how to achieve the perfect settings for their camera. Short answer: there are no perfect settings. If they existed, Fuji could have saved us the trouble of navigating the menu options and simply implemented those ideal settings as the factory default. That said, allow me to suggest some basic settings that are meant to provide good overall performance along with as much flexibility and user-friendliness as possible.

- Many settings (such as film simulation modes, color saturation, contrast, sharpness, noise reduction, film grain effect, etc.) belong in the "JPEG settings" category. They don't affect the RAW files but only affect the out-of-camera JPEGs that are generated during RAW conversion. These settings aren't global or camera-specific—they are *image-specific,* and each image should be adjusted individually.

- In addition to the recommended standard settings, there are many shortcuts and key combinations that can make selecting the optimal camera settings for any situation much easier.

Recommended default settings for your X-T5	TIP 27

There is no perfect set of basic camera settings that could suit all users in all situations. However, the following settings will allow you to use the X-T5 in a flexible, user-friendly manner with good overall performance:

- Select **FINE+RAW** or **NORMAL+RAW** under IMAGE QUALITY SETTING > IMAGE QUALITY. This will get you high-resolution out-of-camera JPEGs (digital prints) *and* flexible RAW files (digital negatives). Using the RAW files, you can create a variety of diverse JPEGs with different looks and settings using the camera's built-in RAW converter (PLAYBACK MENU > RAW CONVERSION). Specifically, you can adjust JPEG parameters such as white balance, film simulation, contrast, brightness, noise reduction, and color saturation. This enables you to create different versions of a shot from a single RAW file; for example, you can make color and black-and-white versions of the same image, including different contrast settings. You don't have to worry about finding the perfect JPEG settings prior to taking a shot because you can always change and optimize those settings afterward in the camera's internal RAW converter.

- **Do *not* use the HEIF format, at least for now.** Instead, set IMAGE QUALITY > SELECT JPEG/HEIF to JPEG. Theoretically, the HEIF format is the superior choice: it's smaller and offers a higher bit-depth with less compression artifacts than JPEG. However, Fujifilm's HEIF format appears to be incompatible with many applications and operating systems. As of June 2023, neither Adobe Lightroom or Capture One Pro 23 could import Fujifilm HEIF files, and macOS itself changes the tonality (contrast, colors) of imported Fujifilm HEIF files, so your images look different (as in, worse) than they looked in-camera. Please note that HEIF (or HEIC) images from Apple devices (iPhones, etc.) work perfectly with Lightroom and Capture One and don't display tonality shifts in macOS or iOS. So, it appears to be a specific issue with Fujifilm's version of 10-bit HEIF images.

- Make sure to use **electronic front curtain + mechanical shutter** as your default shutter setting by selecting SHOOTING SETTING > SHUTTER TYPE > EF+M. Using the electronic shutter (ES) can create all kinds of issues and should be limited to the rare cases where the ES is beneficial, such as shooting with a wide-open aperture (and without an ND filter) in bright daylight, situations that require you to shoot in complete silence (with the alternative of not shooting at all), or situations that require high blackout-free burst rates up to 20 fps. You can also select EF+M+E in SHUTTER TYPE if you want the X-T5 to automatically switch from MS to ES when the shutter speed exceeds 1/8000 sec.

- As a typical standard setting, most photographers use **single shot drive** (select S on the DRIVE dial) and **single shot autofocus** (AF-S; select S with the focus selector on the front of the camera).

- The most flexible AF mode setting is **ALL** (AF/MF SETTING > AF MODE > ALL), so please use this mode as your default setting. This way, you can seamlessly cycle between Single-Point, Zone, and Wide/Tracking AF modes simply by changing the AF frame size (press the focus stick and change the AF frame size with the rear command dial).

- Speaking of the **focus stick**: It's very important that you set it to PUSH > EDIT FOCUS AREA and to TILT > DIRECT AF POINT SELECTION. Please note that this is *not* the X-T5's default setting. However, only this setting ensures that the X-T5 behaves like previous X-T cameras and unleashes all its focus control features. All focus-related tips in this book are based on this focus stick configuration. To access the focus stick configuration page, simply press and hold the stick until the configuration page appears.

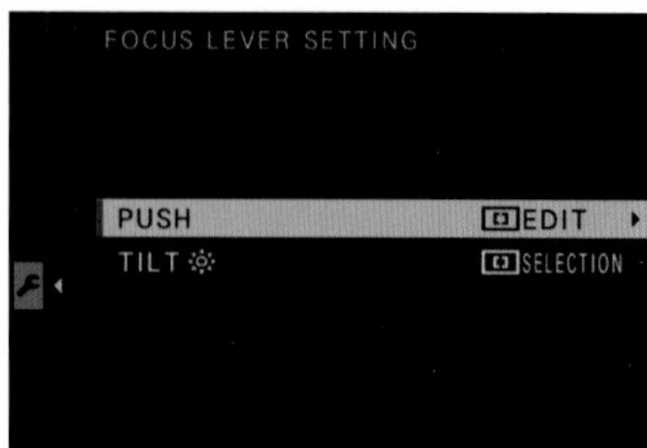

Fig. 37: It's vital that you **configure the focus stick as pictured here**. To do so, press and hold the focus stick until the FOCUS LEVER SETTING page appears.

- Set your X-T5 to **Boost mode** for maximum performance by selecting SET UP > POWER MANAGEMENT > PERFOR-MANCE > BOOST. This option is *not* enabled by default, so you must manually select it. Only Boost mode unleashes the full potential of the camera, offering the fastest available live view readout (EVF FRAME RATE PRIORITY) and best autofocus performance (all Boost mode options). Boost mode uses up more energy, so make sure to carry one or two fully charged replacement batteries.

- Set **Focus Priority** via AF/MF SETTING > RELEASE/FOCUS PRIORITY > FOCUS for both AF-S and AF-C. Focus Priority makes sure that the camera records a picture only when the autofocus thinks that it has locked onto a target. In RELEASE mode, the camera will take the shot even if the autofocus couldn't lock on a target. Please note that if you are using AF+MF mode, AF-S will always operate with release priority. That's why my recommended default setting for AF/MF SETTING > AF+MF is OFF.

- If you want to quickly take a series of single shots, I recommend selecting SET UP > SCREEN SET-UP > IMAGE DISP. > OFF to not interrupt your flow. However, I *normally* set **Image Display** to the shortest available time span of 0.5 SEC. I like to see a quick preview of the final image that represents the camera's exposure and dynamic range (DR) settings. To cancel an ongoing image preview and continue shooting, simply half-press the shutter button.

- Use the VIEW MODE button to activate the **eye sensor,** which will allow the camera to automatically switch between the viewfinder (EVF) and the LCD monitor depending on which view is in use. There's also an alternative mode called EVF ONLY + EYE SENSOR, which is an energy-saving mode. This mode can make it more difficult to operate the camera because the LCD monitor won't be available for changing menus while in shooting mode.

- For **exposure metering**, I recommend using MULTI metering as your default mode. Intelligent matrix metering usually delivers results that don't require a massive amount of exposure correction. You can set the metering mode in the SHOOTING SETTING > PHOTOMETRY menu. That said, if you are like me and shoot everything in manual exposure mode, SPOT metering is usually a better choice.

- Set **white balance** to Auto via IMAGE QUALITY SETTING > WHITE BALANCE > AUTO to let the camera determine and set the correct white balance for a scene. Since you are shooting FINE+RAW or NORMAL+RAW, you can always adjust the white balance later, either with the camera's built-in RAW converter or with external RAW conversion software such as Lightroom. That said, AUTO will deliver very good results in most scenarios.

- Set **Dynamic Range** by selecting IMAGE QUALITY SETTING > DYNAMIC RANGE > DR100% as your default setting. If you require more highlight dynamic range (DR) for a specific subject to avoid blown highlights, you can manually set DR200% (for *one* extra stop of dynamic range in the highlights) or DR400% (for *two* extra stops of dynamic range in the highlights). Setting DYNAMIC RANGE to AUTO is *not* recommended. Extending the dynamic range can bring back texture to otherwise blown-out areas of your shot (such as in white clouds on a sunny day).

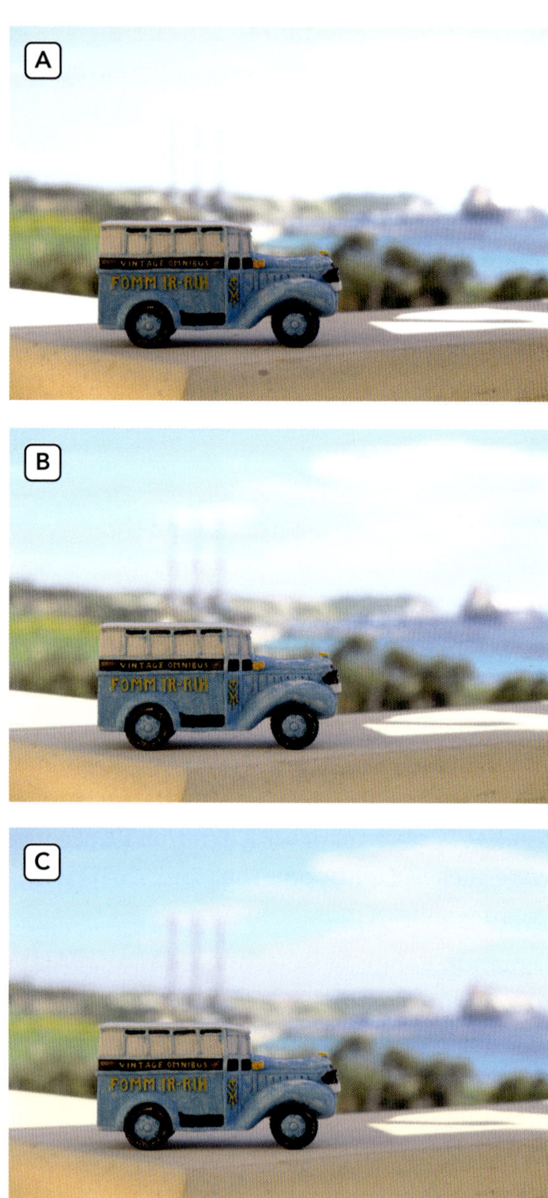

Fig. 38: All Fujifilm X cameras feature a powerful and often misunderstood **DR function** that can increase highlight dynamic range by up to two full stops (EV). The default setting is DR100% (**A**). Seeing blown-out highlights that you do not like? Increase dynamic range to DR200% (**B**) or DR400% (**C**) to get an extra one or two stops worth of highlight detail.

- To use **adapted lenses** with your X-T5, you need either Fujifilm's Leica M adapter or a suitable third-party adapter. To make mechanical third-party adapters work, you must select SET UP > BUTTON/DIAL SETTING > SHOOT WITHOUT LENS > ON. This is necessary because mechanically adapted lenses (and third-party lens adapters) do not feature electronic X-mount contacts, so the lens will not register as being connected to the camera. When you are working with a mechanically adapted lens, you must also enter its focal length in SHOOTING SETTING > MOUNT ADAPTOR SETTING. Without this information, the IBIS will not work correctly. It also ensures that EXIF [24] data will reflect the proper focal length.

- Do you sometimes shoot with very slow shutter speeds lasting several seconds? In this case, I recommend setting IMAGE QUALITY SETTING > LONG EXPOSURE NR > ON to improve the quality of your results. In this **Long Exposure** mode, the camera performs a so-called dark-frame subtraction [25] to reduce noise and eliminate hot pixels. With this process, the total exposure time is at least doubled because the camera is taking the shot twice: once normally and once with a closed shutter curtain. The second shot is then subtracted from the first to improve the overall result.

- I recommend *not* using the AUTO setting for the **brightness control for the EVF** because it tends to show an overly bright live view image in bright sunlight and a subdued image when it's dark. Instead, I select SET UP > SCREEN SET-UP > EVF BRIGHTNESS > MANUAL > 0.

- In this book, we assume that **SHUTTER AF** and **SHUTTER AE** (in the SET UP > BUTTON DIAL SETTING menu) are both set to ON. This ensures that autofocus and exposure (including the working aperture) are locked when you half-press the shutter button in AF-S mode, so the camera is primed for the least possible shutter lag once you fully press the shutter button. In AF-C mode, SHUTTER AF ON means the AF keeps tracking a subject while the shutter button is half-pressed or pressed, and SHUTTER AE ON makes sure the exposure is locked as long as you half-press or press the shutter button.

■ I select SET UP > BUTTON DIAL SETTING > COMMAND DIAL SETTING > *front command dial* 1 > F (aperture) and COMMAND DIAL SETTING > *rear command dial* > S.S. (shutter speed). All related recommendations in this book are based on this setting. In the same menu, my settings for *front command dial* 2 and *front command dial* 3 are ISO and EXPOSURE COMPENSATION, respectively. This means you can cycle between aperture, ISO, and exposure compensation settings by pressing the front command dial. Of course, you are free to set-up your X-T5 differently. Just remember which dial is supposed to perform a specific function that I mention in this book.

<table>
<tr><td>TIP 28</td><td>Avoiding the camera menus: practical shortcuts for your X-T5</td></tr>
</table>

Navigating nested camera menus can be cumbersome. That's why the X-T5 offers the Quick menu (Q button) and user-configurable Fn keys that can provide direct access to important and frequently used camera functions and settings.

The X-T5 also offers seven custom user settings (C1 through C7) that can hold sets of frequently used camera configurations. You can select one of these sets via the Quick menu or an appropriately configured Fn button. Unlike earlier models, the X-T5 treats C1 through C7 like actual camera modes, so you can change your global camera configuration by selecting one of the 7 custom modes.

Finally, the X-T5 offers the MY MENU settings, where you can arrange frequently used menu items on two configurable menu pages for quick and easy access.

Please note that the X-T5 offers two full sets of MY MENU, Quick menu, and custom settings: one for photography and one for video. Depending on the status of the STILL/MOVIE switch, the X-T5 provides the appropriate set of shortcuts and settings.

Sadly, there is only one set of Fn and T-Fn function buttons, so you can't allocate different assignments for photography and video.

Speaking of shortcuts—there are plenty, and most of them are available at your fingertips:

- Pull up the Quick menu, then press and hold the Q button again for a few seconds to directly open the configuration menu for your custom user configurations (C1 to C7).

- Press and hold the Q button while the Quick menu is *not* opened to directly access the Quick menu configuration page, where you can customize the Quick menu to meet your personal requirements. You can assign one of dozens of settings to any of the 16 available Quick menu slots. You can even select NONE, or you can go to SET UP > BUTTON/DIAL SETTING > EDIT/SAVE QUICK MENU to reduce the size of the Quick menu from 16 to 12, 8, or 4 slots. For this book, we use all 16 slots in the camera's STILL mode for photography.

- To review where the Fn and Touch-Fn buttons are located and what's assigned to each of them, simply press and hold the DISP/BACK button until the configuration page appears. In this menu, you can also reassign all Fn and Touch-Fn buttons.

- To confirm a new menu selection in shooting mode, you can either press the MENU/OK button or half-press the shutter button.

- Half-press the shutter button to switch from playback mode back to shooting mode.

- Half-press the shutter button during an ongoing image preview (SET UP > SCREEN SET-UP > IMAGE DISP.) to immediately cancel the preview.

- Half-press the shutter button for a few seconds to wake up the camera from sleep mode.

- In AF-S shooting mode (with Single Point AF) or MF mode, press the rear command dial to zoom into the currently active focus frame. When zoomed-in, you can select various magnification levels by turning the rear command dial. You can also move the focus stick to change the magnified portion of the live view. Please note that this magnifier tool is the default configuration for the rear command dial Fn button. If you assign a different function to the R-DIAL Fn button, this useful zoom shortcut won't be available. Please note that the magnifier shortcut isn't available in AF-S / Single Point AF mode when Pre-AF is on.

- Press and hold the rear command dial in MF mode to cycle between the available manual focus assist modes, such as standard, focus peaking, digital microprism, and digital split image.

- Press and hold the focus stick in shooting mode to access the focus stick options. Make sure that the stick is set to PUSH > EDIT and TILT > SELECTION. This is *not* the factory default setting. However, this setting is required to properly use and benefit from several tips in this book.

- While in shooting mode, press the focus stick to access the FOCUS AREA configuration screen. Here, you can use the focus stick to move the active focus frame or zone, and you can change their size by turning one of the command dials. In this configuration screen, you can press DISP/BACK to center the focus frame or zone. Please note that this shortcut only works with the proper focus stick configuration that I have just described.

- In the FOCUS AREA screen (which pops up when you press the focus stick), you can also use the four selector (arrow or directional) keys to move the AF frame or zone. You can change the size of the AF frame or zone by turning one of the command dials. To reset the size of the AF frame or AF zone, press any of the two command dials.

- In shooting mode, you can move the focus stick directly in eight directions to change the position of the active focus frame or zone. However, their size can't be changed before pressing the focus stick.

- In shooting mode, press and hold the MENU/OK button to lock user-selected camera controls (buttons, dials, menus). Press and hold it again to unlock the camera and restore all controls. You can configure the controls that should be locked in SET UP > BUTTON/DIAL SETTING > LOCK > FUNCTION SELECTION. This is an easy way to temporarily lock specific camera functions or controls and protect them from accidental changes during shooting.

- In playback mode (while viewing an image), turn the front command dial to browse through the images that are on file.

- During playback, you can turn the rear command dial to zoom in and out of an image. By pressing the DISP/BACK button, you can directly return to the standard-size view. Press the rear command dial or the focus stick to zoom in to a 100% view of a shot. You can then zoom in even further by turning the rear command dial. When you are zoomed in, pressing the dial again returns the camera to its regular view, displaying the full image.

- While displaying a RAW image in playback mode, you can press the Q button to directly access the built-in RAW converter. This function allows you to create new

JPEG, HEIF, or TIFF versions of your image using different settings.

- In playback mode, press the upper selector button (or move the focus stick upward) to view the first of two information pages that show additional shooting parameters and the position of the focus point.

- In playback mode, you can use the focus stick as an alternative to the selector buttons and the MENU/OK button.

- Press and hold the playback button in playback mode to directly switch between the two memory card slots (if you are using two cards at the same time).

- For direct access to the SD card formatting menu, press and hold the DELETE (trash symbol) button and the rear command dial together for about three seconds.

TIP 29	Suggested Fn button assignment

Thoughtful assignment of your X-T5's Fn and Touch-Fn buttons will save you many cumbersome trips to the camera menu. You can display and change the assignment of all available Fn buttons in one convenient menu: in shooting mode, press and hold the DISP/BACK button until the configuration page called FUNCTION (Fn) SETTING appears.

Here are my suggested Fn and Touch-Fn button assignments:

- **Fn1: HISTOGRAM.** Your X-T5 features an RGB live histogram with live overexposure warnings, also known as "blinkies." The only way to access this essential feature is via an Fn or a Touch-Fn button, so please make sure it is assigned to one. Personally, I am using Fn1.

- **Fn2: ELECTRONIC LEVEL.** In addition to the regular single-axis indicator, the X-T5 offers a dual-axis electronic level display. The dual-axis indicator helps you correctly align the camera to avoid non-parallel vertical lines, especially in city and architecture shots.

- **Fn3: SUBJECT DETECTION ON/OFF.** This setting allows you to quickly switch the subject detection autofocus on and off.

- **Fn4: RIGHT/LEFT EYE SWITCH.** This button lets you switch eyes in face/eye detection autofocus mode.

- **Fn5: DYNAMIC RANGE.** Fujifilm cameras offer a very powerful and high-quality DR function to extend the highlight dynamic range of an image, so it's a very good idea to keep this function right at your fingertips.

- **Fn6: FACE DETECTION ON/OFF.** This button turns face/eye detection autofocus quickly on and off.

- **Touch-Fn1: DRIVE SETTING.** Accessing the DRIVE SETTING options menu via Fn or Touch-Fn is beneficial because, unlike the regular menu, it is context sensitive and only displays DRIVE options that apply to the DRIVE mode that has been currently selected with the DRIVE dial. For example, in DRIVE mode CH, flicking T-Fn4 will only show you options that apply to high-speed burst mode.

- **Touch-Fn2: PERFORMANCE.** This touch button quickly toggles the camera between Normal, Economy, and the four available Boost modes.

- **Touch-Fn3: D RANGE PRIORITY.** T-Fn3 is one of my "wild card" buttons where I can assign any function that I want to be accessible for a particular task at hand. My current default setting is D RANGE PRIORITY, but it could just as well be WHITE BALANCE or whatever suits the task at hand.

- **Touch-Fn4: AF-C CUSTOM SETTINGS.** AF-C Custom Settings allow fine-tuning the X-T5 for action photography and everything that involves moving subjects. In situations like this, time is of the essence, which is why I want quick, direct access to this menu.

- **AF-ON & AE-L: AF-ON and AE-L.** The dedicated AF-ON and AE-L buttons can also serve as Fn keys, so you can repurpose them as needed. Most users keep the default functions: AF-ON and AE-Lock. However, my *personal* choice for the AE-L button is PREVIEW EXP./WB IN MANUAL MODE. I am shooting everything in manual exposure mode, so I don't need AE Lock—it serves no purpose in mode M.

- **R-DIAL: FOCUS CHECK.** Pressing the rear command dial also serves as an Fn button. The factory default setting is FOCUS CHECK, which allows you to zoom into the live view image on the electronic viewfinder or LCD monitor. Since this is an important and convenient function, I do not recommend changing this default assignment. Please note that all related tips in this book assume that FOCUS CHECK is assigned to the rear command dial button.

- **Q: QUICK MENU.** Fujifilm also allows the Q button to serve as an Fn button. That said, I am happy with its position and don't want to change it. However, if you are coming from the X-T3 or want to use your X-T5 in concert with an X-T3, you might want to remap the button layout of your X-T5 to reflect that of the X-T3.

- **VIEW MODE:** I keep this button in its default VIEW MODE configuration. Of course, if you rarely change the view mode of your X-T5 (it may be in EYE SENSOR mode all the time), you can reassign this button to serve a different purpose. If you change this button, you can still adjust the camera's view mode for shooting and playback in the SET UP > SCREEN SET-UP > VIEW MODE SETTING menu.

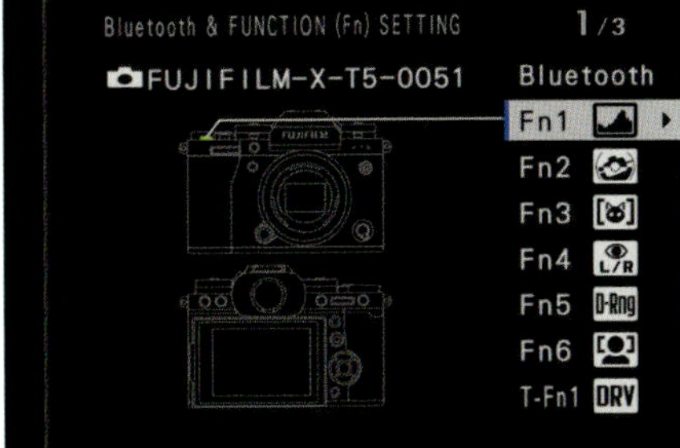

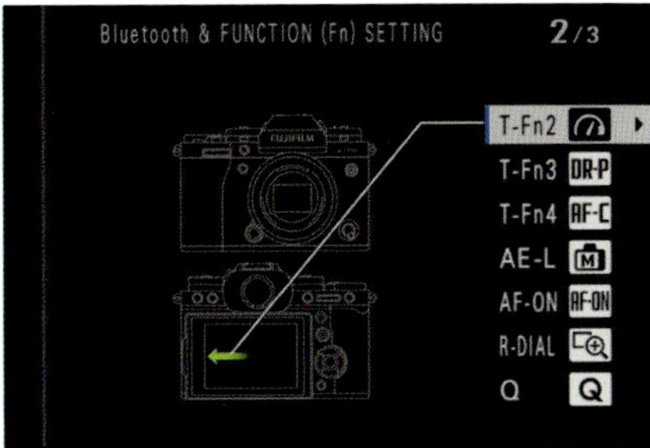

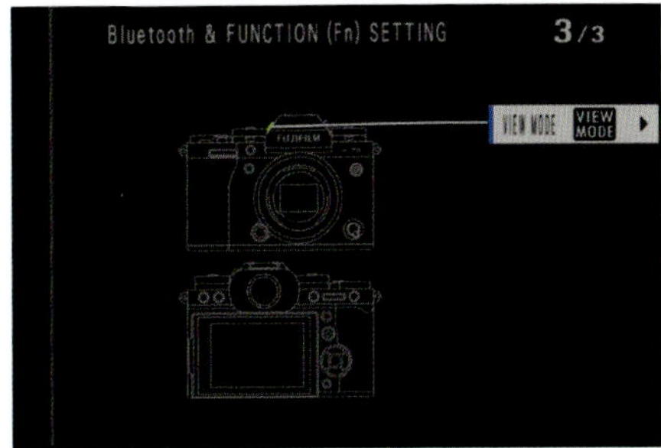

Fig. 39: This is the **Fn button assignment of my X-T5**. To edit the Fn buttons of your camera, press and hold the DISP/BACK button until the configuration page appears.

Please note that using a power zoom lens like the XF18–120mmF4 gives you three additional function buttons on the lens that can be freely configured in your X-T5. You can change the power zoom button configuration in the SET UP > BUTTON/DIAL SETTING > POWER ZOOM LENS FUNCTION (Fn) SETTING menu. Personally, I keep those buttons in their default settings.

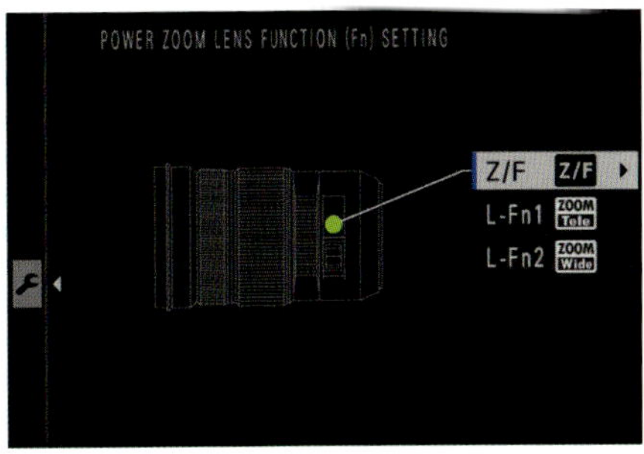

Fig. 40: The X-T5 also lets you configure **Fn buttons on power zoom lenses**.

<table><tr><td>TIP 30</td><td>Recommended My Menu and Quick menu configuration</td></tr></table>

To keep the shooting process effortless and free of interruptions, it's vital to assign frequently used functions to Fn buttons that are easily accessible. However, the number of available buttons is limited. Luckily, we also have My Menu and the Quick menu (Q button) to quickly access frequently used functions and menus that don't fit into the Fn button lineup.

- To configure **My Menu**, select SET UP > USER SETTING > MY MENU SETTING, where you can add new items, rank existing items (i.e., change their position in My Menu), or remove items from the menu.

- To configure the **Quick menu**, press and hold the Q button until the Quick menu configuration page appears. Here you can change each of the 16 slots and assign them either a new function or no function at all (NONE).

Please note that the X-T5 offers independent My Menu and Quick menu configurations for STILL and MOVIE mode. The following figures illustrate the My Menu and Quick menu settings in my X-T5 for STILL mode. Neither is set in stone.

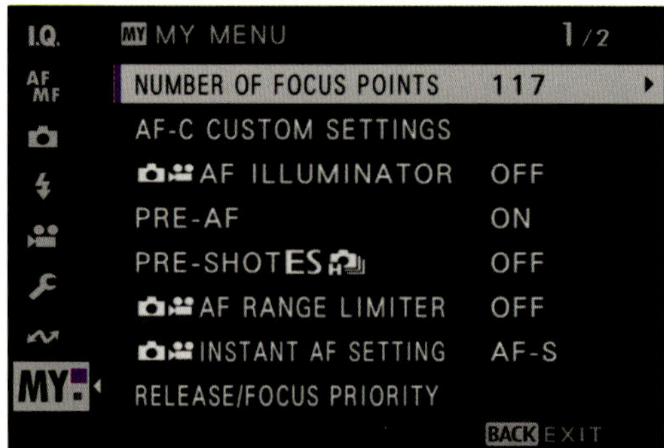

Fig. 41: My Menu in the X-T5 and other current X-series cameras consists of two menu pages with a total of 16 possible entries. I use the first page to quickly change and review settings that are related to focusing and autofocus.

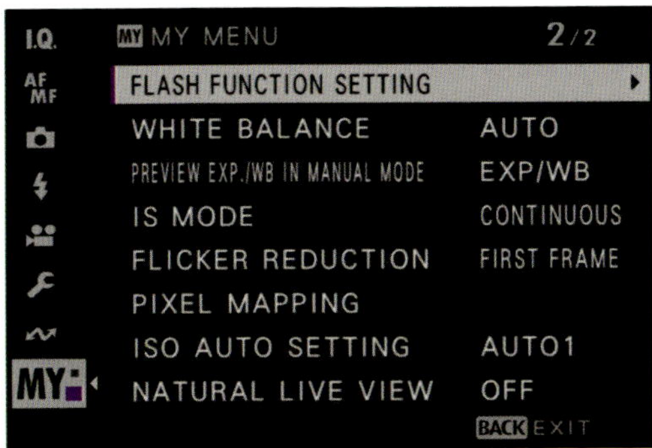

Fig. 42: The second **My Menu** page is reserved for exposure settings and general functions such as IBIS/OIS mode, flash configuration, pixel mapping or white balance options.

Please note that manual exposure mode **M** must be enabled to access the PREVIEW EXP./WB IN MANUAL MODE setting in My Menu.

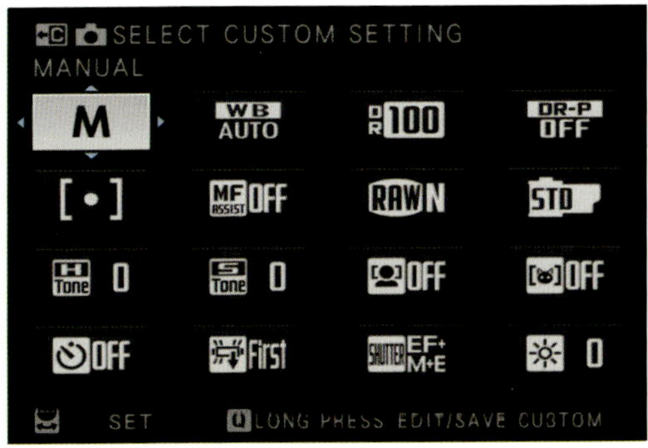

Fig. 43: The **Quick menu** page of my X-T5: Among other things, I want to have direct access to the shutter-type setting and flicker reduction as well as face/eye detection and subject detection options.

| Working with custom settings | TIP 31 |

Beginning with the X-S10, Fujifilm changed their custom settings to "global" camera configurations that contain (as in store and retrieve) most camera settings. Examples of X cameras with global custom settings are the X-S10, X-S20, X-E4, X-H2, X-H2S, GFX100, GFX100S, GFX50SII, and, of course, your X-T5. I assume that all upcoming models will feature them as well.

My recommendation is to set up global custom settings for specific tasks or situations. That way, you can quickly prime your camera for different scenes and subjects. For example, you could set up custom settings for portrait, landscape, action, or long exposure shots. In my experience, it's also useful to set IMAGE QUALITY SETTING > AUTO UPDATE CUSTOM SETTING to ENABLE. This allows you to select a custom setting as your starting point, then fine-tune it for the actual situation at hand. Any changes you make will automatically update that custom setting and refine it.

Of course, too much refining might eventually carry you away from your original custom sets for action, portrait, landscape, etc.—but that doesn't have to be an issue. You can save a copy of all your camera settings (including all your "generic" custom settings) on your Mac or PC with the free FUJIFILM X Acquire app [26] or on your mobile device using the new FUJIFILM XApp. That way, you can modify, adapt, and refine your initial custom settings at will during a shoot. When you are finished shooting a job, simply restore your previously saved full camera settings (including your original custom settings) with FUJIFILM X Acquire. You can even go further and use FUJIFILM X Acquire to swap between different sets of custom settings. After all, 2 × 7 sets (7 sets for video and 7 sets for still photography) may not be sufficient to cover all your shooting needs.

To create a custom setting, select IMAGE QUALITY SETTING > EDIT/SAVE CUSTOM SETTING > CREATE NEW at one of the seven available slots. This saves your current camera settings in this slot. You can name a custom setting by selecting it and choosing EDIT CUSTOM SETTING.

Sadly, the X-T5 stops short of saving *all* camera settings in a custom setting slot. To see what parameters can be saved, you can create a new or select an existing custom setting with IMAGE QUALITY SETTING > EDIT/SAVE CUSTOM SETTING and then pick EDIT/CHECK. The camera will now show you all available menu items. Items that cannot be saved in custom settings are grayed out. In addition to this, you cannot save settings that can also be accessed via "analog" dials and switches. These settings are: aperture, shutter speed, ISO, exposure compensation, DRIVE mode, STILL/MOVIE mode, and focus mode.

To activate a specific custom setting, you can either visit the Quick menu or use IMAGE QUALITY SETTING > SELECT CUSTOM SETTING. You can also assign the custom settings selection to an Fn button (SELECT CUSTOM SETTING) or configure an Fn button to immediately select Custom Setting 1 when that button is pressed (RECALL CUSTOM 1 SETTING). The latter can be helpful in situations that require you to immediately switch to a different camera configuration, for example one for sudden action shot opportunities. To reassign Fn buttons, press and hold the DISP/BACK button until the configuration page appears.

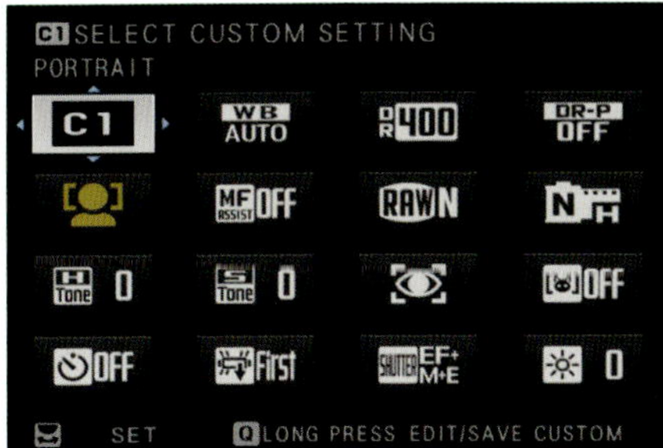
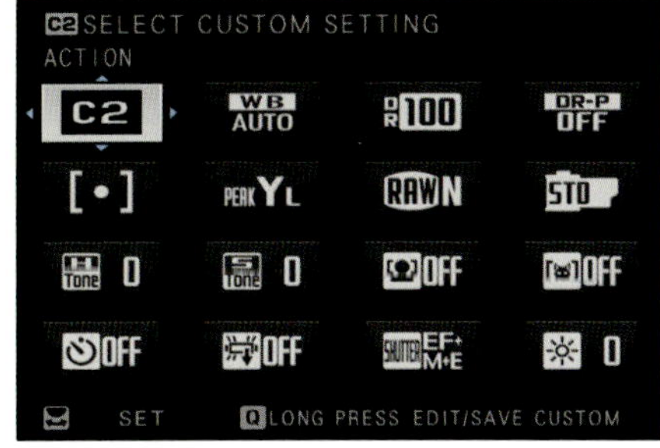

Fig. 44: You can select and activate your custom settings in the upper-left slot of the Quick menu. In this example, I had pre-defined global camera configurations that I named "Action" and "Portrait." Please note that global custom settings extend far beyond the settings that are displayed in the Quick menu. To see what parameters can be saved, you can create a new or select an existing custom setting with IMAGE QUALITY SETTING > EDIT/SAVE CUSTOM SETTING and then select EDIT/CHECK.

<table><tr><td>**TIP 32**</td><td>**Shoot FINE+RAW or NORMAL+RAW!**</td></tr></table>

Should you shoot RAW [27] or JPEG [28]? The best option is to use both formats by setting IMAGE QUALITY SETTING > IMAGE QUALITY > FINE+RAW (or NORMAL+RAW). It doesn't matter if you consider yourself a diehard RAW shooter or a JPEG/HEIF shooter.

This is how **RAW shooters** benefit from shooting FINE+RAW or NORMAL+RAW:

- During external RAW processing, the camera-made JPEG can be used as a (sometimes hard-to-beat) reference image.

- Checking critical focus is only possible at 100% magnification, which only a full-size JPEG can provide. The JPEG that's embedded in the RAW file for preview purposes is too small. Make sure you select one of the available L (Large) options under IMAGE QUALITY SETTING > IMAGE SIZE.

- The IMAGE SIZE menu isn't available in RAW-only mode. Different image formats, such as 1:1 or 16:9, are only available in JPEG/HEIF-only mode or FINE+RAW (or NORMAL+RAW) mode. Autofocus and exposure metering adapt to the currently selected format (aspect ratio) and deliver more accurate readings when you are shooting with odd formats like 1:1. No worries, though: the RAW image is always recorded in the sensor's native 3:2 format, so you don't lose any image information.

This is how **JPEG shooters** benefit from shooting FINE+RAW or NORMAL+RAW:

- Nobody is capable of always setting the *perfect* shooting parameters (exposure, white balance, and dynamic range, as well as JPEG parameters such as film simulation, color, sharpness, noise reduction, shadow and highlight contrast, grain effect, etc.) in advance. FINE+RAW solves this problem by allowing you to change and adjust those settings *after* the fact, either with the built-in RAW converter or with external RAW conversion software. This means you can worry about those JPEG settings later and concentrate on more important factors of your shot, such as focusing, framing, and timing.

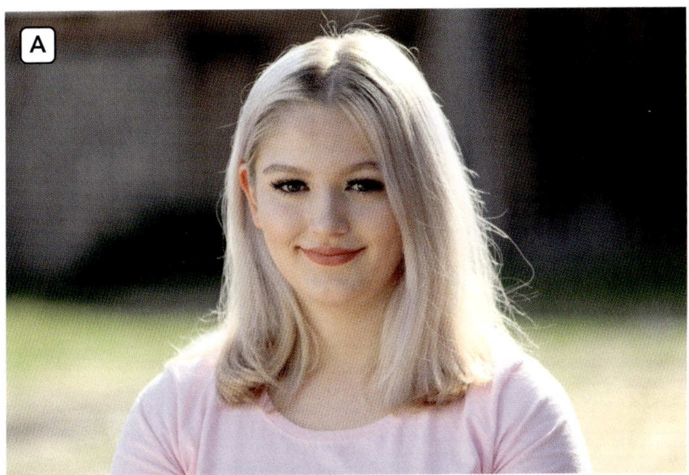

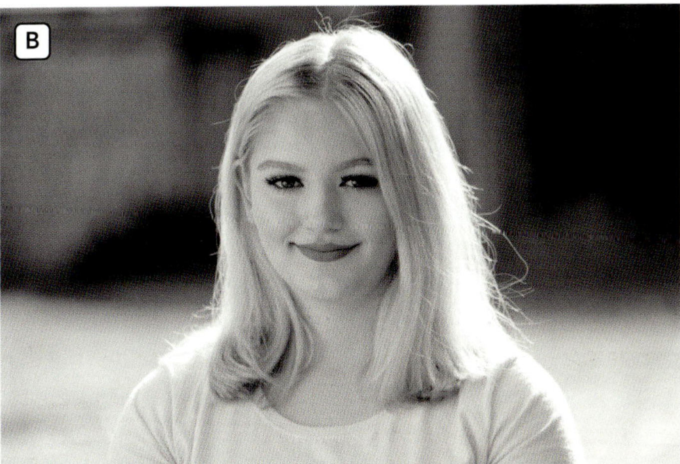

Fig. 45: The X-T5 features a **built-in RAW converter** that allows you to quickly create different versions of a shot and export them in formats like JPEG, HEIF, and TIFF. It only takes a few seconds to modify exposure, contrast settings, and noise reduction of a color image (**A**), or to create a black-and-white version (**B**). All you need is the shot's RAW file.

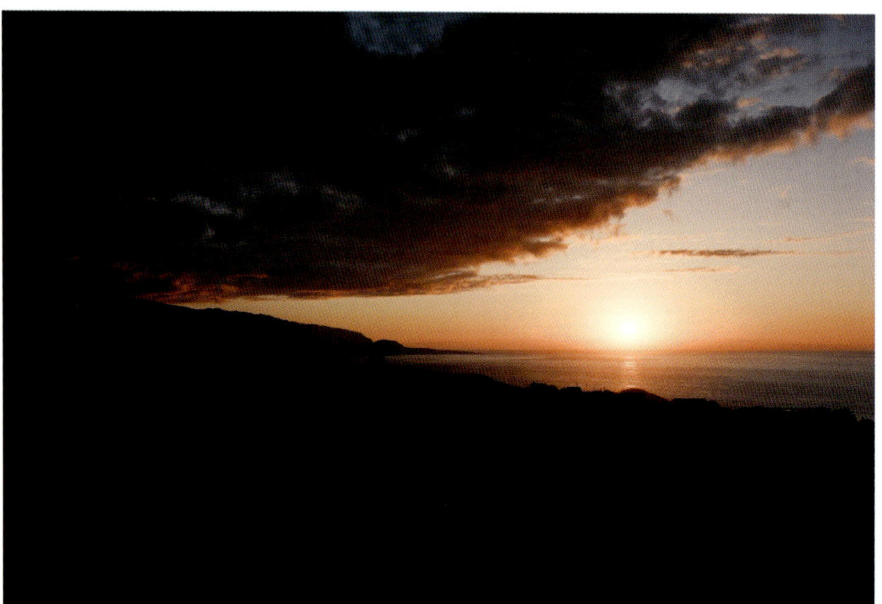

Fig. 46: X-series cameras feature competent JPEG engines with terrific film simulations, but that doesn't mean **JPEG-only shooting** is the best way to go. This JPEG was processed with the Classic Neg. film simulation, and while this result may be exactly what you're looking for, it clearly illustrates the limited dynamic range of regular straight-out-of-camera JPEGs, which often render high-contrast scenes with blown out highlights or blocked shadows (or both). There is no meaningful way to restore what has been lost in processing this JPEG. Instead, you must process the RAW file of this shot.

- Even if you chose the perfect settings in advance, it's possible that you'd like to have more than one version of a shot, such as a color version and a black-and-white version, or versions with different color film simulations. Again, FINE+RAW (or NORMAL+RAW) does the trick because you can use the built-in RAW converter to create (and compare) different JPEG, HEIF, or TIFF versions of a shot.

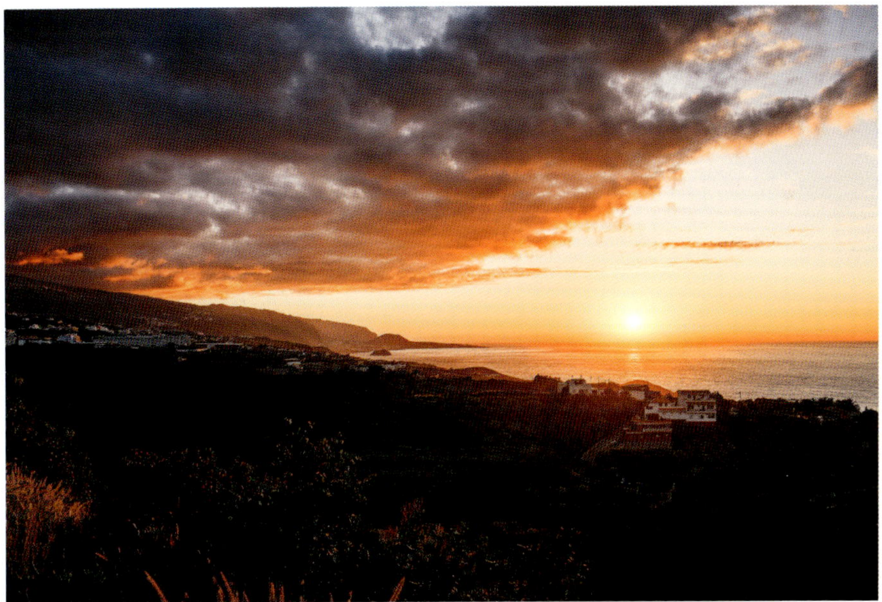

Fig. 47: This is a **Lightroom-processed version** of the RAW file of the previous shot, showcasing the superior dynamic range of the camera's original sensor data. Despite their small size and affordable price, your Fujifilm APS-C camera offers a dynamic range that rivals or even surpasses that of several current full-frame cameras, but you need the RAW file to unlock that potential.

- Progress is continually being made in the digital domain. Things that appear impossible today may be a reality in just a few years. It's perfectly feasible that future RAW converters will be able to extract much better image quality from your RAW files than is possible with today's cameras and RAW processors. It pays to be prepared by archiving the RAW files of your valuable shots. Storage space is cheap; some of your images may be priceless. For example, new AI-based demosaicing, sharpening, and denoising algorithms are now able to produce great results from shots that were considered unusable just a few years ago.

- Your skills may improve as well! Several months or a few years from now, you may be more adept at using post-processing software than you are today. Wouldn't it be sad if you couldn't revisit great shots of the past and process them in a better way? Don't forget, only RAW files contain the full potential of an image. JPEGs and HEIFs are a processed and compressed subset with limited latitude for post-processing. RAW files feature much better tonality and dynamic range. By the way, using the built-in RAW converter of your X-T5 isn't more complex or complicated than using the camera's JPEG settings in the shooting menu (which should be familiar to you as a JPEG shooter).

As you can see, FINE+RAW is the best and most flexible choice. The one detrimental aspect of using FINE+RAW (or NORMAL+RAW) is that it results in larger amounts of data being recorded. This doesn't matter much in practical terms, since your camera can quickly transfer large amounts of data to the memory card. Just make sure to use a fast card.

Let me use this opportunity to address a widespread misconception: RAW files aren't images that you can directly look at. RAWs contain image *data* that still must be *interpreted* or *processed* into an actual image—either in-camera or with external software. Every digital image (including the live view on the monitor, JPEGs from the camera, or TIFF files from Lightroom) is the result of such a translation.

A JPEG shooter who doesn't keep RAW files must settle for only one of the countless possible interpretations of RAW data into an image, and it's extremely unlikely this single JPEG or HEIF from the camera is the best of all possible versions of the image. Basically, discarding the RAW file turns your X camera into an instant camera: you only get one (most likely not the best) image per shot.

*Important: I recommend **not** using the HEIF format to replace JPEGs. Though better than JPEG in theory, there are several* *severe compatibility issues with Fujifilm's specific HEIF files and standard software like Lightroom and Capture One, and even entire operating systems like macOS. Until those have been resolved, choose JPEG in the IMAGE QUALITY SETTING > SELECT JPEG/HEIF menu.*

Compressed or uncompressed RAW files?	TIP 33

The X-T5 offers you a choice of uncompressed and compressed RAW files (IMAGE QUALITY SETTING > RAW RECORDING). Lossless compression cuts the size of RAW files roughly in half, so you can store more of them on a memory card or your computer. The compression also helps speed up camera processes: it takes longer to fill the fast camera buffer, and since the files are smaller, they take less time to transfer to the memory card.

It's important to note that Fujifilm's standard RAW compression is lossless, so there's no difference in image quality between uncompressed and lossless compressed RAWs. The format is widely supported, and RAW converter manufacturers can obtain a free SDK from Fujifilm to support compressed RAW file formats.

The X-T5 also offers a RAW format with *lossy* compression (COMPRESSED). In my experience, this option shaves at least another 10% off the size of a lossless compressed RAW. However, lossy compression means that some image information is discarded. This may become an issue with shots that require extensive post-processing. Is the small size benefit worth the risk? I usually don't think so. That's why I mostly stick with lossless RAW compression. However, if you need fast continuous burst rates, switching from LOSSLESS COMPRESSED to COMPRESSED makes sense. With this configuration and a fast UHS-II card, the X-T5 can sustain a continuous burst rate of 7 fps in RAW-only mode, or in NORMAL+RAW mode, when SEPARATE is set in SET UP > SAVE DATA SETTING > CARD SLOT SETTING.

Windows users should always install the latest version of RAW FILE CONVERTER EX, even if you never intend to use it. This software is available as a free download [29]. It installs a codec that allows Windows to display thumbnail images of compressed Fuji RAW files anywhere on your PC.

TIP 34	Picking different image aspect ratios

The full resolution of the X-T5 (almost 40 megapixels) is available only in its native image format (3:2). However, using a different image aspect ratio (such as 1:1 or 16:9) can still be reasonable. For example, some people prefer to view their images on a 16:9 HD television, while others are fans of the classic (square) medium format look.

No matter what format (aspect ratio) and resolution you choose in IMAGE QUALITY SETTING > IMAGE SIZE, it will only affect the JPEGs coming from your camera. RAW files are always recorded in full resolution in the native 3:2 sensor format. This means that if you kept your RAW files, you could generate new full-size 3:2-format JPEGs with the built-in RAW converter or an external RAW processor.

If you want to compose shots in alternative formats, you should select the desired format in the shooting menu. Here's why:

- The live view in the viewfinder or on the LCD will automatically adjust to the new format, making it easier to compose an image.

- The camera's autofocus frames will adapt to the selected image format.

- The camera's exposure metering and live histogram are based on what's displayed in the live view. Changing the aspect ratio will enhance metering accuracy for the respective format.

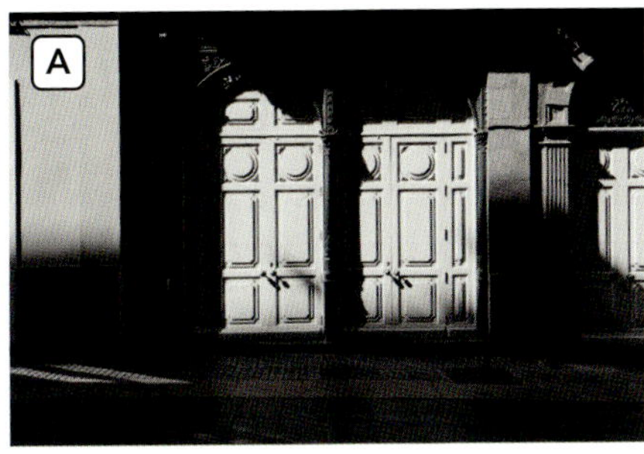
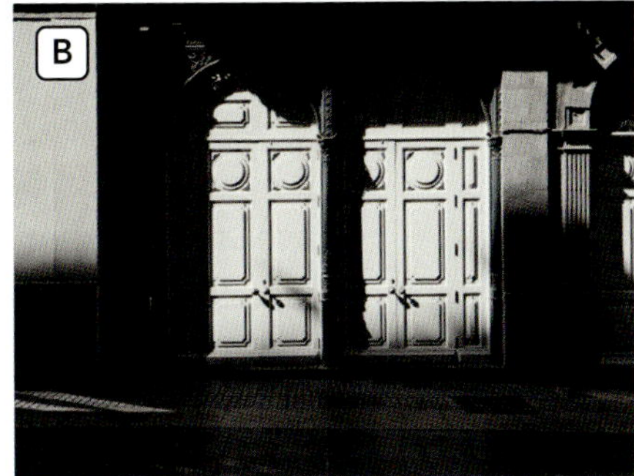
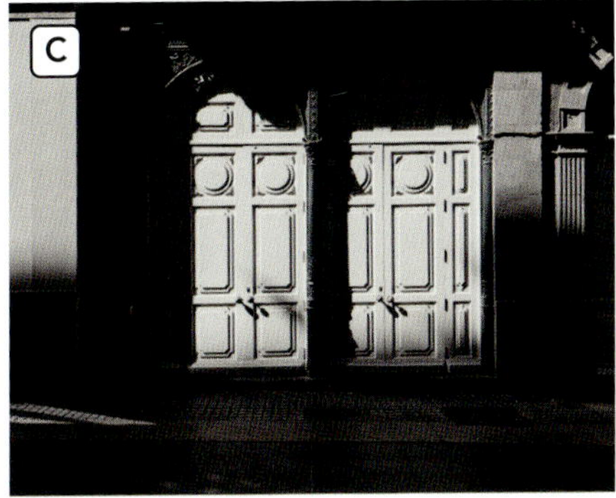
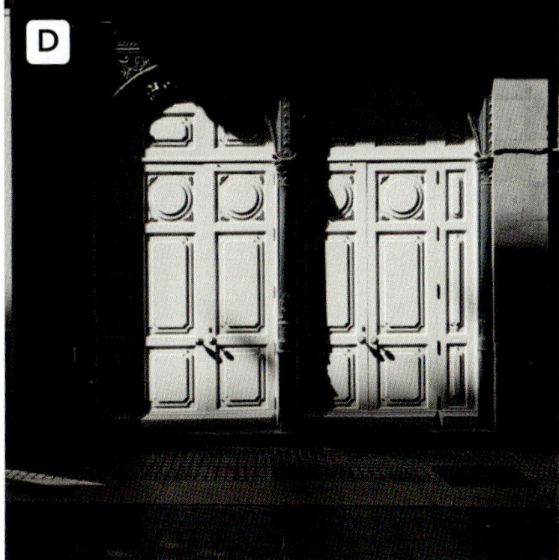

Fig. 48: The X-T5 supports five different aspect ratios and three resolutions for JPEG output. These sample images are all based on the same RAW file, using IMAGE SIZE formats 3:2 (**A**), 4:3 (**B**), 5:4 (**C**), 1:1 (**D**) and 16:9 (**E**).

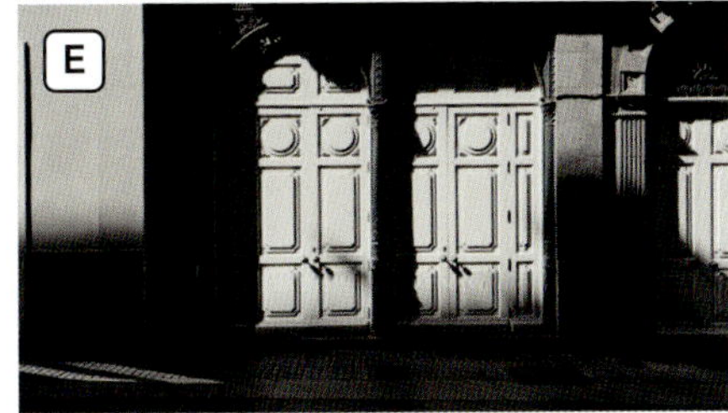

The magical half-press	TIP 35

A basic rule for successfully using mirrorless cameras is minimizing the delay between pressing the shutter button and the camera taking the image. It's about not missing the decisive moment due to shutter lag.

It's up to you to anticipate these decisive moments. By half-pressing the shutter button, you are preparing the camera: exposure and autofocus (unless you are using AF-C) will be set and locked, and the lens aperture will move to its working position. The camera is now ready to record an image with minimal shutter lag—all that's left to do is to fully press the already half-pressed shutter button at the right instant.

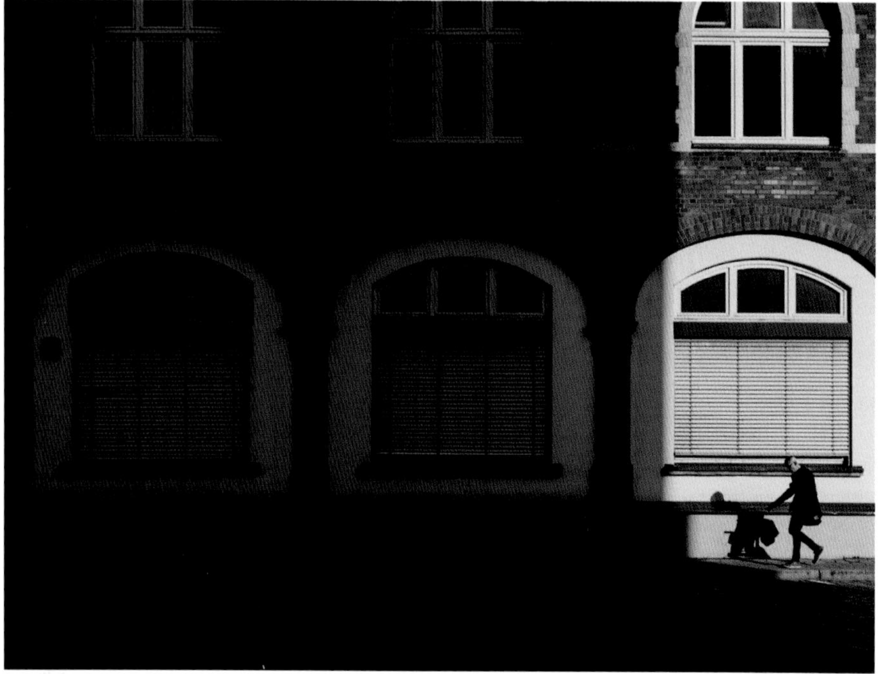

Fig. 49: To make sure your camera is ready when you are, it's useful to prime the camera by **half-pressing the shutter button**.

Don't forget that priming the camera by half-pressing the shutter button only works if SHUTTER AE and SHUTTER AF are set to ON in the SET UP > BUTTON DIAL SETTING menu for AF-S and AF-C.

2.2 MONITOR AND VIEWFINDER

The X-T5 features a large, high-resolution electronic view-finder (EVF) along with an LCD touchscreen. Both can be used for image composition and playback.

Make use of the eye sensor!	TIP 36

Use the VIEW MODE button to activate the built-in eye sensor. The camera will now automatically switch to whichever view (the electronic viewfinder or the LCD screen) is in use when you are taking and reviewing images or making changes to the camera menu.

When you are working with a tripod or holding the LCD display very close to your body, the eye sensor can get confused. In such cases, use the VIEW MODE button to set the camera to LCD ONLY.

If you have reassigned the VIEW MODE button to serve a different function, you can still configure the view mode for shooting mode and playback mode in the SET UP > SCREEN SET-UP > VIEW MODE SETTING menu.

In the SET UP > SCREEN SET-UP > VIEW MODE SETTING > SHOOTING menu, you can press the Q button to limit the available view mode options—so pressing the VIEW MODE button only cycles through the view mode options that you care about.

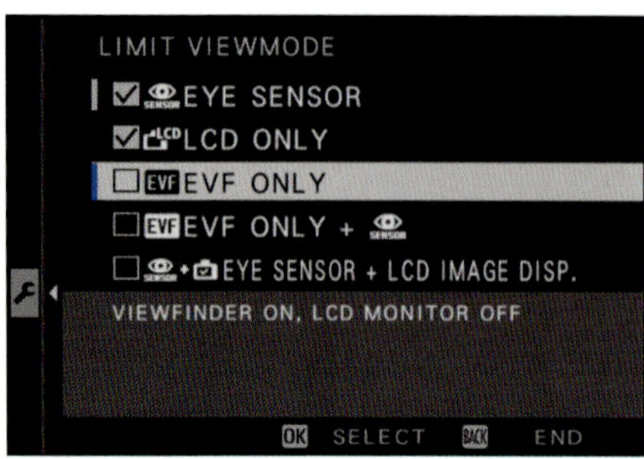

Fig. 50: Pressing the Q button in the SET UP > SCREEN SET-UP > VIEW MODE SETTING > SHOOTING menu leads to the LIMIT VIEWMODE menu where you can configure which of the view mode settings your camera should show or hide in shooting mode. In this example, I have deactivated three of the five view mode options.

Please note that the X-T5 is smart enough to automatically deactivate the eye sensor when the LCD screen has been horizontally unfolded to view it from above.

TIP 37	Instant image review

To instantly review an image right after you have taken it, you can select SET UP > SCREEN SET-UP > IMAGE DISP. and then set a display period of 0.5 SEC, 1.5 SEC, or CONTINUOUS. The image will be displayed in the currently active view (LCD or EVF).

You can cancel an ongoing image review and continue shooting by half-pressing the shutter button. With the CONTINUOUS option, you can also zoom into the displayed image by pressing the rear command dial.

In situations that require you to take a series of shots in quick succession, it may be advisable to switch image review off. To do so, select SET UP > SCREEN SET-UP > IMAGE DISP. > OFF. Even without image review, you can still immediately check your latest shot by pressing the playback button.

Please don't forget that the maximum image magnification (to check critical focus) is only available when the camera is set to record RAW *and* JPEG/HEIF files in size L.

By repeatedly pressing the VIEW MODE button or visiting the SCREEN SET-UP menu, you can enable a different instant review mode named EYE SENSOR + LCD IMAGE DISPLAY. In this view mode, if you take a shot with the EVF and then immediately remove the camera from your eye to review the image you just took on the rear LCD display for the time selected in the SET UP > SCREEN SET-UP > IMAGE DISP. menu. This mode was implemented at the request of former DLSR users who just couldn't help themselves with their so-called "chimping" habit: taking a shot with the viewfinder and immediately reviewing it on the rear LCD display. Of course, with mirrorless EVF cameras, you can simply review your last shot in the electronic viewfinder. The EVF displays the image larger, with higher resolution, without interference from surrounding light, and you save the time and effort of removing the camera from your eye after each shot. That said, the "chimping mode" might still be useful for those who don't want to review every shot but want to check a few specific images.

The DISP/BACK button can be tricky!	TIP 38

The DISP/BACK button serves two different purposes:

- As a BACK button, it returns the camera to a higher menu or selection level without saving any changes you may have made in the menu sub-level.

- As a DISPLAY button, it changes the display mode of the currently active view (LCD monitor or viewfinder).

It's important to remember that changing the display mode only affects the currently active view. For example, to change the display mode of the EVF, the EVF must be in use when you press the DISP/BACK button. This means that when you are using the eye sensor, you must look through the EVF while you are pressing the DISP/BACK button. If you don't, you will only change the display mode of the then active LCD monitor.

When the camera is in shooting mode, the viewfinder and the LCD monitor can each use different display modes at the same time. In playback mode, the EVF and LCD are synched to the same display mode. In this case it doesn't matter which view (EVF or LCD) is active when you change the display mode with the DISP/BACK button.

If you select a display with information overlays in shooting mode, you can choose which elements and indicators will appear in the viewfinder or on the LCD monitor. Select SET UP > SCREEN SET-UP > DISP. CUSTOM SETTING, and then check the items in the list that you want displayed in the EVF and on the LCD. Personally, I check all available boxes except for LIVE VIEW HIGHLIGHT ALERT and, because I don't do video, MOVIE MODE & REC. TIME.

TIP 39	WYSIWYG—What You See Is What You Get!

The EVF and LCD screens of mirrorless cameras normally operate in WYSIWYG mode [30]: What You See Is What You Get. This means that the viewfinder and monitor are always trying to display a live view [31] image that closely resembles the resulting JPEG (or HEIF) image. The live view simulates exposure, colors, contrast, and white balance and, in some cases, dynamic range. When you half-press the shutter button, the camera will set the selected working aperture, so the live view will then also display a preview of the depth of field.

The live view's exposure simulation is quite helpful because it allows you to recognize exposure problems *before* you take the picture. Please note that the live histogram is always based on the contents of the current live view image.

The live view's WYSIWYG simulation is available in all four of the camera's exposure modes: program AE **P**, aperture priority AE **A**, shutter priority AE **S**, and manual exposure mode **M**.

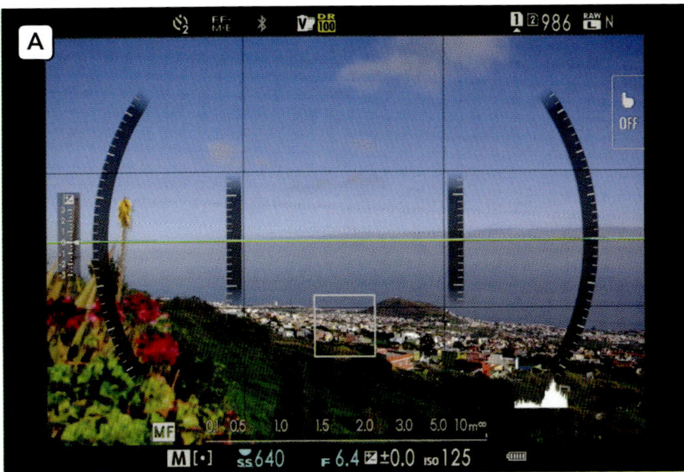

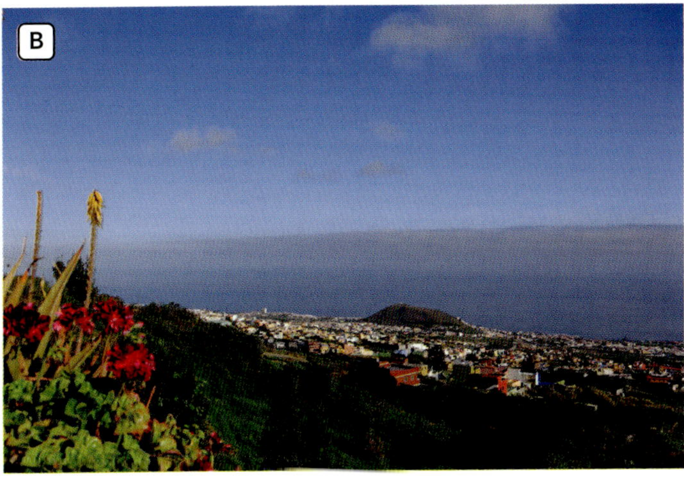

Fig. 51: WYSIWYG: This example illustrates how closely the live view (**A**) represents the JPEG taken from the camera (**B**). The live view doesn't just simulate exposure, white balance, film simulation, and other JPEG settings, it also previews *fixed* dynamic range settings like DR400% or DR-P STRONG.

In manual exposure mode **M**, the X-T5 allows you to switch off the live view exposure simulation by selecting SET UP > SCREEN SET-UP > PREVIEW EXP./WB IN MANUAL MODE > OFF. This way, the camera will always display a usable live view image in manual mode, regardless of the selected exposure parameters (shutter speed, aperture, and ISO). Basically, the live view is switched to AE mode while the camera remains in manual exposure mode. This can be useful in a studio setting with flash photography. For example, you may want to eliminate the surrounding-light component by stopping down the aperture and fully illuminating your subject with strobes.

Please note that in this mode, both the live view and the live histogram aren't representing the actual exposure of your image, so don't forget to switch the exposure simulation back on if you want to work with a proper exposure simulation and live histogram in manual mode **M**.

The live view's exposure simulation may be restricted in situations with very low light and slow shutter speeds of several seconds—the live view and the live histogram may appear darker than the actual result. In such scenarios, you should set the camera to BOOST mode with EVF/LCD LOW LIGHT PRIORITY (SET UP > POWER MANAGEMENT > EVF/LCD BOOST SETTING > EVF/LCD LOW LIGHT PRIORITY). You may also first take a test shot and review it in playback mode. The information display (which you can select with the DISP/BACK button) will show you a playback histogram of the recorded JPEG image. This includes a preview with "blinkies," which indicate blown (overexposed) highlights.

TIP 40	Using the Natural Live View

The so-called Natural Live View disables the WYSIWYG simulation of JPEG settings such as Film Simulation, Tone Curve, or Color. Instead, it will display a rather flat live view image with increased dynamic range in the highlights and shadows, and with colors that are supposed to resemble what our eyes would see through an optical viewfinder. It will also set the live view to Auto white balance, so there will be no simulation of any white balance custom settings or presets. However, all current JPEG and white balance settings will still be applied to the *actual image* that is recorded.

To set the camera to Natural Live View mode, select SET UP > SCREEN SET-UP > NATURAL LIVE VIEW > ON. This setting enables generic-looking previews for color, black-and-white, and sepia shots that do *not* reflect the look of the actual JPEG results.

*Important: The Natural Live View of the X-T5 extends highlight dynamic range by two stops, rendering the live view and live histogram highly inaccurate when shooting with DR100%, DR200%, or DR-AUTO dynamic range settings as well as DR-P WEAK or DR-P AUTO. Do **not** engage the Natural Live View if you want to use the live view and/or the live histogram to judge and set the correct exposure!*

<table><tr><td>Using the LCD touchscreen</td><td>TIP 41</td></tr></table>

The X-T5 features a touchscreen that can perform several functions in shooting mode and playback mode. To use the touchscreen, make sure to select SET UP > BUTTON/DIAL SETTING > TOUCH SCREEN SETTING > *Camera* TOUCH SCREEN SETTING > ON.

In *shooting mode,* you can use the touchscreen to pick a focus frame or zone; to autofocus with the selected focus frame or zone; or to autofocus and shoot with the selected focus frame or zone. These are your options:

- **AREA:** Select a focus frame or zone by tapping once on the LCD touchscreen.

- **AF:** Tap on the LCD touchscreen to pick a focus frame or zone and trigger the autofocus. In MF mode, this option will focus the camera using Instant AF.

- **SHOT:** Tap on the touchscreen to select a focus area or zone, trigger the autofocus through this frame or zone, and take a picture without further delay. In MF mode, this option will immediately take a shot without (re-) focusing.

- **OFF:** Temporarily disable shooting with the touchscreen. This prevents you from accidentally triggering any of the three other touchscreen functions.

Apart from focusing and triggering the camera, the touchscreen offers several additional functionalities:

- In *playback mode,* you can use the touchscreen like a smartphone to browse through images. You can also zoom in and out of an image by double-tapping, or by pinching the image with two fingers. To use the touchscreen in playback mode, make sure to select SET UP > BUTTON/DIAL SETTING > TOUCH SCREEN SETTING > *Playback* TOUCH SCREEN SETTING > ON.

- You can still use the touchscreen when you are shooting with the electronic viewfinder (EVF). In this usage scenario, the touchscreen works like a trackpad that allows you to blindly move the active focus frame. To define the active touchscreen area for EVF operation, select SET UP > BUTTON/DIAL SETTING > TOUCH SCREEN SETTING > EVF TOUCH SCREEN AREA SETTINGS. You will be given a choice of seven active areas and OFF.

- You can also double tap the touchscreen in shooting and playback mode to zoom into the picture. This function has the same effect as pressing the rear command dial in its default FOCUS CHECK configuration. To make sure this feature is available to you in shooting mode, select SET UP > BUTTON/DIAL SETTING > TOUCH SCREEN SETTING > *Camera* DOUBLE TAP SETTING > ON. Double tap also works when you are looking through the EVF if you have defined an active touchscreen area for EVF operation.

- Finally, the touchscreen gives you access to four virtual Fn buttons, so-called Touch-Fn or T-Fn buttons. You can "press" one of these virtual buttons by flicking your finger left, right, up, or down on the screen. You can assign new T-Fn functions by pressing and holding the DISP/BACK button until the FUNCTION (Fn) SETTING screen appears. Please note that T-Fn buttons are available only if SET UP > BUTTON/DIAL SETTING > TOUCH SCREEN SETTING > *T-Fn* TOUCH FUNCTION is set to ON.

2.3 EXPOSING RIGHT

It's not the job of the camera to find and set the correct exposure; it's the job of the photographer. That said, the X-T5 features the usual set of AE (auto exposure) modes: aperture priority **A**, shutter priority **S**, and program AE **P**.

- **Aperture priority A** automatically sets a suitable shutter speed to match a preset aperture based on your exposure.

- **Shutter priority S** automatically sets a suitable aperture to match a preset shutter speed based on your exposure.

- **Program AE P** automatically sets a suitable aperture and shutter speed combination based on your exposure.

- **Auto-ISO** can contribute a suitable ISO setting (within predefined limits). In digital cameras, ISO is the level of signal amplification applied to an image that has been recorded by the camera's sensor. ISO impacts the brightness of the final image (JPEG/HEIF/TIFF and the camera's WYSIWYG live view).

Auto exposure (AE) modes are typically set with the aperture ring on the lens and the shutter speed dial on the camera body: Pre-selecting an aperture and setting the shutter speed dial to "A" activates *aperture priority* mode. Selecting "A" on the aperture ring or lens in concert with a specific shutter speed activates *shutter priority* mode. Finally, selecting "A" on both the lens and the shutter speed dial selects *program AE.*

It is important to understand that these auto exposure (AE) modes (including Auto-ISO) are not responsible for correctly exposing images: exposure is *always* the responsibility of the photographer. AE modes automatically fill variables (such as the shutter speed in aperture priority **A**) in a way that matches the exposure *you* have set. Auto exposure will only deliver good results if the photographer is exposing correctly.

Exposing correctly—how does this work?

Don't panic! Unlike conventional DSLR cameras, your mirrorless X-T5 makes things easy. Four different metering modes (multi, spot, center-weighted, and average), the WYSIWYG live view, and the live (RGB) histogram help you determine the correct exposure for any given scene. If you shoot in one of the three AE modes, the most important tool is the exposure compensation dial, which allows you to correct the metered exposure up to ±3 EV in convenient steps of 1/3 EV. EV means Exposure Value, and 1 EV is equivalent to one full aperture stop. The correct exposure isn't what the camera is metering, it's what *you* make of the metering by adjusting the exposure compensation dial or with manual exposure settings.

TIP 42	Choosing the right metering method

There are up to four different metering methods available to measure the amount of light that goes through the lens and hits the image sensor:

- **Average** metering calculates an unweighted average of the total light that hits the entire sensor area.

- **Spot** metering considers only a tiny percentage of the sensor area. The metering area typically covers a standard-sized focus frame in the center of the image. Alternatively, you can link spot metering directly to the size and position of the active focus frame (in SINGLE POINT AF and MF mode).

- **Center-weighted** metering is a cross between average and spot metering. While it encompasses the entire image area, it puts special emphasis on the image center.

- **Multi** or **matrix** metering calculates a weighted average of the total light that hits the sensor. The weighting is a result of 256 metering areas (the matrix) that the camera evaluates and compares to typical scenarios, which is why multi metering is considered "smarter" than the other methods. For example, multi metering is designed to recognize when you are shooting against the sun.

Average, spot, and center-weighted metering return exposure recommendations based on middle gray. In other words, when you take a picture of a black wall and then a picture of a white wall with auto exposure (AE), the results will both look middle gray. This means:

- If you want the black wall to look black in the resulting image, you must manually adjust the exposure downward.

- If you want the white wall to look bright white in the resulting image, you must manually adjust the exposure upward.

Fig. 52: This illustration shows a black sheet of paper and a white sheet of paper. Both were photographed with the camera's spot metering without any exposure correction. As you can see, the camera delivered a **middle-gray exposure** in both cases. To get an image that reflects the actual brightness of a subject, the metered exposure must be adjusted.

Fujifilm recommends a correction of +1 EV when you are shooting in snowfields, or –2/3 EV when you are shooting subjects in spotlight. Instead of following these rules, I recommend a more precise and methodical course of action using the live view and the live histogram. To minimize corrective adjustments, it's best to select a metering method that fits the subject and the job at hand:

- **Multi** metering is a general-purpose method. Since it is supposed to be "smarter" than the other methods, there's a chance you won't have to apply (m)any corrective adjustments to the proposed exposure.

- **Average** and, to a lesser degree, **center-weighted** metering are rather neutral metering methods that will likely stay more consistent despite small changes in composition (or framing) than multi metering and spot metering. I recommend average metering if you want to take a series of shots of the same subject under similar conditions in one of the auto exposure (AE) modes. In such cases, average metering will help you keep the exposure consistent.

- **Spot** metering bases its measurements on one spot of the overall image. This means you must work very precisely to make sure you are metering the appropriate part (spot) of the scene. The resulting exposure recommendation will expose this spot with middle-gray brightness. For example, if you spot meter a backlit face against the sun, the metered exposure will display the face with middle-gray brightness (or zone 5 in the famous Ansel Adams Zone System [32]). If that's too dark for your taste, you can use the exposure compensation dial to lift the exposure by +1/3 EV or +2/3 EV. On the other hand, if the person has dark skin, you may want to reduce the exposure with a correction in the opposite direction. It's up to you to choose the zone (brightness) of the spot-metered part of the image.

Spot metering is the most powerful and challenging metering method. It's useful when the light is very difficult—too difficult for multi and average metering. Typical examples are isolated bright objects in front of a dark background (and vice versa), such as a musician or an actor on a stage, or strongly backlit subjects. Whenever your exposure must be spot on, spot metering is your friend.

With that said, it's obvious that spot metering requires you to meter very precisely. Even small changes in the camera's direction can lead to dramatic changes in the metered result. Therefore, it can be useful to combine spot metering with the camera's AE-Lock function. AE-L will lock your exposure to prevent it from changing when you alter your composition, or when your subject starts to move away from your metering spot.

The best way to use spot metering is in manual exposure mode **M**. In this mode, metering doesn't affect the exposure because you are manually setting all three exposure parameters (shutter speed, aperture, and ISO). Spot metering in manual mode lets you determine the brightness level of any part of your image for any set exposure: The exposure scale in the viewfinder or LCD tells you exactly how much brighter or darker than middle gray (zone 5) the spot metered object will appear in your shot (either ±3 EV or ±5 EV, depending on your exposure compensation dial mode setting).

Don't forget to *disable* Auto-ISO in manual mode **M**. If you don't, the camera will still operate in some kind of AE mode (I call it "misomatic"); in this mode, the ISO setting will be the exposure variable that's automatically adjusted.

*Important: Multi, average, center-weighted, and spot metering are automatically **disabled** when face/eye detection or subject detection is switched on. In this case, the camera uses a modified version of multi metering that puts particular emphasis on the area of a detected face or subject. When no faces or subjects are detected, the camera always reverts to regular multi metering as a fallback mode, which may be different from the exposure metering mode that you had selected before you switched on face/eye or subject detection.*

TIP 43	Linking spot metering to focus frames

Traditionally, spot metering covers the center of the image with an area that's about as large as a standard-sized focus frame. However, by selecting AF/MF SETTING > INTERLOCK SPOT AE & FOCUS AREA > ON, you can link the spot metering area to the position and size(!) of the active focus frame in Single Point AF and MF mode.

This is a very useful feature if you are using one of the camera's many off-center AF frames, since it's likely that your focus area covers the same part of your subject that is also relevant for exposure metering (such as the brightly lit face of a musician or stage actor who is standing in front of a dark background).

If you want to decouple spot metering from the AF area and limit it to the very center of the frame, make sure to select AF/MF SETTING > INTERLOCK SPOT AE & FOCUS AREA > OFF.

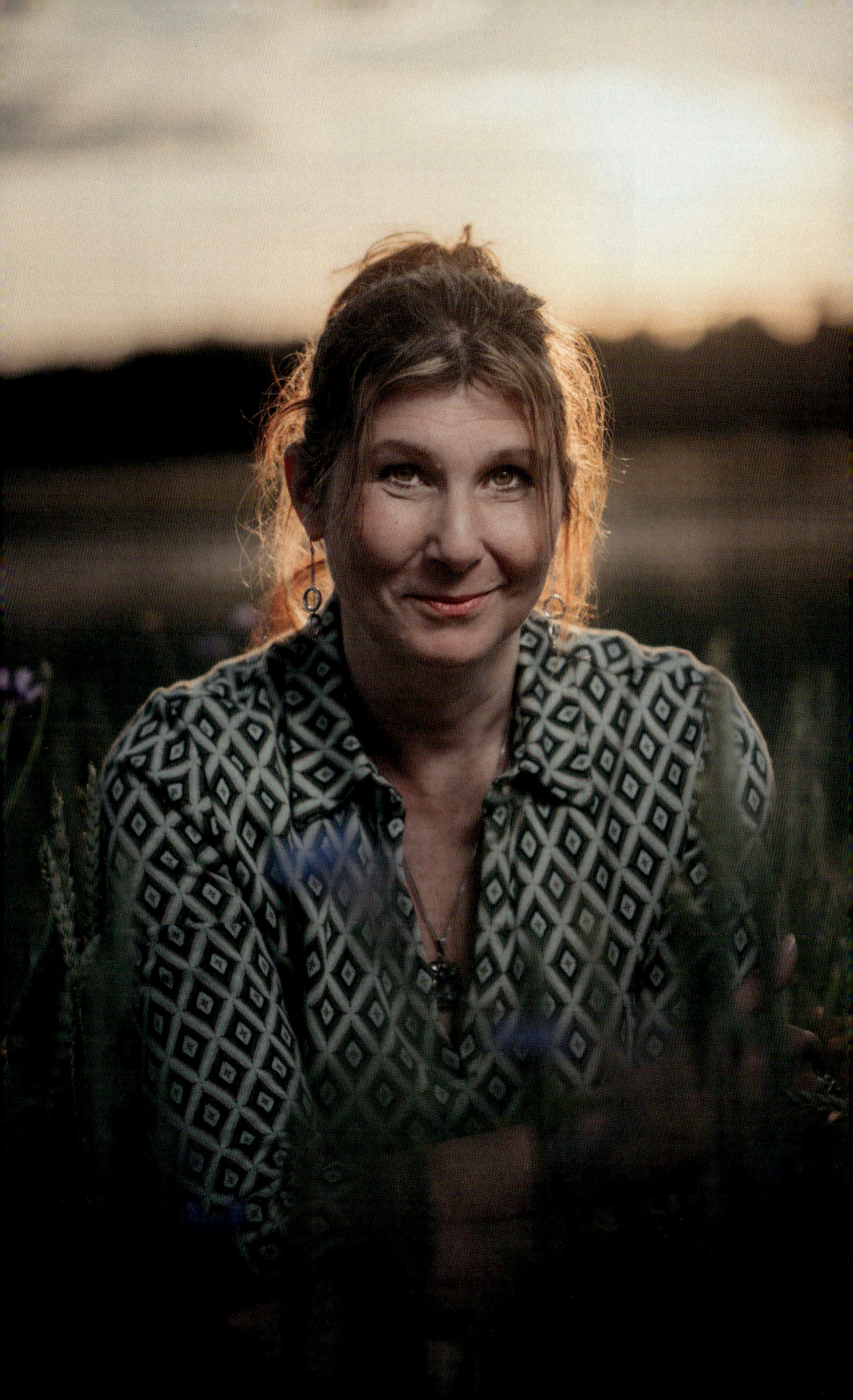

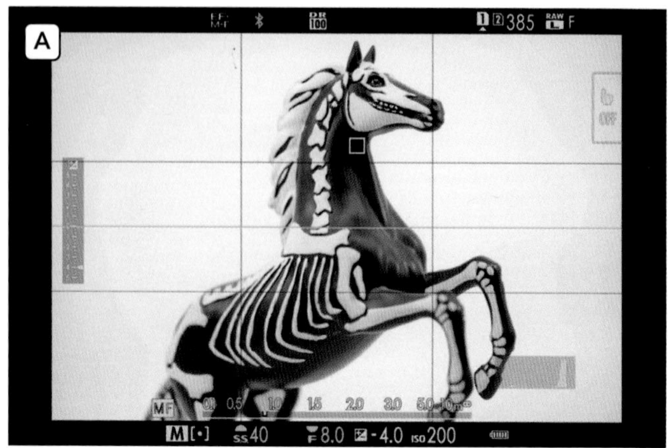

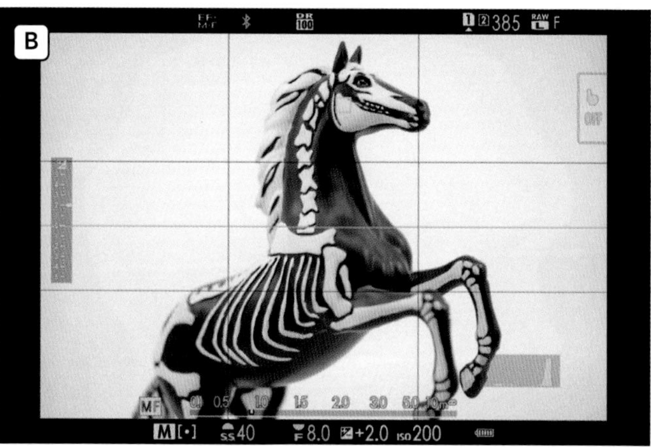

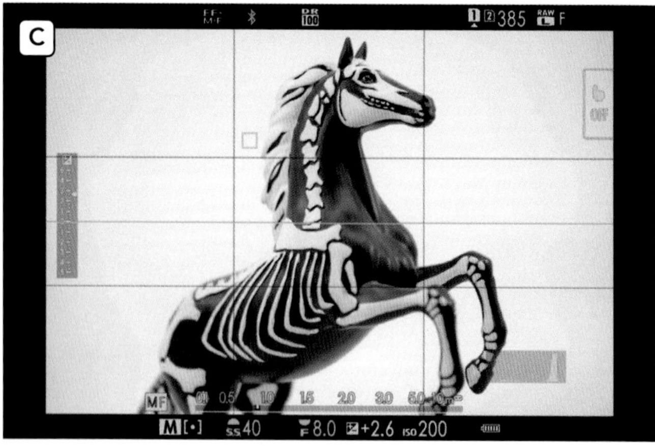

Fig. 53: Spot metering and manual exposure mode: Metering different parts of an image is easy with spot metering. Simply set an exposure (aperture, shutter speed, and ISO), and then point the small spot-metering area at different parts of the scene. The exposure scale in your live view tells you the brightness of any metered spot, with 0 representing middle gray (zone 5 in the Ansel Adams Zone System). To make things easier and most effective, interlock spot metering with the size and position of the currently active focus frame and select the smallest available focus frame size in AF-S or MF mode.

In this example, I spot metered the darkest part of the model horse at −4 EV (**A**), its brightest part at +2 EV (**B**), and the brightest overall part of the scene at +2.66 EV (**C**). This means that the dynamic range of this scene comprises less than 7 EV (2.66 + 4 = 6.66), a range that fits neatly into a regular DR100% JPEG image.

Always remember that the camera will not interlock spot metering with the focus area if you set it to either Zone AF or Wide/Tracking AF. Interlocking only works in concert with Single Point AF or manual focus (MF) mode. And don't forget that spot metering is automatically disabled when either subject detection or face/eye detection are active.

Using the live view and live histogram	TIP 44

Unlike optical viewfinders in DSLRs, the electronic live view of modern mirrorless cameras like your X-T5 provides an accurate simulation of the resulting JPEG image. The live preview encompasses color, contrast, exposure, and effect settings.

In standard display mode, this WYSIWYG preview is complemented by a live histogram [33]. I strongly recommend using the live histogram because it provides a useful overview of the brightness distribution in your scene. It also helps you identify areas of over- and underexposure in advance, so you can take corrective measures:

- If bars are piling up like a bell curve at the right end of the histogram, but are cut off mid-peak, parts of your shot will be overexposed with blown highlights. If this affects important parts of your image, you should correct the exposure downward. Alternately, you can expand the shot's dynamic range by selecting DR200% or DR400% in the respective menu.

- If the histogram leans to the left, leaving plenty of unused space on the right, the shot might end up underexposed. In this case, you can adjust the exposure upward.

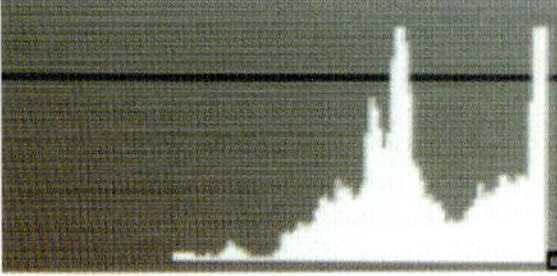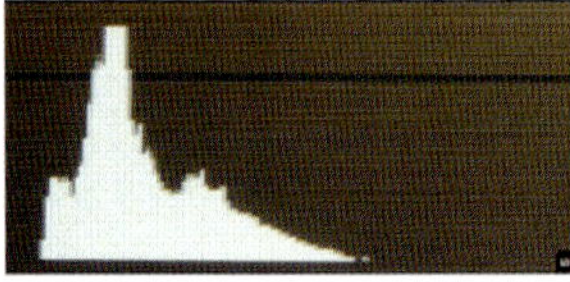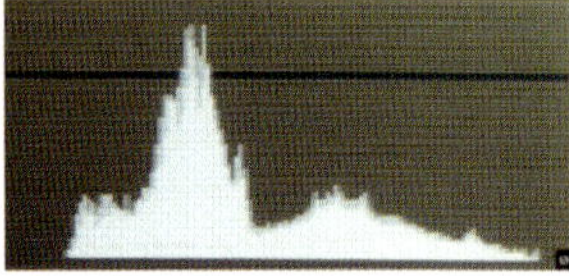

Fig. 54: Three **live histograms** that show overexposure, underexposure, and a balanced exposure of the same scene.

The histogram provides a technical representation of the live view simulation. When the Natural Live View is turned off, both the live view and the live histogram will reflect the current JPEG settings of the camera (white balance, film simulation, color, and highlight and shadow contrast). For example, the VELVIA film simulation delivers more contrast and more saturated colors than ETERNA, and this is reflected in the live view and the live histogram.

It's important to note that the live view and live histogram also represent (simulate) the effect of manual DR200% or DR400% dynamic range settings. However, if you set the camera to DR-AUTO, the live view and live histogram will always display a DR100% preview. DR-P WEAK and DR-P STRONG are also simulated, with DR-P AUTO always showing a DR-P WEAK preview.

The X-T5 also offers an **RGB histogram** [34], which is available only by assigning it to an Fn or Touch-Fn button. The RGB histogram is once again based on the current live view image, so it represents the resulting JPEG image. In fact, the color histogram displays four different histograms at once: overall luminance distribution (a larger version of the standard histogram) and separate histograms for the three color channels: red, green, and blue. That way you can immediately recognize clipping of individual color channels in your JPEG. For example, shooting a red rose, the red channel is the first to clip and, thus, lose texture.

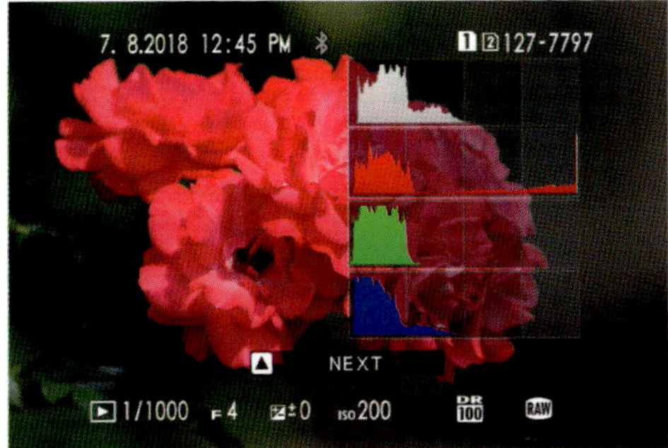

Fig. 55: The **RGB histogram** of this image of a rose illustrates how the red channel is already clipping (indicated by the peaking line at the right edge of the red channel histogram), while green, blue, and overall luminance are barely touching the right half of the histogram. Please note that as long as the Natural Live View is turned off, the histogram always reflects the current JPEG settings (film simulation, contrast settings, color saturation setting, etc.).

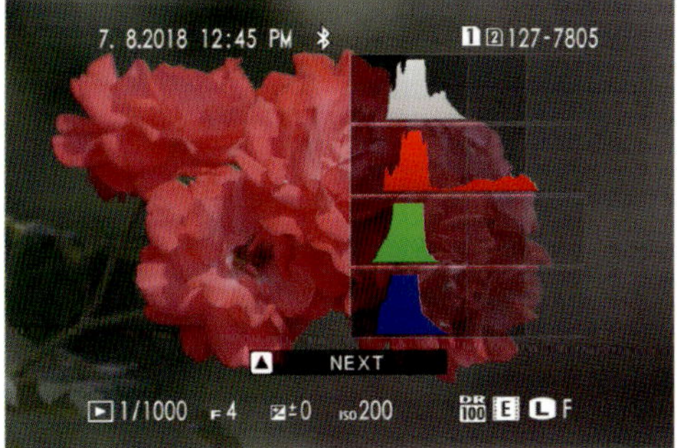

Fig. 56: This is the same RAW image, but this time processed with **flat JPEG settings**: Eterna film simulation, Tone Curve (Shadows) −2, Tone Curve (Highlights) −2, and Color −4. These settings reflect the flattest possible color profile you can achieve in your X-T5, and there's now plenty of additional headroom in the shadows and highlights. Thanks to the much higher dynamic range of the flat JPEG, there's also no clipping of the red channel in the histogram. This flat JPEG reflects the dynamic range of the actual RAW file much better than the camera's default JPEG settings, and many RAW shooters use these or similar flat JPEG settings in concert with the RGB histogram because it makes it easier to determine the optimal exposure, which is right at the sensor's saturation limit.

The RGB histogram also includes "blinkies," which are live overexposure or clipping warnings. If bright parts of your scene start to blink in RGB histogram mode, the blinking areas will be blown out in the resulting JPEG (i.e., losing texture and detail). The blinkies make it easy to set an exposure where important highlights are protected (i.e., not blinking in the RGB histogram view).

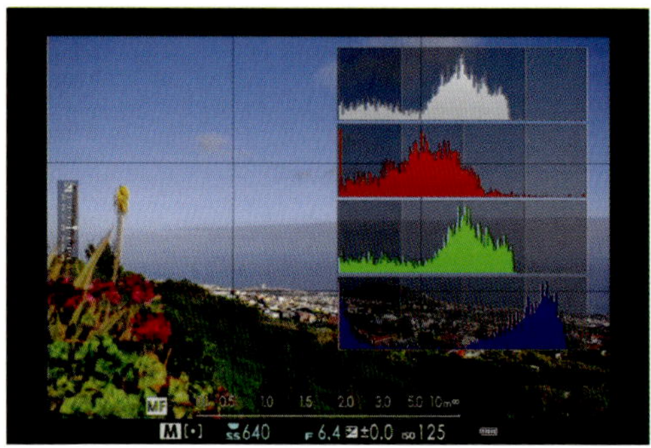

Fig. 57: In shooting mode, the RGB histogram displays a proper representation of the live view contents. This includes exposure, film simulation, contrast / tone curve, dedicated DR / DR-P settings, color saturation, and effect settings like Color Chrome. If parts of your scene are overexposed, the RGB histogram display will show them blinking. Please note that in shooting mode, the RGB histogram can only be activated via a properly configured Fn button or Touch-Fn gesture.

| TIP 45 | Auto exposure (AE) with modes **P**, **A**, and **S** |

The three auto exposure modes of your X-T5 are **P** (program AE), **A** (aperture priority), and **S** (shutter priority).

A brief reminder:

- **Program AE P** will automatically set a suitable aperture and shutter speed combination.

- **Aperture priority A** will automatically set a suitable shutter speed to match a preset aperture.

- **Shutter priority S** will automatically set a suitable aperture to match a preset shutter speed.

To take a picture in one of these modes, you can follow these steps:

- Meter the exposure with one of the metering modes: multi, center-weighted, average, or spot.

- After metering, adjust the exposure to taste using the exposure compensation dial. Use the live view and the histogram to determine the best setting. Remember: it's not the camera that's setting the exposure; it's you. Don't blindly follow what the camera is proposing. Instead, always keep an eye on the live view and the live histogram.

- When you half-press the shutter button, your exposure will be locked as long as you keep the button half-pressed. As long as the shutter button remains half-pressed, you can adjust the framing or composition of your shot without changing the exposure.

- Instead of half-pressing the shutter button, you can also use the AE-L button to meter a scene and lock the exposure. You can configure the AE-L button to either lock the exposure as long as you press the AE-L button (SET UP > BUTTON/DIAL SETTING > AE/AF LOCK MODE > AE&AF ON WHEN PRESSING), or use the button as a toggle to lock and unlock the exposure (SET UP > BUTTON/DIAL SETTING > AE/AF LOCK MODE > AE&AF ON/OFF SWITCH). Personally, I highly recommend the latter option. When the exposure is locked with AE-L, you can still further adjust it with the exposure compensation dial.

- To take the shot, fully press the shutter button.

Metering and exposure are two different things. After metering a scene, the photographer sets the actual exposure with the exposure compensation dial:

- **Metering** is performed using either multi, center-weighted, average, or spot metering.

- Use the **exposure compensation dial** to adjust the metering result. Use the information from the live view and live histogram to adjust your settings. Of course, there are instances where the initial metering is already spot-on, so you won't have to apply any further correction.

- **Expose** the image using one of three AE modes: aperture priority, shutter priority, or program AE.

If you set the exposure compensation dial to its C position, exposure compensation will be performed by one of the command dials with an extended range of ±5 EV instead of ±3 EV. To configure a specific command dial to serve as your exposure compensation dial, go to the SET UP > BUTTON/DIAL SETTING > COMMAND DIAL SETTING screen.

Using auto exposure (AE) modes, the live view will always show the calculated exposure brightness, even when this exposure cannot be realized due to technical limits. For example, the aperture cannot open beyond its maximum "wide open" setting. If the camera's AE encounters such a limit, the affected exposure parameter (aperture or shutter speed) will be displayed in red, meaning that the camera has calculated an exposure parameter setting that isn't practically available. However, the live view acts as if that limit didn't exist.

In manual exposure mode, the live view always represents the actual exposure if SET UP > SCREEN SET-UP > PREVIEW EXP./WB IN MANUAL MODE is set to PREVIEW EXP./WB.

TIP 46	Using manual exposure **M**

In manual exposure mode, you manually specify all three exposure parameters: aperture, shutter speed, and ISO amplification. For this to work, Auto-ISO must be turned off. Otherwise, ISO would become an exposure variable that the camera would automatically fill.

For the live view and live histogram to correctly display the set exposure in manual mode, make sure that SET UP > SCREEN SET-UP > PREVIEW EXP./WB IN MANUAL MODE > PREVIEW EXP./WB is set. I recommend setting the metering to spot metering.

Here's how you can expose in manual mode:

- Select and set an aperture and shutter speed that suit your subject and image idea. Aperture controls the depth of field [35]; shutter speed controls the amount of motion blur [36] and camera shake in your exposure.

- Next, select an ISO value that will yield the desired brightness in your shot. You can (and should) use the live view and live histogram to find a suitable setting. As usual, try not to blow out important highlights. The live histogram is your friend.

- You can check specific parts of your scene by spot metering them. The exposure scale in the live view screen tells you how much above or below middle gray (zone 5) the spot-metered selection will be exposed. This tool helps you ensure that important parts of your image (such as skin tones or snow) will be exposed exactly like you want them to be.

- Finally, you may want to readjust or fine-tune aperture, shutter speed, and ISO according to your metering. Once everything is set, you can take the shot(s).

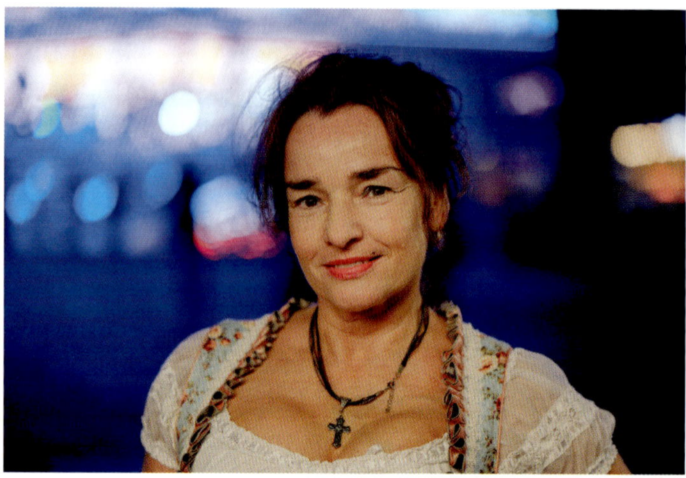

Fig. 58: I shoot in **manual exposure mode** almost all the time. And maybe you should too. Not only can the camera make fewer mistakes when you are in charge, but manual mode also gives you full control over aperture (depth of field), shutter speed (motion blur, camera shake), and ISO (noise level, effective dynamic range). Manual mode also ensures that multiple shots of a scene will have the same consistent exposure, because the exposure doesn't change unless *you* change it. It also forces you to think about your actual exposure parameters: Why are you using a particular setting for aperture, shutter speed, and ISO? Thanks to the WYSIWYG nature of mirrorless cameras, manual exposure mode can help you avoid unpleasant surprises: You *set* the exposure with the dials, you *see* the exposure in the live view, and you *get* the exposure you set and saw in your JPEG.

TIP 47	Using aperture priority A

In aperture priority AE [37], you manually set the aperture [38] and the camera automatically selects a suitable shutter speed based on your chosen exposure (as set with the exposure compensation dial). Which aperture should you select? Let's look at some basics:

- As the aperture gets smaller (i.e., the aperture number gets higher), your depth of field (DOF) [39] increases. DOF is the zone in front of and behind the focus plane that appears in perfect focus when you look at the finished image. In standard display mode, the viewfinder and LCD offer a focus and DOF scale that displays the focus distance as well as the calculated depth-of-field zone that surrounds it.

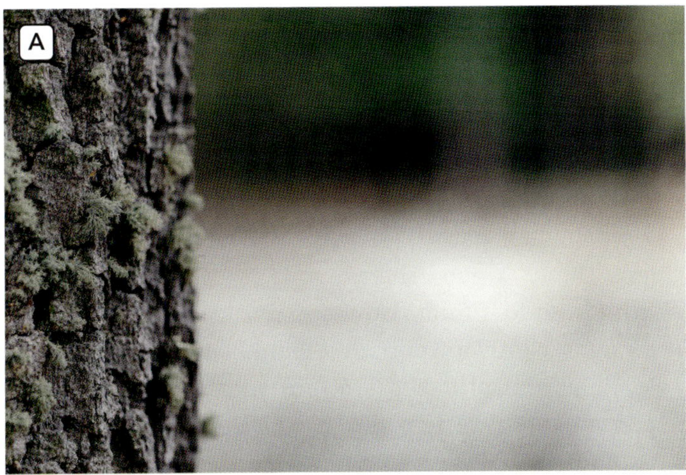

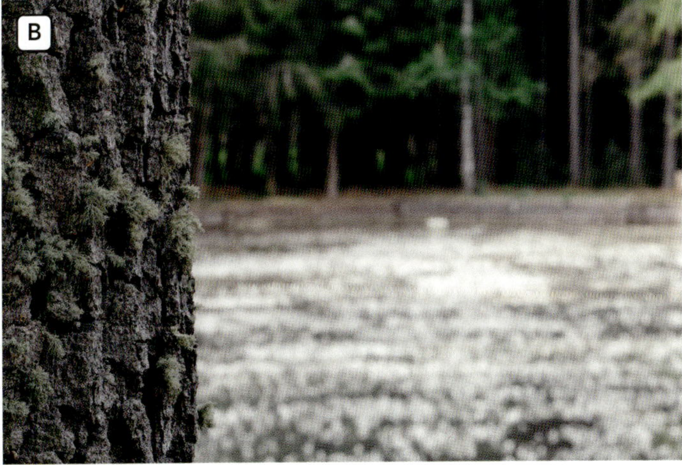

Fig. 59: This example shows the same scene shot twice with the XF90mmF2 R LM WR lens. Image **A** was shot wide open at f/2; image **B** was stopped down to the maximum of f/16. While stopping down clearly increases the depth of field, the look of the remaining out-of-focus area (also known as *bokeh*) is still smooth and silky, which is a trademark of the XF90mmF2 lens. Within the Fujifilm X-mount universe, I consider this the "perfect lens" because it doesn't show relevant weaknesses in any field of use.

- Fast lenses like the XF56mmF1.2 R WR or the XF35mmF1.4 R often exhibit a tight DOF of less than an inch when used wide open, so in a portrait shot, only one of the subject's eyes may be perfectly in focus. If that's the case, you can stop down the lens or change the position of your subject so that both eyes are the same distance from the camera.

- Stopping down a lens to f/8 and beyond leads to increased diffraction blur [40] across the image area. While increasing the depth of field enlarges the in-focus zone, maximum detail within that zone is reduced. In other words, when you shoot with f/22 using a wide-angle lens, there's a good chance your scene will be in focus from front to infinity. However, its overall crispness will be significantly lower than it would be at f/5.6. The Lens Modulation Optimizer (LMO) in your camera can compensate for diffraction blur to a degree, but its effect only extends to JPEGs that are created in-camera. External RAW converters can't support the LMO. However, some external apps offer their own "LMO" profiles. An example for this is PureRAW 3 from DxO, which can easily be integrated into Adobe Lightroom as a plug-in.

- When you shoot wide open or with a high ISO setting, it's possible that the suitable shutter speed is faster than the camera's maximum mechanical shutter speed of 1/8000 sec. If that's the case, the shutter speed will be displayed in red (overexposure warning). You can use shutter speeds beyond the mechanical threshold by activating the electronic shutter.

TIP 48	Using shutter priority S

Shutter priority AE [41] works like aperture priority, except you are manually setting a shutter speed [42], and the camera automatically selects a fitting aperture value based on your exposure. Shutter priority is available only when you're using compatible X-mount lenses with electronic contacts.

Adapted lenses (at least those with mechanical adapters) can only be used with aperture priority or in manual mode.

Setting the right shutter speed depends on two factors:

- Motion blur [43]: The faster your subject is moving, the faster your shutter speed must be to avoid shots with motion blur. This doesn't mean motion blur is always bad; it can be used as a conscious choice to add dynamic punch to your image. For instance, panning [44] the camera blurs the background behind a sharp main subject. Motion blur can be a benefit of long exposures—exposure times [45] of several seconds or minutes can smooth water surfaces, blur cloudy skies, or add star trails.

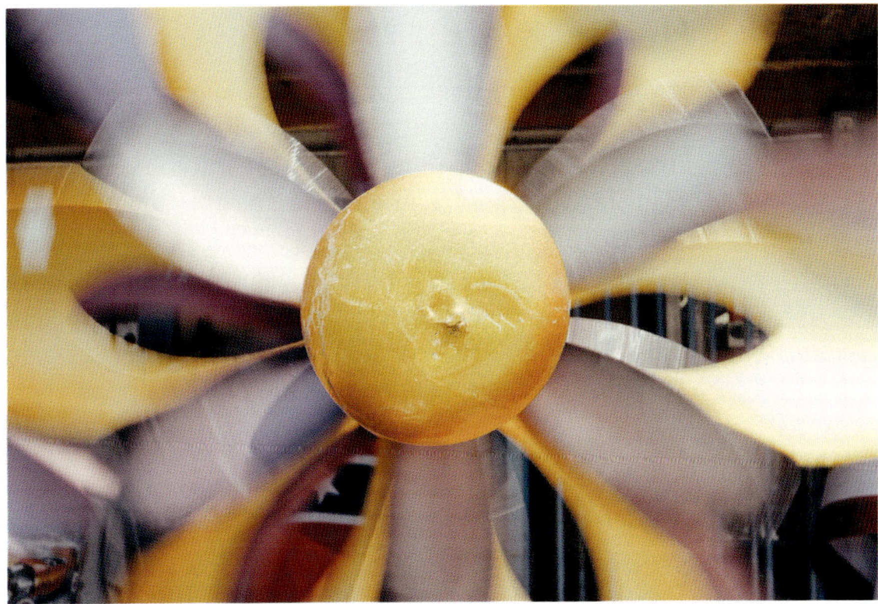

Fig. 60: In this handheld shot of a spinning wind wheel, **motion blur** was a conscious choice. Shot with the versatile XF27mmF2.8 pancake lens at f/13, the selected shutter speed of 1/30 sec. at base ISO was slow enough to illustrate the motion of the propellers around the stationary (and thus sharply focused) node. At the same time, it was fast enough to avoid camera shake which would have blurred the non-moving parts, as well.

- Blur due to camera shake [46]: If you don't hold the camera steady when you take a shot, the resulting image can be blurred. The optical image stabilizer [47] (OIS) and IBIS can help, or you can put the camera on a tripod or a solid surface and use the self-timer or a remote shutter release to take the shot. A rule of thumb suggests using at least the reciprocal of the "full-frame" equivalent focal length as your shutter speed. For example, if you are using a 200 mm lens on your APS-C camera (and the OIS/IBIS has been switched off), your minimum shutter speed should be 1/300 sec., since you must multiply the focal length with the APS-C crop factor [48] of 1.5. Of course, rules of thumb don't apply to everyone in every situation. It really depends on your technique and whether you're blessed with steady hands.

If you set a very slow shutter speed or choose a high ISO setting in shutter priority mode, it's possible that even the smallest aperture opening of your lens will still be too large to avoid overexposure. In this case, the aperture value will be displayed in red.

Since your camera features a dedicated shutter speed dial, you can use it to quickly change the shutter speed in full-stop increments. You can also use the command dial to fine-tune your selection in 1/3 EV intermediate steps.

Hint: Setting the shutter speed dial to **T** (Time) allows you to select the *full* range of available shutter speeds (in 1/3 EV steps) by turning a command dial. You can assign shutter speed control to one of the command dials in SET UP > BUTTON/DIAL SETTING > COMMAND DIAL SETTING. Personally, I always assign shutter speed to the rear command dial.

TIP 49	Using program AE **P** and program shift

In program AE, the X-T5 will automatically pick a combination of aperture *and* shutter speed settings that correspond to your set exposure. This mode can be useful for inexperienced photographers or in situations when you don't have the time or opportunity to manually adjust the aperture or shutter speed.

Like in aperture priority AE, the slowest possible shutter speed in program AE is limited to a maximum duration of 30 seconds. When this (in concert with an already wide-open aperture) is not sufficiently slow enough to achieve the set exposure, the camera will display a red underexposure warning when you half-press the shutter release button.

Even in program AE, you can influence shutter speed and aperture to a degree by using program shift. Program shift allows you to select more suitable combinations of aperture and shutter speed compared to the one originally proposed by the camera's program AE. You can cycle through various combinations of apertures and shutter speeds that all result in the same exposure. When the camera is in program AE mode, you can activate program shift by turning the command dial that is otherwise responsible for adjusting the shutter speed.

Let's say you are shooting a portrait with the XF16–55mmF2.8 R LM WR zoom lens. It's a bright day, so program AE offers a shutter speed of 1/500 sec. with an aperture of f/5.6. However, you prefer to shoot the portrait wide open at f/2.8 to achieve a blurrier background. In this situation, you have two choices: you can either switch to aperture priority mode by manually setting an aperture of f/2.8, or you can use program shift by turning the command dial until the aperture display shows f/2.8. Opening the aperture two stops, from f/5.6 to f/2.8, won't change the original exposure because program shift will automatically adjust the shutter speed two stops from 1/500 sec. to 1/2000 sec.

Important: *Program shift is **not** available if Dynamic Range is set to AUTO or if a TTL flash unit is in use.*

| TIP 50 | Playing it safe with auto exposure bracketing |

As you know by now, the automatic exposure (AE) modes **P**, **A**, and **S** are merely responsible for automatically filling exposure variables. The exposure itself is the responsibility of the photographer. You can use metering (multi, center-weighted, average, or spot), the live view, and the live histogram to determine the correct exposure.

Nobody is perfect! If you want to play it safe, auto exposure bracketing [49] can be a helpful feature. In this mode, the camera takes a series of at least two shots in quick succession, each with a different exposure (known as exposure bracketing). With this method, there will often be one shot with normal exposure, one underexposed shot, and one overexposed shot.

Exposure bracketing is especially useful with subjects that don't move. After you've taken the shot, you can decide which of the differently exposed versions you want to keep.

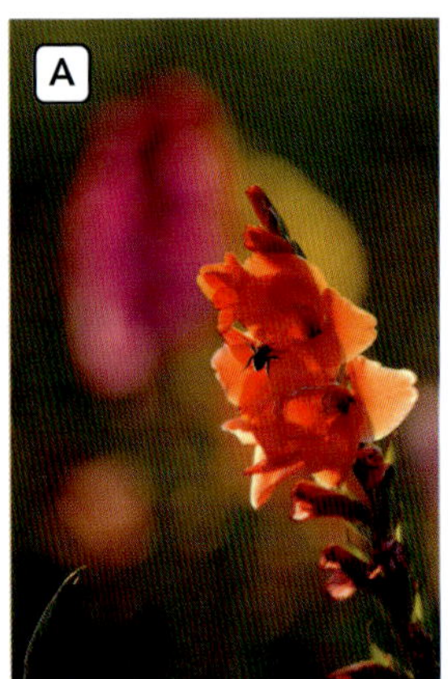
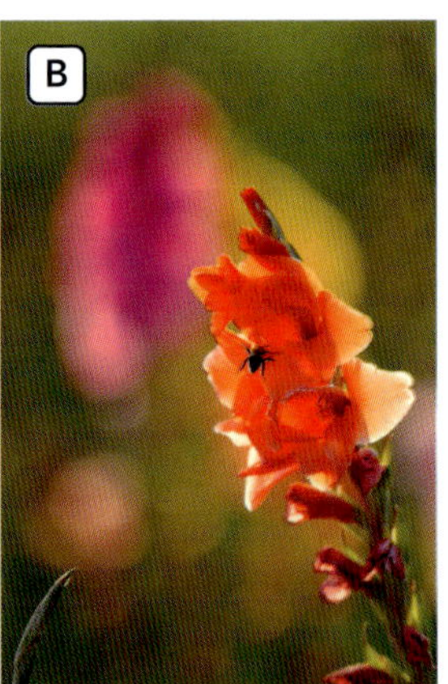
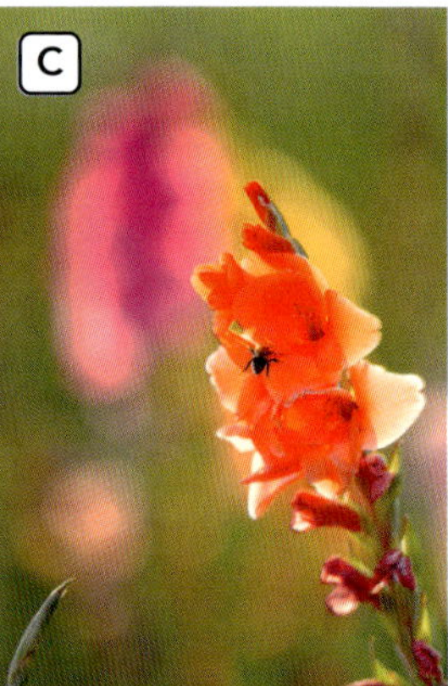

Fig. 61: Auto exposure bracketing automatically takes two or more images with varying exposure. Contrary to its name, AE bracketing even works in manual exposure mode, so you can manually set an exposure (aperture, shutter speed, ISO) you think is right, and AE bracketing will give you additional options with different shutter speeds that are brighter and/or darker than your original exposure. In this example, image **B** shows the originally set exposure. Image **A** was bracketed 2/3 EV darker, and image **C** was bracketed 2/3 EV brighter.

You can activate AE BKT by selecting BKT on the DRIVE dial. You must make sure that AE bracketing is selected in the shooting menu (SHOOTING SETTING > DRIVE SETTING > BKT SETTING > BKT SELECT > AE BKT). You can also configure additional AE bracketing parameters such as the exposure difference between images (SHOOTING SETTING > DRIVE SETTING > BKT SETTING > AE BKT > FRAMES/STEP SETTING).

Long exposures	TIP 51

Long exposures can lead to impressive results. With fireworks, night shots, interesting water surfaces, stars, and clouds, exposure times of several seconds, or even minutes, capture the course of time in a single photograph. Of course, this only works if you put the camera on a tripod or a solid, non-vibrating surface.

You have two basic options:

- Set the shutter-speed dial to **T** (Time) and then use the corresponding command dial to set the shutter speed. To avoid camera shake, use a remote shutter release or the self-timer to take the shot.

- Set the shutter speed dial to **B** (Bulb), then press and hold the shutter button for as long as you want the camera to expose. Obviously, it makes sense to use a remote shutter release that can be locked for the duration of the shot.

For good-quality results, make sure to set IMAGE QUALITY SETTING > LONG EXPOSURE NR > ON. By doing so, the camera will perform a dark-frame subtraction [50] depending on what ISO and exposure time you used. Dark-frame subtraction doubles the duration of the effective exposure, so be patient.

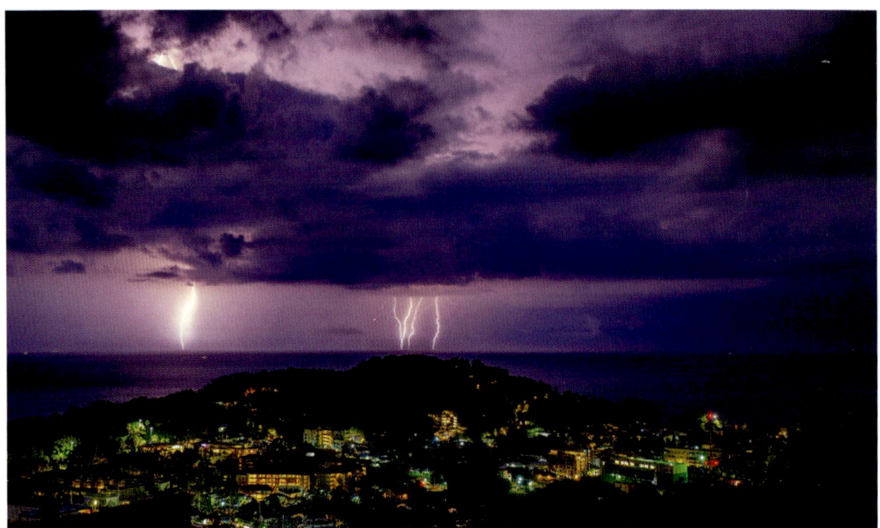

Fig. 62: A **long exposure** of 30 seconds taken in T mode. Make sure to use a tripod for these kinds of shots.

<table>
<tr><td>TIP 52</td><td>Long exposures in bright daylight</td></tr>
</table>

To achieve long exposure times under normal daylight conditions, you can't just stop down the lens. Even at f/22, your shutter speed would still be too fast. Besides, diffraction blur will kick in beyond f/8, so stopping down beyond this point is only recommended when it cannot be avoided.

To realize long shutter speeds in good light, it's best to use a so-called ND filter [51], or neutral density filter. This is a fancy name for a gray filter you can put in front of the lens to block a portion of the light from reaching the sensor.

For example, a filter with an ND 3.0 specification will extend your exposure time by a factor of about 1000 (or 10 f-stops). This means that by using this filter, a scene that would normally require a shutter speed of 1/50 sec. at f/8 can be shot at the same aperture with an exposure time of 20 seconds.

However, there's a catch. Since X-series cameras are equipped with a rather weak infrared (IR) cut filter in front of their sensors, long exposures (typically one minute or longer) in bright daylight should be performed with a regular neutral-density (ND) filter *and* a dedicated IR cut filter in front of the lens. This will help to avoid false colors. Some ND filters already include an IR cut filter.

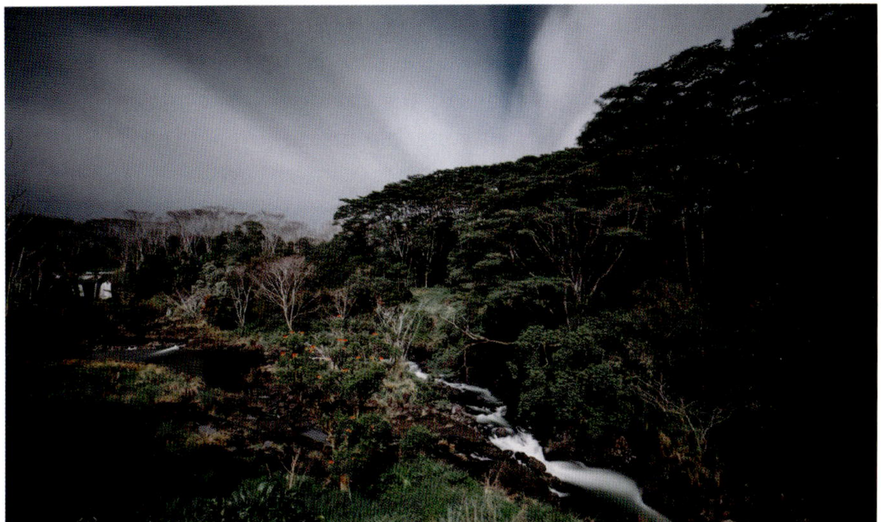

Fig. 63: This **long daylight exposure** lasted almost 4 minutes and was made possible by using a strong ND filter.

ISO settings—what's the deal?	TIP 53

The meaning of ISO in the digital realm is often misunderstood. Unlike film, higher ISO settings *don't* increase the sensor's sensitivity. The sensor in your X-T5 is calibrated to a native ISO 125 (based on the popular SOS standard) [52], and this remains the same no matter what ISO you set.

To be clear, there's no difference between taking a shot with f/5.6 and 1/60 sec. at either ISO L (64) or at ISO H (51200). In both cases, the sensor is exposed to the exact same amount of light (or photons) due to the fixed f/5.6 and

1/60 sec. setting. The amount of light that hits the sensor (the actual exposure) is solely determined by aperture and shutter speed.

So, what exactly is ISO doing? ISO determines the amount of *signal amplification* that's applied to the image. ISO 125, the sensor's native setting, is the camera's basic calibration. At ISO 250, the signal (or sensor data) is amplified by one aperture stop (1 EV) to brighten the image and increase its exposure. At ISO 500, the amplification amounts to two stops (2 EV), and so on. At ISO 12800, the additional amplification of the light recorded by the sensor amounts to almost seven stops. It's not surprising that image quality decreases when ISO amplification increases because noise and artifacts are amplified along with the actual image data.

The amplification we are talking about means brightening the image by increasing its exposure. This concept of amplification isn't limited to the camera itself by setting the ISO—it's also part of the entire workflow from in-camera exposure via RAW file (digital negative) to the final JPEG or TIFF file (digital print). If you are familiar with RAW converters such as Lightroom, you know there's an exposure slider. Moving this slider to the left or right changes the exposure (and hence the ISO brightness) of an image after the fact.

If you take a shot with an ISO 500 setting, you're telling the camera's Auto-exposure (AE) to expose the image two stops darker than it would at its base ISO of 125, then to amplify (brighten) that image two stops to compensate for the underexposure.

Regarding image quality and ISO, there's a basic rule: lower ISO settings lead to higher-quality results—hence the general recommendation to keep the ISO settings as low as possible. However, we obviously can't shoot with base ISO all the time, especially in low-light situations.

There are two basic methods to amplify a digital image:

- **Analog/digital hybrid amplification** *prior* **to writing the RAW file:** This method applies a mix of analog and digital signal processing to amplify or push the image to the brightness level that corresponds to the camera's ISO setting. The digitized result of this amplification/ multiplication process is then saved as a RAW file.

- **Digital amplification (push)** *after* **writing the RAW file:** This method changes the brightness of an image during RAW processing, *after* the RAW file has been generated. Metadata (i.e., instructions) in the RAW file tell the RAW converter what to do. You can also use the camera's built-in RAW converter to adjust the effective brightness (and hence, ISO) of an image after it has been recorded, or simply by adjusting your external RAW converter's exposure slider during RAW processing.

Digital amplification (i.e., multiplication) during RAW processing is beneficial because it's reversible. If the digital amplification was too strong (leading to blown highlights), you can always pull it back again to reduce it. If it was too weak, you can push it up. ISO (i.e., exposure amplification) is a volatile aspect of the photographic process because it can be applied *anytime*: in-camera, prior to writing the RAW file, and later during RAW processing.

The sensor in your X-T5 is a so-called ISO-less sensor. This means there's no significant quality difference between conventional signal amplification prior to writing a RAW file and digital amplification later during RAW conversion. This is great, because it allows you to digitally increase the ISO (i.e., brightness/exposure) of your shots during RAW processing, either in-camera or with external software such as Lightroom. Pushing the exposure up later in your RAW converter won't look much different from choosing a higher ISO setting when you take the shot.

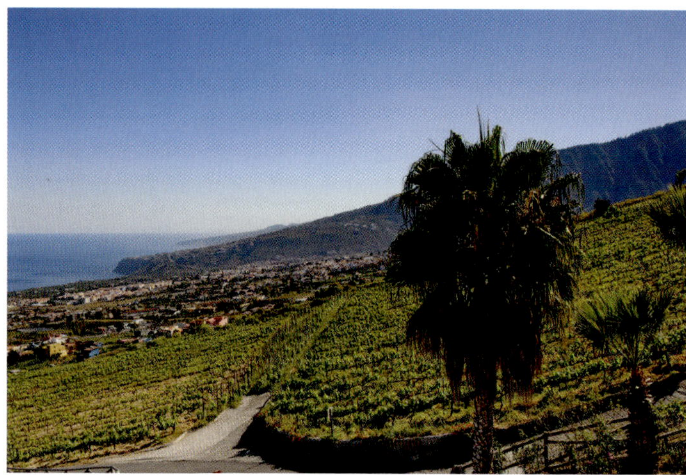

Fig. 64: ISO-less sensor (1): This shot was taken at ISO 2000, with classic analog/digital in-camera amplification. The ISO 2000 result was then burned into the RAW file and the RAW converted to a JPEG.

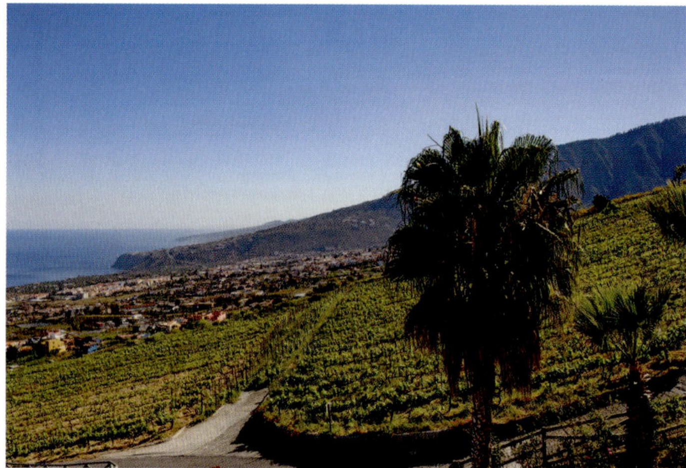

Fig. 65: ISO-less sensor (2): This shot was also *effectively* taken at ISO 2000. However, it was shot with an ISO 125 base setting, using the same aperture and shutter speed as the previous image, effectively underexposing it four stops (4 EV). The amplification from ISO 125 to ISO 2000 took place digitally during RAW conversion, simply by moving the exposure slider 4 EV to the right, thus compensating for the underexposure. You won't be able to see any quality difference between the two shots in this book, so I invite you to look at full-size samples on Flickr [53].

Fig. 66: ISO-less sensor (3): This is the same as the previous shot that was recorded as an ISO 125 RAW file—but without the push of 4 EV that effectively turned it into an image with ISO 2000 brightness.

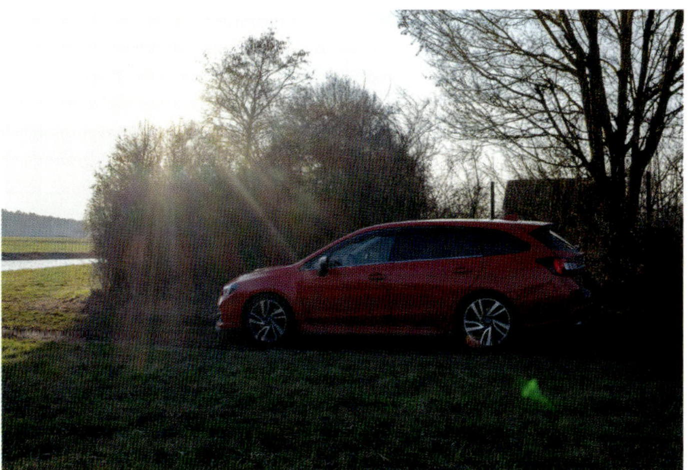

Fig. 67: ISO-less sensor (4): This image was taken at ISO 2000. The exposure was set for the shadows and the car. As you can see, the sky is completely blown and couldn't be recovered during RAW conversion.

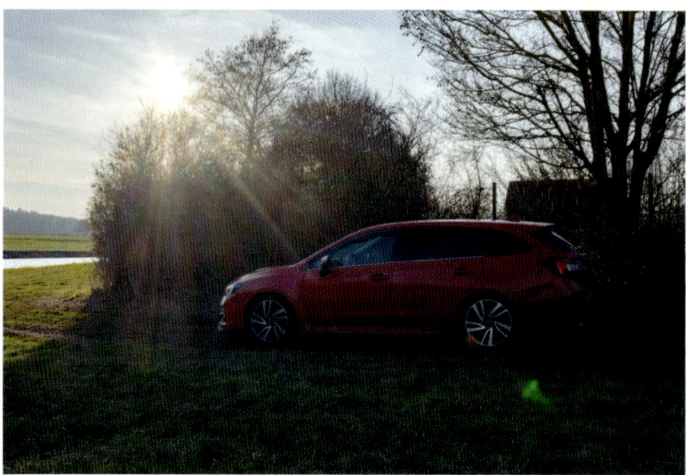

Fig. 68: ISO-less sensor (5): This image was taken at ISO 125, with otherwise the same exposure settings (aperture and shutter speed) as the previous ISO 2000 shot. I also used the same Lightroom development settings as before, with only one difference: the exposure slider was moved 4 EV to the right. This effectively pushes the image data to ISO 2000. Image quality in the shadows and midtones is very similar, but the highlights (sky and clouds) are now fully intact.

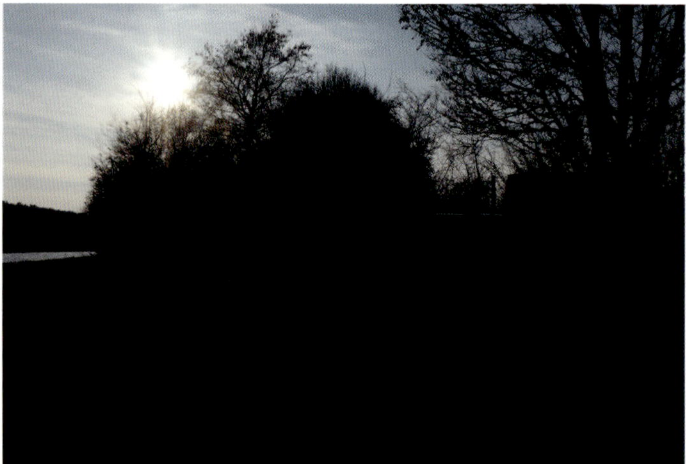

Fig. 69: ISO-less sensor (6): This is the ISO 125 shot from before but processed without the 4 EV exposure push in Lightroom. It shows the actual exposure as it was recorded in the RAW file. It offers 4 EV more highlight dynamic range than the original ISO 2000 shot.

The ISO-less sensor extends the dynamic range of your X-T5. You can now confidently expose for the critical highlights in your scene, thus protecting them from being blown. In step two, you raise the dark (underexposed) parts of the image during RAW conversion. Raising shadows and midtones doesn't produce more visible noise than using a higher ISO setting in the first place.

Of course, it also depends on your RAW converter and how competent it is at raising shadows. Pushing your exposure by 4 EV or even 5 EV is possible if your converter plays along. Basically, you don't just need an ISO-less sensor, you also need an "ISO-less RAW converter."

With Adobe Lightroom, my best experience regarding massive exposure push operations has been with Iridient X-Transformer [54] as an intermediary. X-Transformer not only performs better demosaicing than Lightroom's standard algorithm, it also produces a linear DNG file that is better suited for strong push operations in Lightroom than the original RAF file.

Even better results with very little noise can often be achieved by pushing and processing RAW files with Adobe Lightroom's new AI denoise/demosaicing function. However, this option may produce color shifts and other artifacts with certain shots, so your mileage may vary.

What you should know about extended ISO	TIP 54

You have probably noticed that in addition to the standard ISO settings (ISO 125 to ISO 12800), your X-T5 offers three additional settings: L (64), H (25600), and H (51200).

- **H means High**: In these modes, image data is digitally amplified further. This enormous amplification leads to a visible decrease in image quality. While ISO 25600 is still quite usable (especially for black-and-white JPEGs using the ACROS film simulation), ISO 51200 is only for emergencies.

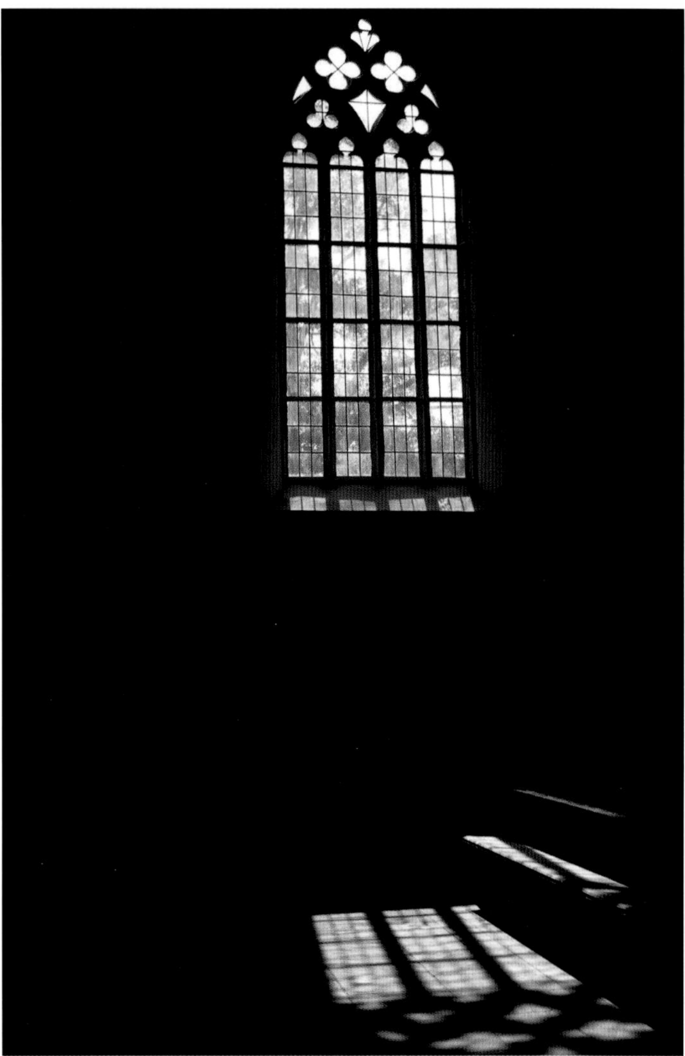

Fig. 70: Extended ISO L can add punch thanks to its decreased dynamic range. To pull it off, set your camera to manual exposure mode, select base ISO 125, and expose the scene to the highlights using the live view and live histogram. Exposing to the highlights means that the brightest, most important parts of the scene are exposed as bright as possible, but without clipping (i.e., losing highlight detail). After the exposure to the highlights is manually set, change the ISO setting from 125 to L (64) without changing aperture or shutter speed. This will increase the contrast of the image by darkening the shadows and midtones one stop, while bright highlights remain where they were.

- **L means LOW**: In ISO L (64) mode, an ISO 125 RAW is over-exposed by one stop. During RAW conversion, the JPEG is pulled down one stop and saved, resulting in an ISO 64 JPEG file. A digital pull is the direct opposite of a digital push operation: Digital pull decreases the exposure of the resulting image. The ISO L (64) RAW and JPEG files contain one stop *less* dynamic range than normal ISO 125 files. This means bright areas like clouds in the sky can easily appear blown out. On the other hand, ISO L (64) can add contrast and punch to scenes with dull lighting and little contrast.

Important: Extended ISO settings are not available when the electronic shutter (ES) is selected.

While shooting in extended ISO L diminishes highlight dynamic range, this fact is *not* reflected in the live view and live histogram. This means the live view and live histogram become pretty much useless for determining the correct exposure to the highlights when you are using ISO L. Only when you half-press and hold the shutter button to lock the exposure will the live view adapt, but at that stage there is no histogram available.

Practically, this means it's not recommended that you use extended ISO L in one of the auto exposure (AE) modes: **P**, **A**, and **S**. Instead, you should first set the correct exposure to the highlights in manual mode **M** at ISO 125 using the live view and live histogram, and then change the ISO setting to ISO L (64) without further adjustments to shutter speed and aperture. This will keep your highlights intact and will add contrast to the image by lowering the midtones and shadows to the new ISO L (64) settings.

The X-T5 also offers extended ISO L (100) and ISO L (80) settings, which are derived from ISO 200 and ISO 160 by first overexposing the shot one stop and then pulling it back down one stop during RAW conversion to match the brightness of the selected ISO L setting of 100 or 80. Doing so deducts one stop of dynamic range. I strongly advise against using these two additional extended ISO L settings.

| TIP 55 | Auto-ISO and minimum shutter speed |

You can automate the task of selecting the best (or lowest) ISO setting possible for any given shooting situation. Auto-ISO is an option with up to three configurable presets (AUTO1, AUTO2, and AUTO3) that can be configured in the ISO menu of your camera (SHOOTING SETTING > ISO AUTO SETTING):

- DEFAULT SENSITIVITY: This is the lower ISO limit. The camera will always try to use this ISO setting if the other parameters permit it.

- MAX. SENSITIVITY: This is the upper ISO limit. The camera's Auto-ISO will never go beyond this level.

- MIN. SHUTTER SPEED: Auto-ISO will automatically increase the ISO setting (up to the MAX. SENSITIVITY threshold) when the minimum shutter speed cannot be realized. There's also an AUTO setting here: If you set MIN. SHUTTER SPEED to AUTO, the camera will adjust the minimum shutter speed depending on the current focal length, using the formula *Minimum Shutter Speed = [1 ÷ (Focal Length × 1.5)] sec.* For example, with a classic XF23mmF1.4 R prime lens, the AUTO setting delivers a minimum shutter speed setting of 1/34 sec.

Obviously, MIN. SHUTTER SPEED is only relevant in auto exposure (AE) modes **A** and **P**, because the shutter speed is already set manually in modes **M** and **S**. Auto-ISO minimum shutter speed makes sure that within the lower and upper ISO limits, the camera will always use a shutter speed that is at least as fast as the set minimum shutter speed.

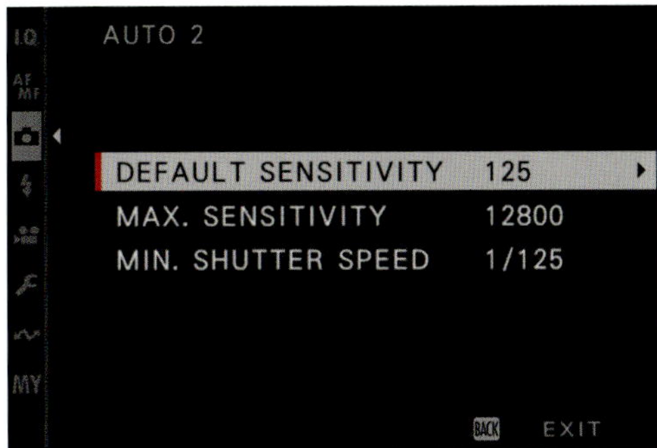

Fig. 71: Auto-ISO works with an ISO range between DEFAULT SENSITIVITY (the bottom) and MAX. SENSITIVITY (the ceiling). It will always try to keep ISO as close to the bottom as possible, but only if the resulting shutter speed isn't slower than the set MIN. SHUTTER SPEED.

Here's an example: Let's say you are shooting in mode **A** (aperture priority) in bright light conditions using f/5.6. Auto-ISO is set to ISO 125 as the lower limit and ISO 12800 as the upper limit. You have set 1/125 sec. as your minimum shutter speed, because you want to avoid motion blur while taking pictures of people walking in the street.

If the scene is brightly lit, there is no problem. The camera will use ISO 125 with shutter speeds at least as fast as 1/125 sec. However, as the sun sets and it becomes impossible to successfully use 1/125 sec. at f/5.6 and ISO 125, Auto-ISO will increase the ISO to ensure the shutter speed doesn't drop below 1/125 sec. This automatic adjustment continues as the light conditions deteriorate until Auto-ISO reaches the upper ISO limit (in our case, ISO 12800). What now? Since the camera can't increase the ISO any further, it will start to reduce the shutter speed to values slower than 1/125 sec. to still ensure a correct exposure.

In mode **S** (shutter priority), the photographer sets the shutter speed. In this mode, Auto-ISO will increase the ISO setting only when the aperture is already wide open and can't be opened further. This can be a problem with fast lenses like an XF56mmF1.2, XF35mmF1.4, or XF23mmF1.4.

When shot wide open, the depth of field of these lenses is quite limited (to say the least). This is why Auto-ISO is better used in modes **P** or **A**, at least in concert with fast lenses.

| **TIP 56** | Auto-ISO in manual mode **M**: the "misomatic" mode |

Manual mode in tandem with Auto-**ISO** provides another auto**MATIC** exposure mode: the so-called "**misomatic**" mode. In this mode, you preselect the aperture and shutter speed, and the camera automatically selects a suitable ISO setting that matches the exposure that has been determined by the currently active metering mode.

To be useful in a misomatic setup, Auto-ISO should be able to use the full ISO bandwidth, so you should configure it with the camera's base ISO 125 as the lower limit and the highest available upper limit (ISO 12800).

Misomatic gives you full manual control over aperture (depth of field) and shutter speed (motion blur and camera shake). You can tailor shutter speed and aperture to the requirements of the task at hand; there will be no surprises. At the same time, you still enjoy the comfort of automatic exposure (AE).

Misomatic also allows you to adjust the camera-metered exposure with the exposure compensation dial. For this to be effective, it's even more important to set the Auto-ISO DEFAULT SENSITIVITY as low as possible and the MAX. SENSITIVITY as high as possible.

If you don't want to spend time with exposure compensation while you are in misomatic mode, you can use Fuji's DR function as a workaround by selecting DR200% in concert with the misomatic. This setting is your insurance against accidental overexposure by the camera's AE, because it gives you at least one stop of extra latitude for after-the-fact overexposure corrections with the internal or an external RAW converter. To correct a poor auto-exposure after the fact, you can use the PUSH or PULL commands of the camera's internal RAW converter or move the exposure slider of your external RAW processing software.

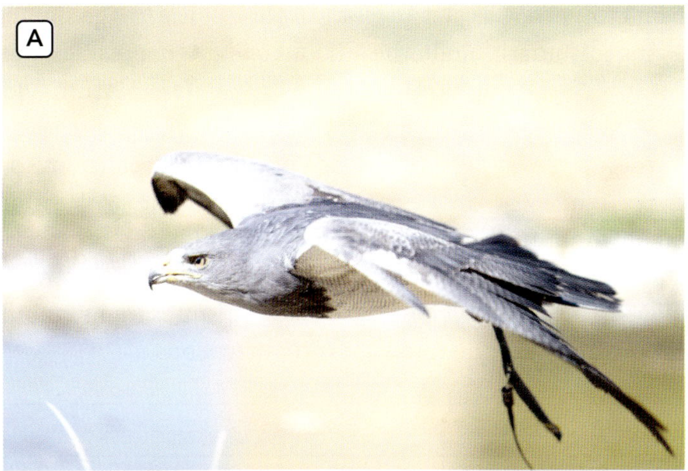

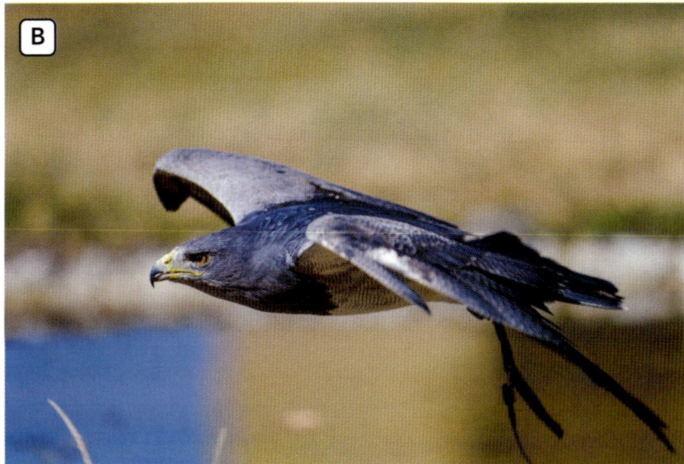

Fig. 72: Misomatic mode combines manual exposure with Auto-ISO. It can be helpful in situations with quickly and suddenly changing light conditions, such as with concerts and other stage events, sporting events, action shots, and street photography. Basically, it's about situations that don't leave you enough time to manually adjust the exposure, and where catching the decisive moment is your priority. In misomatic mode, you can set the desired depth of field (aperture) and motion blur (shutter speed), while the camera auto-exposes the images by applying the right amount of ISO amplification. To protect against accidental overexposure (**A**), you can buy "insurance" by setting the camera to DR200% in misomatic mode. This way, overexposures can be corrected during RAW conversion (**B**).

Don't forget: ISO is just an amplification of the image signal. Using misomatic mode, the amount of light that reaches the sensor is solely determined by your manual aperture and shutter speed settings. It always stays the same, regardless of the automatic ISO setting chosen by the camera. In misomatic mode, the only exposure variable is the amount of signal amplification (i.e., ISO); and with an ISO-less sensor, this variable can also be adjusted later during RAW conversion. In this context, choosing DR200% ensures there's more leeway for after-the-fact exposure corrections.

TIP 57	Extending the dynamic range

If the dynamic range of a scene is larger than the dynamic range of the camera's sensor or image processing, one of the following phenomena occurs:

- The highlights of the image are blown out or appear too bright (overexposed).

- Midtones appear too dark (underexposed), and shadows lose detail in dark areas.

In both cases, the shot's exposure is out of balance. Sadly, it's very difficult (if not impossible) to restore detail in blown highlights. It's much easier to lift underexposed midtones and blocked shadows. This procedure is called *tone mapping*, and it's the only way to access the full potential of a modern digital camera's dynamic range. Tone mapping reassigns certain tonal values of the original exposure, either by employing a tone curve or by using a more complex procedure known as *adaptive* tone mapping, which takes neighboring pixels into account.

To record the full tonal range of a high-contrast scene, it's best to expose the image in a way that preserves the color and texture of the important bright parts of the scene. Of course, doing so can lead to an image with underexposed midtones and blocked shadows that needs further processing to look natural, realistic, and pleasing. You can correct these issues with most external RAW converters.

While every RAW converter is different, most programs offer functions to selectively manipulate the exposure of a shot after the fact. For example, you can change the overall exposure with the exposure slider, and you can restore blown highlights with a highlight recovery slider. Most converters also offer sliders that only target shadow tones.

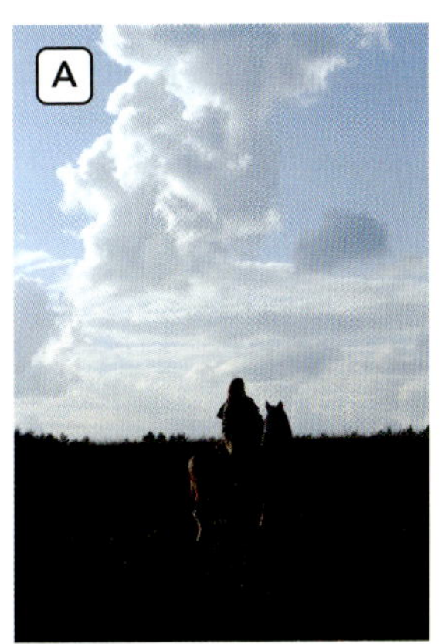
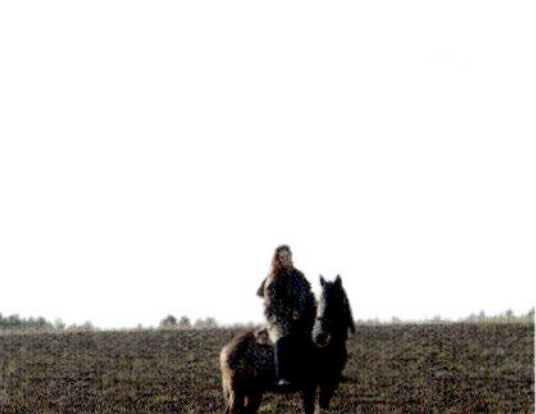
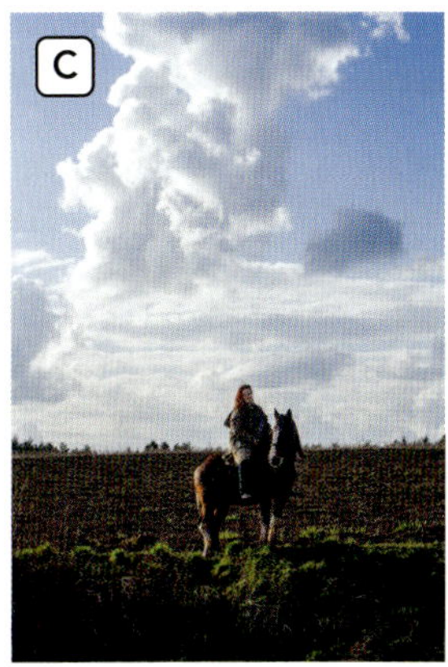

Fig. 73: In many instances, the **dynamic range** of a standard JPEG is smaller than the dynamic range of the scene, so no matter how you expose the scene in your camera, some parts of the resulting image will end up either too dark or too bright (or both). Here's a practical example:

Image **A** was exposed to the highlights, showing color and texture in the blue sky and white clouds. However, the darker foreground is clearly underexposed, resulting in blocked shadows. Horse and rider are almost reduced to a silhouette.

Image **B** depicts the same scene, but this time it was exposed about two stops (EV) brighter, removing blocked shadows and adding detail to the main subject. However, the cloudy blue sky is now overexposed and has all but disappeared.

This is a Catch-22, because no matter how you expose this scene, the JPEG from the camera will always display essential parts either too dark or too bright. Quite obviously, different parts of this scene require different exposures. To pull this off, we use the RAW file of image **A**, which was exposed to preserve the clouds and the sky. By applying tone mapping in a modern RAW converter, we selectively push (brighten) shadows and midtones without further brightening the highlights of the clouds and sky. We can even add additional contrast to the clouds and darken the sky a bit. Image **C** shows the result out of Adobe Lightroom, where different pixels received different levels of (after-the-fact) amplification.

The built-in DR function of your X-T5 can help you automate the tone mapping procedure. It works in two stages:

- The RAW file is exposed one (DR200%) or two stops (DR400%) darker than indicated to preserve bright highlights of a scene that would otherwise be clipped and lost.

- During the RAW conversion in the camera, the underexposed shadows and midtones are digitally amplified by one (DR200%) or two stops (DR400%) to restore their natural brightness, while the (already correctly exposed) highlights are mostly left alone to preserve them.

The resulting JPEG from the camera has undergone a selective exposure correction. The DR function restores the shadows and midtones of a shot that was initially exposed one or two stops darker to preserve the highlights of the scene. Looking at the resulting JPEGs, this leads to an effective gain in dynamic range (DR): one additional stop of highlight DR at DR200%, and two stops of additional highlight DR at DR400%.

In DR-Auto mode, the camera will automatically select a suitable DR setting. Please note that in this mode, the X-T5 will only choose either DR100% (no highlight DR expansion) or DR200% (one stop of highlight DR expansion). DR400% (two stops of highlight DR expansion) is available only when it is manually selected.

You can change the DR settings of your camera in the Quick menu or by selecting IMAGE QUALITY SETTING > DYNAMIC RANGE and then either AUTO, DR100%, DR200%, or DR400%.

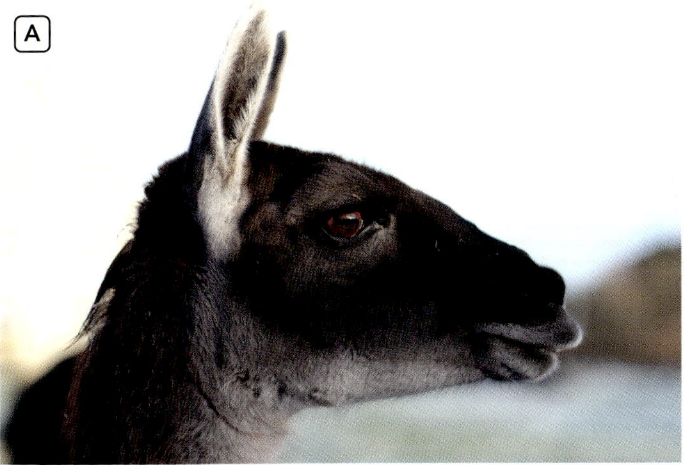

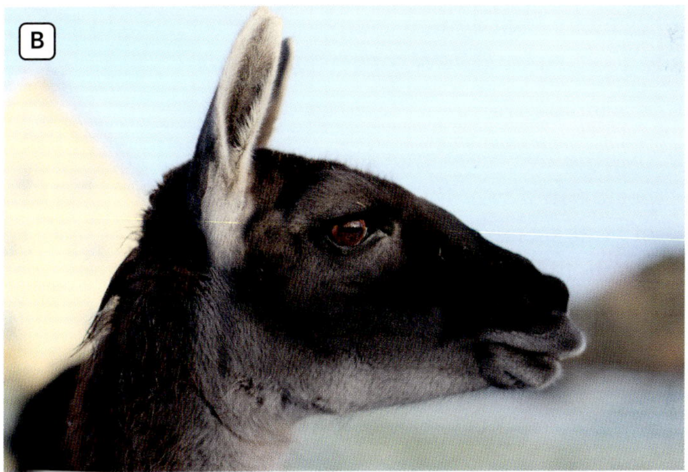

Fig. 74: These examples show the same shot with **DR100%** (image **A**) and **DR400%** (image **B**). At DR100%, the dark llama (our main subject) is correctly exposed in the foreground, but the much brighter colors in the sunny background are almost completely blown out because they were outside of the camera's dynamic range. In the DR400% version of the shot, the exposure (brightness) of the llama didn't change, however, the bright background is now perfectly colored and textured. To pull this off, the camera exposed the RAW file of the scene two stops (EV) darker than indicated, and then boosted shadows and midtones two stops brighter during RAW conversion. The result is a DR400% JPEG with 2 EV of extended dynamic range.

| TIP 58 | Extending the dynamic range for RAW shooters |

RAW shooters typically set the camera to DR100% and perform the tone mapping of their shots later during RAW processing. DR100% provides a realistic live view and live histogram. What You See Is What You Get (WYSIWYG).

The normal strategy of a RAW shooter is to expose toward the critical highlights of a high-contrast scene, making sure that there's sufficient color texture in the bright parts of the shot. This can result in an image with dark midtones and blocked shadows. However, while blown highlights are difficult, or even impossible, to restore, blocked shadows can be lifted (pushed) later. Balanced results from scenes with a very high dynamic range can be achieved in almost any good external RAW conversion software.

Here's what to do:

- Use the live view and live histogram to adjust the exposure in a way that ensures the important highlights of your scene are not blown out. This will preserve the highlights, but it may also lead to darkened midtones and blocked shadows, which you must deal with later during the RAW conversion of your shot.

- After taking the shot, enhance darkened shadows and midtones by selectively lifting the exposure in your RAW conversion software. For example, you could first lift the overall exposure and then restore the highlights with a highlight-recovery slider, or you could lift only the shadow tones with a shadow-tone slider. You can also combine both methods: Many RAW converters are quite flexible and offer several sliders to selectively change the exposure. Lightroom and Adobe Camera RAW (ACR), for example, feature five different controls (exposure, whites, blacks, shadows, and highlights) to perform this task. Whenever you change an exposure slider, you are effectively changing the ISO of any part of the image that is affected by that slider. However, in the digital domain of the RAW conversion stage, nothing is lost, and every-thing is fully reversible. *Selectively* changing the exposure of an image is known as tone mapping.

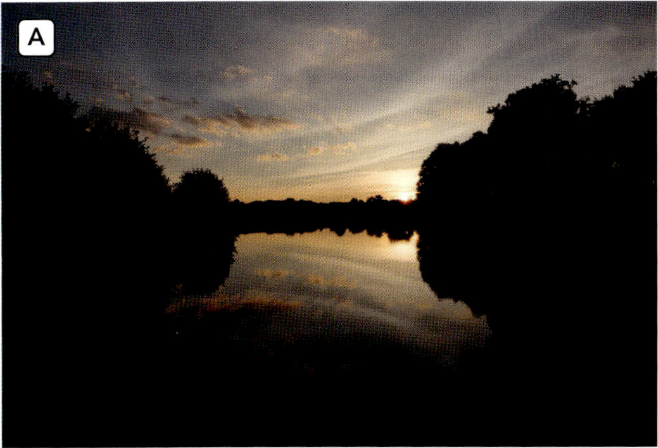

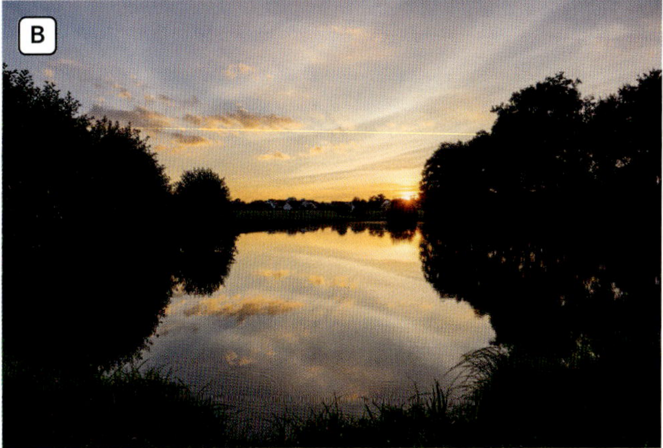

Fig. 75: Image **A** shows an image that has been **exposed to the highlights**. The bright parts are perfectly exposed, but this means that other parts are literally left in the dark. If that's what you want, great! If not, you must apply some tone mapping to the RAW file.

Image **B** shows the same image after tone mapping in Light-room. The dark shadow regions have been lifted, revealing more detail, where the previous image only displayed dark patches. This method is also known as applying adaptive ISO, because different parts of the image received a different degree of exposure-push amplification. While the shadows were pushed up (ISO increase), the highlights mostly remained as they were.

<table>
<tr><td>TIP 59</td><td>JPEG settings for RAW shooters</td></tr>
</table>

The previous tip explained the procedure to capture, compress, and later decompress scenes with high dynamic range. Since our exposure relies on the live view and the live histogram, it's useful to find camera settings that force the live histogram and live view to display as much dynamic range as possible. After all, we are shooting RAW and aren't really interested in the JPEGs from the camera, so we want the live view and live histogram to closely represent the data that will be recorded in the RAW files. This goal can be achieved by choosing JPEG settings in the IMAGE QUALITY SETTING menu that display as much dynamic range as possible:

- Set FILM SIMULATION to ETERNA. This setting results in JPEGs with less contrast than the other film simulation modes.

- Set TONE CURVE (HIGHLIGHTS) to –2. This setting reduces the highlight contrast of the JPEG in the live view and in the live histogram.

- Set TONE CURVE (SHADOWS) to –2. This setting reduces the shadow contrast of the JPEG in the live view and the live histogram.

- If you are shooting scenes with bright and saturated tones of red, blue, or green, you can also dial back the COLOR setting.

The JPEG settings listed above give you a live view and live histogram with maximum dynamic range. JPEGs that are generated with these settings may look flat, but we usually don't intend to keep them anyway. We are only interested in the RAW file, which isn't affected by JPEG settings. However, the live view and live histogram *are* affected, and a flat live view image with a correspondingly flat live histogram is exactly what we want. It helps us to better fine-tune our exposure to preserve important highlights.

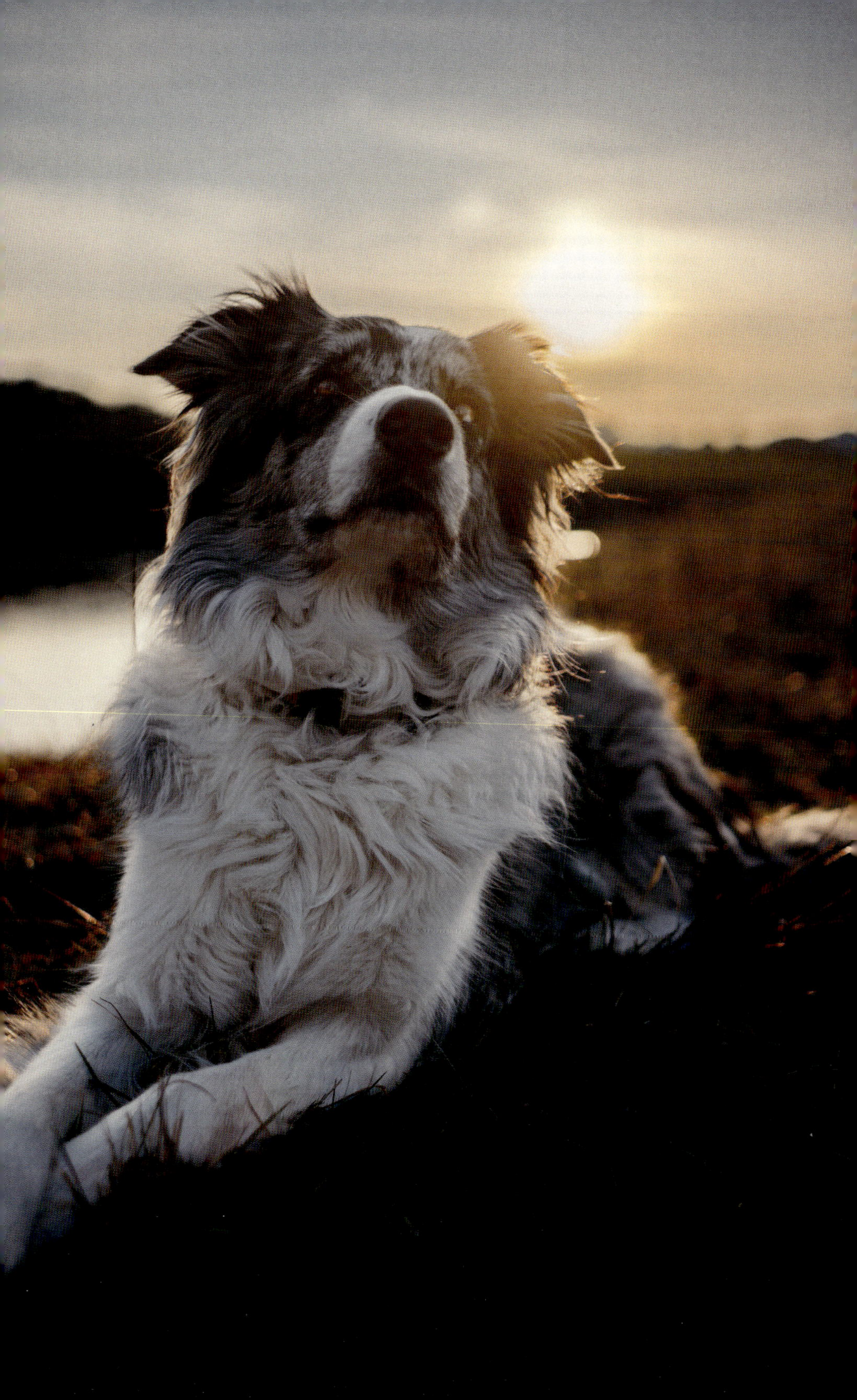

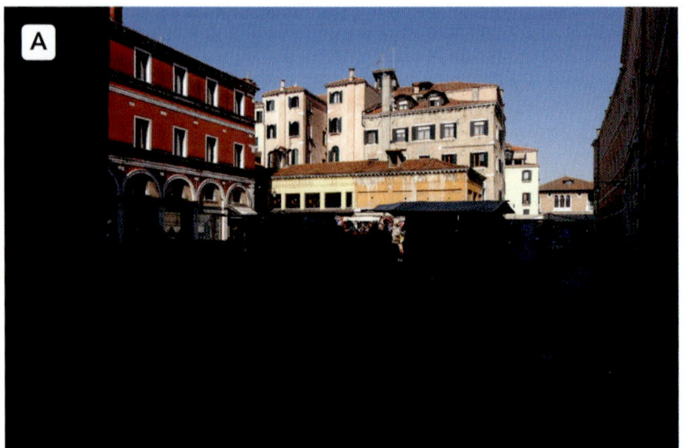

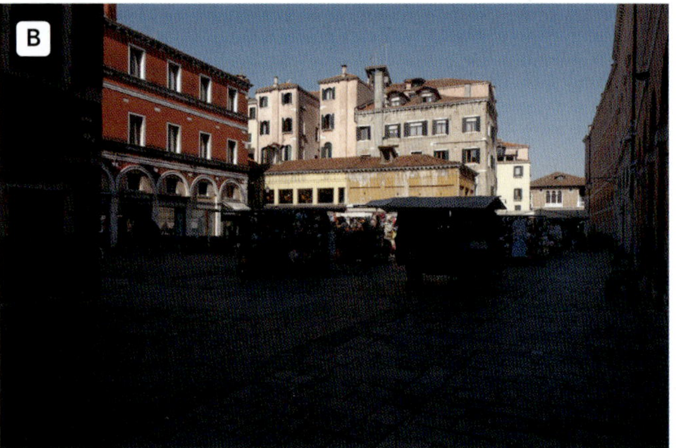

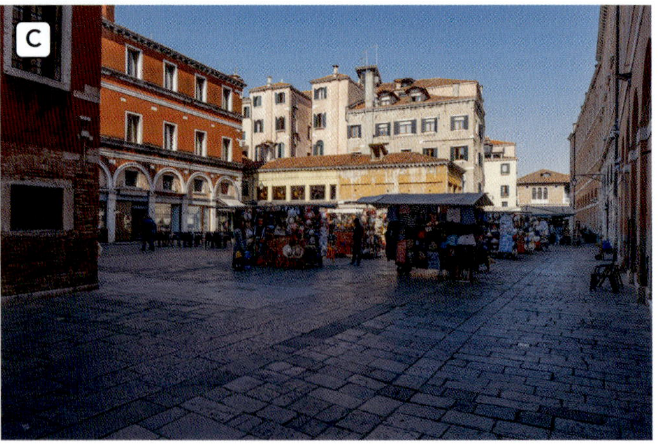

Fig. 76: These examples were all taken using the same exposure settings (ISO, aperture, and shutter speed). The exposure was geared toward the highlights of the sunlit parts behind the much darker foreground.

Image **A** shows how the live view (or JPEG) of the correctly exposed scene looks with the camera's Provia factory setting. While the sunny background is nicely lit, the dark parts are hard to make out. It is difficult to frame this shot.

Image **B** depicts the same scene with the same exposure settings, but this time I used "JPEG settings for RAW shooters" (Eterna, Tone Curve Shadows –2, Tone Curve Highlights –2). These settings deliver a flat live view image (or JPEG) with less contrast and significantly more dynamic range than the camera's default settings. Using flat JPEG settings can be helpful when you compose high-contrast scenes. You can expose to preserve important highlights but still see what you are shooting. Remember: JPEG settings don't affect the RAW data—they only affect how the RAW data is processed in the live view and the resulting JPEG image.

Image **C** is the final result after processing (tone mapping) the RAW file in Adobe Lightroom.

Extending the dynamic range for JPEG shooters	TIP 60

If you prefer to work with JPEGs that come directly from your camera (or want to shoot and keep RAWs *and* JPEGs), you can use Fuji's powerful DR function to capture scenes with high dynamic range. As you know, the DR function employs a two-stage process: reducing the exposure to preserve critical highlights, and then lifting dark shadows and midtones to restore their brightness (exposure) back to realistic-looking levels.

You can simply set the camera to DR-Auto (not recommended), or manually set DR200% or DR400% (recommended) when you take pictures of high-contrast scenes. Remember that DR200% requires a minimum ISO setting of one stop (1 EV) above your camera's base ISO 125, while DR400% requires a minimum ISO setting of two stops (2 EV) above base ISO. This is because the shadows and midtones in your scene will eventually be amplified by one (DR200%) or two (DR400%) ISO stops when the JPEG is created during RAW conversion. In the case of your X-T5, this means that

DR200% requires at least ISO 250, and DR400% requires at least ISO 500.

What if we don't want to just *guess* what DR setting is optimal for any given scene? Can't we use the camera's metering to determine *exactly* how much DR expansion is required? Yes, we can! Here's how:

- To begin with, let's set the camera to DR100% and expose toward the critical highlights of a scene, just like a RAW shooter would do. Assuming you are shooting in one of the AE modes, this will often require you to turn the exposure compensation dial in the negative direction until the live view and live histogram display the scene without blown highlights.

- Next, turn the exposure compensation dial in the opposite (positive) direction until the shadows and midtones are displayed as bright as you want them to appear in the final image. Here's the important part: When you turn the exposure compensation dial up again, count the number of clicks it takes to reach the target brightness of your scene. One, two, or three clicks mean you should set the camera from DR100% to DR200% for one stop of additional highlight dynamic range. More than three clicks mean you should use DR400%. More than six clicks mean that highlights may be blown even when you set DR400%, so you might want to avoid overcompensating beyond six clicks. As you know, each click of the exposure compensation dial equals 1/3 EV (or a third of a stop).

The above describes the procedure for any of your camera's auto exposure (AE) modes **P**, **A**, and **S**, including *miso-matic* mode. Don't compensate with more than six 1/3 EV clicks (that's a total of 2 EV), or your resulting JPEG will be overexposed in the very highlights that you were trying to protect. Instead, try to reduce the shadow contrast by setting SHADOW TONE −1 or SHADOW TONE −2. You can also try a film simulation with less contrast, such as Pro Neg. Std or Eterna.

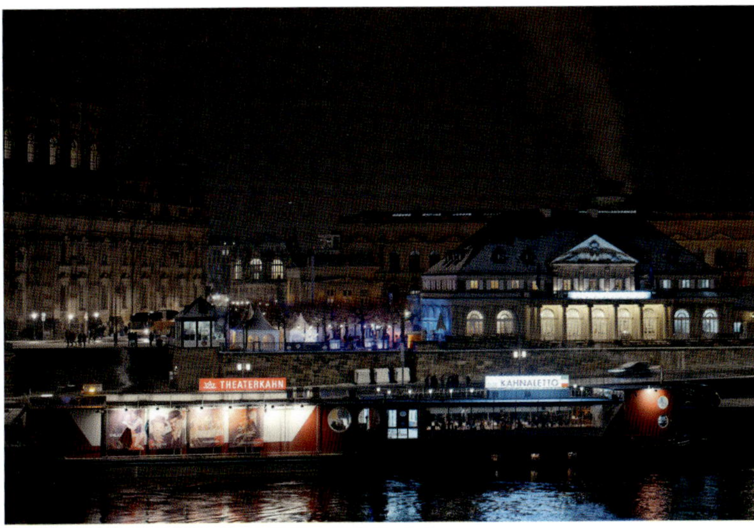

Fig. 77: **Night scenes** with bright lights and high contrast can benefit from a fixed DR400% setting to preserve color and texture in the highlights (Nostalgic Neg., DR400%).

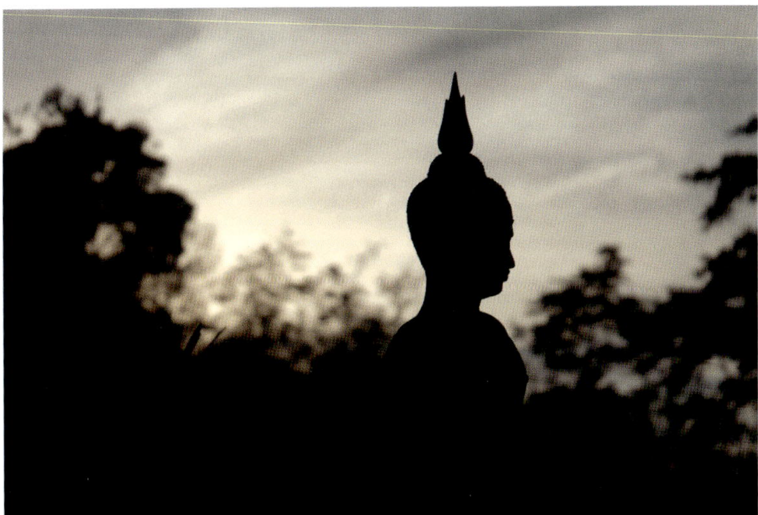

Fig. 78: On the other hand, there are instances where you may want to **maintain maximum contrast** and concentrate on the bright parts of a high-contrast scene. In such cases, a fixed DR100% setting is in order while you are exposing to the highlights (Provia, DR100%).

The two above examples illustrate that DR-Auto is not a "smart" setting; it cannot predict what the photographer has in mind. In both cases, DR-Auto would have picked DR200%—not an optimal setting in either case.

*Important: The X-T5 simulates the effect of manually selected DR200% and DR400% dynamic range settings in the live view and live histogram. However, automatic DR expansion via DR-Auto is **not** simulated in the live view. Instead, the live view and live histogram will display a DR100% simulation, even when DR-Auto eventually decides to take the shot at DR200%.*

In extended ISO L settings, the live view and live histogram wrongly show the dynamic range of a regular ISO setting, giving you the false impression of one stop more highlight dynamic range than what is actually available. Only when you lock the exposure by half-pressing the shutter button will the live view change to display the recorded dynamic range. However, at this stage, there's no live histogram available.

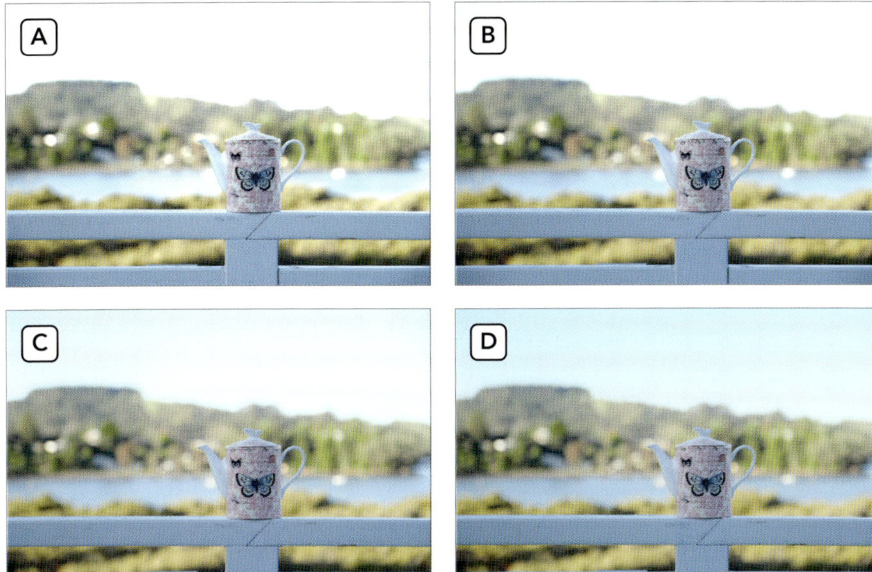

Fig. 79: Comparing dynamic range settings: Image **A** shows a scene taken with extended ISO L (64), f/2.8, and 1/140 sec., which is basically the missing DR50% setting of your camera. Highlight dynamic range is very poor; most bright parts of the image are blown.

Image **B** shows the same subject shot with the camera's base ISO 125 (DR100%), f/2.8, and 1/280 sec. Many parts of the shot are still without texture.

In image **C**, you can see an ISO 250 (DR200%), f/2.8, 1/550 sec. version of the scene, which gives us another stop of highlight dynamic range. In this example, the sky is already looking much better.

Image **D** is an ISO 500 (DR400%), f/2.8, 1/1100 sec. version of our scene, which has two added stops of highlight dynamic range compared to a standard ISO 125 (DR100%) shot. Here, everything is smooth and shiny, with plenty of texture in the sky and bright areas.

These four images were captured with the camera in AE mode **A**.

<table><tr><td>TIP 61</td><td>High-contrast scenes: Using the DR function to the benefit of RAW shooters</td></tr></table>

Fujifilm's DR function works by reducing the indicated ISO level of the RAW file by one (DR200%) or two (DR400%) stops. If you set ISO 500 and DR400% and take a picture, the RAW file of the image will be recorded with ISO 125—two stops darker than it appears in the live view or in the camera's resulting JPEG. Underexposing an image by one or two stops means that one or two stops of additional bright highlights are protected.

In other words, when the DR function is active, the camera's built-in RAW converter (which is also known as the JPEG engine) pushes the shadows and midtones of the underexposed RAW data one (DR200%) or two (DR400%) stops up to ensure that the live view and the resulting JPEG match the indicated ISO setting. It won't push the brightest highlights, though.

For example, if you set ISO 500 and DR400%, the RAW data will be recorded with ISO 125 (to protect two stops of highlights), but the built-in JPEG engine of the camera will make sure the shadows and midtones of the live view and the resulting JPEG image are pushed back up two stops to ISO 500 to compensate for the RAW file's underexposure. However, the brightest highlights of the JPEG will remain at ISO 125.

This is why the minimum ISO settings for DR200% and DR400% in cameras with a base ISO of 125 (like your X-T5) are ISO 250 and ISO 500, respectively. Remember that per definition and convention, ISO settings only apply to the JPEGs generated in the camera, not to the RAW files. It's perfectly normal for the RAW data to be recorded darker or brighter than the indicated ISO level because all ISO settings apply only to JPEGs and the live view, not to RAW data.

Understanding this, it becomes clear that in the X-T5 with base ISO 125, extended ISO L (64) is doing just the opposite of the DR function: it records RAW data one stop brighter at ISO 125, while the JPEG engine pulls down (darkens) the live view and the resulting JPEG one stop to simulate and match the indicated ISO L (64) setting. Overexposing an image one stop brighter in the RAW than it appears in the live view and JPEG also means that one stop of highlight dynamic range is cut off and lost, so selecting ISO L has the same effect as a DR50% setting would have (if that setting existed).

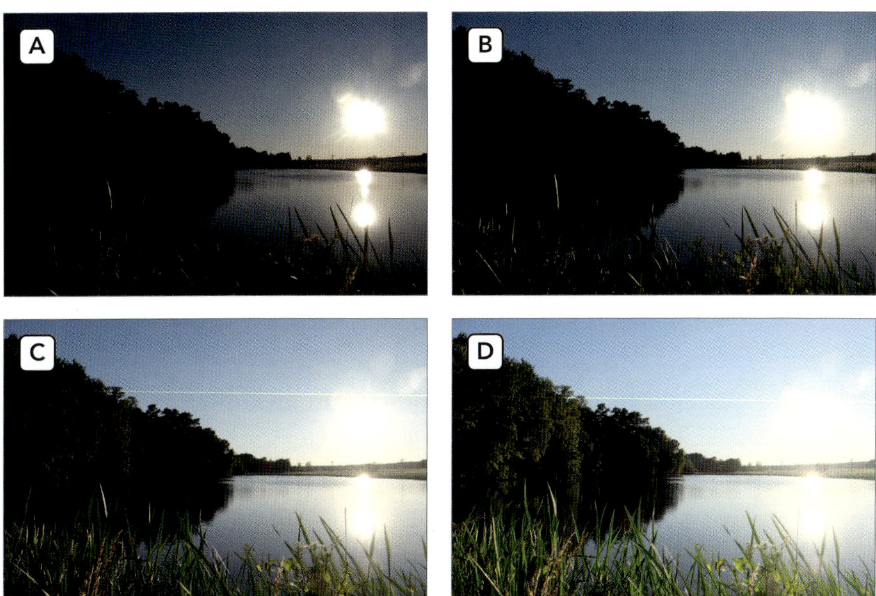

Fig. 80: In this example, I took four images using the same exposure settings: aperture f/11 and shutter speed 1/320 sec. The only differences were four **equivalent ISO and DR settings** that neutralized each other at the RAW level: Image **A** shows the JPEG that resulted from ISO L (64) / DR50%, while image **B** shows ISO 125 / DR100%. The JPEG in image **C** is the ISO 250 / DR200% version, and image **D** was taken with ISO 500 / DR400%.

The four JPEGs are clearly different regarding shadow and midtone brightness, because they must match their respective indicated ISO settings. Obviously, a JPEG taken at ISO 500, f/2.8, 1/500 sec. must look brighter than one taken at ISO 64, f/2.8, 1/500 sec. However, the underlying RAW data is the same in all four instances.

In many practical situations, correctly exposing to the important highlights of a scene results in a live view image that looks very dark in the midtones and shadows, which makes it hard to compose and focus the shot. Using "JPEG settings for RAW shooters" can mitigate this issue, but sometimes it's just not enough. If that's the case, using an equivalent ISO/DR setting can help us out.

For example, the following three exposure settings are perfectly equivalent at the RAW level:

- f/2.8, 1/500 sec., ISO 125 / DR100%
- f/2.8, 1/500 sec., ISO 250 / DR200%
- f/2.8, 1/500 sec., ISO 500 / DR400%

The RAW data for these three shots is the same, only the JPEGs (and hence the live view) look quite different from each other. For example, the live view and JPEG of a f/2.8, 1/500 sec., ISO 500 / DR400% shot looks two stops brighter than the equivalent f/2.8, 1/500 sec., ISO 125 / DR100% version. However, the RAW data of these two shots is the same.

This gives you additional options. For example, you can *manually* expose your scene to its important highlights at ISO 125 / DR100% and then raise ISO one or two stops to 250 or 500, while at the same time changing the DR setting to DR200% or DR400%, respectively. *Increasing* RAW and JPEG ISO two stops from 125 to 500 and *decreasing* RAW ISO two stops by selecting DR400% leaves the RAW data unchanged (+2−2=0). The only thing that has become brighter is the live view and the JPEG from the camera.

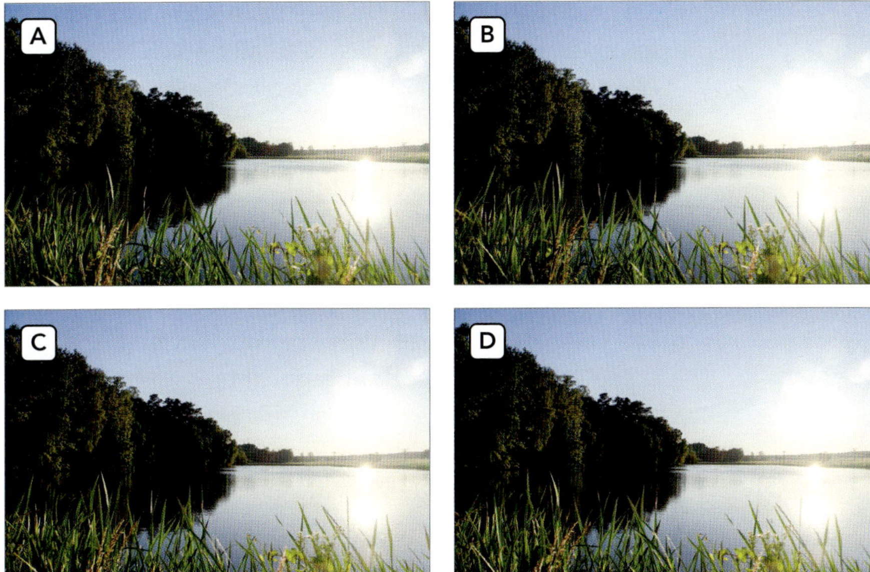

Fig. 81: This example shows the four shots from our previous illustration, all taken with the same exposure settings: aperture f/11 and shutter speed 1/320 sec. This time, however, I processed the RAW files of the four images in Lightroom Classic and applied the same development settings to all of them—with the exception of the exposure slider, which was adjusted to compensate Lightroom's import exposure pull or push that is automatically applied to the RAW data based on the indicated ISO/DR setting.

The Lightroom-processed results from the shots taken with ISO L (64) / DR50% (image **A**, Lightroom exposure slider +3 EV), ISO 125 / DR100% (image **B**, exposure slider +2 EV), ISO 250 / DR200% (image **C**, exposure slider +1 EV) and ISO 500 / DR400% (image **D**, exposure slider 0 EV) look exactly the same. This isn't at all surprising because the RAW data *is* indeed the same.

This discovery can be of tremendous practical benefit if you intend to make the most of your camera's ISO-less sensor and push its dynamic range capabilities to the limits.

The best way to use the DR function for shooting scenes with very high dynamic range is to expose in manual mode **M**. Here's how to proceed:

- Set manual mode **M** and make sure the exposure preview for manual mode is enabled (SET UP > SCREEN SET-UP > PREVIEW EXP./WB IN MANUAL MODE > PREVIEW EXP./WB).

- Deploy "JPEG settings for RAW shooters" by selecting film simulation Eterna, Tone Curve (Highlights) –2, and Tone Curve (Shadows) –2. This step is optional but may be beneficial if the contrast of a scene is very high.

- Set DR100% and manually expose the high-contrast scene to protect important highlights. Use the RGB histogram with the live overexposure warning ("blinkies") and set an exposure that is just rich enough that some of the important highlights in your scene begin to blink. Remember that this is about protecting the *important* highlights. Feel free to overexpose parts of your scene that aren't worth saving, like the sun in a backlit daylight scene.

- Now that your exposure to the scene's critical highlights is manually set and locked, the live view may look too dark to comfortably frame the scene. So, let's add the DR function to the mix. First, increase ISO as needed by either one or two full stops (1 or 2 EV). Then neutralize this ISO change by also increasing DR by the same amount (either DR200% or DR400%). For example, you can raise ISO from 125 to 500 (i.e., a two-stop ISO *increase* applied to the RAW, the live view, and the JPEG) while also raising DR from DR100% to DR400% (i.e., a two-stop ISO *decrease* that is applied only to the RAW file, but not to the live view and the JPEG).

- Having completed the previous step, the RAW remains as it was, but the live view looks either one or two stops brighter than before. That's great for demanding, high-contrast scenes, because not only can we perfectly expose to their important highlights, but we can also still see what's going on in those really dark parts of the scene.

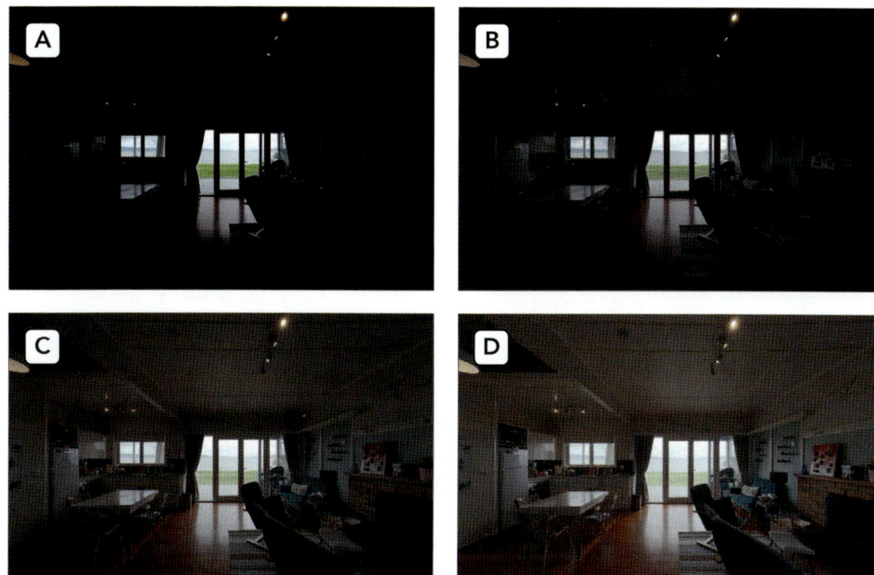

Fig. 82: This high-contrast interior example was shot at f/9 and 1/60 sec. in manual exposure mode. Image **A** shows the scene as it looked with Provia factory settings and base ISO 125. Image **B** shows the same image, but now with "JPEG settings for RAW shooters": film simulation Eterna, Tone Curve (Shadows) −2, and Tone Curve (Highlights) −2. While these are perfect settings for *exposing* a high-contrast scene toward its important highlights, the live view still looks a tad too dark to comfortably *frame* the scene. Luckily, we now know what to do. We can increase ISO / DR in tandem by one stop to ISO 250 / DR200% (image **C**) or two stops to ISO 500 / DR400% (image **D**) to get a brighter live view (and brighter JPEGs) without affecting the perfect RAW exposure that was determined and set using the base ISO / DR100% live view from image **A**.

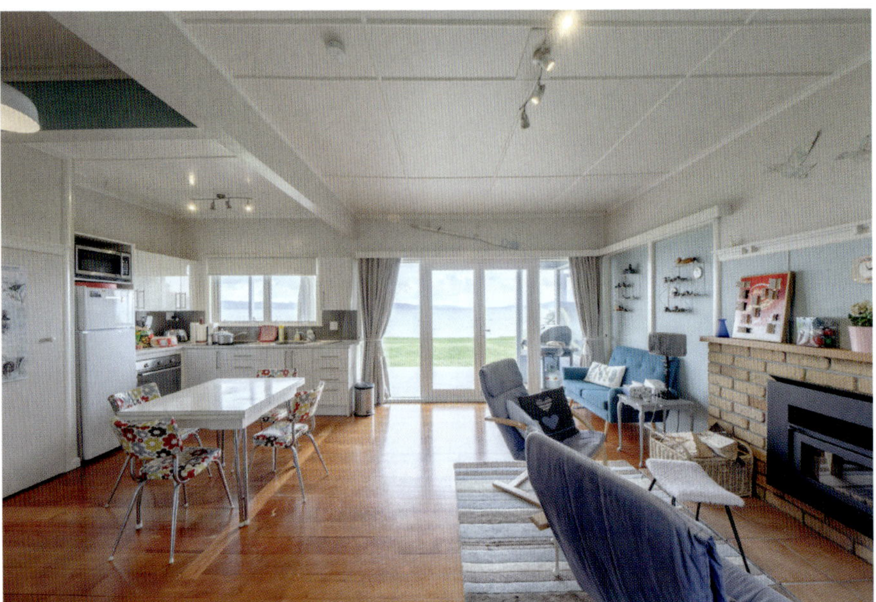

Fig. 83: This example shows the previous image after processing (tone mapping) the RAW file in Adobe Lightroom.

Using manual mode M to expose high-contrast scenes is highly recommended because you can easily split the process into two stages. First, you determine and set the correct exposure to protect important highlights of the scene using DR100% and "JPEG settings for RAW shooters." After the exposure is set, you can concentrate on brightening the live view to a more useable level by increasing ISO one or two stops while also raising DR to either DR200% or DR400%. With the brighter live view, you can easily compose the scene, focus it, and take the shot at the right moment. Not only can you now see what's going on in the shadows and midtones of the scene, the camera's auto white balance will also do a better job when it's not fishing in the dark. This is an accurate, reliable, and straightforward process, and I use it frequently with great success.

As an alternative to raising ISO and DR in tandem (which brightens the live view without affecting the RAW exposure), you can also expose high-contrast scenes in manual mode **M** and then turn off the exposure preview after determining the correct exposure. Here's how it works:

- Set manual mode **M**, DR100%, and turn *on* exposure preview (SET UP > SCREEN SET-UP > PREVIEW EXP./WB IN MANUAL MODE > PREVIEW EXP./WB).

- Like before, expose toward the important highlights of your scene and set a suitable exposure (ISO, aperture, and shutter speed).

- If the live view appears too dark, turn *off* exposure preview in manual mode (SET UP > SCREEN SET-UP > PREVIEW EXP./WB IN MANUAL MODE > OFF) and take your shots. The easiest way to do this is by assigning the manual exposure preview function to an Fn button. Personally, I have assigned the exposure preview toggle to the AE-L button of my X-T5 because I'm mostly shooting in manual mode, where the classic AE-Lock function is not available, anyway.

Turning off exposure preview in manual mode forces the live view to behave like it was in one of the three auto-exposure (AE) modes **P**, **A**, or **S**: the live view image will automatically change its brightness toward a middle-gray exposure (depending on the scene and the selected exposure metering method), but without affecting the actual exposure of the shot.

Using this rather simple procedure may sound quite appealing, but it has one major drawback: the JPEGs of your shots are still recorded rather dark (exposed to the highlights), making it difficult, or impossible, to immediately check critical focus and other details. You'd first have to push each image in the built-in or an external RAW converter. If you take a lot of images using this method, it can become quite a chore to browse through all your dark images and select the keepers.

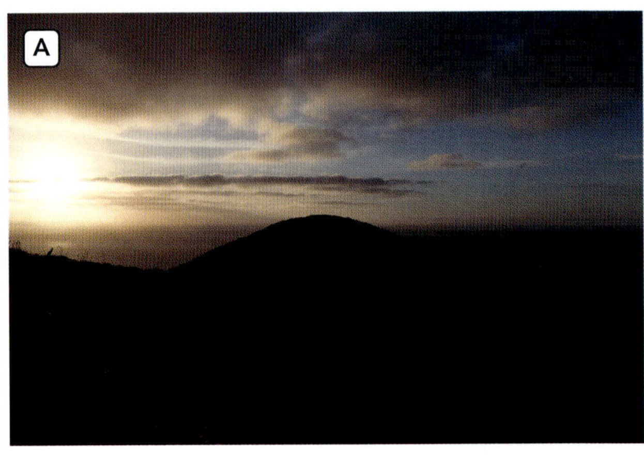

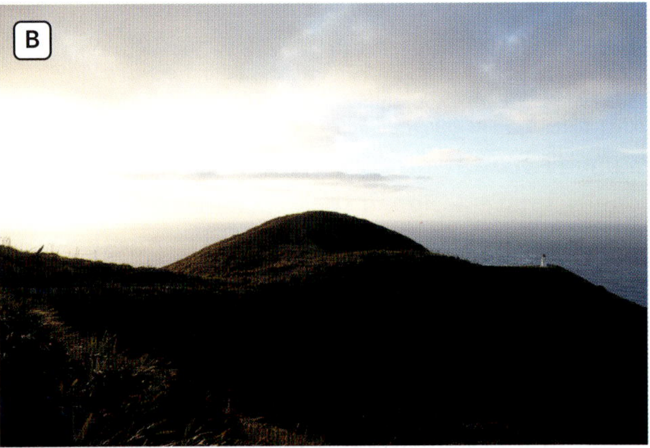

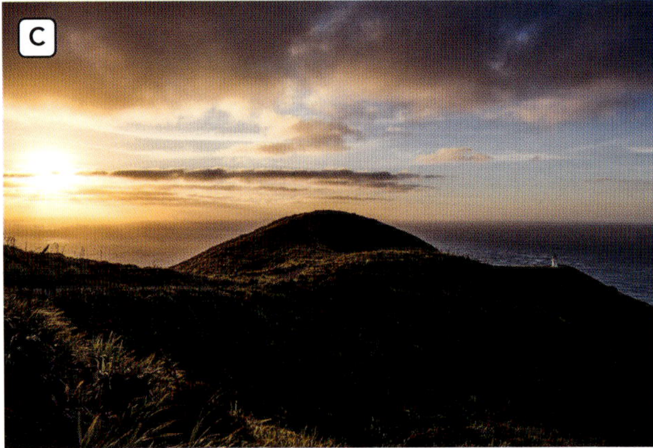

Fig. 84: This example shows a typical sunset shot with very high dynamic range. To protect the bright colored areas around the sun, I selected manual mode and exposed to the critical highlights. Sadly, this also resulted in a dark live view that made it very difficult to frame the scene (**A**). By **disabling the exposure preview for manual exposure mode**, I achieved a much more usable live view image (**B**) that allowed me to compose the scene. Image **C** shows the shot after processing the RAW file in Adobe Lightroom.

DR versus DR-P	TIP 62

In addition to the DR function with its DR-Auto, DR100%, DR200%, and DR400% options, your X-T5 also features a function called DR-P, which stands for Dynamic Range Priority.

If you activate DR-P in the IMAGE QUALITY SETTING menu, it replaces the classic DR function, so you can't use both functions together. It's either the one or the other. Setting DR-P to anything but OFF automatically overrides and cancels your DR settings.

The AUTO, WEAK, and STRONG options of DR-P correspond to the DR-Auto, DR200%, and DR400% settings of the DR function, while OFF relays control back to whatever regular DR settings you have selected. This also means that DR-P WEAK and DR-P STRONG have the same minimum ISO requirements as DR200% and DR400%.

So, what exactly is the difference between DR-P and DR? It's rather mundane: DR-P *combines* regular DR settings with different contrast settings into a package that can't be untied later. For example, DR-P WEAK combines DR200% with TONE CURVE (HIGHLIGHTS) −2 and TONE CURVE (SHADOWS) −2. Correspondingly, DR-P STRONG results in an image that combines DR400%, TONE CURVE (HIGHLIGHTS) −4, and TONE CURVE (SHADOWS) −4. (These two −4 settings aren't available in the menu, but the camera can still access them internally.)

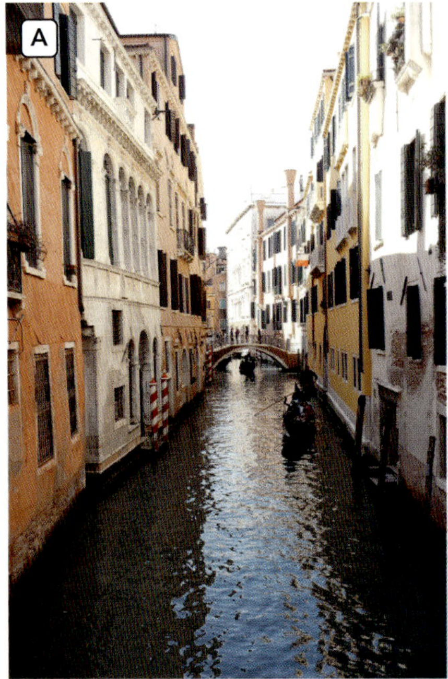

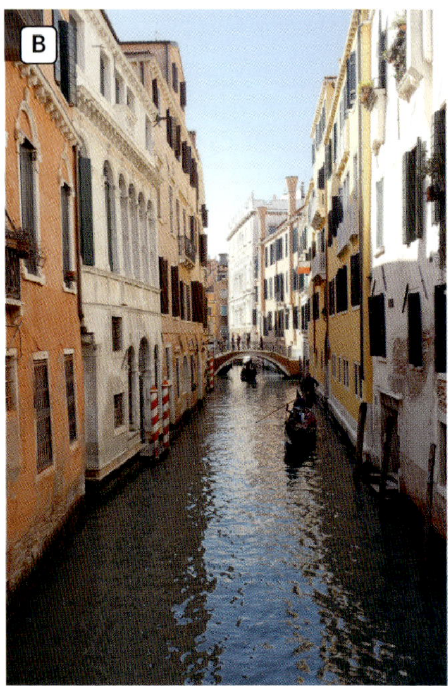

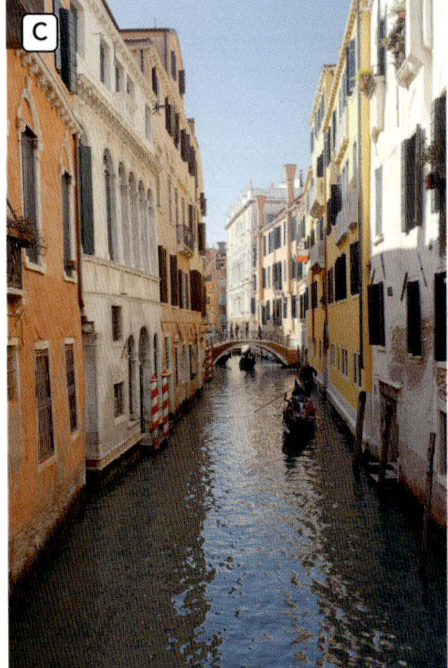

Fig. 85: This **Dynamic Range Priority** comparison shows straight-out-of-camera JPEGs of a high-contrast scene with DR-P OFF / DR100% (**A**), DR-P WEAK (**B**), and DR-P STRONG (**C**) settings. These JPEGs were created in-camera using the same RAW file.

Please note that DR-P AUTO will record a shot with either DR-P WEAK or DR-P STRONG, but never with DR-P OFF. The live view in DR-P AUTO always represents a DR-P WEAK setting, even if DR-P STRONG is eventually used and recorded. Hence, never use DR-P AUTO when you want to use the live view or live histogram to determine the exposure.

Shooting RAW, you can change your mind later and reduce or remove DR-P from a newly generated JPEG in the camera's built-in RAW converter. Select the image in playback mode and press the Q button to access the RAW conversion menu, then scroll to D RANGE PRIORITY and select a new DR-P setting. Selecting OFF automatically enables the DYNAMIC RANGE and TONE CURVE menu items, where you can adjust dynamic range and contrast settings independently from each other.

Using the built-in RAW converter, you can only *reduce* dynamic range of newly created JPEGs, not add to it. For example, if you shot an image with DR-P STRONG, you could later reduce DR-P to WEAK or (with DR-P OFF) select either DR400%, DR200% or DR100%. However, shooting with DR-P WEAK only leaves you with DR-P OFF and DR200% or DR100% as editing choices. DR-P STRONG or DR400% won't be available.

Instead of editing images with the Q button using the camera display or EVF, you can also revisit RAW files stored on your PC and create new JPEGs with different contrast settings using the free FUJIFILM X RAW STUDIO [55] software.

Using DR-P for high-contrast daylight scenes	TIP 63

The new global custom settings of the X-T5 make it difficult to quickly switch between standard settings and "JPEG settings for RAW shooters" because they not only encompass JPEG settings but pretty much all camera settings. This is a problem when you only want to change JPEG settings but not everything else.

With custom settings out of the picture, is there another quick way to handle high-contrast scenes in the live view? Yes, there is! Let's assume the most common case, which is daylight scenes that can be exposed to the critical highlights at the camera's base ISO setting of 125. Here's how you prepare your camera:

- Set your X-T5 to manual mode **M**.

- Set ISO to 500.

- Set DR-P to STRONG.

- Set ISO back to 125. The camera will automatically revert to DR100%.

- Select PROVIA or another film simulation that you like for your scene or topic. There's no need to employ specific "JPEG settings for RAW shooters" such as ETERNA and TONE CURVE (SHADOW TONE / HIGHLIGHT TONE) reduced to −2.

Preparing your camera like this makes exposing and shooting quite easy and straightforward:

- Expose for the critical highlights of your scene by setting your desired aperture and selecting a shutter speed that doesn't clip bright parts that you want to keep. Use the live RGB histogram with blinkies to find this exposure.

- If the WYSIWYG image in your live view looks good, you can now take the shot.

- However, if it looks too dark, change ISO from 125 to 250. Do not change aperture or shutter speed. The camera will automatically switch to DR-P WEAK and display a brighter live view. If that brightness is enough for you to compose and take the shot, do so now.

- However, if the live view still looks too dark, change ISO from 250 to 500. Do not change aperture or shutter speed. The camera will then automatically switch to DR-P STRONG and display an even brighter live view image with little contrast and allow you to compose the contents of even challenging high-contrast scenes. Take the shot at your convenience.

- When you are done shooting that scene or subject, switch ISO back to 125. The camera will automatically revert to DR100% and you are good to go to measure the exposure of your next subject.

This simple method uses ISO-equivalent ISO/DR-P combinations to produce a live view and JPEGs that contain and capture much more dynamic range than "regular" JPEGs. An added benefit of this are RAW files that are much more flexible than regular DR100% RAW files when you want to process them in-camera with the built-in RAW converter. Even though the RAW image data itself doesn't change with ISO-equivalent settings, the RAW *metadata* does. A shot with DR-P STRONG in the metadata gives you more options: For example, you can reprocess it with DR-P WEAK, DR-P OFF / DR400%, DR-P OFF / DR200%, or DR100%. You can also combine these settings with PUSH/PULL exposure changes of up +3 EV and down to −2 EV.

In other words: Shooting with ISO 500 / DR-P STRONG instead of ISO 125 / DR100% (and otherwise identical exposure settings) gives you much more freedom with in-camera RAW conversions. Your built-in JPEG engine becomes more powerful and can handle high-contrast scenes that would otherwise be impossible to grasp with JPEGs created in-camera.

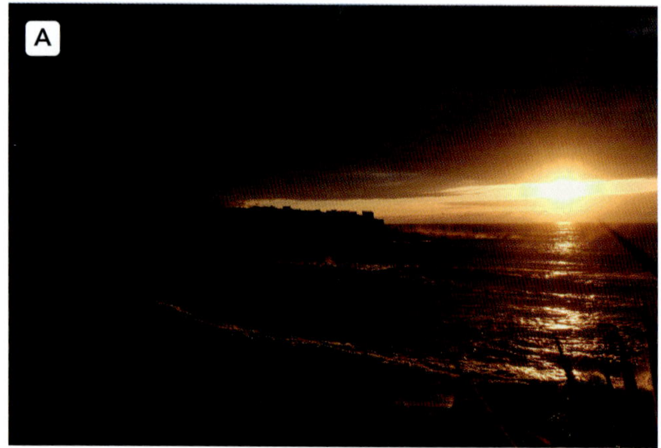

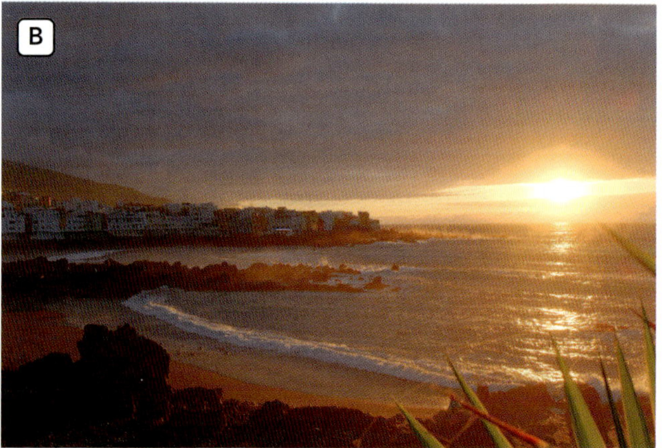

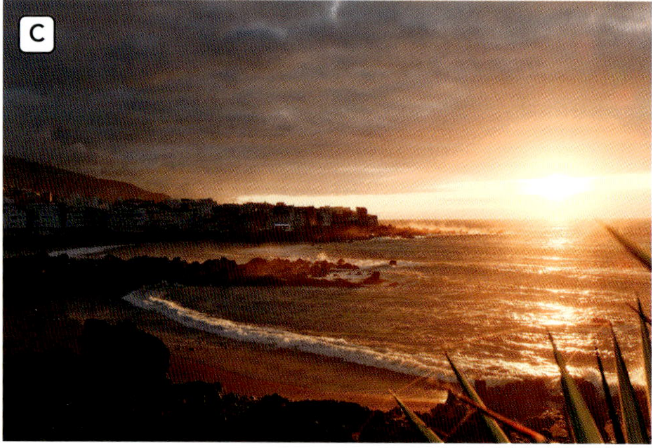

Fig. 86: This demanding sunset scene was shot and processed entirely inside my X-T5, using an XF16–80mmF4 kit zoom at f/9 and 1/200 sec. Image **A** shows how I exposed the scene to preserve the critical highlights with PROVIA default settings at base ISO 125 / DR100%. Image **B** shows how I composed and took the shot with ISO-equivalent settings at ISO 500 / DR-P STRONG (still using PRO-VIA and f/9, 1/200 sec.), and image **C** is a straight-out-of-camera JPEG from reprocessing the image B RAW file in-camera "to taste" with the following changes: CLASSIC Neg., DR400%, AUTO WB AMBIENCE PRIORITY, WB SHIFT R: +2 / B: −2, SHADOW TONE −1.5, COLOR +4, SHARPENING +1 and CLARITY +5.

Dual conversion gain and how to use it	TIP 64

We already know that your X-T5 uses a base ISO of 125. However, there's also what's called "dual conversion gain"—a second (higher) base ISO level. In our case, this additional base ISO level is automatically activated when you set ISO 500 (or higher) at DR100%.

Dual conversion gain (DCG) reconfigures the sensor for low-light use: read noise is further reduced, which means you can extract additional dynamic range in situations with very little light.

Normally, you wouldn't care about dual conversion gain because the camera is performing everything automatically. There is no "on/off" switch or menu: simply set a minimum of ISO 500 / DR100% (or ISO 1000 / DR200%; or ISO 2000 / DR400%) and dual conversion gain will be active.

You can make use of this second DCG ISO level in the same way you use base ISO 125 to extract as much dynamic range from high-contrast scenes as possible. However, in this case, we are talking about situations with very little light; scenes that one would usually expose with very high ISO settings such as 6400, 12800, or even 25600.

Instead of setting these high ISO values, you can just as well set the camera to ISO 500 / DR100% (or to equivalent ISO-level settings of ISO 1000 / DR200% or ISO 2000 / DR400%) and shoot away, while protecting as many highlights as possible. Of course, you can also use DR-P WEAK instead of DR200%, or DR-P STRONG instead of DR400%.

I will give you a practical example. I attended an evening get-together in an ancient wine cellar that was illuminated by only a few candles. I shot several candid portraits of the attendees using manual mode **M** with fixed settings of ISO 500, f/2.8 (wide-open), and 1/20 sec. (my slowest usable shutter speed for handheld shooting of living subjects). To see the image that I was composing, I turned *off* the exposure preview in manual mode.

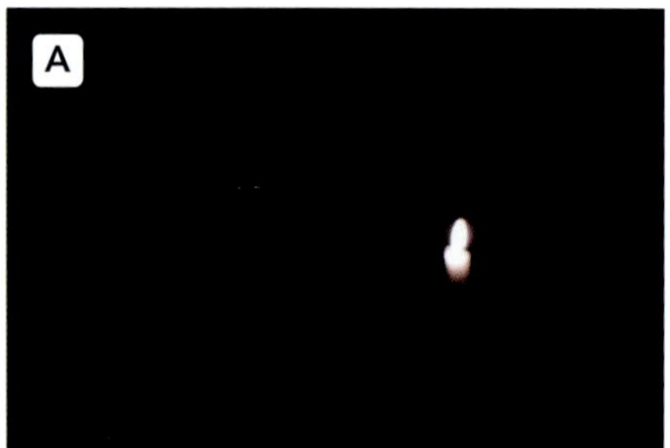
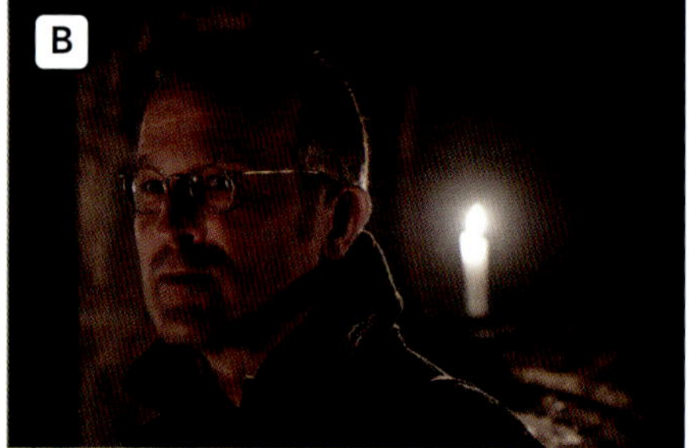

Fig. 87: This **dual conversion gain** example shows a low-light shot as it was taken with a 55mm focal length, f/2.8, 1/20 sec., and ISO 500 / DR100% (the camera's additional "dual gain conversion" base ISO level). The unprocessed result (**A**) looks really dark. The only part that is clearly visible is one of the few candles that were lighting the scene.

Image **B** shows the same shot after processing the RAW file in Lightroom Classic. Pushing the brightness of the face up from ISO 500 resulted in equivalents of at least ISO 12800, while the already-bright parts of the candle remained at ISO 500 to protect as much of its texture and tones as possible. It's the usual tone mapping procedure, and it gives you a glimpse of the dynamic range reserves available in Fuji's X cameras. You just need to be bold enough to unleash them.

Dual conversion gain results in a small noise advantage. It's not much, but it can be essential in situations where you must push shadows up 4 or 5 stops during RAW processing (or when you need to take images at very high ISO levels like 12800 and above).

In low-light situations that require higher ISO levels, you can use ISO-equivalent DR-P settings based on your camera's dual conversion gain level of ISO 500:

- Set your X-T5 to manual mode **M**.

- Set ISO to 500, which is your camera's DCG level.

- Set DR100% and DR-P OFF.

- Select PROVIA or another film simulation that you like for your scene or topic. There's no need to employ specific "JPEG settings for RAW shooters" such as ETERNA and TONE CURVE (SHADOW TONE / HIGHLIGHT TONE) reduced to –2.

After this preparation, you can measure the exposure and start shooting:

- Expose for the critical highlights of your scene by setting your desired aperture and selecting a shutter speed that doesn't clip bright parts that you want to keep. Use the live RGB histogram with blinkies to find this exposure.

- If the WYSIWYG image in your live view looks good, you can now take the shot.

- However, if the live view looks too dark, change ISO from 500 to 2000 and select DR-P STRONG. This will considerably brighten the live view and the associated JPEGs. Do not change aperture or shutter speed. Take the shot at your convenience.

- When you are done shooting that scene or subject, switch ISO back to 500 and select DR-P OFF and DR100%. You are now good to go to measure the exposure of your next subject.

Hint: If your scene is very dark, make sure to select EVF/LCD LOW LIGHT PRIORITY in SET UP > POWER MANAGEMENT > EVF/LCD BOOST SETTING and enable BOOST mode in SET UP > POWER MANAGEMENT > PERFORMANCE.

TIP 65 | **Creating HDR images with the X-T5**

A popular method of capturing high-contrast scenes is HDR photography. HDR [56] means High Dynamic Range: multiple images of a scene are taken at different exposure levels and then they are merged into a single image with extended dynamic range. The merging process can be facilitated with specialized software, such as Photomatix Pro by HDRsoft.

Typically, HDR requires a minimum of two different exposures of a scene, but some photographers don't stop there. They take five, seven, or even nine different exposures, each separated from the other by (usually) one stop or 1 EV (exposure value).

Here's a procedure that you can use to quickly generate nine different exposures of a single scene:

- Put the camera on a tripod or a similar device.

- Connect a remote shutter release or set the self-timer to 2 seconds to avoid camera shake.

- Set the camera to aperture priority **A**, select BKT on the DRIVE dial and make sure that AE BKT is set in SHOOTING SETTING > DRIVE SETTING > BKT SETTING > BKT SELECT.

- Choose a low ISO setting (such as base ISO 125). Don't use extended ISO L, though!

- Deactivate any DR expansion by setting the dynamic range to DR100% and DR-P to OFF.

- Select a suitable aperture for your shot and scene and use manual focus. If you like, you can also use adapted manual focus lenses.

- Set AE BKT (auto exposure bracketing) to nine shots with a variation of ±1 EV (SHOOTING SETTING > DRIVE SETTING > BKT SETTING > AE BKT > FRAMES STEP SETTING).

- Select AVERAGE exposure metering.

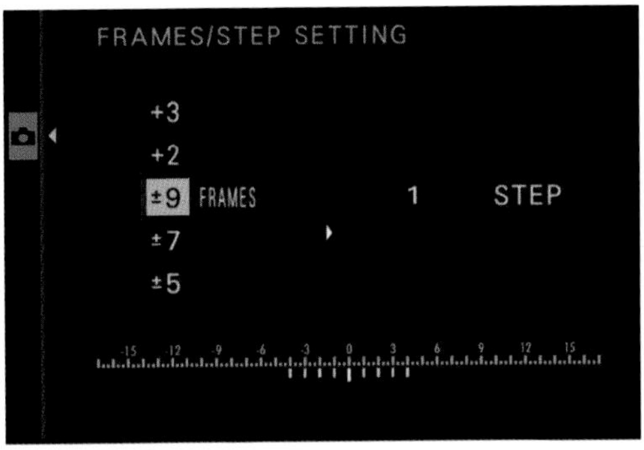

Fig. 88: In this FRAMES/STEP SETTING screen, AE BKT has already been set up to take nine images with a step of 1 EV. The images will cover exposures ranging from −4 EV to +4 EV.

Having prepared the camera for HDR, you can now capture the actual images:

- Set the exposure compensation dial to neutral (0), manually focus the scene and press the shutter release. Make sure to either use a remote shutter release or the self-timer. The camera will now record nine images ranging from −4 EV to +4 EV.

This procedure results in nine different exposures that you can merge using the HDR software of your choice. The resulting image will have an additional dynamic range of ±4 EV.

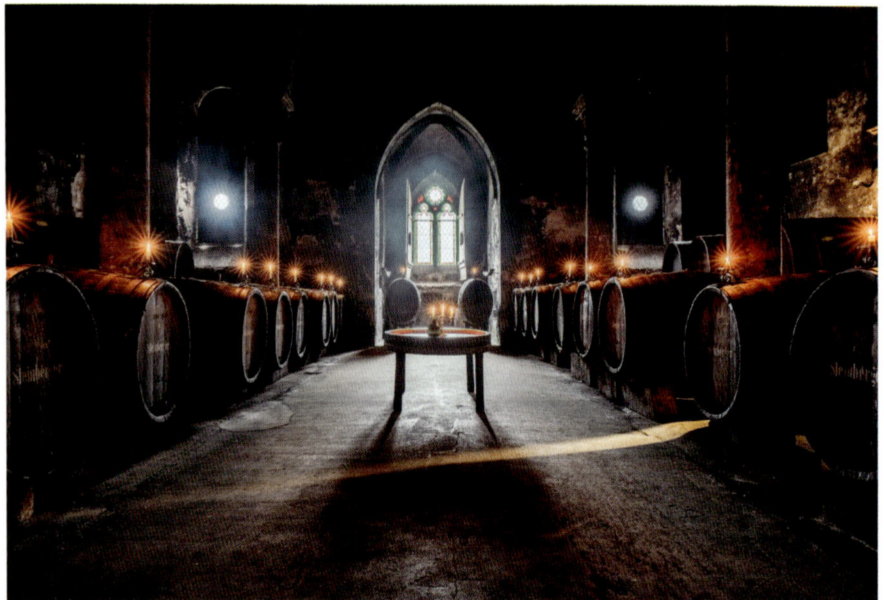

Fig. 89: This rather extreme **HDR image** consists of seven RAW shots, each taken with an exposure difference of 2 EV and merged in Lightroom Classic.

| TIP 66 | HDR: the handheld way |

Thanks to the ISO-less sensor in the X-T5, you can effectively take handheld HDR shots by combining two or three differently exposed RAW files into one HDR-DNG file in Lightroom or Adobe Camera RAW.

Let's start with how to prepare the camera for this endeavor:

- Set the X-T5 to aperture priority **A**, select BKT on the DRIVE dial, and make sure that AE BKT is set in SHOOT-ING SETTING > DRIVE SETTING > BKT SETTING > BKT SELECT.

- Select a low ISO setting, such as ISO 125. Don't set extended ISO L.

- Make sure the dynamic range is set to DR100% and DR-P is OFF.

- Pre-select a suitable aperture.

- Set AE BKT with a variation of +3 FRAMES and a 2 STEP in the SHOOTING SETTING > DRIVE SETTING > BKT SETTING > AE BKT > FRAME/STEP SETTING menu.

- You may also want to use the "JPEG settings for RAW shooters" setup: film simulation ETERNA, TONE CURVE (SHADOWS) −2, and TONE CURVE (HIGHLIGHTS) −2. This may help you frame the scene and determine the best exposure to the highlights.

Now let's take our HDR shots:

- Expose to the highlights! Using the live view and live histogram, frame your scene, and turn the exposure compensation dial until highlights you want to preserve aren't blown.

- Focus and press the shutter button to take the shot, and don't recompose the scene while doing so. Hold the camera very steady while it takes a quick burst of three consecutive AE bracketing shots (each with a different exposure).

- Import the RAW files of the three bracketed shots into Lightroom or Adobe Camera RAW, where you can merge them into a single HDR-DNG file using the HDR function. You can then process the HDR-DNG file in Lightroom like any normal RAW file.

By combining three shots with an exposure difference of 2 EV between each, we dramatically enhance the overall dynamic range of the image. Since the shots were taken in a quick burst with maximum continuous drive speed, there's also little or no motion blur in the resulting DNG composite image. This trick can even work for (slowly) moving subjects, especially since Lightroom's HDR merge tool includes automatic deghosting.

The darkest of the three shots is perfectly exposed to the highlights, while the other two exposures bring 2 EV and 4 EV less noise to the table. Since our ISO-less sensor provides very little sensor read noise, we can easily push the brightest of the three RAWs up another 3 EV without sacrificing too much image quality. This adds up to a whopping 7 EV of *additional* dynamic range, which should be enough to overcome almost every dynamic range challenge you may encounter in your photographic life. Even better, you can use this process for handheld shots—just make sure the shutter speed of the brightest shot is still fast enough to prevent blur caused by camera shake.

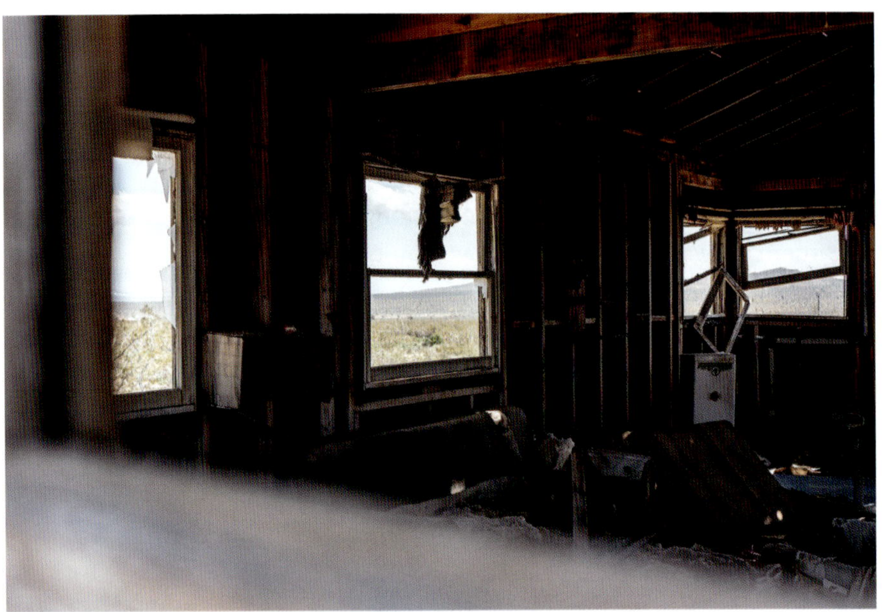

Fig. 90: This **handheld HDR** consists of the original "exposed-to-the-highlights" image, plus two additional shots that were exposed 2 EV and 4 EV brighter. Lightroom was used to merge the RAW files into a single HDR-DNG file. The result looks clean and noiseless in the shadows, with plenty of fine texture and no tonal gaps.

| Using the built-in HDR function | TIP 67 |

The built-in HDR function of the X-T5 hides in the DRIVE dial. To activate it, set the DRIVE dial to HDR and select one of the five available HDR options in SHOOTING SETTING > DRIVE SETTING > HDR MODE: AUTO, 200%, 400%, 800% or 800%+.

Fujifilm's HDR feature follows a concept that is very similar to its long-established DR function: It adds highlight dynamic range by exposing shots darker than indicated by the EXIF data, live view, and camera settings. The main difference between HDR and DR is that DR works with a single shot, whereas HDR works with three frames: one "master frame" that is exposed with the selected and indicated settings, and two additional frames that are exposed darker than the master frame.

In HDR mode, the camera merges the three differently exposed frames to produce a composite JPEG, HEIF, or TIFF file with enhanced highlight dynamic range. It also saves a container-style RAW file that includes the RAW data of the three differently exposed shots. As a result, HDR RAW files are roughly three times the size of a regular single-shot RAW file.

- HDR AUTO automatically selects either 200%, 400%, or 800% based on the contrast range of the scene in the live view. I don't recommend using this setting.

- HDR 200% expands the highlight dynamic range of the scene by one stop. The JPEG result will look very similar to using DR200% with the same (or equivalent) exposure settings (aperture, shutter speed, ISO).

- HDR 400% expands the highlight dynamic range of the scene by two stops. The JPEG result will look very similar to using DR400% with the same (or equivalent) exposure settings (aperture, shutter speed, ISO).

- HDR 800% expands the highlight dynamic range of the scene by three stops. There is no equivalent DR setting in the X-T5. However, if you still use an older X-series compact camera with a 1-inch EXR sensor (like the X10, XF1, or X-S1), you can achieve similar results by setting this camera to DR800%.

- HDR 800%+ works like HDR800 but adds additional shadow dynamic range (and a small amount of additional highlight dynamic range) to the JPEG by flattening the tone-curve during internal RAW processing. It also appears to internally change the CLARITY setting.

My preferred HDR capture setting is HDR 800%+, usually in concert with a low-contrast film simulation like ETERNA or PRO NEG. STD. I recommend HDR 800%+ because it encompasses HDR 800%, HDR 400%, and HDR 200%. This means that you can convert an HDR 800%+ shot to HDR 800%, HDR 400%, or HDR 200% anytime later using your camera's internal RAW converter.

Please note that this is a one-way street: It's *not* possible to change a shot taken with HDR 200% to HDR 400%, or to reprocess an HDR 800% image as HDR 800%+ after the fact. However, you can always reprocess an HDR 800%+ image as HDR 800%, HDR 400%, or HDR 200%, including changing the film simulation, SHADOW/HIGHLIGHT contrast, and CLARITY settings in the process. The sky's the limit.

Here's how you prepare your X-T5 for HDR shooting:

- Set the camera to manual exposure mode **M** and make sure that RAWs *and* JPEGs are recorded simultaneously (IMAGE QUALITY SETTING > IMAGE QUALITY > FINE+RAW).

- Please check that the exposure preview in manual exposure mode is enabled (SET UP > SCREEN SET-UP > PRE-VIEW EXP./WB IN MANUAL MODE > PREVIEW EXP./WB).

- Make sure that the RGB histogram with "blinkies" (visual overexposure warning) can be activated by pressing one of your camera's Fn buttons. On my X-T5, I have assigned this function to the Fn1 button. To replicate this assignment, press and hold the DISP/BACK button until the FUNCTION (Fn) SETTING page appears, then select Fn1 > HISTOGRAM in the menu.

- It's vital that the Natural Live View is *disabled* (SET UP > SCREEN SET-UP > NATURAL LIVE VIEW > OFF).

- To make things easier, set the film simulation to ETERNA (IMAGE QUALITY SETTING > FILM SIMULATION > ETERNA). You can also set HIGHLIGHTS and SHADOWS to −2 in the TONE CURVE menu (IMAGE QUALITY SETTING > TONE CURVE).

- To measure the exposure of your high-contrast scene, select a *regular* shooting mode, e.g., DRIVE dial > STILL IMAGE (S) and DR100% (IMAGE QUALITY SETTING > DYNAMIC RANGE > DR100%). Do ***not*** yet set the camera to HDR mode!

Since this is also my recommended "RAW shooter" setup for regular, non-HDR photography, nothing is really new so far. To measure and set the exposure of a scene for HDR-mode photography, you can follow these steps:

- Set a manual exposure that preserves the critical highlights of the scene. If possible, use the camera's ISO 125 base setting. If you need a higher ISO setting, I recommend the X-T5's dual conversion gain setting of ISO 500. Press Fn1 to activate the RGB histogram and the "blinkies", then set the brightest possible manual exposure (aperture and shutter speed) that doesn't blow important highlights of the scene. In other words: Make sure that critical highlights of your scene don't blink in the live view. To be accurate and useful, this determination requires a DR100%

setting and a disabled Natural Live View. Also make sure that you are in a regular non-HDR shooting mode.

- After setting the "perfect" exposure for the critical highlights, decrease the shutter speed by *three* full stops to compensate the camera's shutter speed increase in HDR 800%+ mode. For example, when your exposure for the highlights was 1/250 sec. at f/8 and ISO 125, change it now to 1/30 sec., f/8, and ISO 125.

- Select DRIVE dial > HDR to engage HDR 800%+ mode. You can change the HDR mode in SHOOTING SETTING > DRIVE SETTING > HDR MODE, so reaffirm that 800%+ is selected there.

- Press the shutter button to take the shots. Hold the camera very still or use a tripod. In our example, the camera will take three frames with different exposures ranging between 1/30 sec. and 1/250 sec. The three exposures will be saved in a RAF container file, and the camera will also create a composite HDR JPEG file with enhanced dynamic range.

HDR JPEGs exhibit a small crop because the camera requires extra space to realign the three individual frames, hinting that Fuji's HDR function is meant to be suitable for hand-held shooting. However, whenever possible, you should use HDR in tandem with a tripod.

Please remember that HDR 800% and HDR 800%+ result in a minimum shutter speed that is three stops slower than your initial exposure for the critical highlights of your scene, so camera shake and/or motion blur can become an issue.

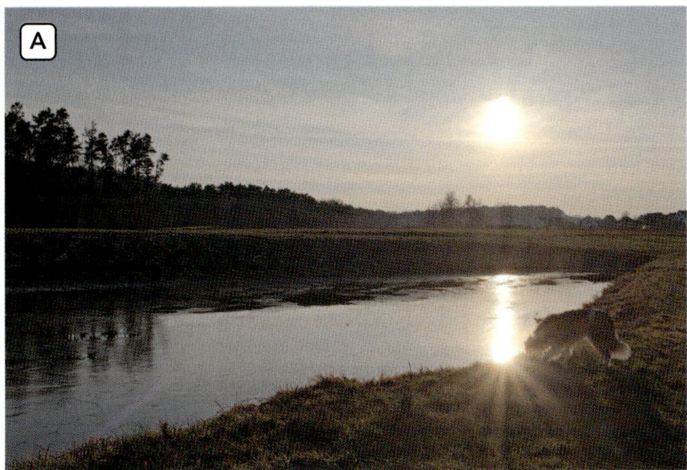

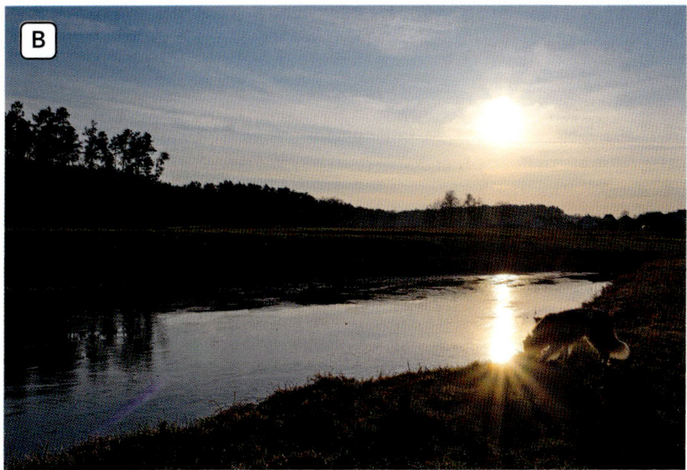

Fig. 91: Fuji's **HDR mode** takes three shots at different exposure levels: one shot at the set exposure, and two darker shots to protect highlights. In HDR 800% and HDR 800%+ mode, the darkest frame is recorded three stops darker than the set exposure level. To compensate, I manually decreased the shutter speed three stops. Image **A** shows the straight-out-of-camera HDR 800%+ JPEG in concert with ETERNA. Using the built-in RAW converter, you can also save HDR composites as "16-bit" TIFF files and further process them with any software. In this case, I used Adobe Lightroom to turn the straight-out-of-camera HDR 800%+ ETERNA TIFF into a punchier shot (image **B**).

Compared to a single exposure JPEG with PROVIA factory settings, composite HDR 800%+ JPEGs with ETERNA contain between four and five stops of additional dynamic range. Three stops are owed to the additional exposures, the remainder is due to ETERNA's flat contrast profile and the particularly flat tone curve of HDR 800%+.

In a way, an HDR 800%+ ETERNA composite looks like ungraded F-Log video recordings. Like F-Log, HDR 800%+ ETERNA provides a flat profile with maximum tonality, which makes it very suitable for further post-processing. In this context, our best option is to reprocess the HDR 800%+ RAF using the camera's built-in RAW converter (PLAYBACK MENU > RAW CONVERSION) and save it in the 16-bit TIFF format. To retain as much fine detail as possible, you can also set NOISE REDUCTION to −4 in the RAW conversion menu.

A flat "16-bit" TIFF from the X-T5 only contains 10 actual bits of tonality per color channel. This translates to 1024 brightness levels for red, green, and blue. Practically, this is perfectly sufficient because of the "flatness" of the file. You can further process (or "color grade") flat HDR 800%+ TIFFs in pretty much any image processing software.

As mentioned before, you can reprocess the original HDR 800%+ RAF in your camera with different parameters to alter the result. For example, you can increase the contrast by changing the film simulation from ETERNA to PROVIA or CLASSIC CHROME, or by downgrading HDR 800%+ to HDR 800% and at the same adjusting the settings for CLARITY and TONE CURVE (HIGHLIGHTS / SHADOWS) to your taste. To make this procedure more comfortable, I recommend using Fuji's free X RAW STUDIO [57] software to remotely control the X-T5's built-in RAW converter. That way, you can safely store your HDR RAW files on your PC or Mac.

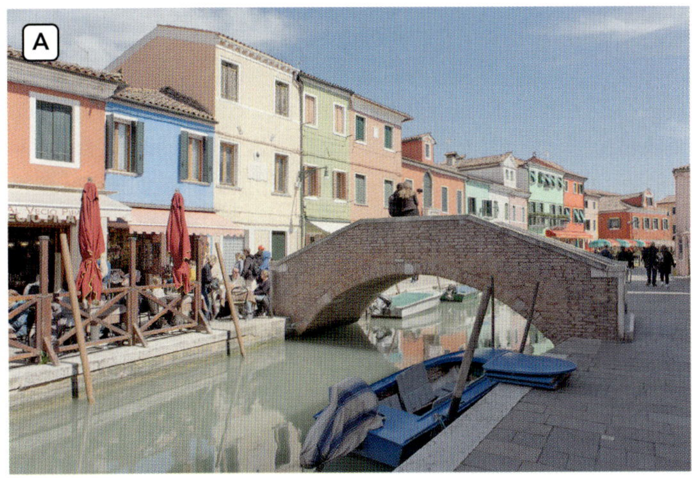

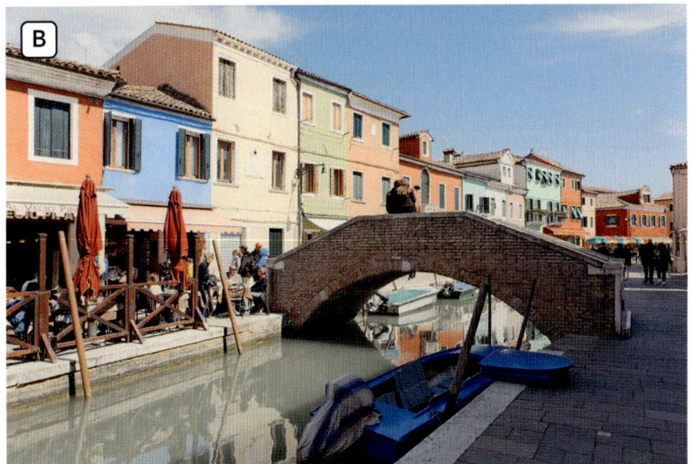

Fig. 92: Here's another X-T5 HDR example: Image **A** shows the HDR 800%+ ETERNA straight-out-of-camera image—it resembles the look of an ungraded F-Log video recording. Image **B** shows the straight-out-of-camera JPEG after reprocessing the HDR 800+ RAW in-camera with X RAW STUDIO. I reprocessed the file with these settings: HDR 800, PULL −1 EV, NOSTALGIC Neg., WB SHIFT R:0 / B:+1, HIGHLIGHT TONE −2, SHADOW TONE −2, COLOR +1, SHARPENING +2, HIGH ISO NOISE REDUCTION −4, CLARITY +4.

TIP 68 In-camera HDR vs. Adobe HDR-DNG

The built-in HDR function is an addition and alternative to more conventional HDR methods. The most effective and conventional method is recording different RAW files through exposure bracketing and merging them into an HDR-DNG file. The industry standard here is Adobe Lightroom, with HDR RAW file merging capabilities that are superior to those of Capture One Pro.

So, how does Lightroom's HDR-DNG feature compare with the X-T5's internal HDR function?

- Fujifilm's internal HDR-RAF files can only be processed in-camera to produce HDR output in formats like JPEG or TIFF. External converters like Lightroom and Capture One Pro can open HDR-RAFs, but they can edit only one of the three exposures that they contain. This makes HDR-RAFs

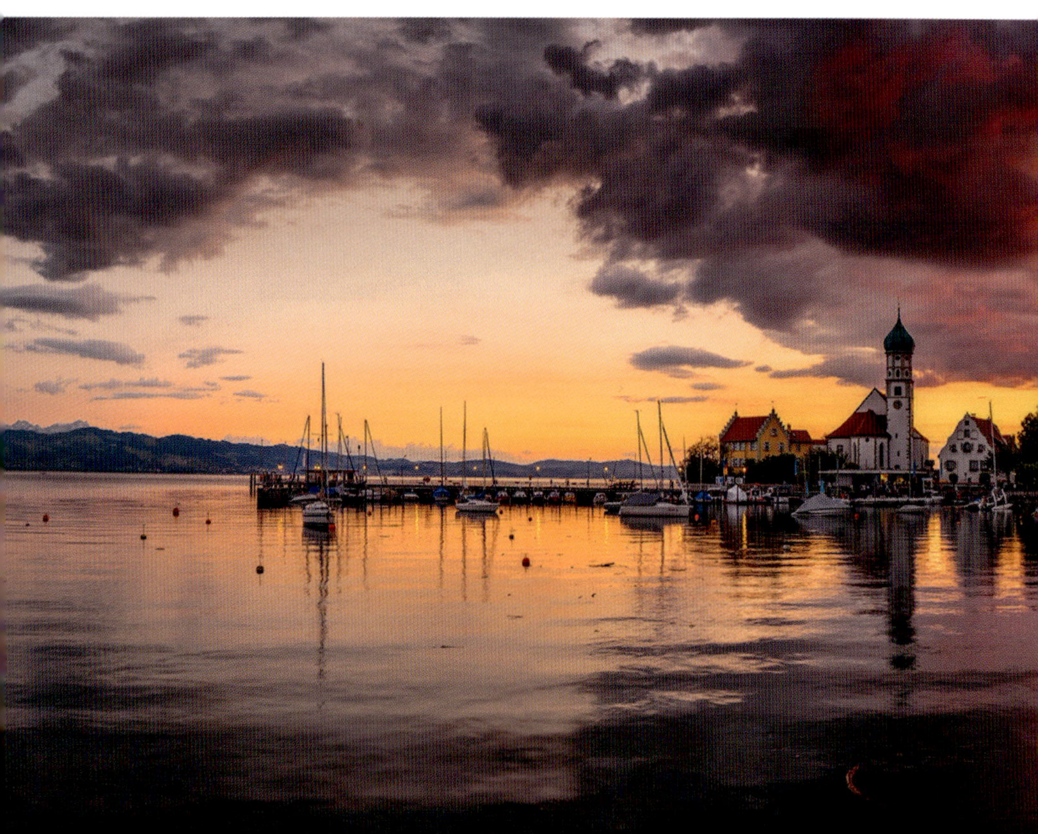

basically useless outside of the camera. On the other hand, HDR-DNGs created in Lightroom can be processed in Lightroom like regular RAF files, including access to all Fujifilm film simulations, white balance, lens corrections, sharpening, and noise reduction tools.

■ The camera's built-in HDR function is limited to a maximum of three stops of additional dynamic range (HDR 800%). This range can be further extended by choosing a flat film simulation (ETERNA) and selecting HDR 800%+ to add flat contrast curve settings to the merged result. On the other hand, Lightroom can process and merge any number of differently exposed RAF files that can deliver much more than just 3 EV of extra dynamic range. If you need it, you can add 5, 7, or even 10 stops of additional DR. In that regards, Lightroom's HDR function is also much more flexible than the equivalent function in Capture One Pro.

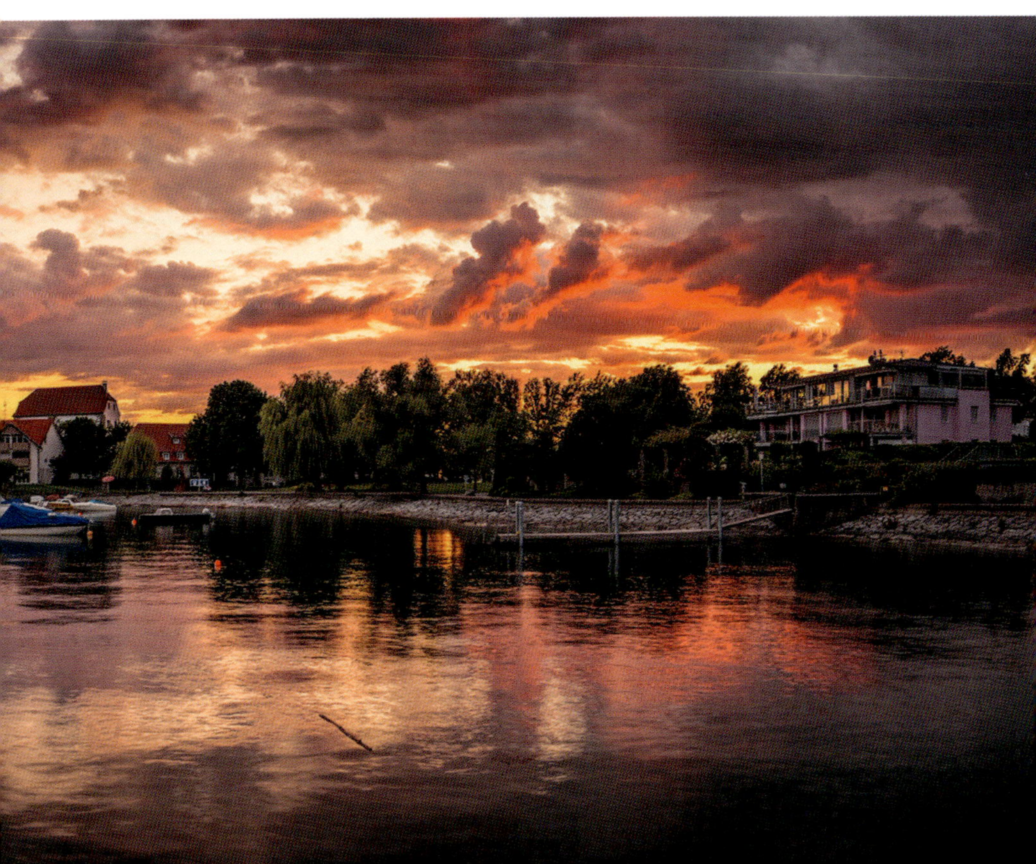

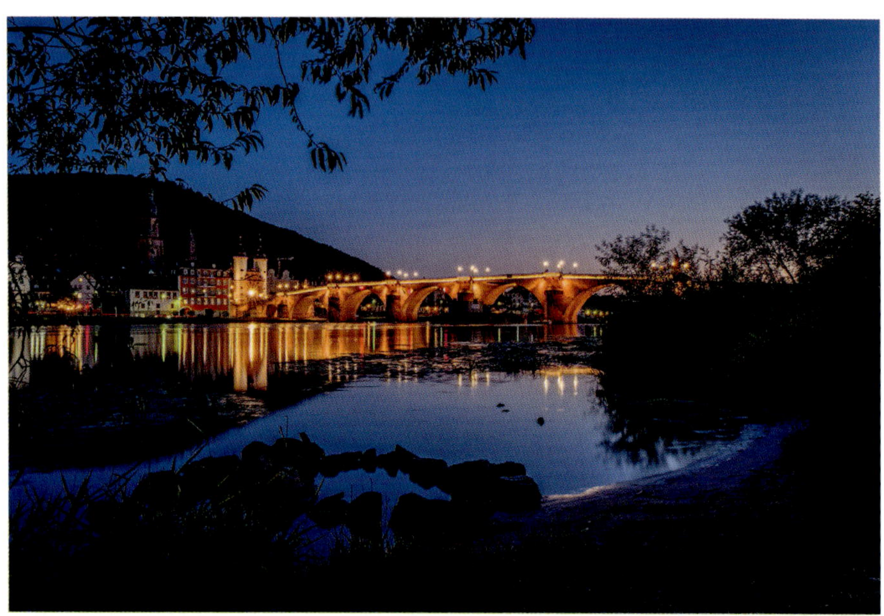

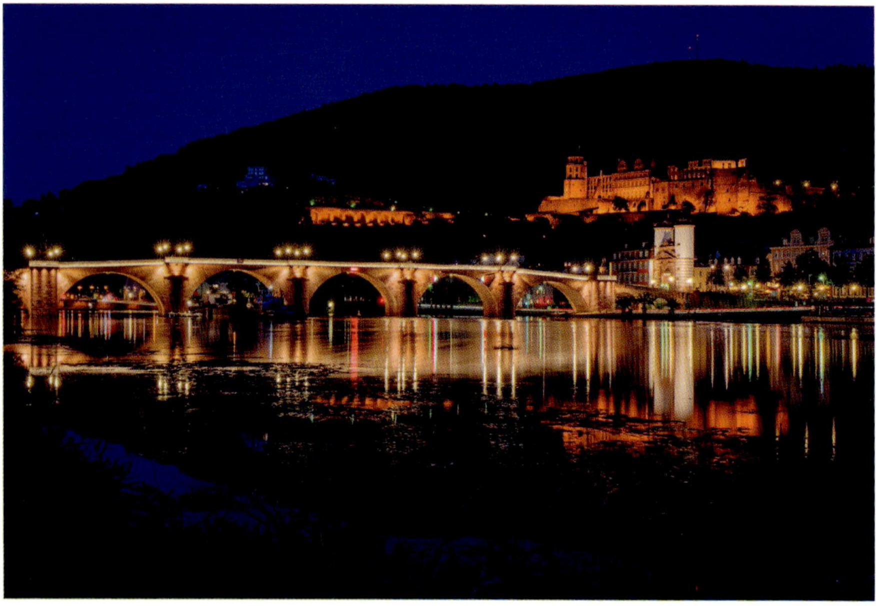

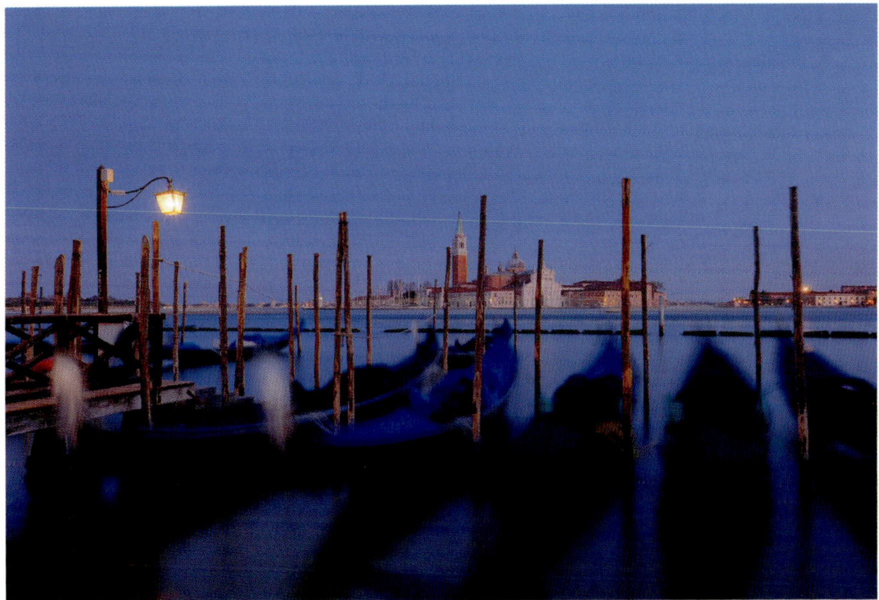

Fig. 93: These five examples illustrate how Adobe Lightroom can be used to create **HDR and HDR-Panorama images** by merging differently exposed RAW files. In Lightroom, HDR-DNGs, Panorama-DNGs, and HDR-Pano-DNGs can be edited like regular RAF files.

- Since HDR-RAFs coming from the X-T5's internal HDR function cannot be externally processed (so far), the best way to use this data outside of the camera is by exporting an HDR 800%+ TIFF image in 16-bit quality with the camera's built-in RAW converter. You can subsequently edit the flat TIFF in Lightroom, Capture One, or any other program of your liking. However, TIFF images already come with a film simulation, white balance, sharpening, and noise reduction baked in, so your options are limited compared to HDR-DNG files out of Lightroom. HDR-DNGs are more versatile and behave like regular RAF files.

Personally, I rarely use the built-in HDR function due to its various limitations. Instead, I take a bunch of different exposures of a scene and merge the RAW files in Lightroom, thus creating an HDR-DNG or even an HDR-Panorama-DNG file.

TIP 69	Electronic shutter (ES) and electronic first curtain shutter (EFCS)

The electronic shutter (ES) offers three advantages: it is completely silent, it eliminates vibrations from shutter shock, and it allows shutter speeds as fast as 1/180,000 sec. That's great in situations where you want to be particularly stealthy, or when you want to use fast lenses (like the XF56mmF1.2 R WR) with a wide-open aperture in bright light and spare yourself the hassle of attaching an ND filter.

You can set which shutter type the camera is supposed to use in SHOOTING SETTING > SHUTTER TYPE. There are six available options:

- **MS**: The camera is using only the mechanical shutter. This is the default setting.

- **ES**: This setting switches the camera to the electronic shutter with shutter speeds up to 1/180,000 sec. Extended ISO settings aren't available in ES mode, and you cannot fire a flash when the ES is in use.

- **EF**: This switches the X-T5 to electronic front curtain shutter (EFCS). The EFCS combines some advantages of the ES with some benefits of the MS: it reduces vibration and eliminates shutter shock by replacing the mechanical first shutter curtain with an electronic version. However, the second shutter curtain remains mechanical, thus avoiding issues caused by electronic rolling shutter. The drawback: In concert with fast shutter speeds, it can impact the look of out-of-focus areas (bokeh) in a negative way.

- **M+E**: In this mode, the camera combines the mechanical (MS) and the electronic shutter (ES). It will automatically switch to ES for shutter speeds faster than the X-T5's maximum mechanical shutter speed of 1/8000 sec. Flash photography is possible, but only within the envelope of the mechanical shutter.

- **EF+M**: This mode combines the electronic first curtain shutter (EFCS) with the mechanical shutter (MS). The X-T5 will generally use the EFCS, but for shutter speeds faster than 1/2000 sec., it will switch to the MS. This helps avoiding bokeh quality issues that occur with the EFCS at very fast shutter speeds.

- **EF+M+E**: This setting combines the electronic first curtain shutter (EFCS) with the mechanical shutter (MS) and the electronic shutter (ES). The X-T5 will generally use the EFCS, but for shutter speeds faster than 1/2000 sec., it will switch to the MS. Furthermore, it will automatically switch to ES for shutter speeds faster than the maximum mechanical shutter speed of 1/8000 sec. Flash photography is possible, but only within the envelope of the mechanical shutter.

To manually access shutter speeds beyond the camera's mechanical limit, you can set the shutter-speed dial to **T** and then browse through all available shutter speeds with the command dial in 1/3 EV steps.

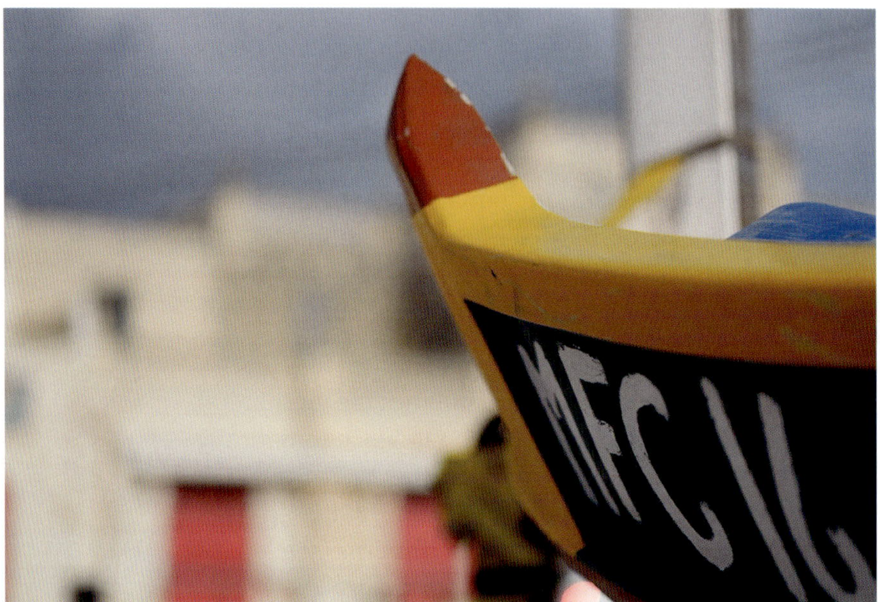

Fig. 94: The **electronic shutter** is a practical option for shots taken with fast lenses in bright light when the maximum mechanical shutter speed simply isn't fast enough to avoid overexposure.

Please note that even at 1/180,000 sec., the electronic shutter needs some time (approx. 1/30 sec. or even longer) to capture all image contents. This effect, known as *rolling shutter* [58], can lead to weird distortions when you are taking pictures of fast-moving subjects, including panning the camera. In addition, image quality will deteriorate when the ES is used in concert with pulsing or flickering artificial light sources. The long readout time and the rolling shutter are also responsible for the restrictions regarding flash photography.

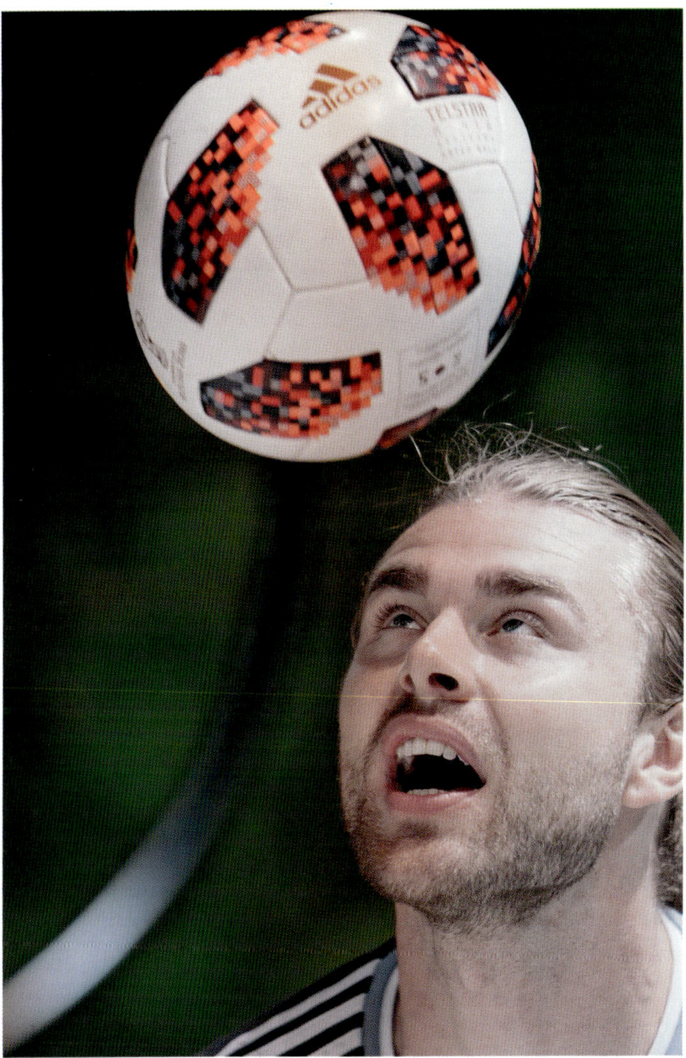

Fig. 95: The **distortion effect** of electronic rolling shutters becomes quite visible in scenes with fast-moving subjects like this football.

The **electronic first curtain shutter (EFCS)** combines some advantages of the ES with some benefits of the MS: it reduces vibration and eliminates shutter shock by replacing the mechanical first shutter curtain with an electronic version. However, the second shutter curtain remains mechanical, thus avoiding issues caused by electronic rolling shutter. The EFCS can also reduce the blackout period in the EVF and emits a subtler mechanical shutter noise.

With very fast shutter speeds, using the EFCS can potentially be detrimental to image quality (especially the bokeh). That's why there's also the EF+M setting that automatically switches back to the MS when the shutter speed exceeds 1/2000 sec. Personally, I now use EF+M+E as my default setting.

Please note that in the X-T5, shutter type must be set to ES (not M+E or EF+M+E) to be able to access the camera's blackout-free high-speed burst modes of 15 fps (without image crop) and 10/13/20 fps (with an image crop of 1.29x). Despite the high nominal speed of these burst modes, rolling shutter distortion and image striping due to pulsing artificial light may be an issue, so please be careful with the ES setting when you are shooting fast action, panning the camera, or shooting under artificial light.

TIP 70	Using flicker reduction features

Is it safe to use the mechanical shutter or electronic first curtain shutter in situations with pulsing artificial light? The answer is yes *and* no. Because pulsing light sources have the nasty habit of continuously going on and off, the scene (your subject) is illuminated with varying amounts of light that fluctuate 100 or 120 times per second along with the phase frequency of the electric AC grid. Even in manual exposure mode **M**, shooting the same scene multiple times with the same exposure settings can result in inconsistently exposed images, depending on your shutter speed and how lucky you are to randomly catch a brighter or a darker portion of the pulsating light.

While this flicker phenomenon is invisible to the human eye, your camera will be affected by it as soon as you select faster shutter speeds. In such cases, the camera can record only a random portion of the light's pulsating on/off cycle.

This is where **flicker reduction** comes into play. You can find it under SHOOTING SETTING > FLICKER REDUCTION.

When you take a shot, flicker reduction forces your camera's exposure to coincide with cyclic peaks of the AC current phase. In other words, shots are delayed until the pulsating light happens to illuminate the scene with maximum brightness. With flicker reduction, your series of exposures will look bright and uniform.

In a world of pulsing energy-saving light sources, flicker reduction is an essential feature. However, make sure to use it only in situations that require its magic. In natural daylight (or artificial light that doesn't pulse), flicker reduction is not only useless; it will also slow down your camera.

The X-T5 offers two options for flicker reduction: FIRST FRAME and ALL FRAMES. ALL FRAMES corresponds to the regular FLICKER REDUCTION ON setting in older X camera models, meaning the camera is synchronized with the main frequency before every single shot it takes, even during high-speed bursts that will inevitably be slowed down because of this. FIRST FRAME only performs this analysis before the first shot of a burst. It's my standard setting, I regard it as a good compromise.

Flicker reduction is not available in concert with the electronic shutter (ES). You can only use it with the mechanical shutter (MS) or the electronic first curtain shutter (EF), including EF+M. In mixed modes that encompass the ES (such as EF+M+E), flicker reduction is automatically disabled if the shutter speed exceeds 1/8000 sec.

The X-T5 incorporates an additional flicker reduction setting that can help you synchronize your shutter speed with pulsating light from LEDs and other sources: SHOOTING MENU > FLICKERLESS S.S. SETTING. If you turn this option ON, your manual shutter speed settings change in a few ways: Your

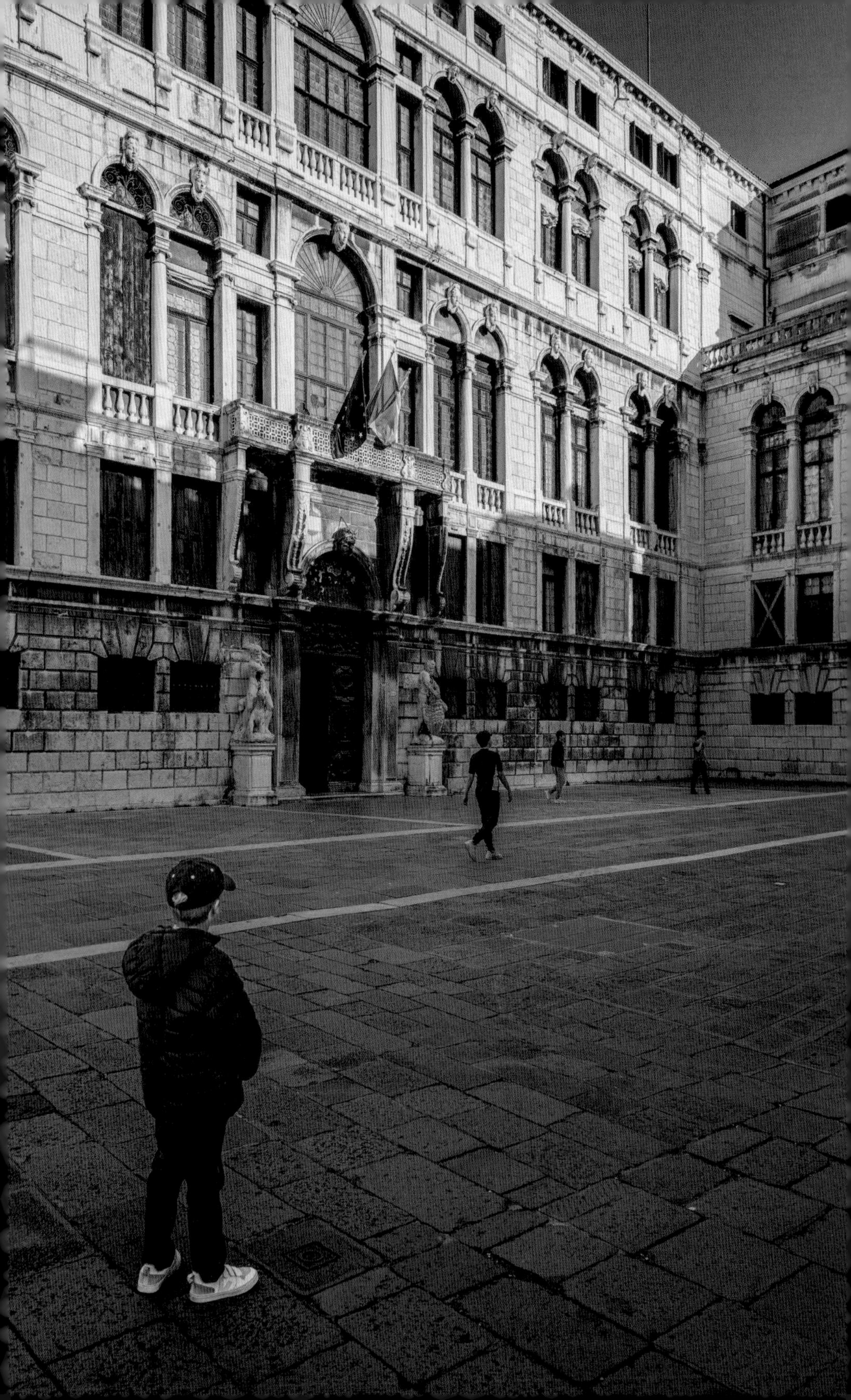

minimum shutter speed (in STILL photography mode) is now 1/50 sec., and you can fine-tune the shutter speed in fractional increments to harmonize it with flickering light sources. This option only works in exposure modes M and S. It is also available in concert with the electronic shutter.

Using Multiple Exposure mode	TIP 71

Multiple Exposure overlays up to 9 individual shots and creates a composite JPEG or HEIF file. It also saves single RAW files of each shot, so you can also process and overlay the individual shots externally on your computer. You can activate the function with SHOOTING SETTING > MULTI EXPOSURE > ON, then choose one of the overlay options (ADDITIVE, AVERAGE, LIGHT, DARK).

The live view shows you the progress of your multi exposure series. This is very helpful for composing overlay images and once again provides true WYSIWYG. However, the result is just one JPEG or HEIF file that cannot be replicated in-camera with different parameters, so make sure to select the image size and quality settings that you need before taking the overlay shots. Of course, you can always process and overlay the single RAW files in Photoshop or a similar app.

Using PIXEL SHIFT MULTI SHOT	TIP 72

In this mode, the X-T5 takes 20 shots, using its in-body image stabilization (IBIS) to move the image sensor by half a pixel with each shot. Each frame is recording as a RAW file. You then need the free Fujifilm Pixel Shift Combiner software [59] to combine the RAWs to a DNG file with a resolution of either 40 MP or 160 MP. Finally, this DNG file can be processed in Lightroom or Capture One. This DNG file will also exhibit better dynamic range than a single shot.

After all, it's based on 20 shots that, in total, collected 20 times a much light as a single exposure.

To activate Pixel Shift Multi Shot, select SHOOTING SET-TING > PIXEL SHIFT MULTI SHOT and choose an interval setting. Typically, you want to select SHORTEST INTERVAL here. When you release the shutter button, all 20 shots will be taken with the electronic shutter (ES) using the same focus distance and exposure settings.

As of now, Pixel Shift Combiner does a terrible job correcting artifacts that are a result of camera movement, subject movement, or even light changes that occur during the acquisition of the 20 RAW files. Here are a few tips that may help you get usable results:

- Place the camera on a sturdy tripod and avoid any kind of vibration during the image acquisition process. Choose solid ground and don't move while the camera is working. The slightest interference can ruin the series for Pixel Shift Combiner, at least in its current state (June 2023).

- Avoid any light changes during the image acquisition process.

- Make sure that your subject doesn't move or exhibit motion blur. Water, leaves, moving cars, or people may result in image artifacts.

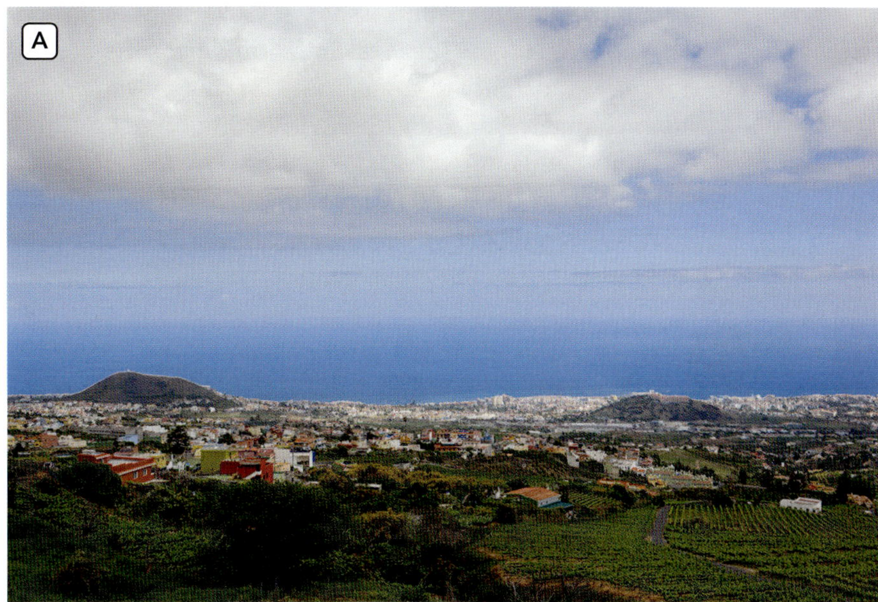

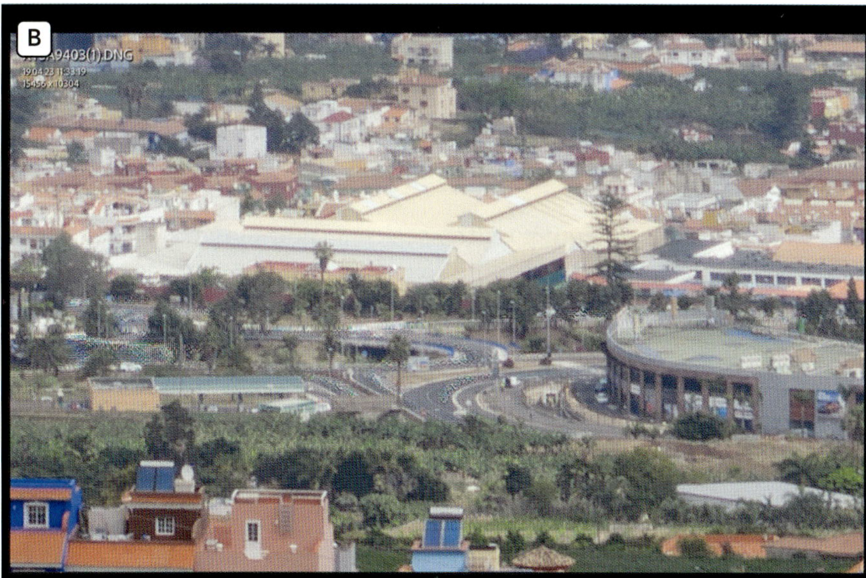

Fig. 96: Pixel Shift Multi Shot may sound like a good idea for landscape photographers who like to work from a tripod and appreciate high-resolution shots with up to 160 MP (image **A**). However, even the slightest camera vibration or subject movement can cause artifacts, as seen in the enlargement (image **B**).

I want to reiterate that the issue with Pixel Shift Multi Shot isn't the camera; it's the Pixel Shift Combiner software and its current inability to compensate for tiny movements or light changes. Hopefully, this will be improved in future versions of this software.

Please note that Pixel Shift Combiner offers a Help menu that is a comprehensive user guide with plenty of additional tips on setting up the camera and combining the images.

<table><tr><td>TIP 73</td><td>Adv. Filters: exposing with creative filters</td></tr></table>

Advanced Filters are a collection of creative effect filters. Gimmicks, you may rightfully say, but they can be fun to play with. To access the filters, turn the DRIVE dial to the ADV. Position and select one of 13 filter options in SHOOTING SETTING > DRIVE SETTING > ADV. FILTER SETTING.

Here's the good news: Adv. Filter doesn't just create a JPEG or HEIF file showing the effect, it also saves a RAW file that you can revisit later to generate a "regular" image without fancy filter effects. You can do so using the built-in RAW converter or an external RAW converter like Lightroom. That said, there are two things that you should keep in mind:

- Depending on the selected filter option, Adv. Filter also adjusts the auto-exposure of your shot. For example, LOW-KEY will expose a scene much darker than HIGH-KEY. This means that depending on the filter you choose, the exposure of the RAW file will also differ. To rule out exposure changes due to a specific filter selection, you can use manual exposure mode **M**.

- The RAW file that is created along with the effect JPEG cannot be used to create other Adv. Filter effects because the camera's built-in RAW converter doesn't offer any Adv. Filter options. You can only use the built-in RAW converter to create "regular" JPEG, HEIF, or TIFF images.

| Motion panoramas | TIP 74 |

MOTION PANORAMA works like the panorama function in your smartphone: while you pan the camera in a horizontal or vertical motion, the X-T5 takes a series of images and stitches them together in a panoramic JPEG file. After selecting Panorama on the DRIVE dial, you can choose between two sizes (M and L), and you can specify the direction of your panning motion (left, right, up, and down). You can use a vertical motion horizontally by holding the camera upright.

Here are a few tips for getting the best results with motion panoramas:

- Since MOTION PANORAMA results in only a JPEG file (no RAW), JPEG parameters such as white balance and film simulation must be set *before* taking the shots.

- Exposure, white balance, and focusing remain constant during the recording of a motion panorama. This applies to all focus modes (AF-S, AF-C, and MF). That's why it's important to set a focus distance and depth of field that work for the entire panoramic scene.

- Panoramas tend to extend over a wide area with varying light conditions and strong changes in contrast. In such cases, it's smart to shoot with an extended DR setting, such as DR200% or DR400%. In addition to that, the exposure should be set in a way that suits the entire panoramic image, not just a small part of it. The edges of a panorama are rarely representative; it's usually better to base your exposure on the main part of the image in the middle. Motion panorama works with all four exposure modes, so shooting it in manual mode **M** may be the smartest option. Please note that motion panorama only works with multi metering.

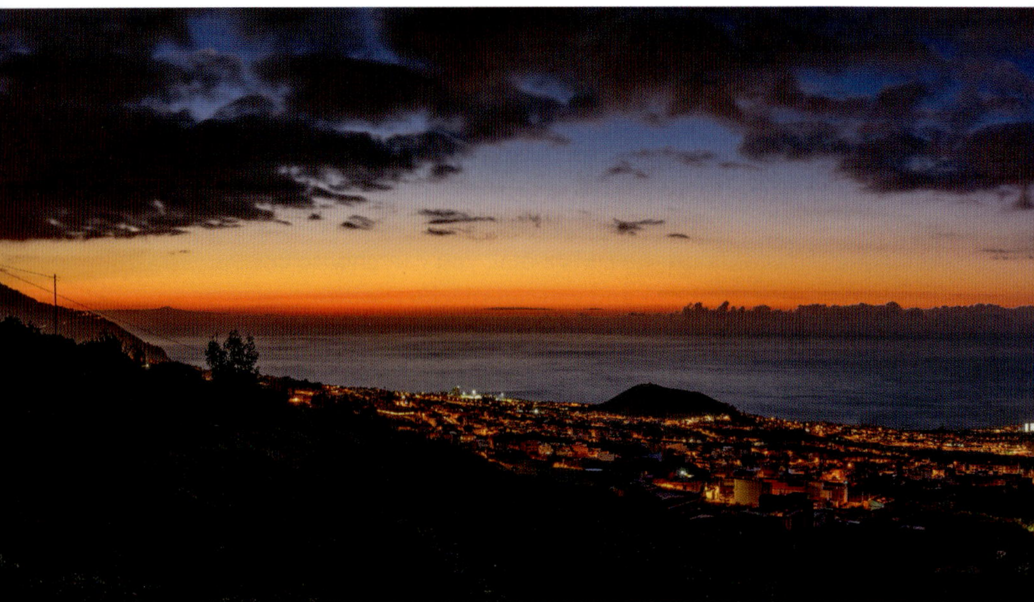

Fig. 97: Motion panorama is a "quick and dirty" method to produce panorama JPEGs. It's like shooting panoramas with a smartphone, and to be honest, modern smartphones often do a better job. If you are into high-quality results, let me propose an alternative: shoot the panorama manually and merge the RAW files with software like Adobe Lightroom. For this example, I took eight shots with a small tripod (exposing each shot for 15 sec.), denoised the files with Lightroom's new AI function and merged the denoised DNGs into a Lightroom Pano-DNG with approx. 100 MP.

- If you decide to *not* manually set exposure, white balance, and focus, point the camera toward a representative part of the panoramic scene, then lock focus, exposure, white balance, and DR by half-pressing the shutter button. Then pan to the point where you'd like to start the panning action (while holding the shutter button half-depressed), press the shutter button fully, and start panning. Don't forget that SHUTTER AE must be set to ON to lock the exposure of the panorama by half-pressing the shutter.

- Avoid scenes that contain a lot of motion. Moving objects (people, vehicles, etc.) can lead to ghosting artifacts,

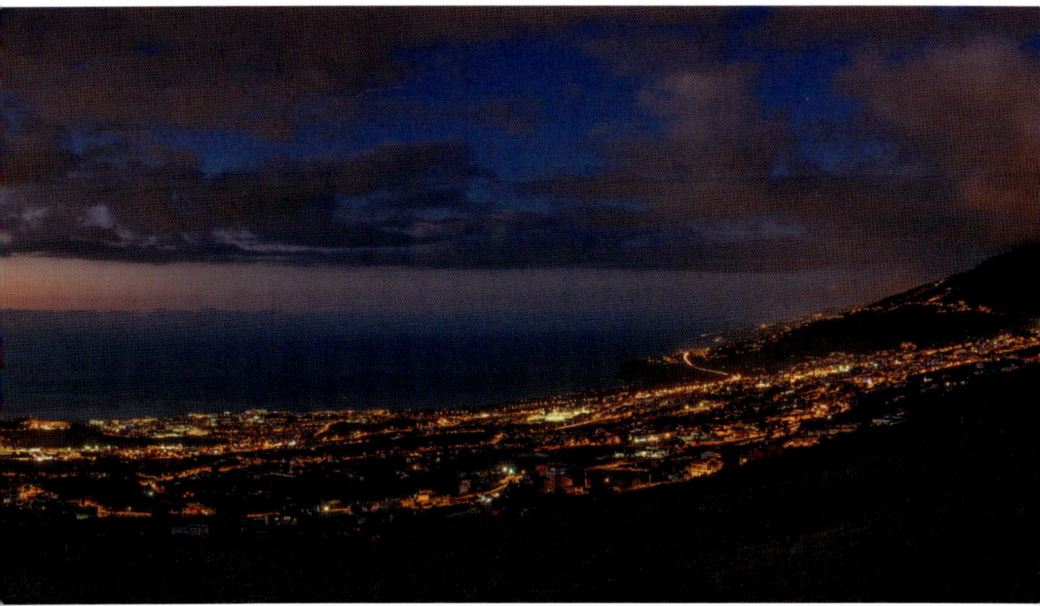

which is when moving objects (partially) appear in more than one spot of the final panorama.

- Keep a healthy distance to the panoramic scene. Don't shoot panoramas in close quarters. Also make sure that you have sufficient depth of field. Wide-angle lenses are better suited for this job than normal or telephoto lenses.

- Make sure that the shutter speed is fast enough to avoid motion blur from panning. Don't pan too fast!

- Always pan with the EVF (camera held to your eye), not with the LCD display (arms stretched in front of you).

- While panning, stand parallel to the panoramic scene and always stand on level ground.

- Try to ignore the time delay that may occur between the currently recorded image and what's displayed in the EVF. Keep panning the camera in a smooth motion until the camera stops taking frames.

- Use a tripod and make sure the camera is leveled to the horizon.

- Immediately check your finished panorama in the camera's viewfinder after you have captured it. Look out for stitching errors and ghosting artifacts. Do this while you are still on location, not at home when it's too late to reshoot a panorama that went wrong.

2.4 FOCUSING WITH THE X-T5

The X-T5 features a hybrid autofocus system that combines CDAF and PDAF. CDAF, PDAF, and hybrid AF? It can be quite confusing.

- **CDAF** means **C**ontrast **D**etection **A**uto**F**ocus and is a standard in mirrorless cameras. CDAF is available throughout the entire sensor area (117 or 425 AF frames in Single Point mode or 117 AF frames in Zone and Wide/Tracking mode). It works quite precisely but is not particularly fast.

- **PDAF** means **P**hase **D**etection **A**uto**F**ocus and used to be the standard AF in DSLRs. Since the X-T5 is mirrorless, its PDAF works directly on the sensor and covers its entire area. PDAF is fast and particularly good at tracking moving subjects. It can predict where a moving object will be a split second from now, a feature that can be quite useful when you shoot in burst mode.

- **Hybrid AF** means that the X-T5 automatically chooses and combines available AF methods (CDAF or PDAF) for the current subject and the current light conditions.

CDAF and PDAF: what's the difference?	TIP 75

Both AF methods offer distinct qualities that can be useful during your daily shooting:

- CDAF focuses on surfaces and works best with areas that offer a lot of contrast. CDAF doesn't work well for a solid white or black wall, but for a checkered wall, it works great. It's the same with clothing: solid colors may be tough, but patterned clothes work wonderfully. CDAF operates with a trial-and-error approach: it keeps adjusting the focus until it finds the distance setting with the utmost contrast. CDAF doesn't directly go to the optimal focus setting. This results in heightened autofocus motor activity and visible focus hunting while the AF iterates back and forth until it finds the optimal focus position.

- PDAF loves focusing on edges, especially vertical edges (or horizontal ones if you hold the camera upright). Unlike CDAF, PDAF can directly determine the distance to an object, so there's no need for focus hunting. This is why PDAF is considerably faster.

- Both methods depend on sufficient light to work with maximum efficiency. The brighter a scene is and the more contrast it has, the better the AF will work. Bright lenses with large maximum aperture openings are beneficial because they allow the AF to work with more light and less depth of field, which helps increase the precision of the autofocus. It's worth noting that most lenses are darker near the edges than they are at the center (this effect is called vignetting), so in poor light, the autofocus may work less efficiently with focus frames that are located far off center.

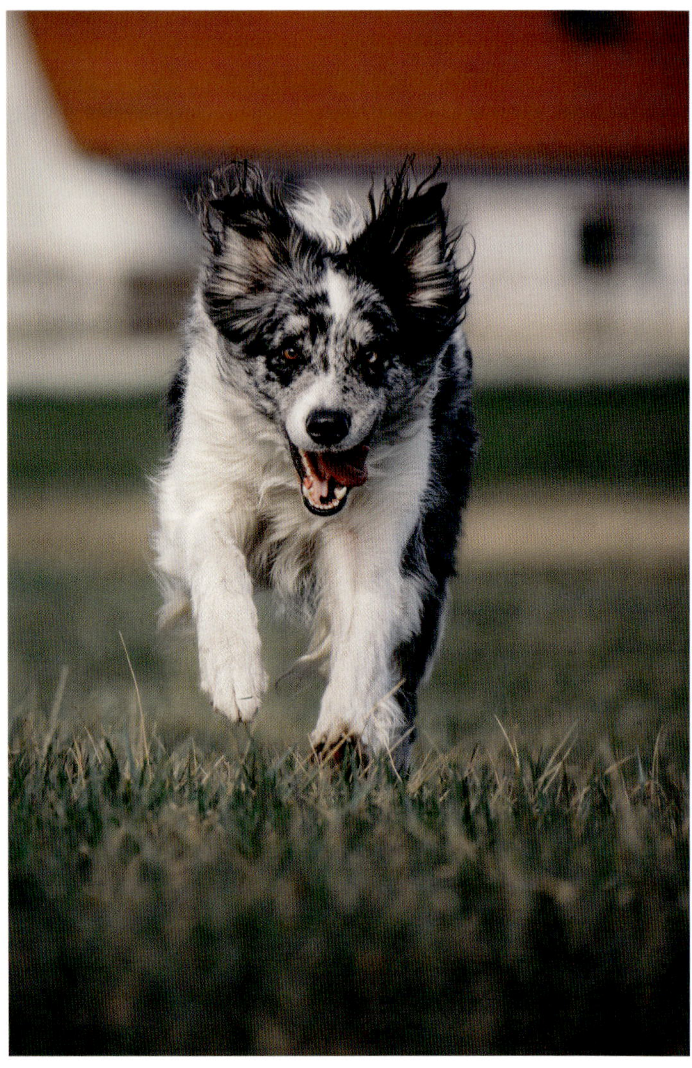

Fig. 98: Tracking fast-moving subjects like this running dog is a job for the **phase detection autofocus** (PDAF).

<table><tr><td>AF-S or AF-C?</td><td>TIP 76</td></tr></table>

Your X-T5 features two basic AF modes that can be selected with the focus mode selector at the front of the camera:

- **AF-S (AF Single) is meant for stationary subjects**. When you half-press the shutter button, the camera will focus on the object covered by the active AF frame and lock the distance (as long as you keep the shutter button half-pressed). You can either fully press the shutter button to take the shot, or you can take your finger off the shutter release and try again.

- **AF-C (AF Continuous) is meant for moving subjects**, especially those that move toward or away from the camera. When you half-press the shutter button, the camera starts focusing on the object covered by the active AF frame and continuously adjusts the distance to the moving object while you keep the shutter button half-pressed.

While AF-C focuses using the set working aperture, AF-S can open the aperture beyond the working aperture to improve the AF performance in poor light. This also improves the focusing accuracy due to the reduced depth of field caused by the wide-open aperture.

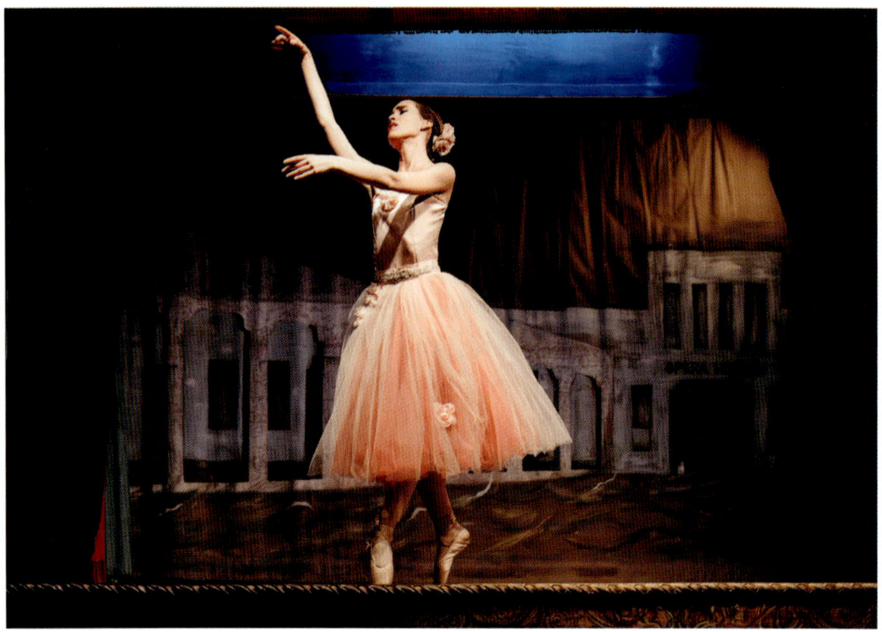

Fig. 99: When shooting with **AF-C in poor light**, it helps to keep the aperture wide open.

| TIP 77 | Single Point AF vs. Zone AF vs. Wide/Tracking AF |

AF/MF SETTING > AF MODE lets you choose between SINGLE POINT, ZONE, or WIDE/TRACKING autofocus. The X-T5 also offer an ALL option, which lets you seamlessly select one of the three AF modes simply by changing the size of the focus frame or zone. You should definitely set your camera to ALL.

- **Single Point AF** mode is my recommended AF setting for most applications. In this mode, you can manually select one of up to 425 available focus frames. Try to avoid old habits like using only the center frame in concert with the focus-and-recompose [60] technique. It's better to *first* compose the shot and *then* select a suitable AF frame that covers the part of the image you want to be in perfect focus. This helps you avoid focus errors that invariably occur when you pan the focus plane. Such focus errors may be irrelevant with long focal lengths and small aperture openings (larger depth of field) but focus errors can be quite unpleasant with wide-angle lenses, a wide aperture opening (small DOF), and in situations with a short distance between the camera and the subject. Single Point AF can be used in concert with both AF-S and AF-C.

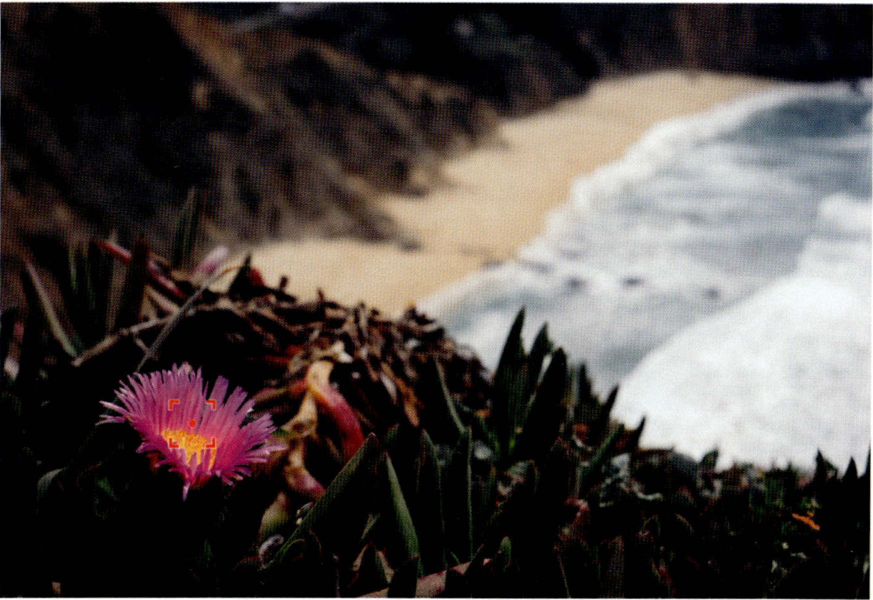

Fig. 100: Shooting with **minimal depth of field**, you can't afford to use a focus-and-recompose habit because it would quickly lead to soft results that appear out of focus. Instead, compose the shot, and then focus using a single focus frame that covers the part of the image that is supposed to be in focus.

■ You can think of **Zone AF** as an extension of Single Point AF. Basically, an AF zone is a particularly large AF frame that consists of a matrix of smaller AF points. Zones are available in sizes that cover 3 × 3, 5 × 5, or 7 × 7 out of a total of 117 AF points. Like Single Point AF frames, AF zones can be moved around within the image area. Since they are larger than focus frames, AF zones make it easier to focus on moving subjects. In Zone AF mode, the camera will usually start looking for something to focus on in the center (crosshairs) of the selected zone and will then expand its search toward the edges of the zone until it finds a target. Like Single Point AF, Zone AF works in concert with either AF-S or AF-C.

■ When you combine **Wide/Tracking AF** mode with **AF-S**, you get *Wide AF* mode. The camera scans the entire image frame and automatically selects several focus frames. It's a bit like rolling dice, since the camera is simply looking for areas it can easily focus on. It doesn't know what's important in a scene. This changes when Wide/Tracking is used in concert with **AF-C**: this results in *Tracking AF* which offers real 3D tracking of moving objects; that is, objects that not only move toward or away from the camera, but also left, right, up, and down within the image frame. To track such an object, select Wide/Tracking and AF-C and pick one of the available AF points. To start the tracking process, make sure the selected point covers the moving object you want to track. Half-press the shutter button to start the tracking process. While you keep the shutter button half-pressed, the camera will automatically follow the selected subject as it moves across the image area.

<table>
<tr><td>TIP 78</td><td>Correct focus stick configuration</td></tr>
</table>

For the best results, you must configure the focus stick in a way that's different from the factory default setting. *Without these settings, many of the following tips and procedures will not work, so please make sure that we are all on the same page.*

To adjust the focus stick configuration, press and hold the focus stick until the FOCUS LEVER SETTING configuration menu appears. Now select the following options:

- PUSH > EDIT FOCUS AREA. This setting ensures that pressing the focus stick takes you to the FOCUS AREA screen where you can adjust the size and position of the focus frames. You can also quickly change the AF mode, given that AF mode ALL has been selected in the AF/MF SETTING > AF MODE menu.

- TILT > DIRECT AF POINT SELECTION. This setting allows you to directly more the focus frame or zone around simply by tilting the focus stick. This is the easiest way to adjust the position of the focus frame.

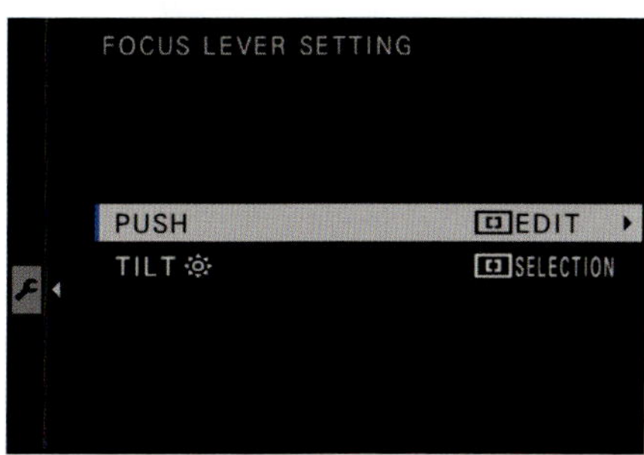

Fig. 101: This **focus stick configuration** gives you direct access to all options.

<table><tr><td>Selecting an AF frame or AF zone</td><td>TIP 79</td></tr></table>

The X-T5 allows you to use the focus stick or the touchscreen to select a focus frame or zone. Make sure that the focus stick is configured as described in the previous tip.

- Pressing the focus stick opens the FOCUS AREA screen, where you can move around the focus frame or focus zone by tilting the stick in any direction. You can change the size of the frame or zone by turning the front or rear command dials. In AF mode ALL, doing so also changes the AF mode (Single Point, Zone, Wide/Tracking). In the FOCUS AREA screen, pressing the rear command dial resets the size of the zone or frame to their default values. Pressing DISP/BACK centers the position of the AF frame or zone.

- You can also *directly* move the focus frame or zone around simply by tilting the focus stick without pressing it first. This is the easiest way to adjust the position of the focus frame. However, to have additional options like changing the size of the frames, you must first press the focus stick to get to the actual FOCUS AREA screen.

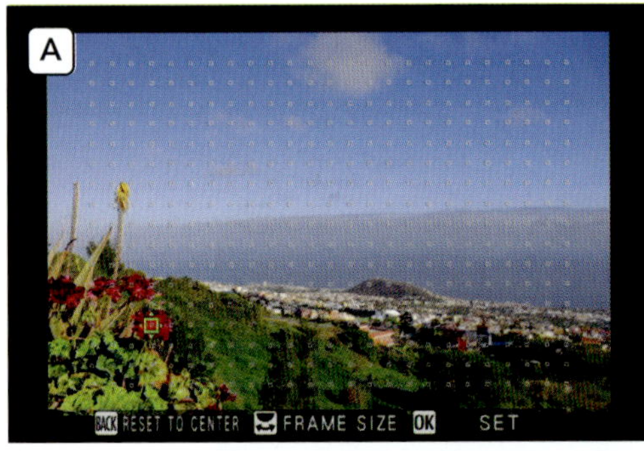

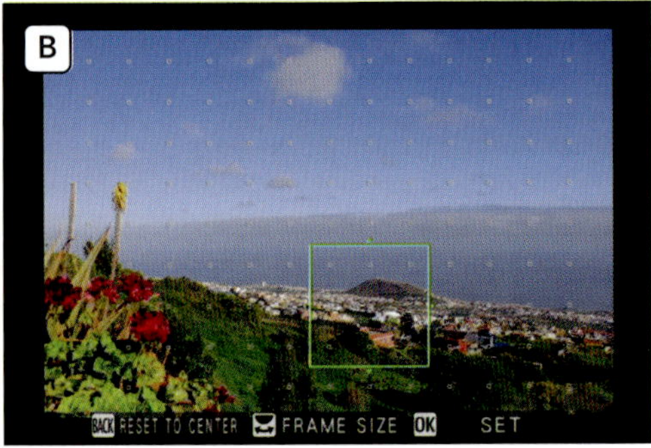

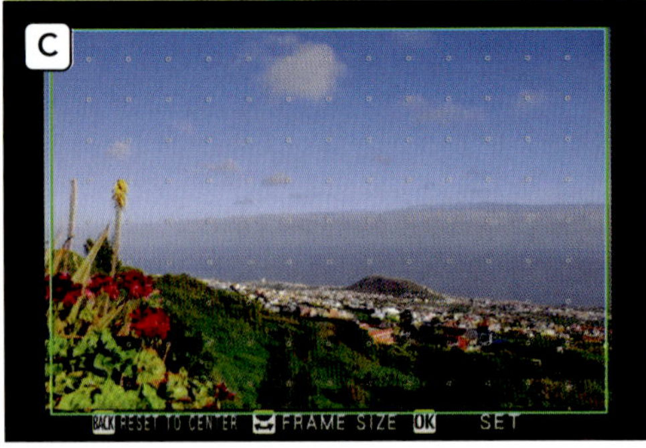

Fig. 102: Pressing the focus stick opens the **FOCUS AREA screen**, where you can select a focus frame or AF Zone and change their sizes. Using the convenient AF mode ALL, changing the size cycles through AF modes Single Point AF (**A**), Zone AF (**B**), and Wide/Tracking AF (**C**).

You can also use the touchscreen to change the position of a focus frame or zone. Make sure the touchscreen-AF interface is set to AREA mode, and then tap anywhere on the screen to select an AF area or zone.

You can even use the touchscreen like a trackpad to change the position of the focus frame or zone when you are looking through the electronic viewfinder (EVF). You can select the active trackpad area with SET UP > BUTTON/DIAL SETTING > TOUCH SCREEN SETTING > EVF TOUCH SCREEN AREA SETTING.

Of course, for all of this to work, the touchscreen must have been enabled in the first place, so make sure that SET UP > BUTTON/DIAL SETTING > TOUCH SCREEN SETTING > *(camera symbol)* TOUCH SCREEN SETTING is set to ON.

Choosing a suitable AF frame or AF zone size	TIP 80

The X-T5 offers 117 or 425 different AF frames in Single Point AF, and each frame comes in six sizes. You can change the size of an AF frame by pressing the focus stick and turning one of the command dials left or right to decrease or increase the frame size.

AF frame size affects the efficiency of CDAF and PDAF. A basic rule to follow is: *Make your AF frame as large as possible and as small as necessary.*

This is why:

- With a larger AF frame size, the camera has more to work with and a better chance to find contrast in a target, especially when the light conditions aren't optimal. There's also a better chance the camera will be able to use the faster PDAF method. When PDAF isn't possible, the camera will fall back to the slower CDAF.

- With a smaller AF frame size, the autofocus becomes more accurate. A small AF frame gives you better control over *exactly* what the camera is focusing on. Avoid AF frame sizes that are larger than the part of your image that needs to be in focus. For example, if your AF frame is larger than the head of the person you are focusing on, there's a chance that the camera will instead focus on the background behind them, especially if that background contains a lot of contrast.

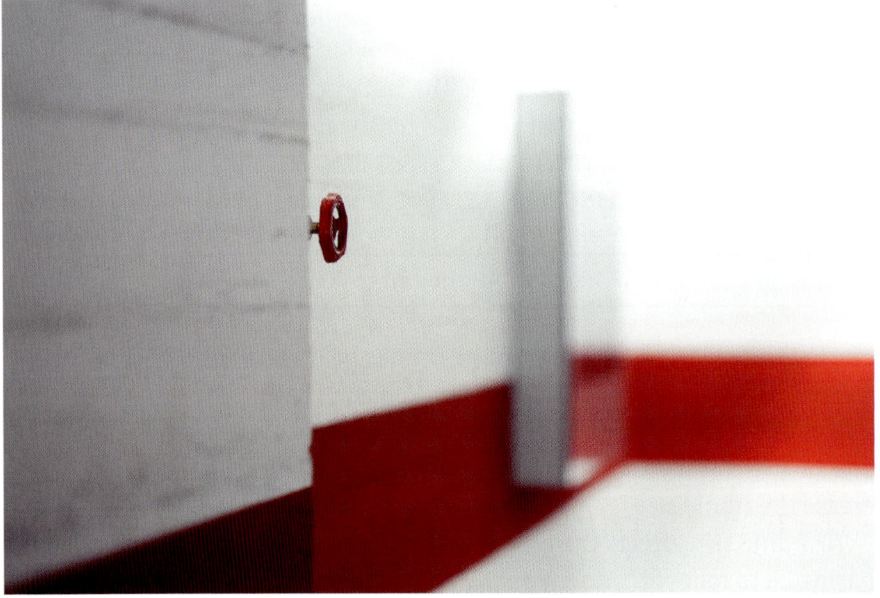

Fig. 103: To get tiny parts of an image in perfect focus, it's best to choose a **small AF frame size**.

In a similar fashion, you can change the size of AF zones by pressing the focus stick and then turning the command dial left or right. You have a choice of three AF zone sizes: 3 × 3 (default), 5 × 5, or 7 × 7 out of 117 frames.

Since we can regard AF zones as very large AF frames, the same rules apply. Larger zones are more convenient, and they potentially offer a faster AF response, but they are also potentially less accurate than smaller zones.

<table><tr><td>**Manual focus and DOF zone focusing**</td><td>**TIP 81**</td></tr></table>

Manual focus (MF) mode offers several focus aids:

- A magnification tool with several magnification levels.
- Focus peaking (Focus Peak Highlight) with two strength levels and optional colors.
- Digital split image.
- Digital microprism.
- An electronic distance scale with depth-of-field indicators.
- Instant AF: autofocus in MF mode that is triggered by pressing the AF-ON button in manual focus mode.

The electronic distance scale can help you define a focus zone with a predetermined depth of field (DOF). The X-T5 offers two DOF scales: a *pixel-based* scale (recommended) and a *film-format based* scale (not recommended). If you opt for PIXEL BASE in AF/MF SETTING > DEPTH-OF-FIELD SCALE, everything inside the DOF zone will look pixel-sharp even when the image is magnified to a 100% view. Please don't confuse manual zone focusing with Zone AF—they are completely different things.

Here's a zone-focusing example using an 18 mm lens manually set to 5 m and stopped down to f/8. The DOF bars will show a depth-of-field zone that begins at around 4 m and ends at around 10 m. This means everything located within this zone (between 4 and 10 m) will appear equally in-focus in the final image. You only have to make sure that your subject is inside that zone when you press the shutter button.

A special case of manual zone focusing is when setting the hyperfocal distance [61]. This is the distance setting with the maximum DOF (all the way to infinity). Again, the electronic DOF scale can be very helpful: you can manually set the distance where the blue DOF bar on the right touches the infinity mark. For example, using an 18 mm lens at f/16, the hyperfocal distance is located at approximately 8 m, with the pixel-sharp DOF zone extending from approx. 4 m to infinity.

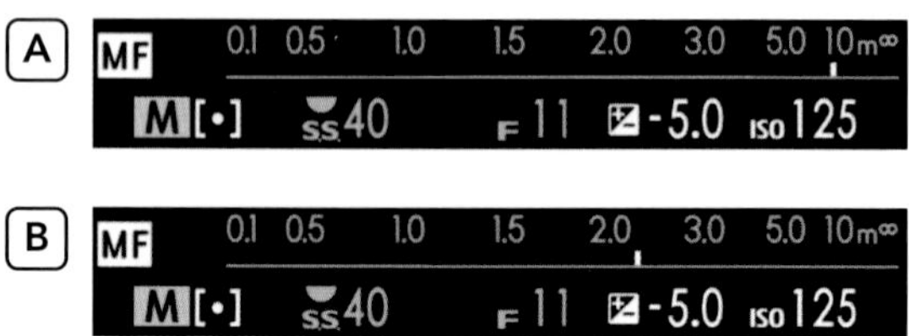

Fig. 104: Setting the **hyperfocal distance** with the electronic distance and DOF scale: instead of focusing on a predetermined distance, manually change the focus distance until the DOF bar touches the ∞ mark on the right end of the scale. This gives you the hyperfocal distance for a given aperture and focal length. This illustration shows the hyperfocal distance of a wide-angle lens (16 mm) at f/11 for both the PIXEL BASIS option (**A**) and FILM FORMAT BASIS option (**B**).

Please note that depth of field is very much dependent on the circle of confusion (CoC) [62]. Fujifilm uses a very conservative CoC that guarantees pixel-sharp results even when the DOF zone is viewed at 100% magnification on a computer screen. Fuji is literally using the sensor's physical resolution as a benchmark. In PIXEL BASIS mode, everything that's located inside the electronic DOF zone will be rendered as sharp as the sensor can resolve it. In the age of pixel peeping, this is as good as it can get.

You should know that the engraved analog distance and DOF scales on the XF14mmF2.8, XF16mmF1.4, and older XF23mmF1.4 version follow a different rule: the FILM FORMAT BASIS option. They are based on a much less conservative circle of confusion that is several aperture stops more generous than the electronic PIXEL BASIS scale. You can change the electronic scale to FILM FORMAT BASIS (and hence use a less conservative scale with all your lenses) in AF/MF SETTING > DEPTH-OF-FIELD SCALE. However, I want to reiterate that I do not recommend this setting. Instead, I recommend using the PIXEL BASIS scale.

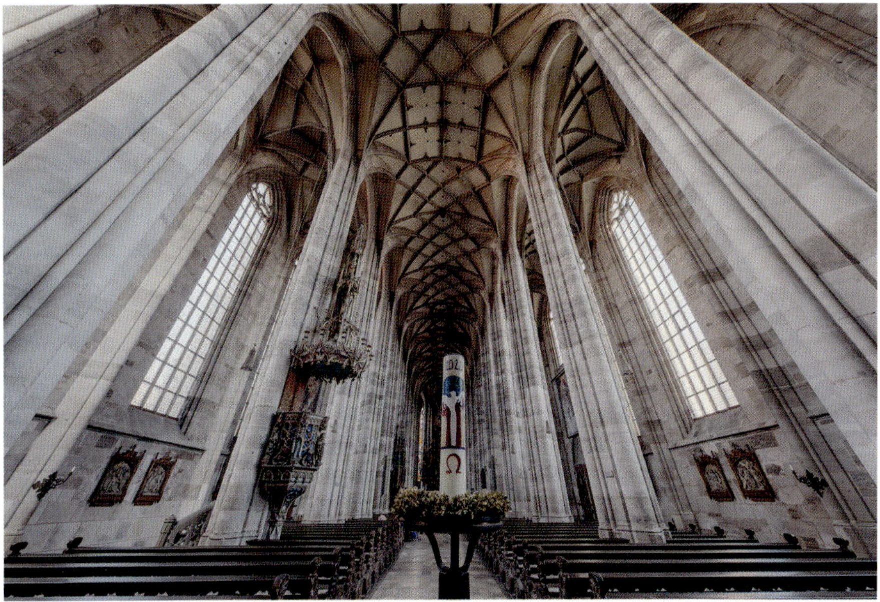

Fig. 105: This shot was manually focused by setting the **hyperfocal distance** on the camera's electronic PIXEL BASIS focus distance scale.

<table><tr><td>Manual focus assistants</td><td>TIP 82</td></tr></table>

The X-T5 features several MF assistants:

- **Focus Peaking** (or Focus Peak Highlight) emphasizes the edges of objects when they are in focus. This method is especially useful in concert with longer focal lengths and bright lenses with little DOF.

- **Digital Split Image** tries to simulate the split image indicator of manual focus SLRs. It works best with vertical lines (or horizontal lines when the camera is held in portrait orientation).

- **Digital Microprism** simulates a microprism that used to be popular in the manual-focus SLR days.

To quickly switch between the available MF assistants, press and hold the rear command dial for about a second while you are in MF mode. For this to work, FOCUS CHECK must have been assigned as the Fn button to the rear command dial.

You can watch a short video [63] demonstrating different manual focus assistants. There's also a video demonstrating the "real thing": actual analog split image and microprism focusing in an old Minolta SLR [64].

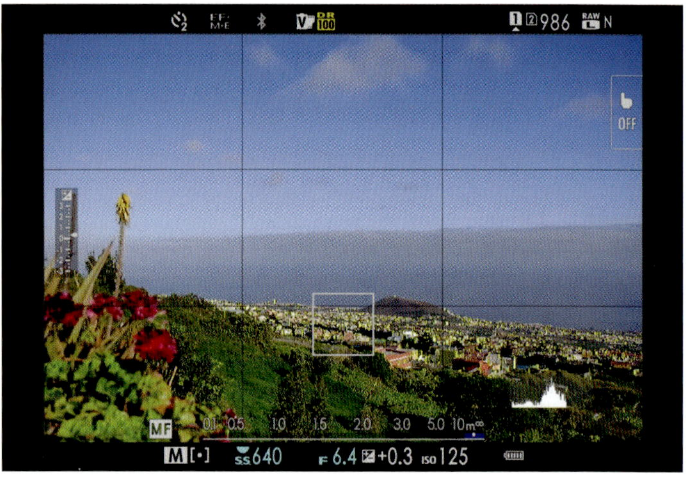

Fig. 106: Focus peaking is my favorite among the available manual focus aids. In this example, I opted for yellow outlines to indicate the areas of the scene that are in focus.

TIP 83	Using the Focus Check magnifier tool

The magnifier tool is helpful for checking if the current focus is spot-on. Press the rear command dial (either in AF-S/ Single Point AF or in MF mode) to magnify the area that is targeted by the selected focus frame. Of course, this assumes the rear command dial is operating with its default FOCUS CHECK Fn button assignment.

You can change the magnification level by turning the rear command dial. You can also combine focus check with any available MF assistants (focus peaking, digital split image, and digital microprism). Please note that in digital split image and digital microprism mode, only *one* magnification level is available.

By selecting AF/MF SETTING > FOCUS CHECK > ON, the magnifier tool is *automatically* activated when you turn the manual focus ring of a lens in MF mode. You can immediately cancel any automatic focus check by half-pressing the shutter button.

There are up to 425 different focus frames available in manual focus mode. The active frame indicates which part of the image will be magnified when focus check is activated. As usual, you can change the active frame by moving the focus frame around with the focus stick.

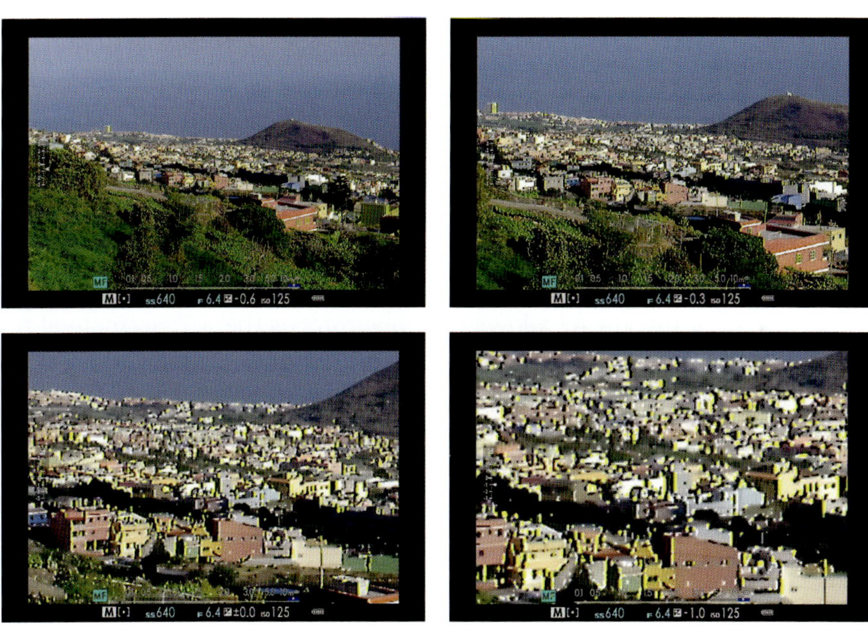

Fig. 107: The X-T5 offers several **magnification levels**. To make things easier, the magnification can be combined with focus peaking. You can also move the magnified area with the focus stick or touchscreen while Focus Check is zoomed into the frame.

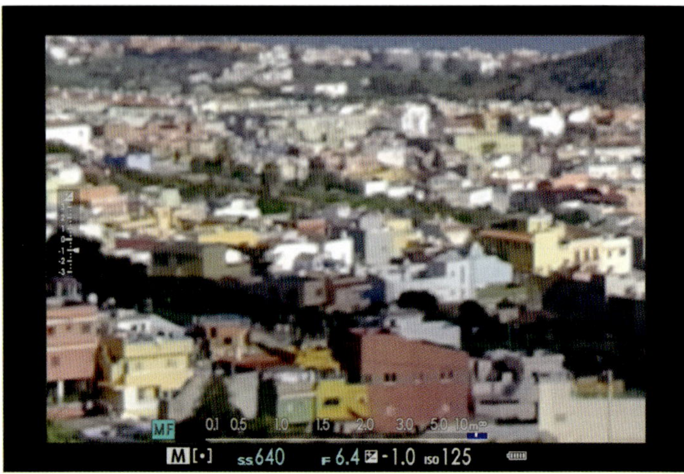

Fig. 108: Without focus peaking, the X-T5's maximum Focus Check magnification level reveals a weakness of the tool: the image is rather soft and makes it difficult to find the perfect focus setting.

Please note that Focus Check is not available in AF-C mode, or when PRE-AF has been turned on.

TIP 84	Using Instant AF-S and Instant AF-C

Instant AF allows you to autofocus the X-T5 in manual focus mode by pressing the AF-ON button. Instant AF always works with a wide-open aperture. Like the regular autofocus, its efficiency depends on the size of the selected focus frame.

Instant AF is the most precise AF method available, but it is a bit slower than the camera's regular autofocus. It can be combined with conventional manual focusing: you can use Instant AF to quickly autofocus on an object, and then manually fine-tune the focus by turning the focus ring and using MF assistants like the magnifier and focus peaking.

Sadly, this convenient method of fine-tuning Instant AF with manual focus is *not* available when you are using lenses with manual focus clutches (e.g., XF14mmF2.8, XF16mmF1.4, and the older version of the XF23mmF1.4).

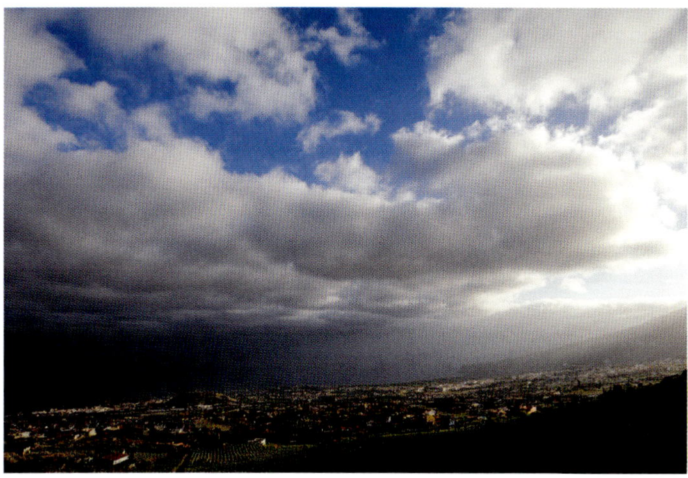

Fig. 109: Instant AF forces the lens to focus with a wide-open aperture. This AF method is particularly accurate when you shoot with a stopped down wide-angle lens.

Instant AF normally functions like AF-S, but you can also set it to continuous autofocus with AF/MF SETTING > INSTANT AF SETTING > AF-C. In this mode, Instant AF will track the subject distance with AF-C while you keep the AF-ON button pressed in manual focus mode.

Unlike normal AF-C (that focuses with the working aperture), Instant AF-C can focus with a wide-open aperture, making it an option for stage and concert photography with moving subjects in poor light, where you want to shoot with AF-C and a stopped-down lens. Just keep the AF-ON button pressed for continuous instant autofocus as you press the shutter button at the right moment.

Note that Instant AF-C stops focusing when you half-press the shutter button. To avoid unnecessary time lags between focusing and shutter release, it's best to first activate Instant AF-C by pressing and holding the AF-ON button (or any other designated Instant AF button) to continually focus and then *fully press* the shutter button to take a shot. In other words: skip the half-press and go all the way.

<table><tr><td style="background:#a4c639;color:white">**TIP 85**</td><td>**Using AF+MF**</td></tr></table>

AF+MF allows you to manually focus in AF mode by turning the focus ring, all while holding the shutter button half-pressed. Select AF/MF SETTING > AF+MF > ON to enable this feature. To use AF+MF, your camera needs to be in AF-S autofocus mode.

Here's how it works:

- Autofocus on your subject as usual in AF-S mode by half-pressing the shutter button.

- Once the autofocus has been confirmed (green square[s]) or not confirmed (red AF warning), keep the shutter button half-pressed and rotate the focus ring of your lens to *manually* adjust the focus distance until you are satisfied. If focus peaking is enabled, it will automatically engage when the focus ring is rotated and manual focus (MF) kicks in. You can also use the Focus Check function (AF/ MF SETTING > FOCUS CHECK > ON) to automatically magnify the focus area when you turn the focus ring. For this to work, make sure that AF-S and Single Point AF are set. You can also combine Focus Check magnification with focus peaking. Turn the rear command dial to change the magnification factor and press the rear command dial to manually enable/disable the live view magnification. Remember that all this must be performed while you hold the shutter button half-pressed, so this might require some practice.

- When you are happy with your manual focus adjustments, fully press the half-pressed shutter button to take the shot.

I see three main applications for AF+MF:

- **Manual focus in situations when autofocus fails**: Instead of losing time by changing the focus mode from AF to MF, you can immediately focus manually when the camera's

AF fails to acquire the subject. Simply adjust the focus manually using the focus ring.

- **Correcting the camera's autofocus**: There are instances when you might want to fine-tune the autofocus of your camera by adjusting it manually. Again, focus peaking is available to make things easier, and you can enable Focus Check to automatically show a magnified view of the focus area when you turn the focus ring.

- **Shifting the depth-of-field (DOF) zone or setting the hyperfocal distance**: After half-pressing the shutter button, AF+MF lets you quickly shift the DOF zone toward or away from the camera by turning the focus ring. The electronic distance scale on the screen can be quite helpful here. For example, you can set the hyperfocal distance [65] by shifting the right tip of the DOF bar to touch the infinity mark of the electronic distance scale.

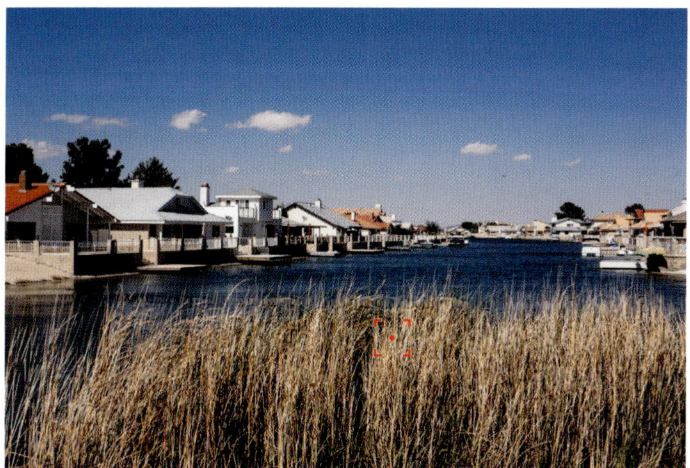

Fig. 110: In this example, I autofocused on the reeds by placing the AF frame right over them. I used a small aperture of f/9 for a decent amount of depth of field (DOF). Since the portion of the DOF zone that extends in front of the reeds toward the camera is useless in this case, I manually shifted the DOF zone away from the camera using **AF+MF**. The resulting DOF zone starts at the reeds and extends all the way back.

At first glance, the MF component of AF+MF may look like your regular manual focus, but it's not. While genuine MF is performed at a wide-open aperture, the MF part of AF+MF is performed at the selected working aperture. That's because the shutter button is half-pressed, so the camera has already been primed to take the shot with minimal shutter lag.

This also means the EVF/LCD will display a live view image that shows the actual depth of field of the resulting image, and focus peaking will show a larger area as being in focus when you stop down the lens. This can make it more difficult to nail your manual focus adjustment.

AF+MF also works with clutch-type lenses such as the XF14mmF2.8, XF16mmF1.4, and the older of the two XF23mmF1.4 lenses. These lenses feature a clutch to mechanically switch between MF and AF mode. Since the focus ring of these lenses can be turned only when the clutch is in the MF position, you need the following configuration to get AF+MF to work:

- Enable AF+MF in AF/MF SETTING.

- Select AF-S on the camera and MF on the lens (by pulling the clutch mechanism toward the camera).

- Use AF+MF as described above.

Here are a few tips regarding AF+MF and clutch lenses:

- Make sure the manual focus ring of the lens has sufficient play to the left and right so you can make the necessary MF adjustments.

- The distance and DOF markings on your clutch lens are meaningless when in the AF+MF configuration. Instead, use the electronic distance/DOF scale that's displayed in the camera's viewfinder or on the LCD.

- To use clutch lenses in manual focus mode when AF+MF is set to ON, both the lens *and* the camera must be set to MF.

Important: *Switching on AF+MF in the menu internally sets AF-S PRIORITY SELECTION to RELEASE priority. This means that the camera may **not focus correctly** in AF-S mode if you swiftly and fully press the shutter release button (basically skipping the half-press phase and the autofocus confirmation). For this reason, I recommend **not** using AF+MF in the X-T5.*

Pre-AF: a relic of the past	TIP 86

Pre-AF brings the AF-C of first-generation Fujifilm X cameras (like the X-Pro1) to more current models like your X-T5. With Pre-AF set to ON, the camera will continuously focus on whatever is covered by the active AF frame, even when the shutter button is *not* half-pressed.

Pre-AF burns plenty of power because the autofocus in the lens is always working. On the other hand, using it can potentially result in a quicker AF response, and it can help face/eye detection and subject detection find a target. When you are shooting action with telephoto lenses, Pre-AF may be particularly helpful—remember to pack a few extra batteries. I usually set this option (AF/MF SETTING > PRE-AF) to OFF.

Using face/eye detection and subject detection	TIP 87

Face detection and subject detection are combined autofocus and exposure metering modes. They even affect auto white balance. You can activate face/eye detection with AF/MF SETTING > FACE/EYE DETECTION SETTING > FACE DETECTION ON and picking one of the four eye detection options.

Here's what it does:

- The camera scans the scene and detects human faces, heads, and bodies. It automatically focuses on one of the detected subjects when the shutter button are half-pressed. When more than one face or person are detected, the camera tends to focus on the one that's closest to the focus frame or zone of the underlying autofocus focus mode. This person/head/face/eye will be highlighted with a white frame.

- Face detection and subject detection use a custom version of weighted multi metering that puts an emphasis on the selected subject. The goal is to deliver an exposure that is biased to the subject. It may also influence the camera's auto white balance.

Face detection and subject detection are both a blessing and a curse. They are a blessing when they work because they focus directly on a subject or object and make sure that they are "correctly" exposed. It's a curse when the detection goes wrong because it doesn't just mean the focus might miss its mark; it may also mess up your exposure metering and change your auto exposure.

The good news is that in many cases, face and subject detection work. For example, face detection even works with people who only show their profiles to the camera, persons wearing glasses, and even persons that turn away from the camera. In such cases, face detection will focus on the head or on the entire body.

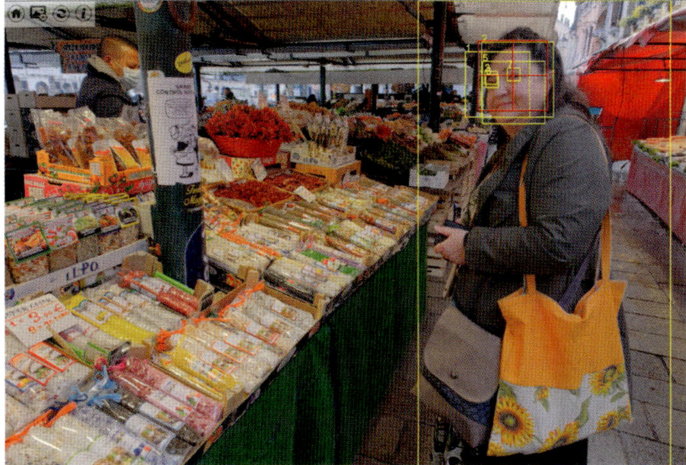

Fig. 111: Face detection is great for scenes with one or more people looking at (or showing their profile to) the camera. Fifth-generation X cameras like the X-T5 feature enhanced face and subject detection that's based on machine learning. For example, the face/eye detection algorithm can also detect and direct the autofocus to the head, torso, or entire body of a person.

Here are a few helpful tips regarding face and subject detection:

■ If you want to take face detection and subject detection exposure metering out of the equation (and I highly recommend that you do), you can set the camera to manual exposure mode **M**. While the *metering* will still be affected in this mode, the *exposure* itself will not. Alternatively, you can use the AE-L button to meter and lock the exposure and prohibit face or subject detection from interfering with it while AE-L is active. You can still adjust your locked exposure with the exposure compensation dial.

■ Spot, center-weighted, and average metering aren't available when face or subject detection are active. The camera is always using a derivate of multi metering.

- When face or subject detection fail to detect a suitable target in the scene, the camera will automatically fall back to the selected regular AF mode: Single Point, Zone, or Wide/Tracking. At the same time, exposure metering reverts to regular multi metering.

- Face and subject detection can and should be assigned to function (Fn) buttons.

- Face detection and subject detection cannot be active at the same time. It's either one or the other. However, you can regard face/eye detection as simply another subject detection mode. There's no difference in camera behavior between face/eye detection and the six subject detection options (ANIMAL, BIRD, AUTOMOBILE, MOTORCYCLE&BIKE, AIRPLANE, TRAIN). That said, FACE/EYE DETECTION offers additional options such as selecting the left or right eye or switching off eye detection altogether.

- Subject detection will only detect the currently selected subject type. For example, if you select MOTORCYCLE&BIKE, the camera will not look for and detect trains, cars, planes, or animals. However, it may very well detect a person riding a bike and focus on their head, helmet, or face. If they come close enough, the camera may even focus on that person's eye.

- Fujifilm is always enhancing and expanding the face and subject detection functions to make them more useful and effective. For example, BIRD mode includes insects, and AIRPLANE mode includes helicopters and drones. Further improvements may already have been implemented through firmware updates when you read these lines.

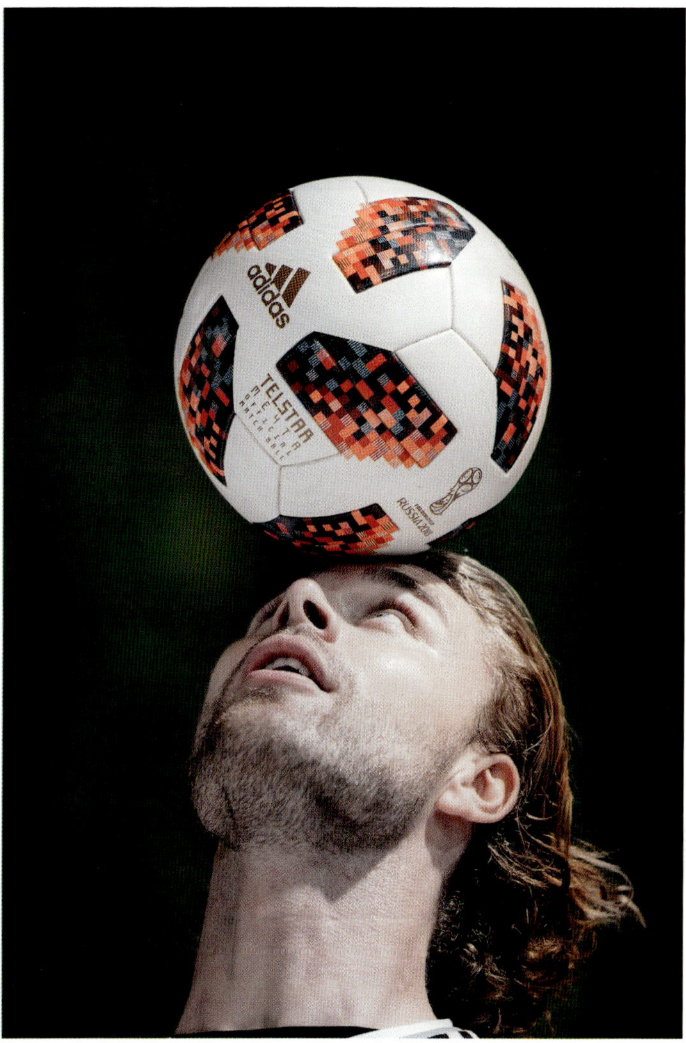

Fig. 112: For persons who are moving around, the X-T5 is fast enough to track their faces with **AF-C and face/eye detection**.

Face detection accuracy can be improved with the optional eye detection feature. To activate it, select either LEFT EYE PRIORITY or RIGHT EYE PRIORITY. You can also select EYE AUTO to make the camera focus on the eye that's closest to the camera or select EYE OFF to deactivate eye detection during face detection.

In the viewfinder, the camera will highlight a detected eye with a small square and will focus on it when you half-press the shutter button. I usually set this function to EYE AUTO. You can still toggle between the left or the right eye by assigning RIGHT/LEFT EYE SWITCH to an Fn button of your liking.

TIP 88	Face and subject detection and the underlying fallback autofocus mode

With face and subject detection, the underlying fallback AF mode is the autofocus mode that you have selected before you activate face detection or subject detection on top of it:

- Single-Point AF
- Zone-AF
- Wide-AF (in concert with AF-S)
- Tracking-AF (in concert with AF-C)

Face/subject detection AF and the underlying AF mode work together in two ways:

- The size and the position of the focus frame (Single-Point AF), the focus zone (Zone-AF) or the tracking frame (Tracking-AF) determine the area and vicinity where face detection and subject detection are looking (and not looking) for suitable targets. It also determines on which of multiple suitable targets to focus. For example, if face detection finds a group of three people, the camera will focus on the face that's closest to the position of the underlying focus mode's focus frame.

- If face detection or subject detection fail to find or track a target for whatever reason, the autofocus automatically falls back to the underlying AF mode: Single-Point AF, Zone-AF or Wide/Tracking AF.

Based on the above, here are a few tips on how to use face/subject detection in concert with underlying AF modes:

- To make the camera scan the entire image frame for subjects, you can select Wide-AF as your underlying AF-S mode. In AF-C, the widest scan area is provided with Zone-AF and a centered 7×7 zone square.

- To direct face or subject detection to a *specific* subject inside your frame, you can use Single-Point AF or Zone-AF with a small or regular frame size and position that frame close to your chosen subject.

- Always remember that the position and size of the underlying AF mode's focus frame or zone will be used in cases when no subject can be detected, or when subject tracking is interrupted or fails. The underlying AF mode is your fallback AF mode. For example, when you are shooting portraits with face/eye detection in AF-S, you might want to select a small Single-AF frame as your fallback AF mode and position that frame over the face or (if possible) an eye of your subject.

- If a face or subject has been detected and you half-press the shutter button, the camera will keep tracking the selected subject no matter what until you release the shutter button. Of course, if subject tracking fails, the camera will fall back to the underlying autofocus mode. If your underlying AF mode is Tracking-AF, the autofocus will store and track the pattern that exists at the position where face or subject detection tracking stopped working. This means that when you are tracking moving subjects in AF-C mode, it may be a good idea to use Tracking-AF as your underlaying AF mode.

- Face and subject detection are meant to make your life easier. But *easier* isn't always *better*. In many situations and with some practice, you may do a better job than the camera—not only detecting suitable subjects, but also positioning a perfectly sized focus frame over them. This is especially true for stationary subjects that can be shot in AF-S mode. I use subject detection mostly in scenarios where I cannot always keep a regular focus frame or zone on a moving subject. However, I am always selecting a suitable fallback AF mode and trying to keep the focus frame or zone of the fallback mode on target in case the camera's "smart" subject tracking fails. In other words: Don't rely too much on the camera to do your job.

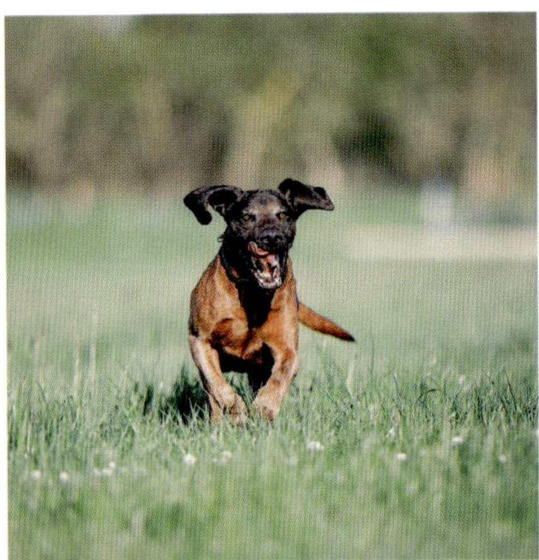

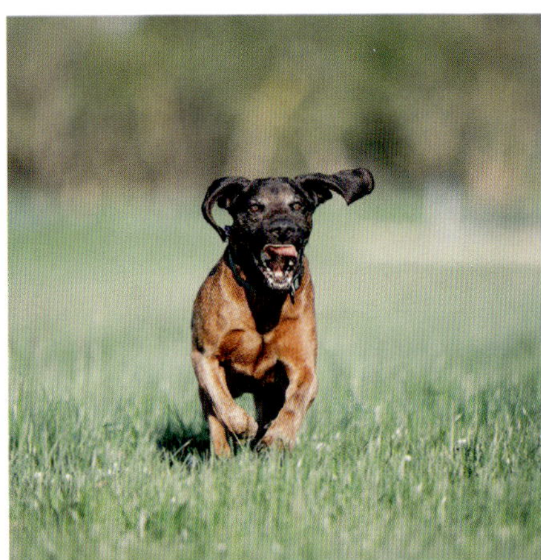

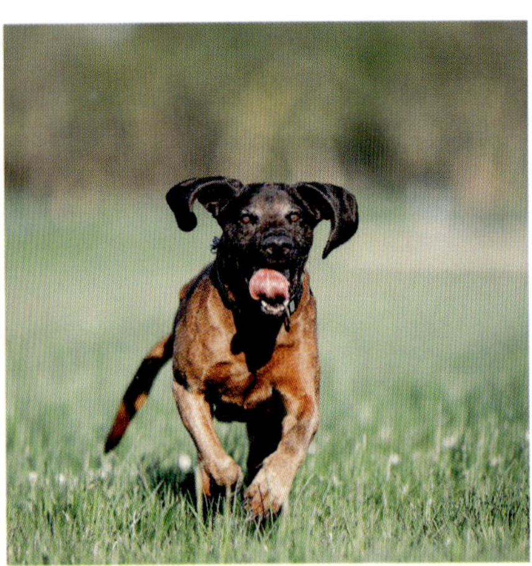

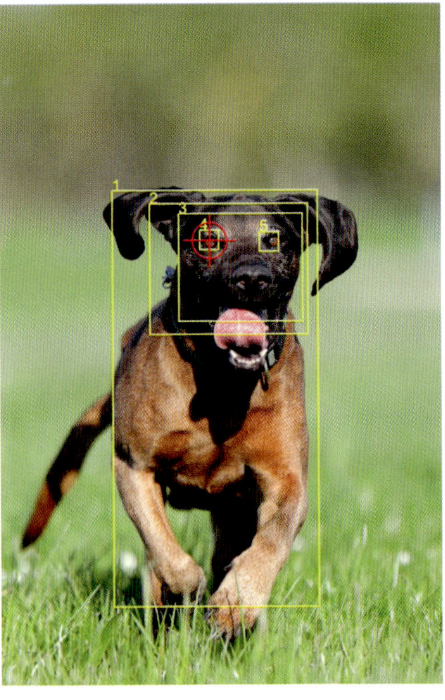

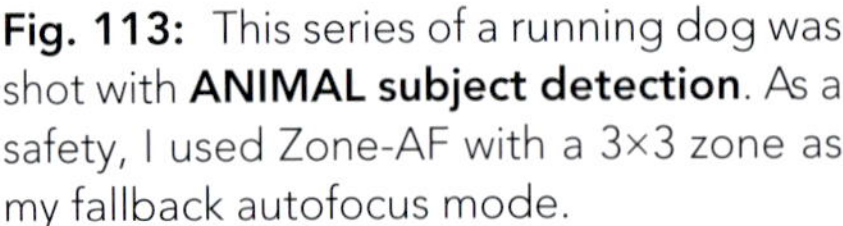

Fig. 113: This series of a running dog was shot with **ANIMAL subject detection**. As a safety, I used Zone-AF with a 3×3 zone as my fallback autofocus mode.

<table><tr><td>**Using AF-ON (back-button focusing)**</td><td>TIP 89</td></tr></table>

AF-ON brings back-button focusing to your X-T5, a common practice among DSLR users. Simply put, AF-ON assigns the camera's autofocus to a function button. Press that button, and the camera starts focusing. Release it, and the focusing stops at the current focus position—until you press the AF-ON button again.

In other words: AF-ON performs the same autofocus function as half-pressing the shutter button (assuming that SHUTTER AF ON is set in the SET UP > BUTTON/DIAL SETTING menu). In AF-S mode, pressing AF-ON will perform a single focus search and lock the distance. In AF-C mode, AF-ON will continuously focus on a target as the button is kept pressed (just like half-pressing the shutter button).

In the X-T5, the AF-ON function is already pre-assigned to the AF-ON button. You can press and hold AF-ON while you simultaneously press the shutter.

- In AF-S, pressing and holding AF-ON will focus the camera and lock that focus while AF-ON is held, so simultaneously half-pressing or pressing the shutter button won't interfere with your locked focus.

- In AF-C, pressing AF-ON means that the camera keeps tracking your target as long as AF-ON is pressed and held.

- In manual focus (MF) mode, AF-ON turns into Instant AF.

If you are a "religious" back-button-AF user (some DLSR converts are), you may find it more comfortable to entirely disable the shutter button's AF functionality by selecting SET UP > BUTTON/DIAL SETTING > SHUTTER AF > OFF for AF-S and/or AF-C, so AF-ON will be the only available method to autofocus in AF-S or AF-C mode.

| TIP 90 | Focusing in poor light |

Low light can lead to poor contrast along with more photon noise, making it more difficult for the camera to find and lock the correct autofocus distance. However, the amount of light (and hence noise) that reaches the sensor depends not only on the brightness of a scene, but also on the brightness of the lens. The XF56mmF1.2 is 3.5 stops or EVs (exposure values) brighter than the XF18–55mmF2.8–4 kit lens in its 55 mm position. So, with the XF56mmF1.2 lens, the same scene can look 3.5 stops brighter to the camera's autofocus system. You can guess which lens will perform better when the lighting gets tough.

Don't be confused by appearances—it's true that the live view image in the viewfinder will look equally bright with both lenses, but that's only because the camera is electronically amplifying the live view display as needed. However, the autofocus needs *actual* light and contrast. When the light is poor, it's vital to target surfaces with contrast and, if possible, use a larger AF frame size.

One way of tackling a tough lighting situation is by using fast lenses, like an XF56mmF1.2, XF35mmF1.4, or XF23mmF1.4. You can also generate light—the camera's AF assist lamp can illuminate a subject to help the autofocus find better contrast. Be aware that the AF assist lamp can be easily blocked by an attached lens hood. Watch out for this and remove the lens hood if necessary. Since the AF assist lamp tends to concentrate on the center of the image, it works best in concert with one of the more central AF frames. To use the AF assist lamp, make sure to set AF/MF SETTING > AF ILLUMINATOR > ON.

An alternative to using the AF assist lamp is using a flashlight to temporarily illuminate a subject. If you are indoors, you can try turning on the lights in the room for a moment and using AF-Lock to lock the focus. Just make sure to meter and set the exposure *after* the lights are off again.

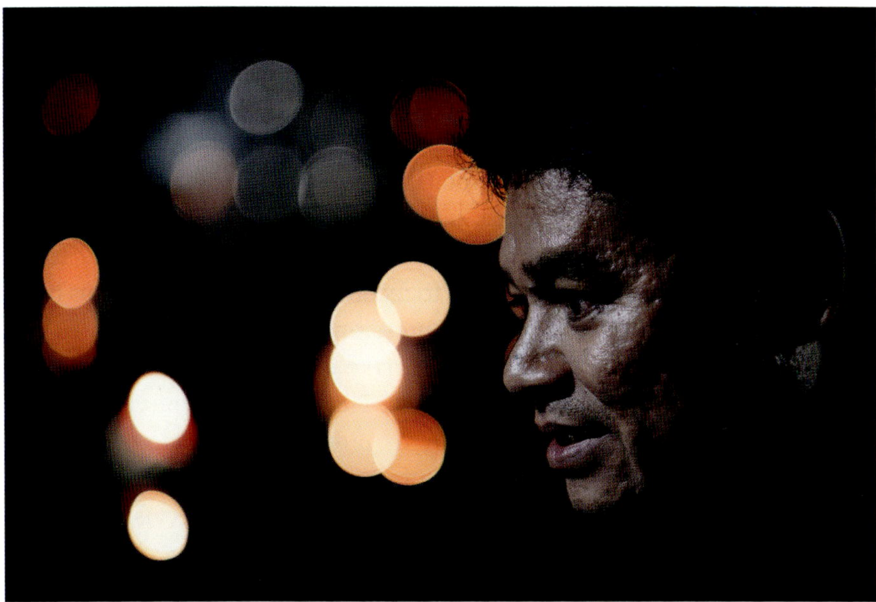

Fig. 114: In this **low-light shot**, the fast XF56mmF1.2 R lens made it easier on the autofocus system to find its target in AF-S mode. In AF-S mode, low-light AF performance isn't related to the set working aperture, but to the maximum wide-open aperture that is available. In this example, it wouldn't have made a difference if I had set the aperture to 1.2 or 5.6 or 8, because in AF-S mode, the focusing system can temporarily open to the widest lens aperture.

Important: If you intend to stop down the aperture of your lens in poor lighting, make sure to use either AF-S or manual focus with Instant AF-S or Instant AF-C as your focusing mode. Why? Because Instant AF always focuses wide open. Try to avoid regular AF-C, because this mode will usually focus with (or closer to) your stopped-down working aperture, which will make things more difficult for your camera since less light will reach the sensor.

| TIP 91 | Macro: focusing at close distances |

The biggest challenge with shooting macro is the lack of depth of field (DOF). The slightest movement may cause the shot to be out of focus. That's why macro photography is usually performed using a tripod and manual focus, often with Instant AF, Focus Check (magnifier tool), and focus peaking. It's vital not to recompose after the focus has been set. To get a visual impression of the current DOF, you can half-press the shutter (make sure SHUTTER AE is ON) or assign PREVIEW DEPTH OF FIELD to one of your Fn buttons.

Macro shots usually require you to stop down the lens to increase the DOF. Since this can result in slower shutter speeds, it's important to make sure the subject isn't moving too fast or out of the focus plane. Shooting a close-up of a flower in the wind may not yield excellent results.

If you don't want to use manual focus in macro mode, you can also focus automatically. Here's how:

- Set AF-S and Single Point AF and select a small AF frame size.

- Reposition the small AF frame to exactly cover the part of the image you want to be in focus. Quickly take the shot after you half-press the shutter—don't recompose.

- You can check your focus with the magnifier tool before taking a shot by pressing the rear command dial. After doing so, you can change the magnification factor by turning the command dial.

- Try not to shoot handheld; it's better to use a tripod.

- Stop down the lens and visually check the depth of field by half-pressing the shutter button or using the DOF preview function (remember that function can be assigned to any Fn button).

- Make sure there is sufficient light and try to shoot subjects that don't move in and out of the focus plane.

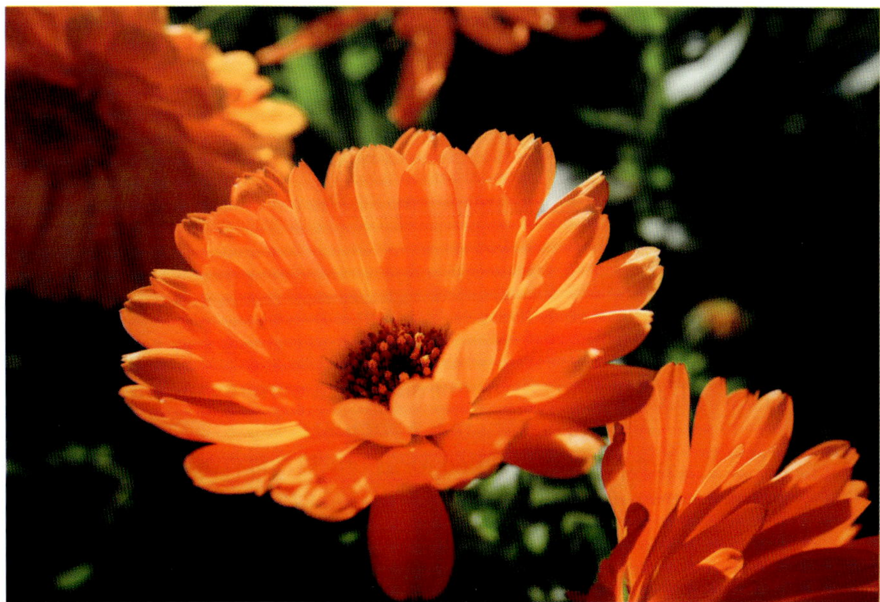

Fig. 115: Macro shots can be quite challenging due to their lack of DOF. This is why a tripod is highly recommended. With a little bit of luck, handheld shots like this example are possible, as well. I took this one with the XF30mmF2.8 R LM WR Macro at f/7.1.

You can add macro capability to many of your existing XF and XC lenses by using Fujifilm's electronic macro extension tubes MCEX-11 and MCEX-16. You can download a PDF file [66] from Fujifilm's website that provides a chart that shows how these extension tubes enhance the magnification factor of compatible lenses. Please note that the camera's electronic DOF/distance scale doesn't reflect the use of macro extension tubes.

Focus Bracketing	TIP 92

The need for greater depth of field (DOF) [67] is a common issue for macro and landscape photographers. With increasing sensor resolution, diffraction blur [68] becomes a serious limitation. To avoid visible diffraction with your

40 MP APS-C sensor, you should avoid stopping down your lenses beyond f/8.

Even worse, many lenses have their "sweet spot" (the critical aperture delivering the best resolution and sharpness) [69] about two stops down from their maximum wide-open aperture. For example, my XF27mmF2.8 pancake delivers its maximum resolution around f/5.6.

For macro and landscape photographers, stopping down the lens to f/16 or f/22 often isn't an option due to quality considerations. Not to mention that even at f/22, depth of field would still not be sufficient in many macro situations.

What to do? There is a popular solution among ambitious photographers called *focus bracketing* [70], in which multiple images are taken at various focus distances and they are later are merged (i.e., *stacked*) into a single image that displays increased depth of field. The series of individual source images can be merged in Photoshop or in other specialized software such as Helicon Focus [71]. This technique is referred to as *focus stacking*.

Focus bracketing helps you automate the generation of the source material you need for focus stacking. To configure focus bracketing in your X-T5, select SHOOTING SETTING > DRIVE SETTING > BKT SETTING > FOCUS BKT.

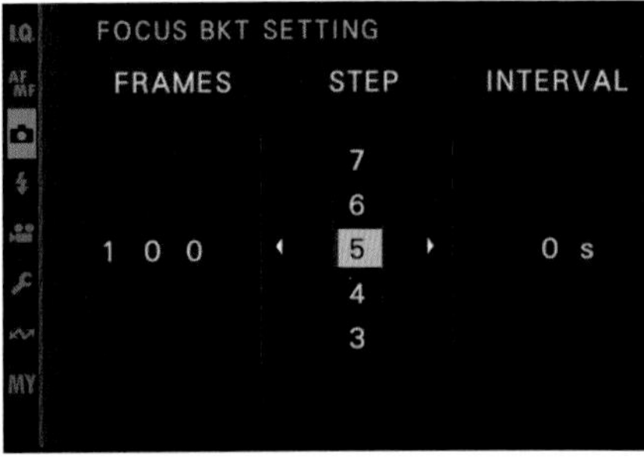

Fig. 116: The **manual focus bracketing** configuration screen allows you to set the number of frames the camera should automatically take (FRAMES), the focus difference between individual shots (STEP), and the pause between individual shots (INTERVAL). The latter is useful so that the camera can settle down after each shot to avoid shutter-induced vibration. It's also recommended to activate the electronic first curtain shutter (EFCS) or even the electronic shutter (ES).

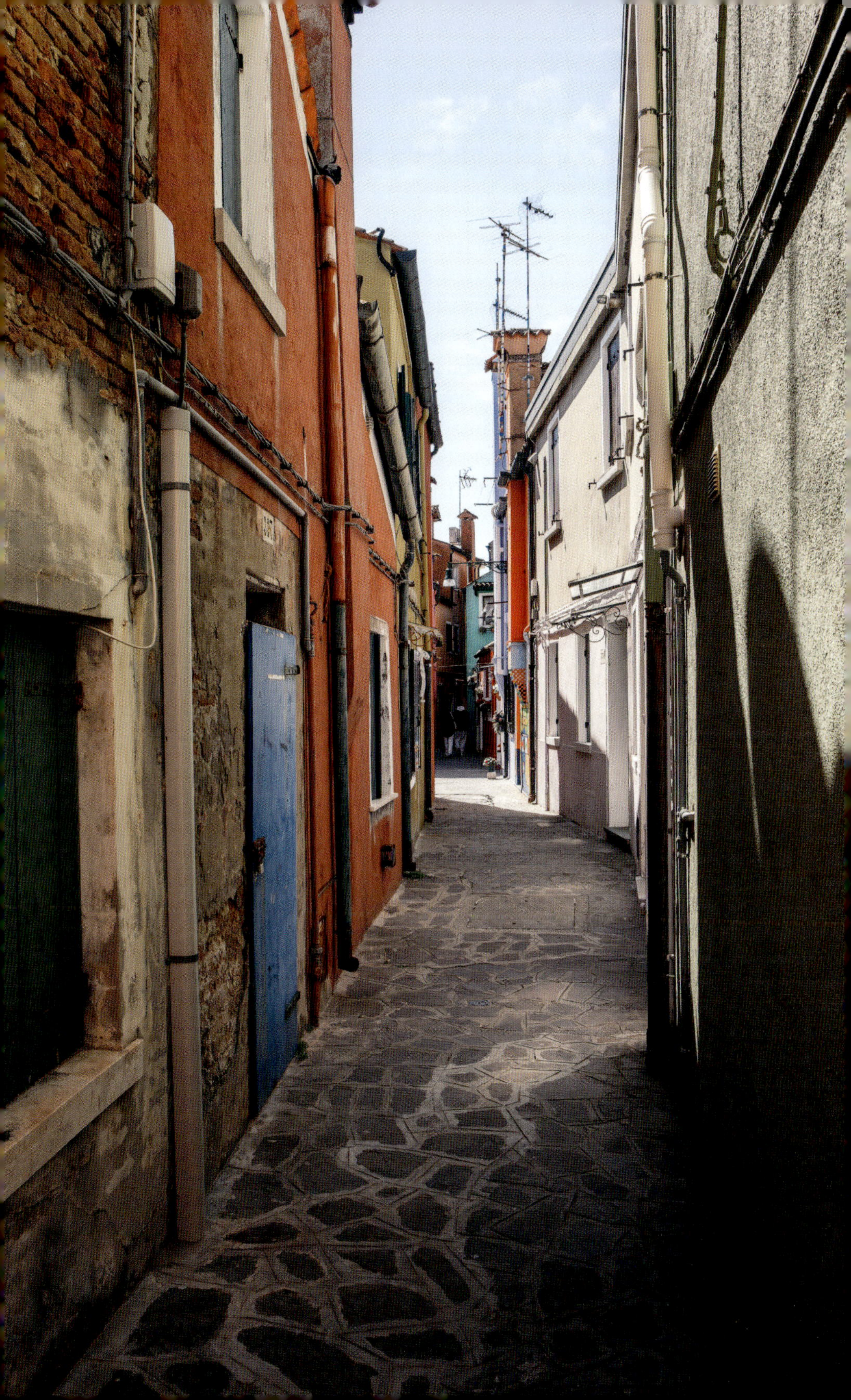

To initiate focus bracketing, it's best to select MF and manually focus on the nearest point of the subject you want to have in perfect focus. It's also recommended to stop down the lens to its "sweet spot." With macro lenses, this is typically two stops down from their maximum aperture opening. Wide-angle lenses often deliver peak performance three or four stops down.

Depending on your needs and time restraints, you can experiment with various step settings. To start the sequence, make sure the camera is in BKT mode (DRIVE dial) and that FOCUS BKT is selected as the BKT MODE, and then press the shutter button. The camera will take the set number of images or stop when it reaches infinity—whatever occurs first.

When the camera has finished recording the source images, you can merge them in Photoshop or in specialized focus-stacking software like Helicon Focus.

Sounds cumbersome? It is! Luckily, your X-T5 also features an *automatic* focus bracketing mode, where you can manually set a starting point (the closest focus distance) and an end point (the furthest focus distance) for a given scene or subject. The camera will then automatically take the required number of shots at varying distance settings so cover the area between the start point and the end point. All that's left for you to do is specify the shooting interval between consecutive bracketing shots. If you use the electronic shutter, you can pick a shooting interval of zero without suffering shutter shock vibration.

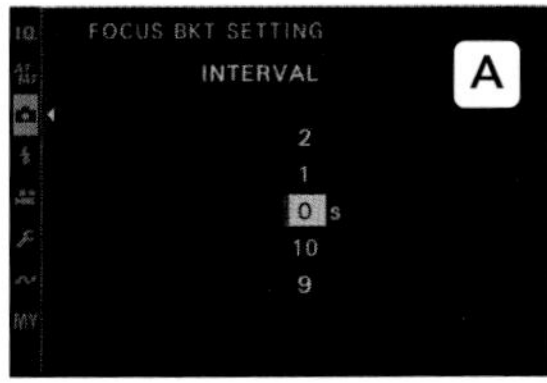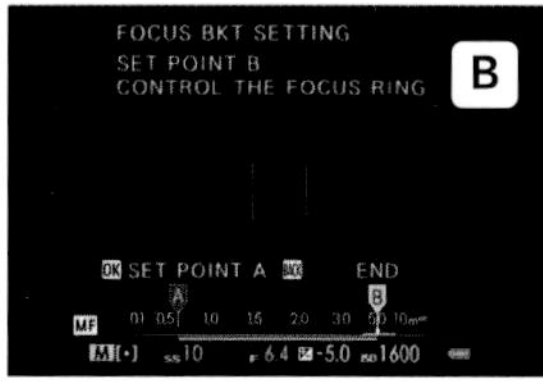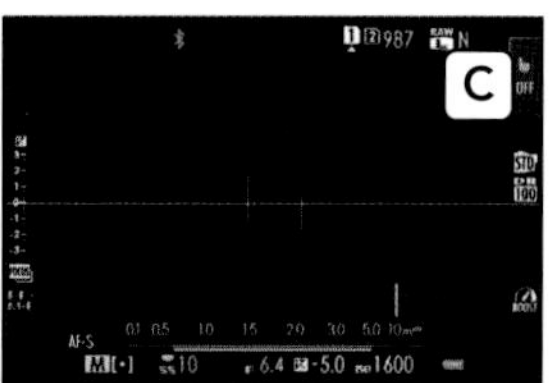

Fig. 117: Focus Auto Bracketing facilitates the image acquisition process and automatically captures the number of shots that are required to cover a user-defined distance range. In your X-T5, the focus bracketing settings menu is hidden under SHOOTING SETTING > DRIVE SETTING > BKT SETTING > FOCUS BKT, followed by three different settings pages.

After selecting AUTO as your focus bracketing mode, the camera opens the next settings page where you can specify the INTERVAL. This is the time lag between consecutive acquisition shots. Your options range from 0 to 10 seconds. Ideally, you should select a zero interval to mitigate the risk of subject motion blur (**A**). On the other hand, using the mechanical shutter can lead to shutter shock that can't be compensated by a tripod or the IBIS/ OIS. This means that using the electronic shutter (ES) is the best way to go—but only when your light source isn't flickering. If you are using a flash, the ES isn't an option at all. You can still use the electronic first curtain shutter (EFCS), though. In any case, make sure that the interval is long enough so your flash has sufficient time to recycle between shots.

After setting and confirming the INTERVAL time, the next FOCUS BKT SETTING screen (**B**) prompts you to manually set the focus bracketing range and asks you to enter corresponding "A" (near) and "B" (far) points. This is performed by turning the manual focus ring of your attached lens. Sadly, this process is not very intuitive: The camera asks you to toggle between the "A" and "B" points with the OK button and to confirm your finished range setting with the BACK button. To facilitate the range setting process, you can use a manual focus assistant like focus peaking, so make sure to enable it in the AF/MF SETTING > MF ASSIST menu before entering the FOCUT BKT SETTING process. You can also use the magnifier tool to zoom in and out.

Having set and confirmed your focus bracketing range, the camera will now display a yellow line below the live view's distance scale that indicates the bracketing distance range (**C**).

Once everything is set up properly, you can just press the shutter button and the camera will automatically record the required number of shots that cover the preset focus distance range based on the current aperture setting.

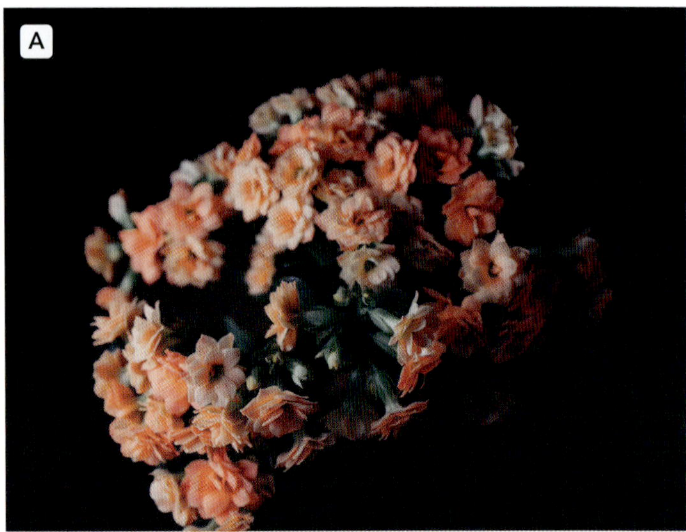

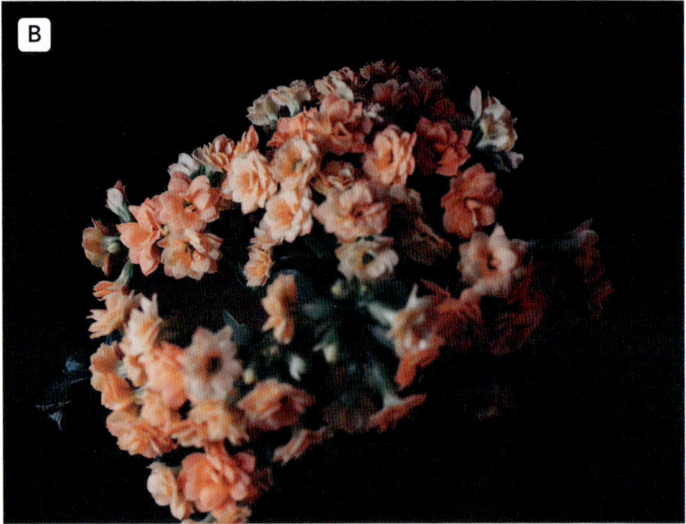

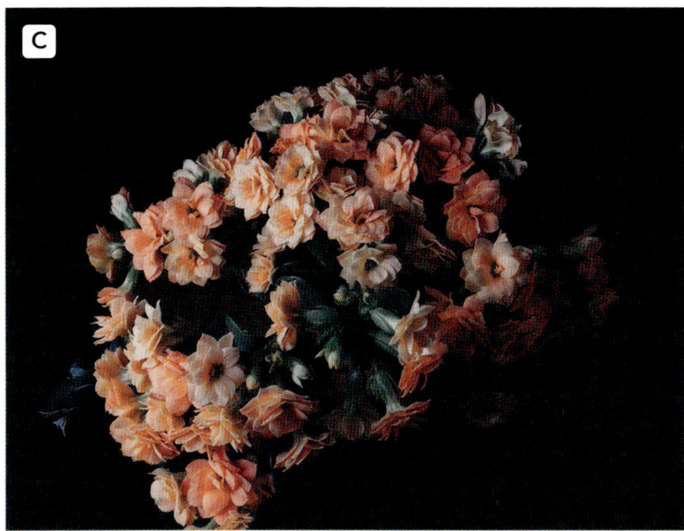

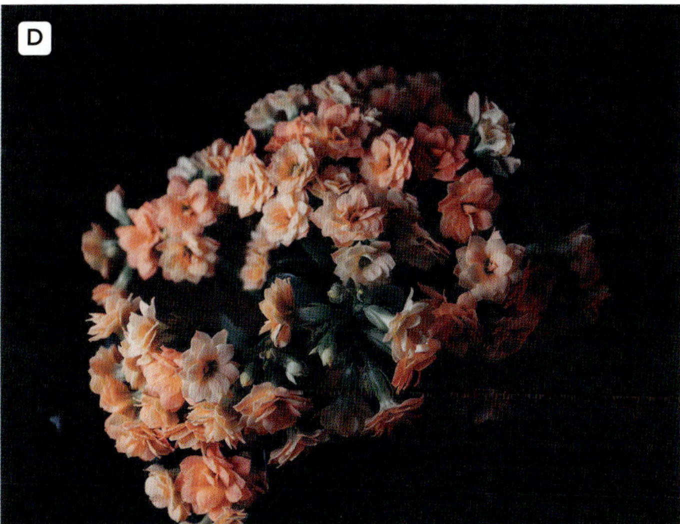

Fig. 118: I used AUTO focus bracketing to record an in-focus image of these artificial flowers. I used an XF30mmF2.8 R LM WR Macro lens at f/6.4, 1/25 sec. and ISO 125. Image **A** shows the near point, image **B** the far point of my focus bracketing series. Image **C** shows the result after merging (stacking) the 27 acquired RAF files with Helicon Focus software and exporting a linear DNG file that I could process in Lightroom with the same RAW development settings that I used with a single shot (**D**) out of the bracketing series.

TIP 93	Limiting the autofocus range

Limiting the autofocus range can speed up the focusing process and avoid misfocused images. The X-T5 offers you two ways to accomplish this:

■ Go to AF/MF SETTING > AF RANGE LIMITER and select a range preset or select/set define a CUSTOM focus range. This is the *camera-based autofocus range limiter*.

■ Use the dedicated focus range limiter switch that is available on some macro and telephoto lenses like the XF80mmF2.8 Macro, the XF200mmF2, or the XF70–300mm zoom. This is the *lens-based autofocus range limiter*.

The camera-based and lens-based AF limits work independently from each other. An active camera-based AF limit is indicated by a yellow line below the focus distance scale in the live view. However, there's no indicator for an active lens-based focus limit, so always check the position of that limiter switch.

Important: *Activating subject detection or face/eye detection overrides (disables) any selected camera-based AF range limit, meaning the camera will use the full AF range. However, face/eye and subject detection do **not** override lens-based focus limitations.*

By limiting the autofocus range, you can make sure that the camera is literally focusing on "where the action" is, ignoring possible distractions.

TIP 94	Focusing on moving subjects (1): the autofocus trick

Consider these "rules:" use AF-S (Single) for stationary subjects; use AF-C (Continuous) for subjects that move toward or away from the camera. However, as usual, there are no rules without exceptions. Meet the so-called "autofocus trick" or "shutter mash" technique. It employs AF-S to focus on moving subjects and has been an option since the early days of the X100 Classic and the X-Pro1. Here's how:

- Set the camera to AF-S and single shot drive mode (S).

- Make sure that Boost mode is switched on and that AF/MF SETTING > RELEASE/FOCUS PRIORITY > AF-S PRIORITY SELECTION is set to FOCUS.

- Use Single Point AF or Zone AF. Select an AF frame or zone position and size that cover the part of the moving subject you want to be in focus.

- Set a suitable exposure and make sure the shutter speed is fast enough to avoid unwanted motion blur. Many action shots require shutter speeds of 1/1000 sec. or faster.

- Follow the moving subject in the viewfinder, making sure the selected AF frame or AF zone always covers the part of the subject that needs to be in focus. Do *not* half-press the shutter button!

- *Fully* press the shutter button in one swift motion when you want to take the shot. The camera will need some time to focus, so make sure the focus frame remains positioned on the moving subject while the camera is focusing. As soon as the camera can lock the focus, it will automatically take the shot.

The AF trick, also known as *shutter mash*, is based on the camera's autofocus priority logic. When you release the shutter, the camera *first* attempts to lock the focus and *then* takes the shot. Since the delay between having locked the focus and releasing the shutter is very short, the moving subject ends up being in focus most of the time. This means the AF trick works best with aperture settings that offer sufficient depth of field, and with subjects that don't move too quickly toward the camera.

A negative aspect of this method is the delay between fully pressing the shutter button and the camera taking the shot. This makes it challenging to hit decisive moments and requires some amount of foresight from the photographer.

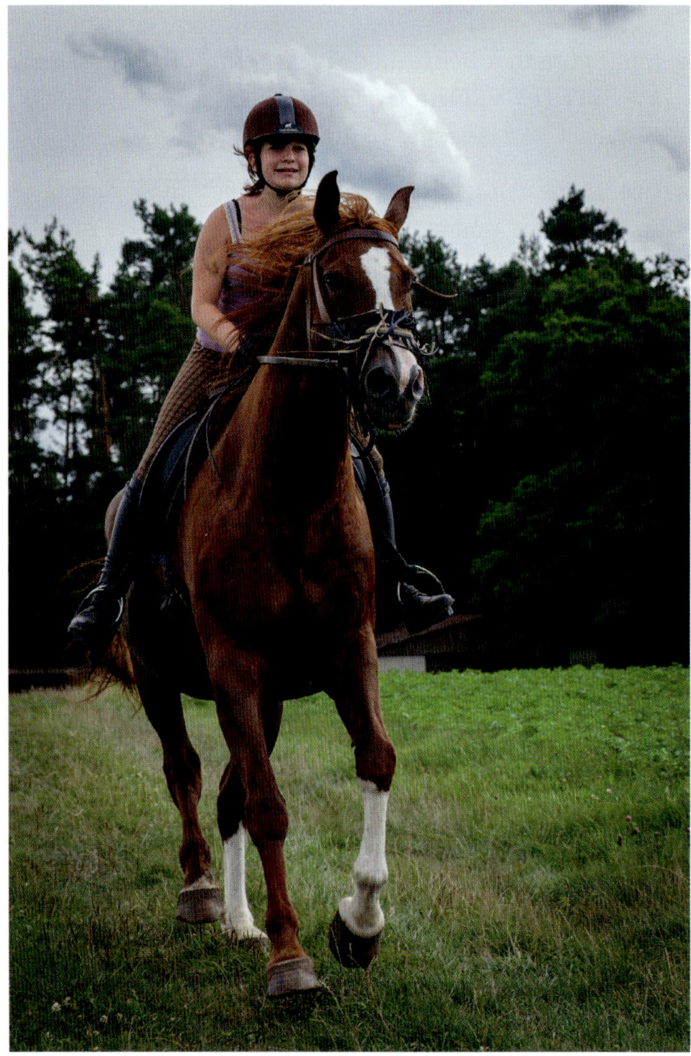

Fig. 119: A running horse captured using the **autofocus trick** or **shutter mash technique**.

The autofocus trick has been around for more than a decade. Initially, it was the *only* way to autofocus on moving subjects with X cameras. Of course, this has changed over the years, and the shutter mash technique has now taken a back seat compared to other methods that involve AF-C, including 3D subject tracking. Mirrorless cameras have come a long way.

However, this method is still useful. Imagine you are shooting portraits, a landscape, or a city view in AF-S mode. Suddenly, you encounter an unexpected moving subject, like a bird, a moving vehicle, or a running person that looks interesting. There's no time to switch autofocus modes. You must take the shot immediately, or the opportunity will be lost. In those scenarios, the autofocus trick can be quite helpful because you don't have to change any settings. Just point the AF-S focus frame or zone at the target and fully press the shutter button, while following the target with the focus frame until the camera takes the shot.

Focusing on moving subjects (2): the focus trap	TIP 95

Setting up a focus trap is about pre-focusing on a location that a moving object will eventually pass through. This method can be useful with sports and other action that runs along a pre-determined course (track, street, trail, etc.).

This is how it works:

- Set the camera to manual focus (MF).

- Pre-focus on the location where you want to capture the moving subject. Select an aperture with sufficient depth of field (DOF) to make sure all relevant parts of the object will be in focus.

- Half-press the shutter button when the moving subject is approaching the location you have in focus. The camera will lock the exposure and set the working aperture (assuming SHUTTER AE is ON).

- Fully press the shutter button as soon as the subject is about to cross the in-focus location.

There's only a very small shutter lag between half-pressing and fully pressing the shutter button. Depending on how fast the subject is moving, it may be necessary to fully press the shutter button a split second before it is in the optimal position.

Alternatively, you can set the camera to high-speed burst mode, increasing the chance that one or two frames will successfully capture your fast-moving subject as it crosses your focus trap.

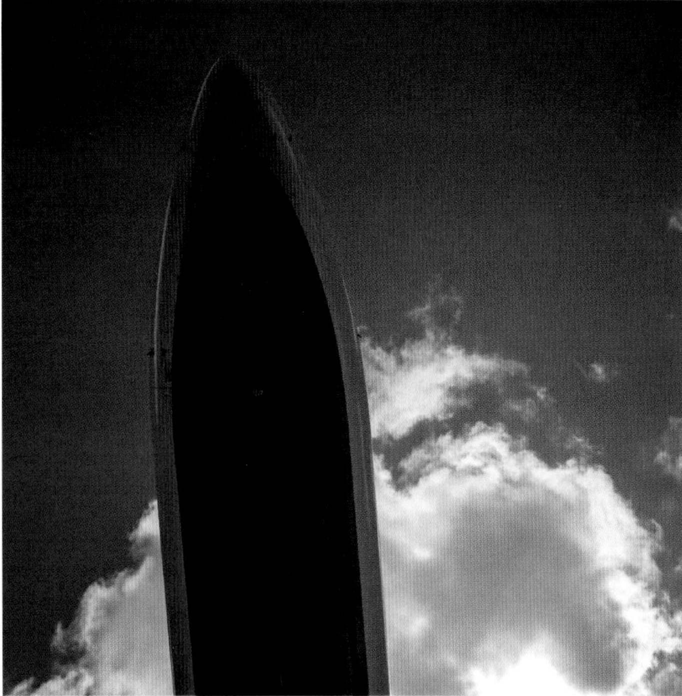

Fig. 120: Focus trap: To capture this landing Airbus A330 as it was flying over me at only a few meters, timing was essential. Instead of using autofocus, I pre-focused the 18 mm lens with sufficient depth of field and waited for the right moment with my camera primed and the shutter half-pressed. At the decisive moment, I fully-pressed the shutter button.

You can also trap moving subjects in a preset focus zone. Stop down your lens enough to create a sufficiently large DOF zone, and then wait until a subject enters the zone. This method is often used by street photographers with wide-angle lenses (typically 16–23 mm) who can't afford to miss the decisive moment.

A variant of this method is panning [72] the camera with a slow shutter speed and a small aperture (plenty of DOF). The slow shutter speed makes sure that the background is blurred while the subject remains in focus.

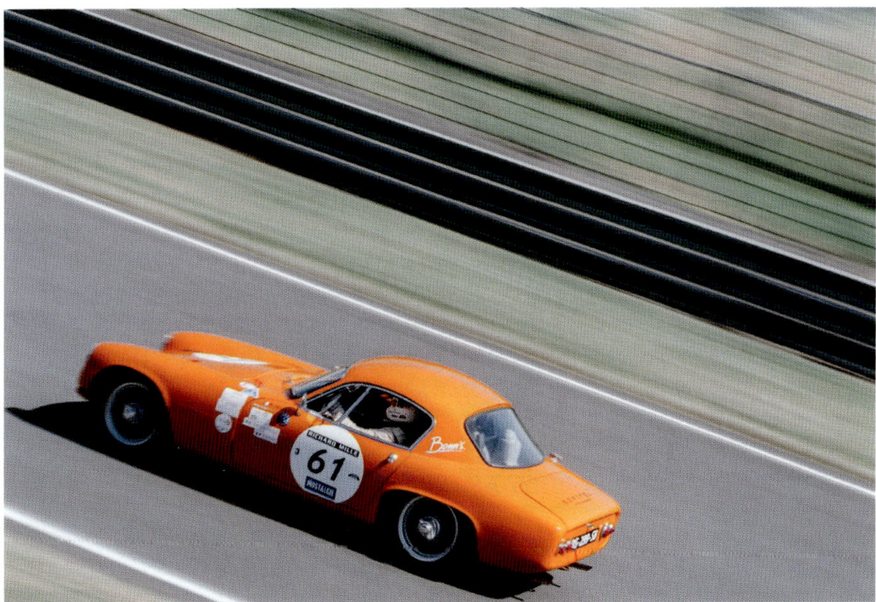

Fig. 121: Panning the camera at 1/60 s in synch with a racecar. The slow shutter speed resulted in f/18 and there was more than sufficient DOF using a focal length of 50 mm.

Focus traps work with all lenses, including mechanically adapted manual focus lenses.

TIP 96 | Focusing on moving subjects (3): Autofocus tracking using Single Point AF, Zone AF, or Tracking AF

Predictive PDAF (phase detection autofocus) allows you to track moving subjects in three-dimensional space. Since the camera can calculate the movement of the subject, it can automatically pre-focus on the predicted distance and compensate for any inherent shutter lag.

The X-T5 features predictive PDAF that covers the entire sensor area, so you don't have to restrict AF frames or zones—the entire sensor is the PDAF area!

Let's start with the **Single Point AF** and **Zone AF** modes:

- Set the focus to AF-C and make sure Boost mode is set.

- Set the camera to burst mode. I recommend a CL setting of 7 fps that displays a real-time live view image between shots. I also recommend using the EFCS to minimize the blackout time in the live view.

- Select a suitable autofocus frame or zone size. Since PDAF covers the entire sensor area of the X-T5, there are no restrictions regarding size and position of the AF frame or zone.

- Position the AF frame or AF zone to directly cover the subject or the part of the subject you want in focus. Half-press the shutter button, and the camera will start tracking the subject covered by the AF frame or AF zone.

- Keep the shutter button half-pressed as you follow the moving subject with the selected AF frame or AF zone.

- Fully press the shutter when you want to start taking the series of exposures. The actual burst speed (frame rate) depends on how well the camera can track the subject. As the camera is taking pictures, keep the selected AF frame or AF zone on the part of your image that is supposed to be in focus. This may be challenging at first, so practice is important.

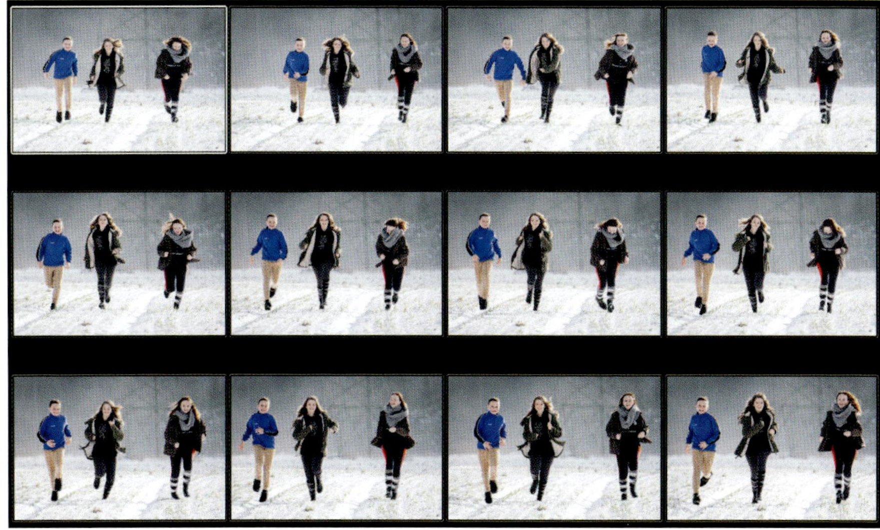

Fig. 122: AF tracking with AF-C and burst mode: The predictive autofocus was tracking one of the kids with the selected AF zone while they were running toward the camera. To make this kind of shot work, it's vital to follow the subject with the active AF frame or AF zone, making sure it's always covering the part of the subject that is supposed to be in focus.

In principle, AF-C tracking also works in single shot mode (DRIVE mode **S**—not to be confused with the focus mode **S**). In this case, the camera takes a single frame when the shutter button is fully pressed and then ends the tracking.

As an alternative to tracking moving subjects using Single Point and Zone AF, you can use **Wide/Tracking AF** mode in concert with AF-C. This mode enables real 3D tracking; meaning the camera isn't merely tracking a subject's changing distance from the camera (z-axis), but it also tracks its left/right (x-axis) und up/down (y-axis) movements inside the image frame.

Here's how it works:

■ Set the focus mode to AF-C and make sure that Boost mode is active.

- Set the camera to **Wide/Tracking AF** and select a slow burst mode (CL).

- Select one of the available tracking AF points. The point you select will serve as a starting point for your tracking action, so position it in a way that suits your composition.

- To identify your target, make sure the selected AF point covers the object you want to track and then half-press the shutter button. While you keep the shutter button half-pressed, the camera will use pattern recognition to automatically follow the object as it moves around in the frame (or as you move the camera).

- Fully press the shutter button and keep it pressed to take pictures at the selected burst rate. The camera will continue exposing images until you release the shutter button.

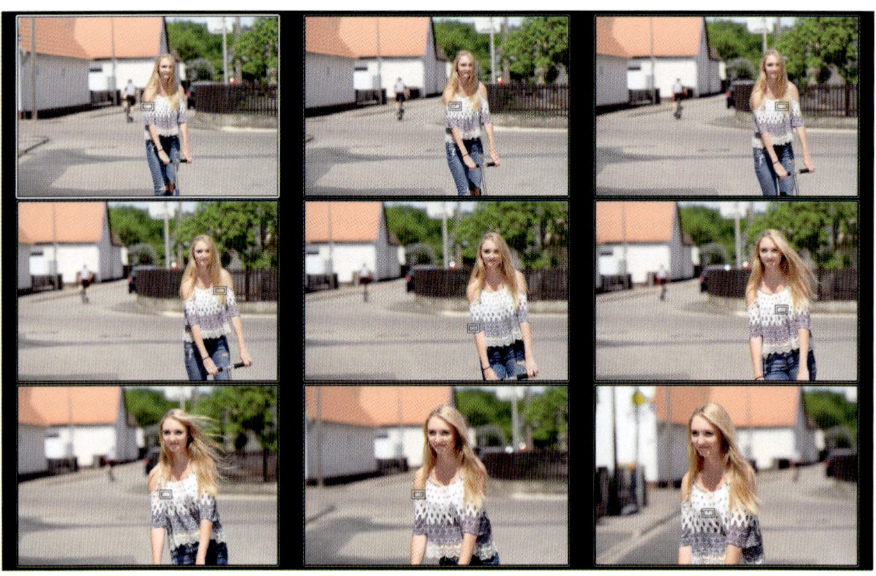

Fig. 123: AF-C in concert with **WIDE/TRACKING** and burst mode can track a subject in 3-dimensional space. To accomplish this, the camera is using pattern recognition to follow the designated subject as it moves.

Performance-wise, AF-C tracking mode has long been a weakness with many X cameras. This has changed for the better with the X-T5. The same is true for AF-C tracking with face detection and subject detection. The X-T5 offers much-improved AF-C tracking in concert with these modes.

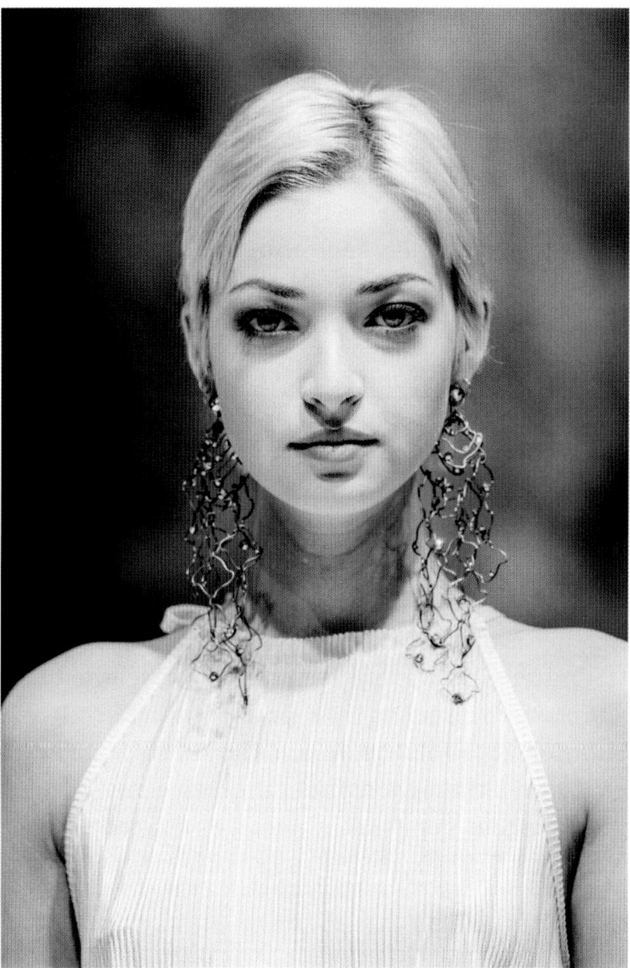

Fig. 124: AF-C in concert with face detection has traditionally been a weakness of older X-series cameras. However, modern bodies like the X-T3, X-T4, and X-T5 offer decent face- and eye-detection tracking. This catwalk demonstration was shot wide open with the XF200mmF2 R LM OIS WR telephoto lens.

TIP 97 Tracking-AF vs. face/eye and subject detection tracking

Combining Wide/Tracking-AF mode with AF-C will get you Tracking-AF. Combining face/eye detection AF or subject detection AF with AF-C will get you something very similar. So, what are the differences?

- Tracking-AF requires *you* to identify the target and show it to the camera by pointing the focus frame at it. When you half-press the shutter button, the camera will "learn" the color/contrast pattern beneath the focus frame, memorize it, and focus on it. As long as you keep the shutter button half or fully depressed, the focus frame follows that pattern around the entire image area, providing the autofocus system continuously with a target to focus on.

- Face/eye detection and subject detection combined with AF-C basically does the same as regular Tracking-AF. The main difference is that the camera identifies suitable targets (faces, animals, cars, etc.) that are in the vicinity of the focus frame. By changing the size and position of the underlying focus frame or focus zone, you can direct the system to a different target, or you can select one of multiple available targets. When you half-press the shutter button, the camera memorizes the selected target and starts focusing on it. As long as you keep the shutter button half or fully depressed, the selected subject will be followed throughout the entire image area, providing the autofocus system continuously with coordinates to focus on.

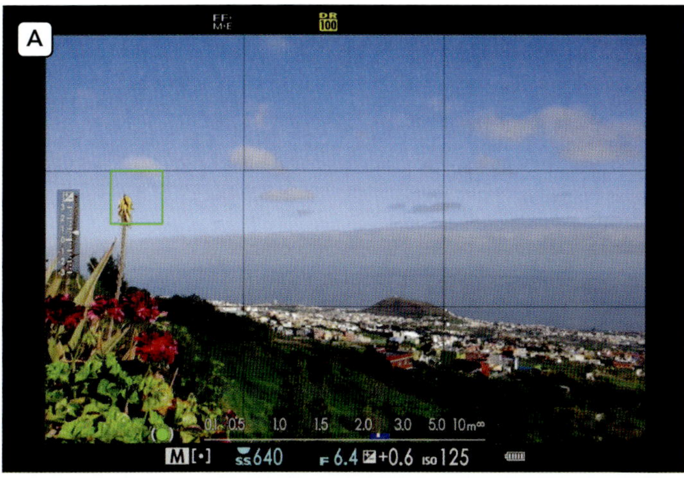

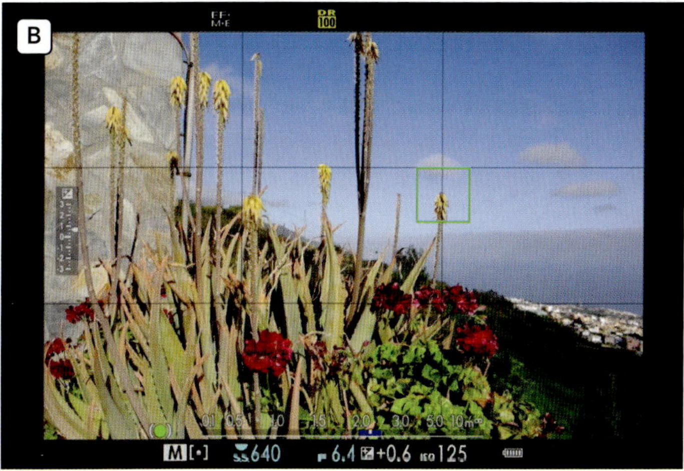

Fig. 125: In Tracking-AF, you are identifying the target by pointing the focus frame at it and half-pressing the shutter button (**A**). When the target moves around the frame (or when you move the camera and reframe the target, like in this example), Tracking-AF will stay on the target and focus on it for as long as you keep the shutter button half-depressed (**B**).

Due to the similarity between these modes, it may sometimes be a good idea to select Tracking-AF as your underlying fallback AF mode and select face/eye detection or subject detection on top of it. This way, the camera will use face/eye tracking or subject tracking for suitable targets but can automatically fall back to regular Tracking-AF if a subject target has been (temporarily) lost. In that case, Tracking-AF will take over and continue tracking the target starting right at the position where face/eye detection or subject detection have lost theirs.

| TIP 98 | Using AF-C custom settings |

The X-T5 features three PDAF parameters that allow you to customize the AF-C's behavior for a specific task or application:

- **Tracking Sensitivity** (TS) specifies whether the camera should switch its focus to a different subject or retain its current focus to wait for the subject to reappear. This control is useful when the subject you are focusing on disappears behind an obstacle or goes out of the frame, or when you aim at a new target with a different distance. Selecting 0 (zero) makes the camera switch its focus immediately to the new distance, while choosing 1–4 progressively extends the time it will retain the "old" focus distance. Technically speaking, tracking sensitivity 0 will not predict an autofocus target's position when it's temporarily lost or obscured by something else. Tracking sensitivity settings of 1, 2, 3, and 4 will predict a lost or obscured target's position for another approximately 0.4 seconds, 0.7 seconds, 1.0 second, and 1.3 seconds, respectively, before the AF-C locks onto the new target distance.

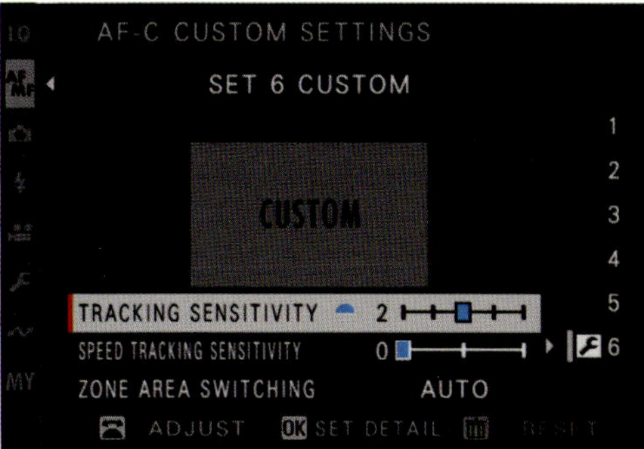

Fig. 126: By selecting a higher **TS** setting, the camera will wait a moment or two before it switches the continuous autofocus to a new target distance. The default setting is 2, which means the camera will give you about 0.7 seconds to re-aim the focus frame or zone back on your subject after you have lost sight of it. Higher TS settings are useful in situations where you want to track a specific subject with as little interference as possible.

- **Speed Tracking Sensitivity** (STS) controls the camera's tracking characteristics based on changes to the subject's speed. Selecting 0 (constant speed), the camera expects a steady movement when it predicts the subject's distance. Select 1 or 2, and the camera takes speed changes more and more into account when it's predicting subject movement, making it suitable for suddenly accelerating or decelerating targets, like race cars or a flower in the wind.

- **Zone Area Switching** (ZAS) is available only in Zone-AF mode and specifies which part of the focusing zone should be given focusing priority. CENTER maintains focus on the center of the zone. FRONT switches the focus to the closest subject (or the closest part of a subject) anywhere inside the zone area, which (in concert with a TS setting of 0) is great for immediately capturing new targets that suddenly move into a zone. AUTO tracks the subject you first focused on while it remains inside the zone area.

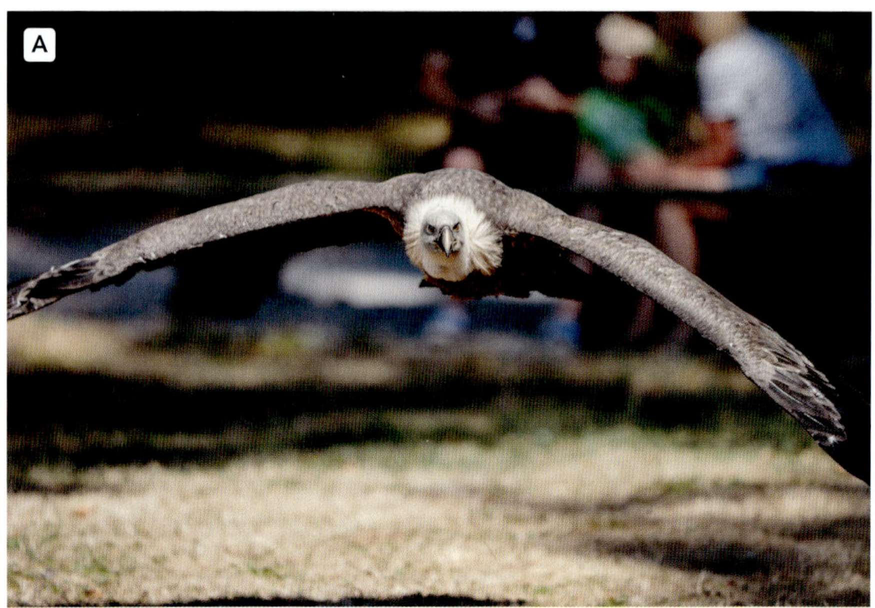

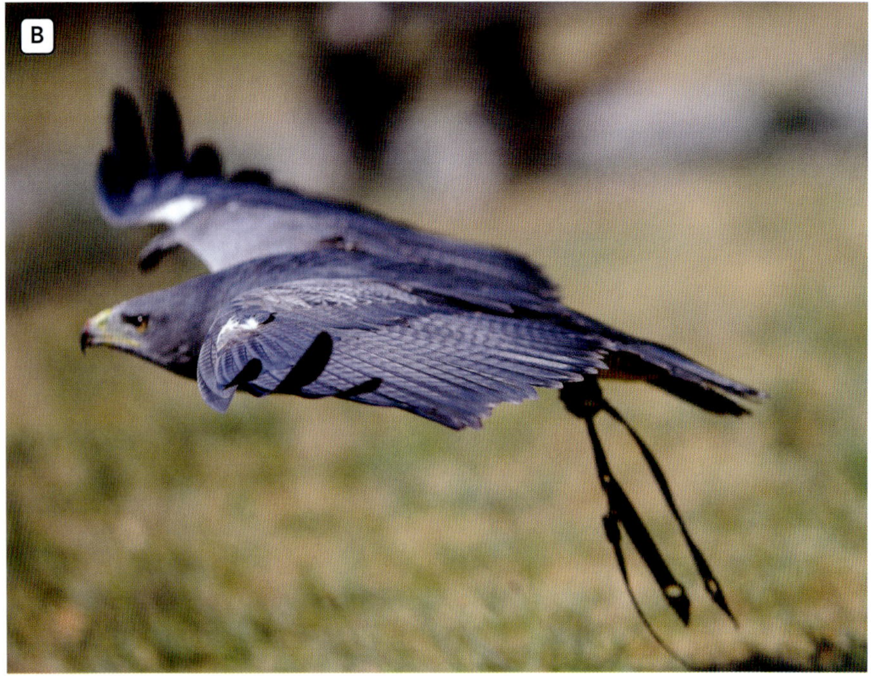

Fig. 127: By selecting FRONT as your **ZAS** setting, you can force the camera to focus on whatever part of the image inside your selected AF zone happens to be closest to the camera. In the case of the vulture that was flying toward the camera (**A**), a ZAS FRONT setting allowed me to focus on the bird's head and beak instead of the more prominent wings. However, using the same settings in a fly-by situation (**B**) only shifted the focus toward the left wing, which was closest to the camera within the 3 × 3 zone I had selected.

The X-T5 offers several presets that cover typical AF-C shooting scenarios. Select AF/MF SETTING > AF-C CUSTOM SETTINGS, and then pick one of the following available parameter sets:

- SET 1: MULTI PURPOSE is the default setting and is our general AF-C setting. It's a great choice for situations where you don't have a clear understanding of how a specific custom setting could improve the AF-C performance. Its parameter settings are TS 2, STS 0, and ZAS AUTO.

- SET 2: IGNORE OBSTACLES & CONTINUE TO TRACK SUBJECT keeps the focus on a subject even when it has temporarily left the frame or has been obscured by obstacles. This can be useful for following a specific target with the camera and ensuring that the target isn't dropped when it's temporarily obscured by people, trees, or other obstacles that block the line of sight to your target. Its parameter settings are TS 3, STS 0, and ZAS CENTER.

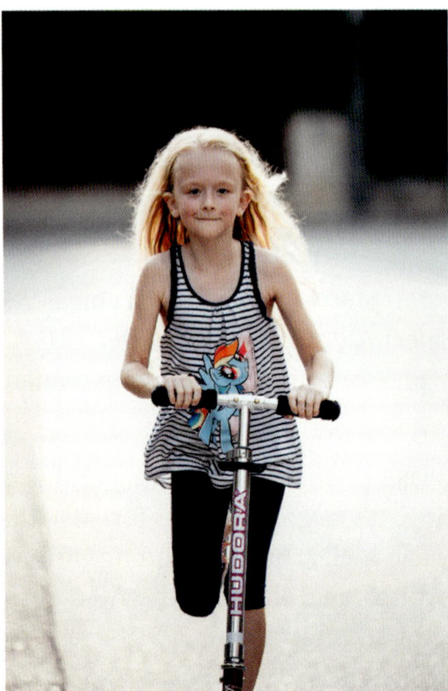

Fig. 128:
Set 2 is a good choice when you want to track a specific, steadily moving subject without interference, like this girl riding a scooter through the shot.

- SET 3: FOR ACCELERATING/DECELERATING SUBJECT is your typical racetrack mode. It takes changing relative speeds of subjects moving toward the camera into account. Whenever you have targets that rapidly accelerate or decelerate, this mode can be useful, especially in concert with XF lenses featuring high-speed linear autofocus motors. Its parameter settings are TS 2, STS 2, and ZAS AUTO.

- SET 4: FOR SUDDENLY APPEARING SUBJECT allows the camera to instantly focus on a subject that enters the focusing area, with priority given to any object (or any part of it) that is closest to the camera. It is ideal for subjects that suddenly appear in the focusing frame. Its parameter settings are TS 0, STS 1, and ZAS FRONT.

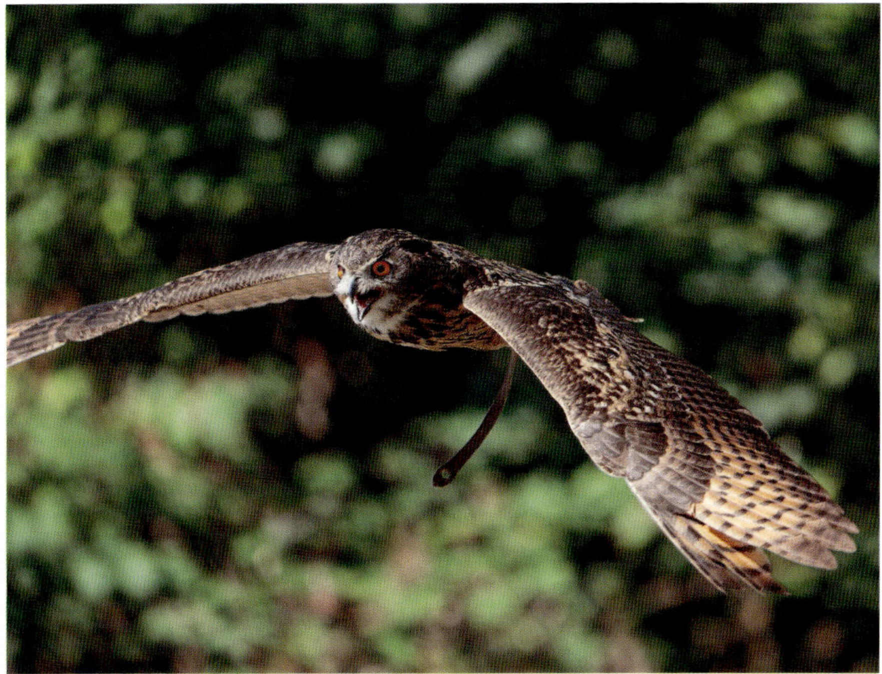

Fig. 129: Set 4 makes sure that the AF-C immediately focuses on what's closest to the camera (as long as it's located anywhere inside the selected AF zone).

- SET 5: FOR ERRATICALY MOVING & ACCEL./DECEL. SUBJECT is suitable for subjects that are moving at varying speeds in different directions, coming in and out of the focusing area. It is optimized for shooting field sports like soccer or tennis. Of course, this also applies to playing kids or dogs. Its parameter settings are TS 3, STS 2, and ZAS AUTO.

- SET 6: CUSTOM stores your own setting for the three AF-C subject-tracking parameters: TRACKING SENSITIVITY (TS), SPEED TRACKING SENSITIVITY (STS), and ZONE AREA SWITCHING (ZAS). Use this preset to manually create optimized settings for the specific movement characteristics of your subject.

TIP 99 | Focus Priority vs. Release Priority

By selecting focus priority for AF-S and AF-C you can reduce the number of out-of-focus pictures on your memory card. Here is how to set it up:

- Set AF/MF SETTING > RELEASE/FOCUS PRIORITY > AF-S PRIORITY SELECTION > FOCUS to prevent the camera from taking the shot before it has finished focusing.

- Set AF/MF SETTING > RELEASE/FOCUS PRIORITY > AF-C PRIORITY SELECTION > FOCUS to make sure the camera takes pictures in AF-C mode (particularly in concert with burst mode) only when the autofocus can lock onto something. By default, the camera is set to release priority, following the motto, "better a misfocused shot than no image at all." Since I am no fan of misfocused shots, my cameras are set to focus priority for both AF-S and AF-C.

Important: When AF+MF is active in AF-S mode, the camera will always use AF-S Release Priority, even if the menu setting says Focus Priority. This can lead to misfocused images because the camera can now take pictures before the autofocus has finished its job.

TIP 100 | Using Pre-Shot ES

Pre-Shot ES is a "time machine" that allows you to capture moments you just missed. It only works in concert with the electronic shutter (ES) and high-speed burst mode (CH). Pre-Shot ES takes advantage of the X-T5's electronic shutter and new processor, which allow for faster burst mode settings (10, 13, or 20 frames per second) that work with a 1.29x crop. You can also use 8.9 or 13 fps without a crop.

Pre-Shot ES compensates for the reaction time between recognizing a sudden event and actually pressing the shutter release button. With extremely quick subjects, that delay can cause you to miss your ideal moments.

In Pre-Shot ES mode, the X-T5 starts recording and buffering images as you half-press and hold the shutter release button. As long as you keep your finger pressed halfway down, the camera keeps recording images into its buffer. It will continue to refresh the buffered content (FIFO: first in, first out) so that you always have several frames stored in the buffer.

When a sudden event happens and you fully press the shutter to capture it, the camera will not only take new images from that moment forward, it will also write the previously buffered images onto the memory card. It will continue to capture and write new images to the card while you hold the shutter release all the way down.

In effect, Pre-Shot ES allows you to go back in time and capture the moment or moments right *before* you fully pressed the shutter release button. Normally, those moments would be lost due to the inevitable reaction time of the photographer and camera. You can activate Pre-Shot ES with SHOOTING SETTING > PRE-SHOT ES > ON, but only when the camera is set to ES-only and CH high-speed burst shooting.

Since Pre-Shot ES only works in concert with the electronic shutter, it is subject to rolling shutter artifacts such as object distortion (when you are panning the camera or with subjects that move very fast) and an uneven exposure (banding) under pulsing artificial light. This rolling shutter effect may be more pronounced if you shoot without the 1.29x crop.

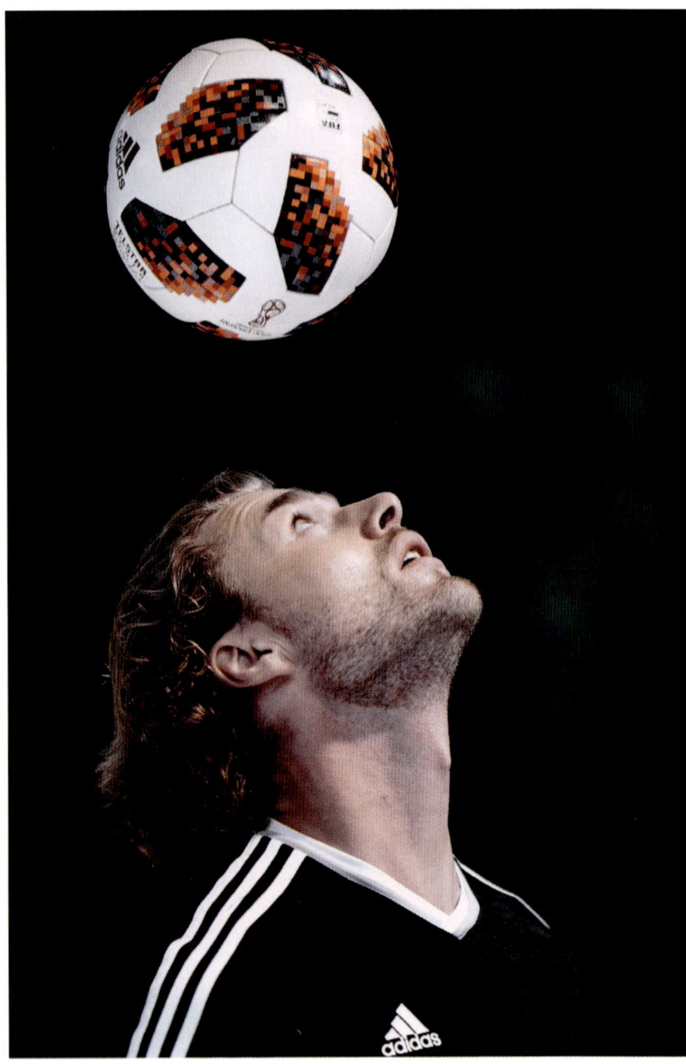

Fig. 130: Missing a decisive or unexpected moment? **Pre-Shot ES** allows you to go back in time and capture it.

TIP 101	Using Sports Finder Mode

Sports Finder Mode adds a 1.29x crop to your resulting image. The crop is indicated through a bright white frame in the live view. Sports Finder Mode only works in concert with the mechanical shutter (MS) or electronic first curtain shutter (EFCS). It can help you reduce your reaction time in situations with moving objects that suddenly appear in the live view, because it allows you to see beyond the final image frame. This is like the bright frame in the optical viewfinders of the X100 or X-Pro series.

In Sports Finder Mode, the camera's AF tracking extends beyond the indicated bright frame, making it possible to track objects that are outside the active image area. This is also why I am covering this feature here in the focus section of this book and not in the section about the viewfinder.

You can activate Sports Finder Mode with SHOOTING SETTING > SPORTS FINDER MODE > ON.

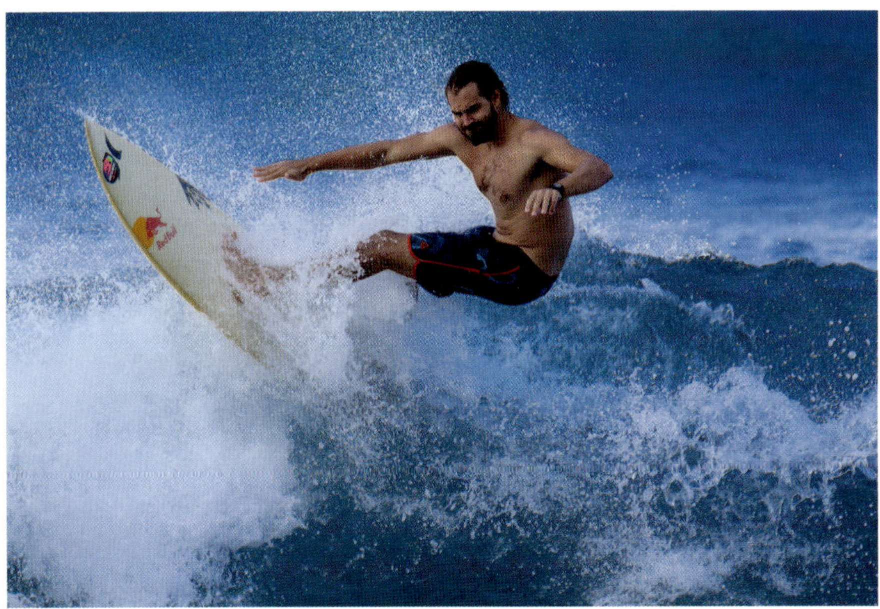

Fig. 131: Sports Finder Mode adds a 1.29x crop to the image. The downside is a decrease in resolution. Since the effect is the same as cropping an image in post-processing, the actual benefit of Sports Finder Mode is its ability to let you see beyond the final (cropped) image borders and to allow the autofocus to track subjects beyond these borders. Please note that unlike using the digital teleconverter or a non-standard image format (like 1:1), Sports Finder Mode also crops the RAW data.

2.5 WHITE BALANCE, JPEG PARAMETERS, AND RAW CONVERSION

A great feature of all X-series cameras is their ability to set white balance [73] and JPEG parameters before *and* after you take a shot, thanks to the built-in RAW converter. This gives you full control over the JPEGs that are generated in your camera.

It's not necessary to anticipate and set the perfect settings for each shot in advance because you can always generate different JPEG, HEIF, or TIFF versions of a shot with the internal RAW converter. For example, you could create a version with bold Velvia colors, or a black-and-white version with strong contrast and minimal noise reduction. As long as you have access to the RAW file, you can change all JPEG parameters after the fact and you can use the RAW file to create as many different-looking JPEGs, HEIFs, or TIFFs as you want.

Using the built-in RAW converter in the playback menu is quite easy because it offers the same functions that are available in shooting mode.

IMAGE QUALITY SETTING menu	RAW CONVERSION menu
(Exposure Comp. Dial)	PUSH/PULL PROCESSING
IMAGE SIZE	IMAGE SIZE
IMAGE QUALITY	IMAGE QUALITY
SELECT JPEG/HEIF	FILE TYPE
DYNAMIC RANGE	DYNAMIC RANGE
D RANGE PRIORITY	D RANGE PRIORITY
FILM SIMULATION	FILM SIMULATION
WHITE BALANCE	WHITE BALANCE
(incl. WB SHIFT)	WB SHIFT
COLOR	COLOR
SHARPNESS	SHARPNESS
TONE CURVE (HIGHLIGHTS)	TONE CURVE (HIGHLIGHTS) / HIGHLIGHT TONE
TONE CURVE (SHADOWS)	TONE CURVE (SHADOWS) / SHADOW TONE
HIGH ISO NR	HIGH ISO NR
GRAIN EFFECT	GRAIN EFFECT
MONOCHROMATIC COLOR	MONOCHROMATIC COLOR
COLOR CHROME EFFECT	COLOR CHROME EFFECT
COLOR CHROME FX BLUE	COLOR CHROME FX BLUE
SMOOTH SKIN EFFECT	SMOOTH SKIN EFFECT
CLARITY	CLARITY
LENS MODULATION OPTIMIZER	LENS MODULATION OPTIMIZER
COLOR SPACE	COLOR SPACE

Notable differences between shooting mode and after-the-fact RAW conversion in playback mode affect only a few items in this list:

- **Exposure corrections** made *before* you take a picture can affect aperture, shutter speed, and ISO. **Push/pull processing** applied *after* you have taken a picture affects only the ISO amplification. Effectively changing the ISO via push/pull processing also doesn't change the nominal ISO value in the EXIF data [74] of the JPEGs. Instead, Push/Pull processing in the internal RAW converter has the same effect as moving the exposure slider in external RAW conversion software, such as Lightroom, Silkypix, or Capture One.

- *Before* you take an image, you can select from four **dynamic range** options: AUTO, DR100%, DR200%, and

DR400%. DR200% exposes the RAW file one ISO stop darker than indicated; DR400% exposes it two ISO stops darker. DR-Auto automatically selects either DR100% or DR200%. *After* you have taken an image, you can still select different DR settings in the internal RAW converter. However, you can only *reduce* the DR after the fact; you cannot increase it. If you are working on a RAW file that was recorded with DR400%, you can reprocess it to create JPEGs with DR400%, DR200%, or DR100%. A DR200% RAW file can be reprocessed with DR200% or DR100%, but not DR400%. And a DR100% RAW file can only be reprocessed with DR100%. The same restrictions apply to the D RANGE PRIORITY settings STRONG, WEAK, and OFF.

Additionally, the RAW conversion menu offers options to change the HDR mode and the digital teleconverter setting. Again, you can only *downgrade* these settings after the fact. For example, if you recorded an image in HDR 800%+, the RAW conversion menu lets you downgrade this setting to HDR 800%, HDR 400%, or HDR 200%. If you shot it in HDR 400%, you can only downgrade to HDR 200%.

In a similar fashion, if you shot with the digital teleconverter, you can turn it off after-the-fact in the RAW conversion menu. However, you cannot *add* the digital teleconverter later.

The correct **white balance** ensures that neutral (white or gray) areas of an image appear without color tints, regardless of the light conditions. At the same time, the results are usually not supposed to look clinically neutral. Your X-T5 masters this task quite well, so you can rely on the Auto white balance setting to get it right most of the time.

However, "most of the time" is not "all the time." There are instances when the white balance is off, or when you *want* it to be off. For example, you may want to emphasize a sunset with a warmer white balance. In such cases, it makes perfect sense to manually set the white balance in advance or after the fact.

The X-T5 offers a variety of options to manually set the white balance, as follows:

- Several white balance presets for typical situations, such as sunny weather (Fine), cloudy skies (Shade), and tungsten light (Incandescent).

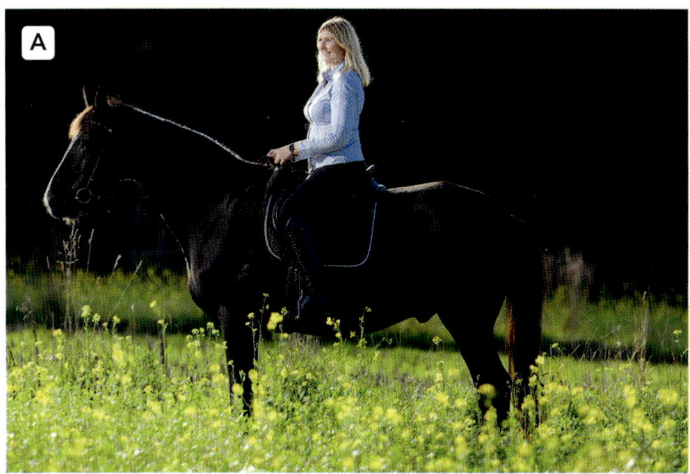

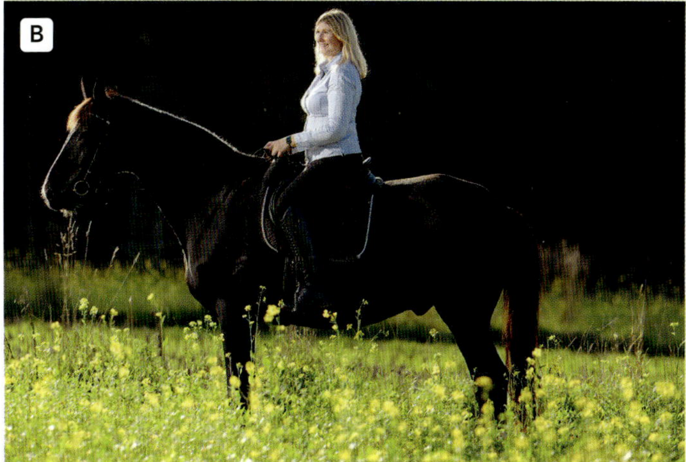

Fig. 132: AUTO white balance isn't always right, especially when ambient light is mixed with non-TTL flash light. However, you can always adjust white balance later with the built-in, or an external, RAW converter. In this case of two straight-out-of-camera JPEGs, a simple **white balance preset** change in the camera from AUTO (**A**) to SHADE (**B**) did the job and created a warmer look. All other settings remained the same.

- A Kelvin option to manually set the color temperature.

- Custom white balance that meters a white or neutral surface (like a white wall) under the current light conditions. This way, the camera can adjust the white balance to make the surface appear neutral. The X-T5 features three independent slots for your custom WB settings.

- You can also bias the camera's AUTO white balance to prioritize either the mood of a scene (AUTO AMBIENCE PRIORITY) or to achieve a more neutral result (AUTO WHITE PRIORITY).

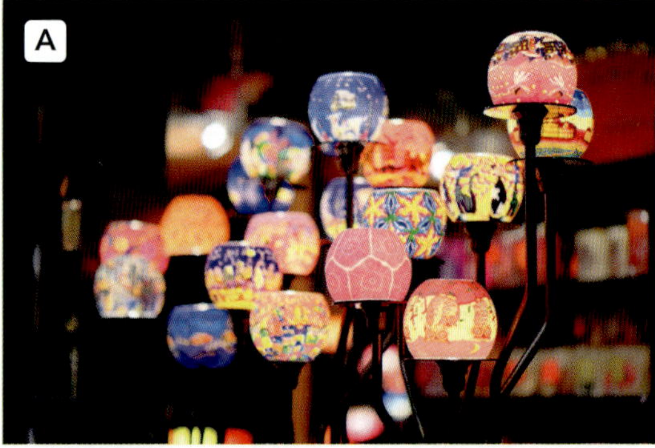

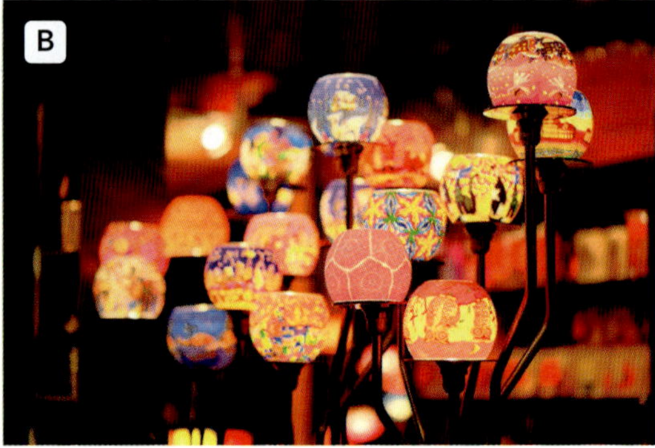

Fig. 133: In the X-T5, AUTO white balance encompasses three menu options: AUTO WHITE PRIORITY, the regular AUTO mode, and AUTO AMBIENCE PRIORITY. This example with straight-out-of-camera Velvia JPEGs shows the difference between AUTO WHITE PRIORITY (**A**) and AUTO AMBIENCE PRIORITY (**B**) for a moody night shot of lights at a Christmas market.

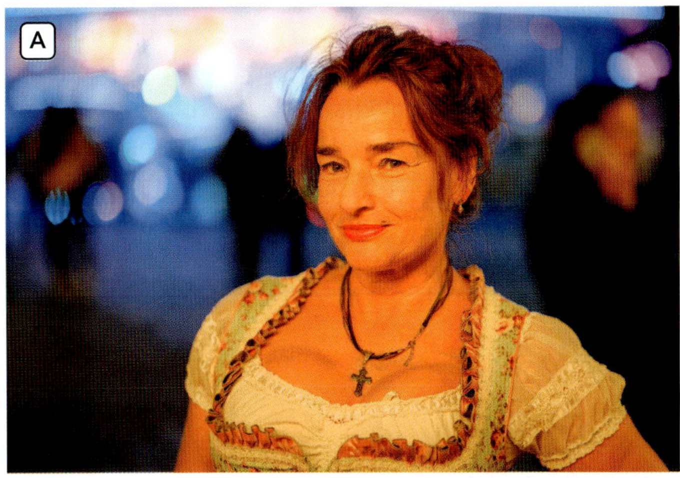

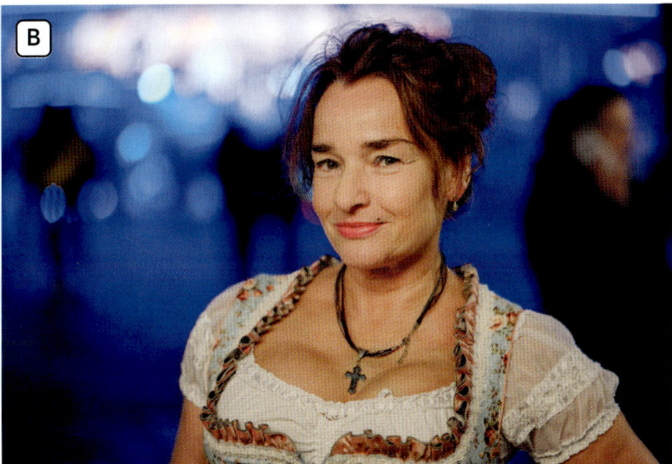

Fig. 134: Two versions of the same shot processed with **different white balance settings**. Image **A** shows the WB Auto setting; image **B** shows the same shot after a manual white balance adjustment in Lightroom. While white balance can also be adjusted with the camera's built-in RAW converter, extensive changes like this one are easier to accomplish with external RAW conversion software.

TIP 102   Custom white balance: a little effort can go a long way.

This useful function is only available *before* you take a shot, because you are metering the white balance of the actual scene. Custom white balance allows you to calibrate the camera's white balance toward a part of your scene you want to appear neutral in the final image.

Here we go:

- Select IMAGE QUALITY SETTING > WHITE BALANCE > CUSTOM. The X-T5 allows you to set and save three different custom white balance settings at the same time (CUSTOM 1–3).

- Point the camera toward a surface you want to use as a neutral reference—for example a white wall or a gray card [75]. Make sure the surface is large enough to be fully covered by the white balance metering frame in the viewfinder. Move closer to your subject or zoom in if you need to.

- Fully press the shutter button to meter and set the new custom white balance. The live view will change accordingly and will simulate the adjusted color temperature. If you are happy with the result, confirm it by pressing the OK button.

You can use the same procedure with a firing flash unit. In this case, the custom white balance will meter the mix of light from the flash with the ambient light that hits your neutral reference surface.

Don't worry! You are under no obligation to use the custom white balance later during RAW conversion. It's simply one of many options, and you can always adjust it later as you please. For example, you can use the built-in RAW converter with a manual KELVIN setting or select one of the white balance presets (FINE, SHADE, FLUORESCENT LIGHT

1–3, INCANDESCENT, and UNDERWATER). You can even apply AUTO white balance anytime later because the camera will always save its automatic white balance reading for later use by the internal RAW converter. This includes the AUTO white balance options for AMBIENCE PRIORITY and WHITE PRIORITY.

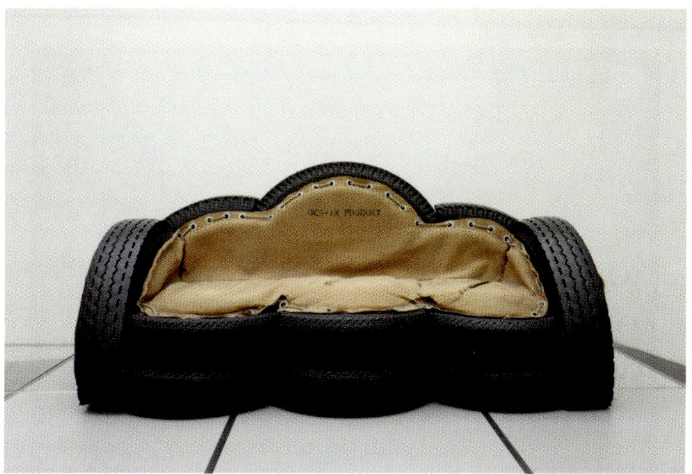

Fig. 135: A **custom white balance** setting was used to take this shot. The wall behind the sofa served as a neutral reference.

Changing color tints with WB SHIFT	TIP 103

WB SHIFT lets you correct (or introduce) a color tint in any shot. You can adjust the color tint as an addition to any white balance setting—either before you take a shot, or in the built-in RAW converter.

You can individually set a *different* white balance shift for each of the camera's white balance options (Auto, Kelvin, WB presets, and Custom white balance settings). You can do this by adjusting the setting between green and red on the X-axis and between yellow and blue on the Y-axis of the display that automatically appears when you select one of the white balance options.

I recommend a neutral setting here to avoid confusion. As mentioned before, there's a different white balance shift setting for each of the white balance options, meaning the camera can store up to a dozen white balance shift settings at once. This makes it too easy to forget a previously set correction, which is why I recommend introducing white balance shift only during RAW conversion.

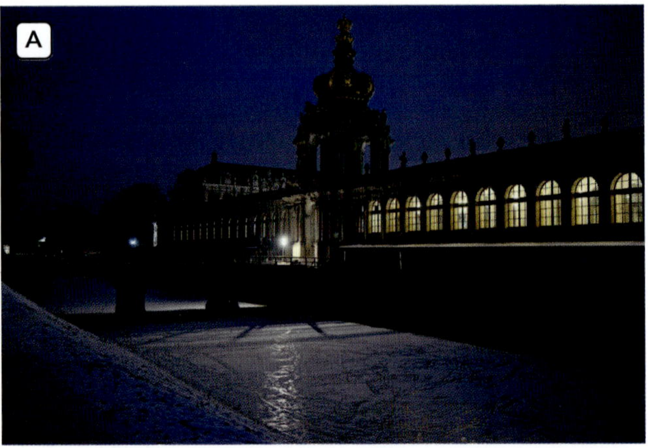

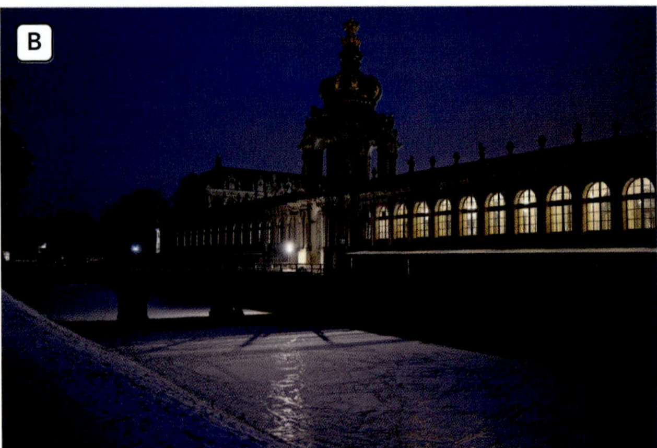

Fig. 136: WB SHIFT in action: Image **A** shows a straight-out-of-camera image (SOOC JPEG) with the INCANDESCENT white balance settings. Image **B** is the same shot, again straight out of camera and with INCANDESCENT white balance, but with an additional WB SHIFT of BLUE +3 and RED +4.

Important: *When you process a RAW file externally with Lightroom or similar software, any WB Shift settings that were active when you took the image will usually be disregarded. However, Capture One Pro is an exception to this rule and honors WB Shift settings automatically.*

White balance and monochrome images	TIP 104

You may think white balance adjustments don't affect black-and-white images because monochrome shots only consist of neutral shades of gray. In reality, your white balance settings still affect the *underlying* color information that your monochrome conversion is based on.

Black-and-white photography is color photography with an additional dimension of difficulty. This added dimension is determining how specific grayscale levels are assigned to specific colors. Since your white balance settings affect the colors of the underlying shot, they also affect the grayscale tones of the color-to-monochrome conversion.

Black-and-white images can be created either in-camera (with the MONOCHROME and ACROS film simulations) or externally with RAW conversion software such as Lightroom, Capture One, or Silkypix. When you set your X-T5 to ACROS or MONOCHROME, it is still recoding RAW *color* images, which are then converted into black-and-white JPEGs, HEIFs, or TIFFs.

Knowing this, you can manipulate the look of your black-and-white conversions by changing the white balance during RAW conversion—either in-camera or externally in your post-processing software. In-camera with the built-in RAW converter, you can use one of the white balance presets, or you can select a manual Kelvin setting between 2500K and 10000K.

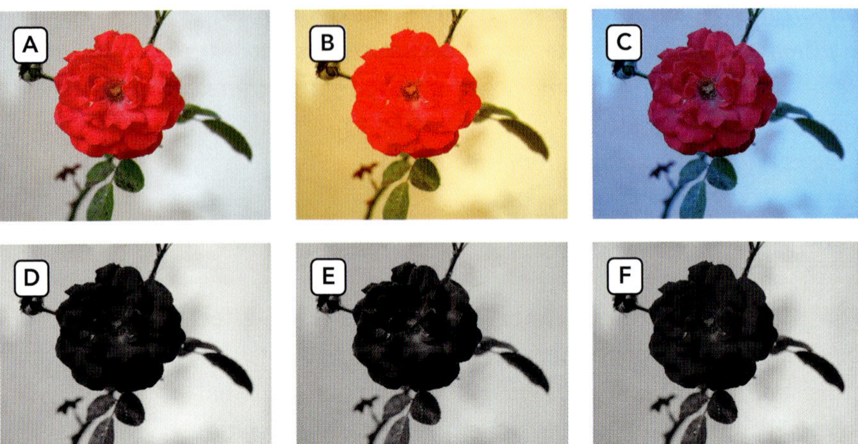

Fig. 137: White balance and monochrome: In the upper row, this illustration shows the same color image with Auto white balance (**A**), a 2500K setting (**B**) and a 10000K setting (**C**). The lower row exhibits monochrome conversions of the above images (**D**, **E**, **F**); all three made with a MONOCHROME+G FILTER film simulation and a SHADOW TONE +4 setting. The various underlying white balance settings have a visible impact on the appearance of the monochrome conversions.

TIP 105	Using film simulations

The importance of film simulations for the overall look of a JPEG is often underestimated. Film simulations influence color grading, color saturation, dynamic range, and contrast in the resulting JPEGs. Picking a film simulation should always be the first step when adjusting JPEG parameters. As with all JPEG settings, film simulations have no effect on the actual RAW file (the digital negative). They only affect the JPEGs, HEIFs, and TIFFs that are generated in the camera (the digital prints).

Here are the available film simulation options:

■ PROVIA is the standard, all-purpose setting. The name reminds us of Fuji's popular Provia slide film.

- ASTIA is another color slide film derivate with softer highlights and pleasing skin tones. It's often used for portraits but can also work with landscape shots that feature vegetation and blue sky.

- VELVIA is a very contrast-heavy, color-saturated derivate of the legendary Fuji Velvia slide film. It's mostly used for landscape and nature shots and is rather unsuitable for portrait work.

- CLASSIC CHROME reminds us of the golden era of color magazine photography. The distinctive look of Classic Chrome is equally suitable for landscapes and portraits.

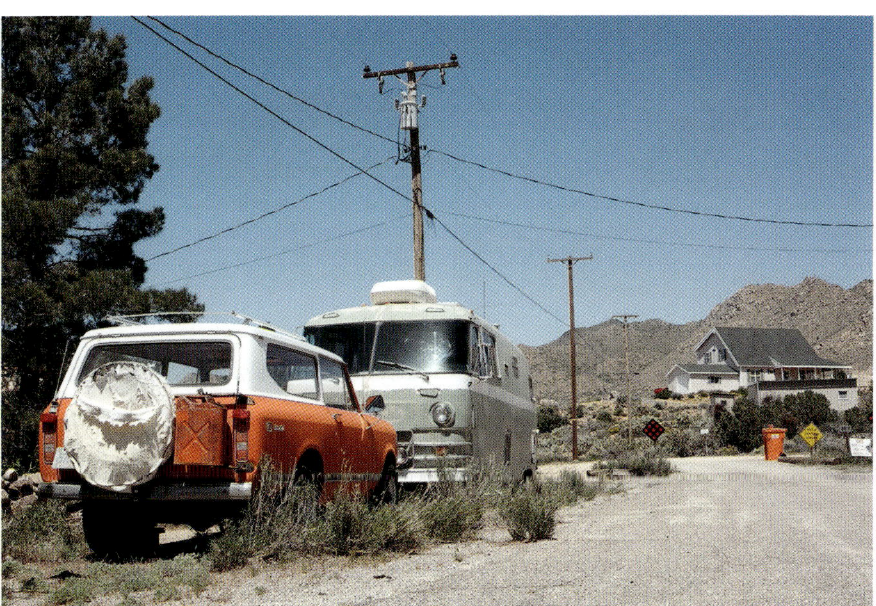

Fig. 138: The distinctive look of **CLASSIC CHROME** has earned it much popularity in a very short time.

- CLASSIC NEG. is based on Fujifilm's popular Superia color negative film. It features a quite unique look with distinct green and red tones.

- PRO NEG. HI is derived from a professional color negative film that was specifically made for portraits. It delivers accurate and pleasing skin tones with nice contrast and adds some punch to the image without adding too much color to faces.

- PRO NEG. STD is a rather neutral film simulation. Featuring flat contrast, subdued colors, and high dynamic range, it can look dull at first, but the JPEGs are usable for further post-processing. Fuji recommends this film simulation for studio portraits in a flash setup.

- NOSTALGIC NEGATIVE is like PRO NEG. STD, but with warmer tones and a more vintage look. I specifically like it for fall colors and to mitigate stark contrasts.

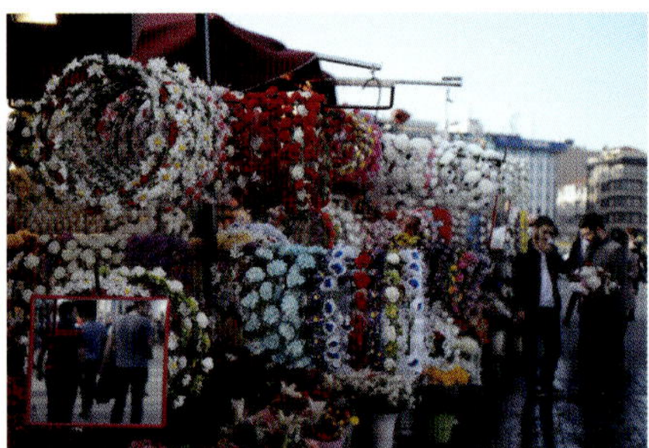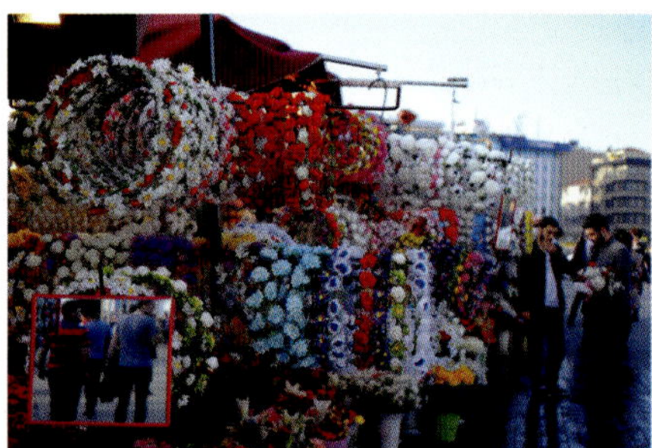

Fig. 139: Antagonists: PRO NEG. STD and VELVIA illustrate the spectrum of Fuji's various film simulation modes. On the left you can see the PRO NEG. STD version of a shot, and on the right its VELVIA cousin.

- ETERNA is the most neutral film simulation. Though Eterna was designed as a flat and desaturated film simulation for video production, it's also our preferred low-contrast, high dynamic range profile for RAW photography.

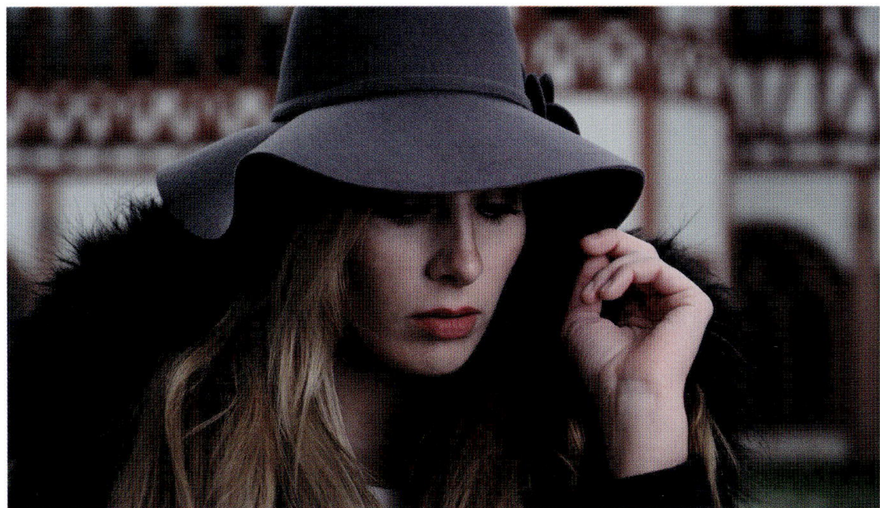

Fig. 140: ETERNA is a flat film simulation profile with a cinematic look. It is named after Fujifilm's discontinued Eterna motion picture film. With low contrast, high dynamic range, and desaturated colors, it's ideal for video production work. That said, it can also be used as a flat RAW shooter profile (along with Tone Curve (Highlights) −2 and Tone Curve (Shadows) −2 settings), or for neutral, cinematic JPEGs like this sample image.

- ETERNA BLEACH BYPASS is a desaturated and much more contrasty version of ETERNA. It delivers a gritty, cinematic look.

- MONOCHROME is Fuji's standard black-and-white conversion. Black-and-white photography is based on assigning specific gray levels to specific colors of a scene. To increase the contrast, many photographers combine MONOCHROME with increased TONE CURVE (HIGH-LIGHTS / SHADOWS) settings. Additionally, noise reduction is often decreased to reveal more detail and display more noise, which gives the appearance of film grain.

- MONOCHROME+Ye FILTER adds a digital yellow filter to the black-and-white conversion. This typically results in a slight increase of contrast because yellow parts of the scene will be represented by brighter gray tones.

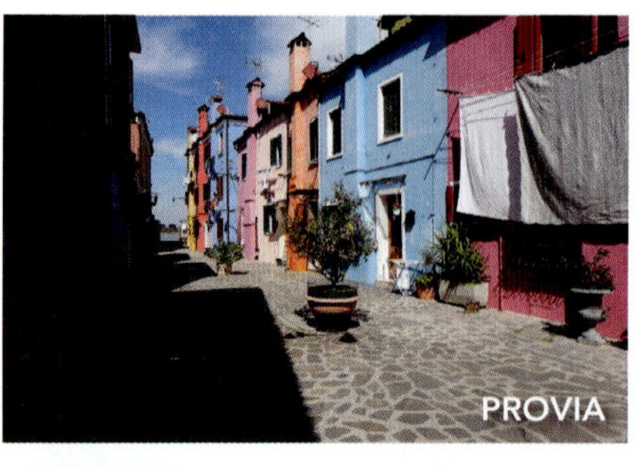
PROVIA

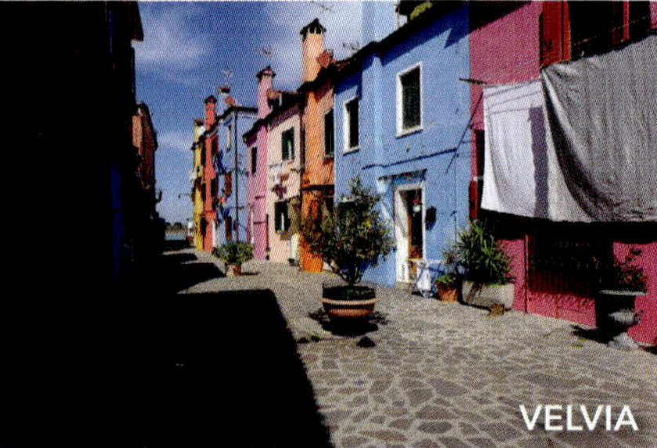
VELVIA

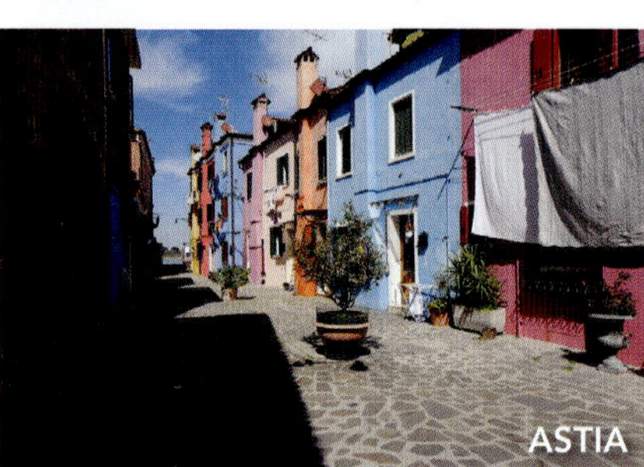
ASTIA

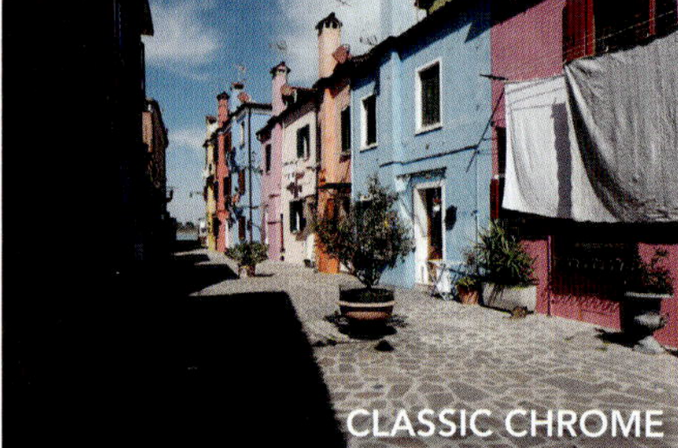
CLASSIC CHROME

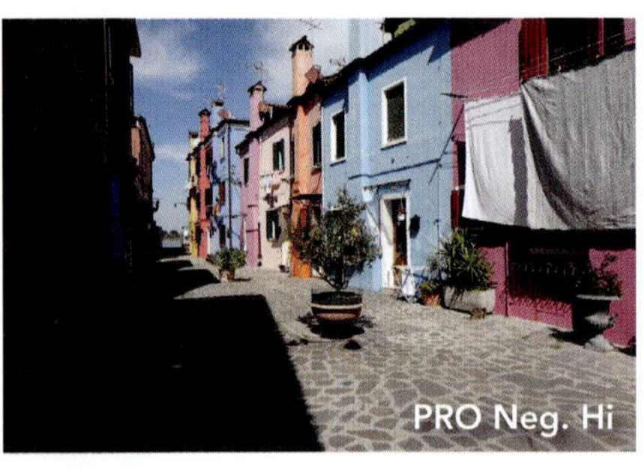
PRO Neg. Hi

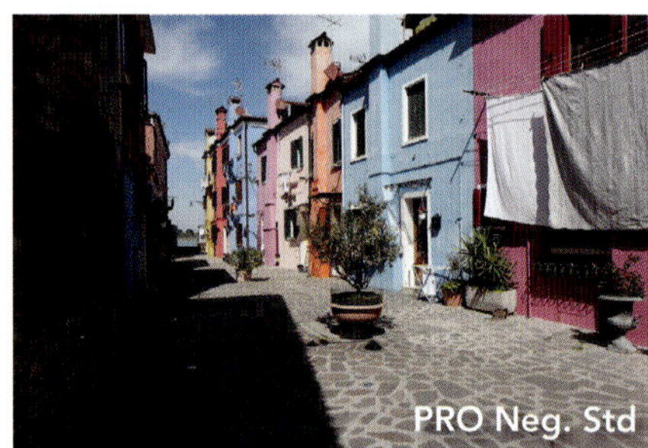
PRO Neg. Std

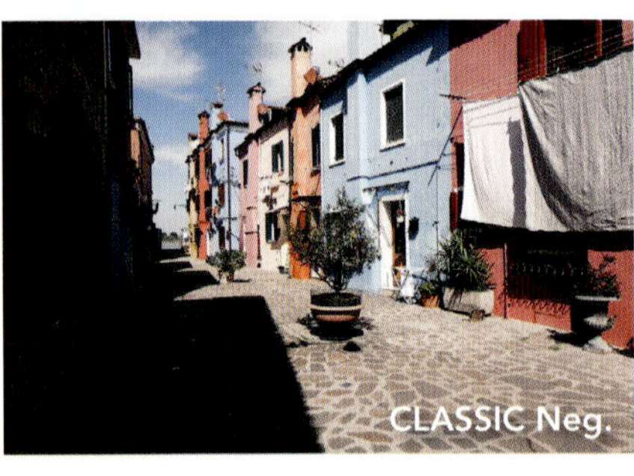
CLASSIC Neg.

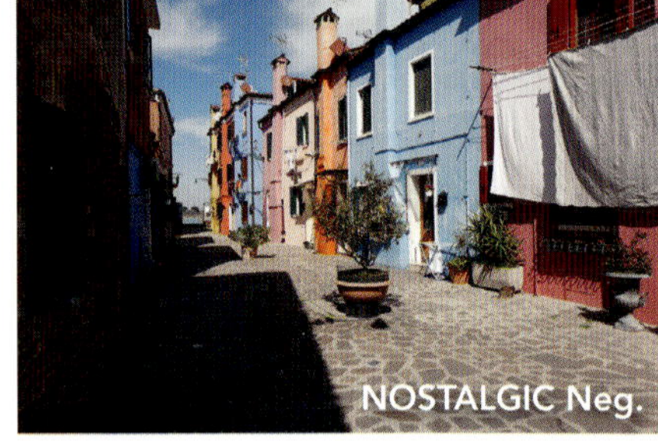
NOSTALGIC Neg.

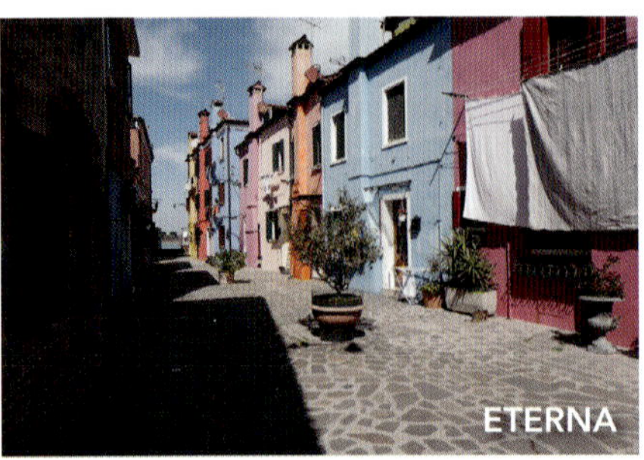
ETERNA

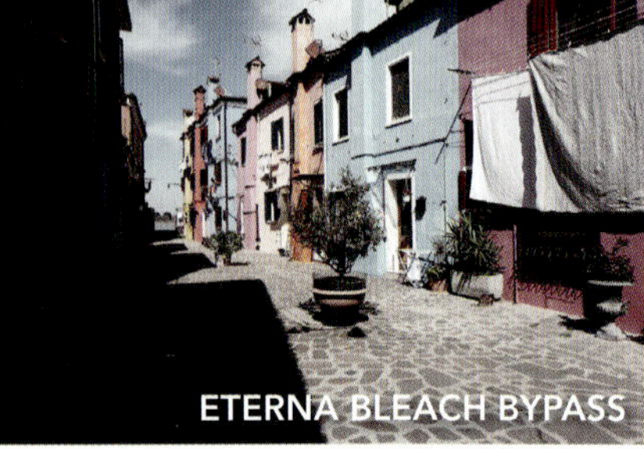
ETERNA BLEACH BYPASS

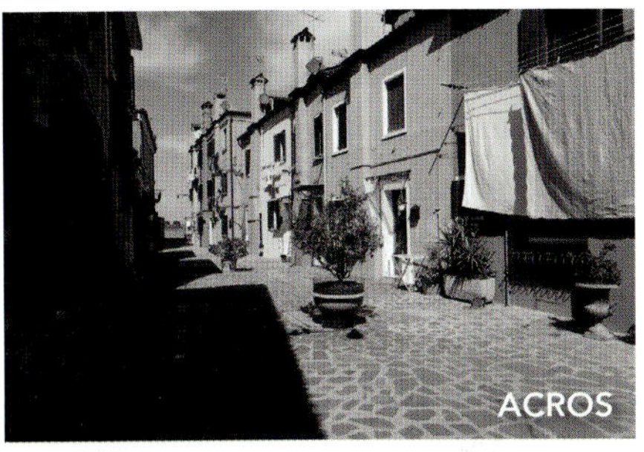

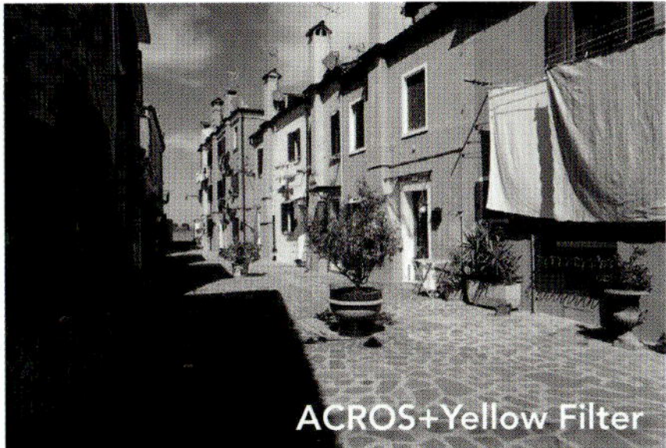

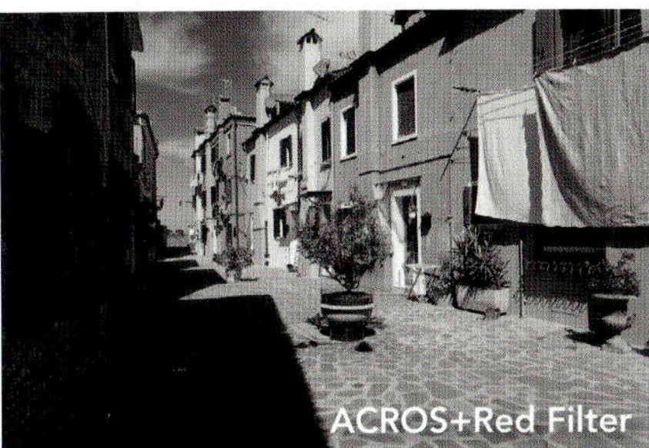

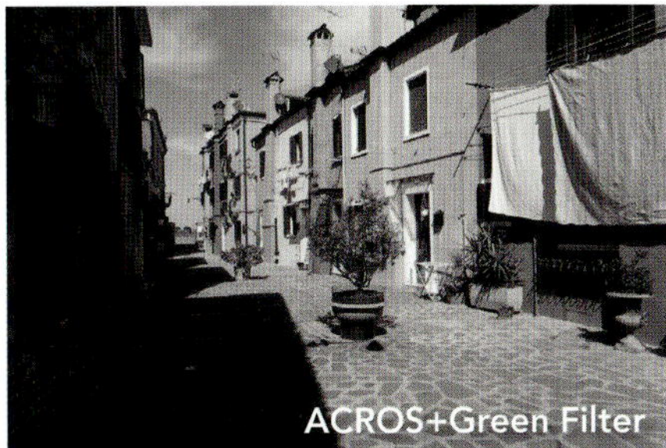

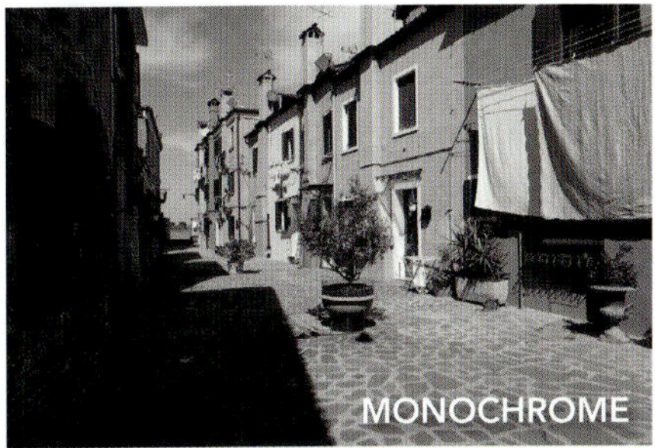

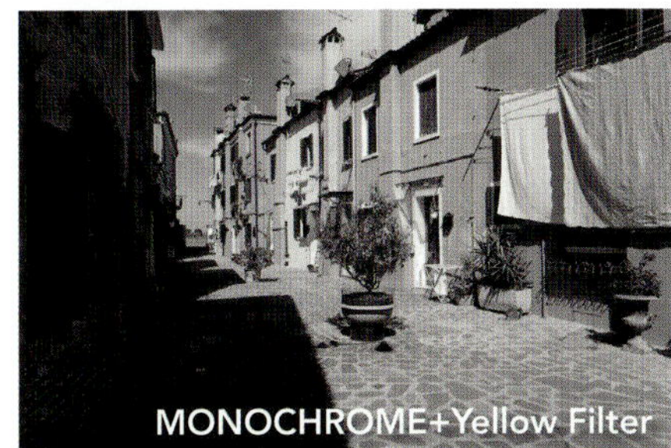

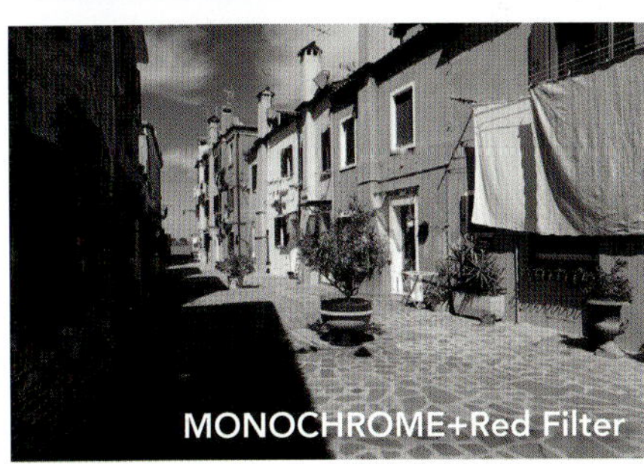

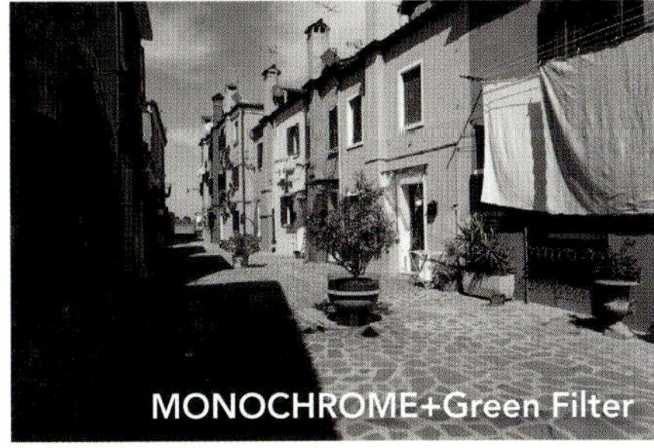

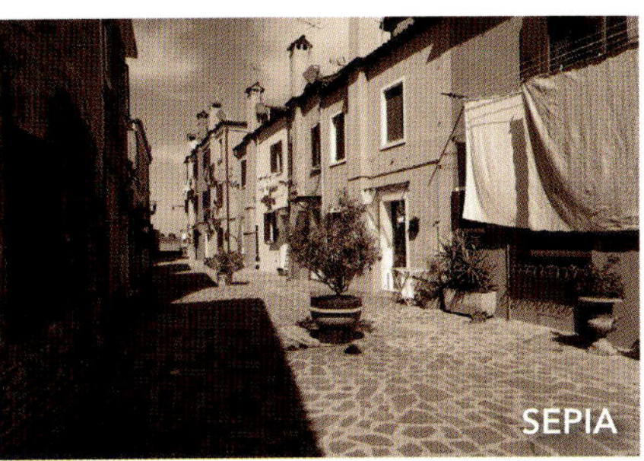

Fig. 141: Comparing all 19 film simulations: These straight-out-of-camera JPEGs illustrate the same shot in all 19 film simulations that are available in the X-T5.

- MONOCHROME+R FILTER adds a red filter to the black-and-white conversion. This means that skin tones will become brighter, which will camouflage reddish skin impurities. Conversely, blue skies will be darkened, adding contrast between clouds and the sky.

- MONOCHROME+G FILTER adds a green filter to the black-and-white conversion. This filter will add texture to skin tones and can potentially emphasize imperfections.

- SEPIA results in a sepia-toned monochrome JPEG for a vintage-looking touch.

- ACROS is a more sophisticated alternative to the regular MONOCHROME settings and is available in four versions: no filter, or with either a yellow, red, or green filter. It reminds us of Fujifilm's analog Acros film and offers a quite cinematic look. This is partly because ACROS includes a noise-dependent analog film grain simulation that transforms regular image noise into analog-looking grain.

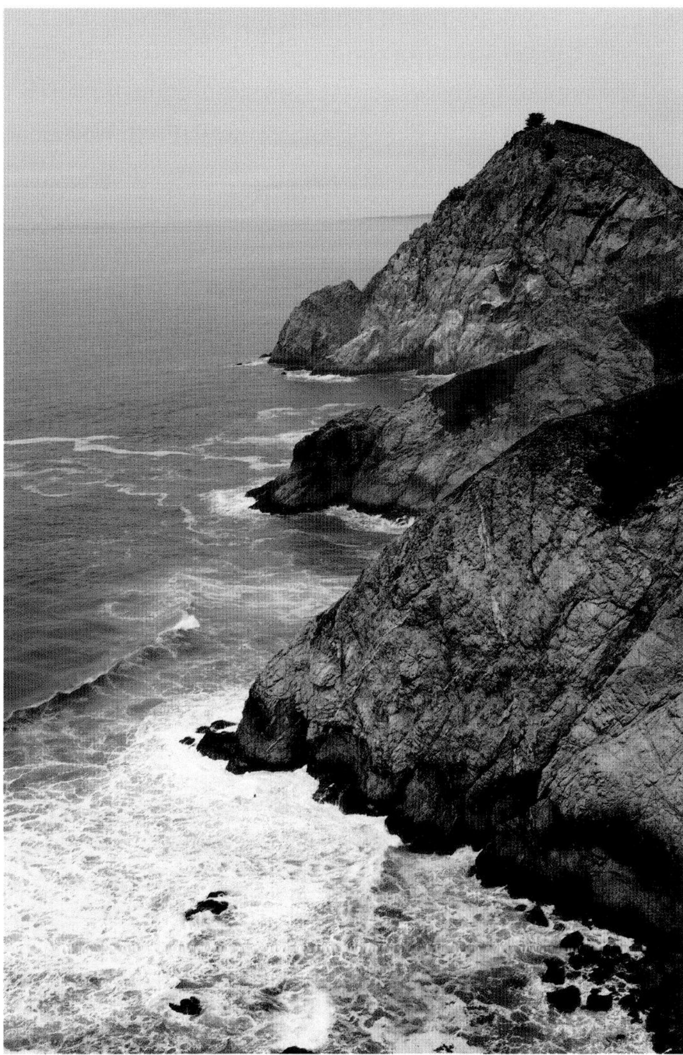

Fig. 142: ACROS has quickly become a favorite among X-series users. Due to its high processing requirements, this sophisticated monochrome film simulation is only available in cameras that are equipped with X-Processor Pro, X-Processor 4, or X-Processor 5.

The noise-dependent analog film grain simulation of ACROS is based on innovative noise shaping. To make the grain visible, your image must contain some noise, so it's best to set in-camera noise reduction to a minimum (–4). Even at base ISO, there's already a subtle difference between ACROS and the regular MONOCHROME film simulation—if you set noise reduction to –4 to give the noise-shaping algorithm something to work with.

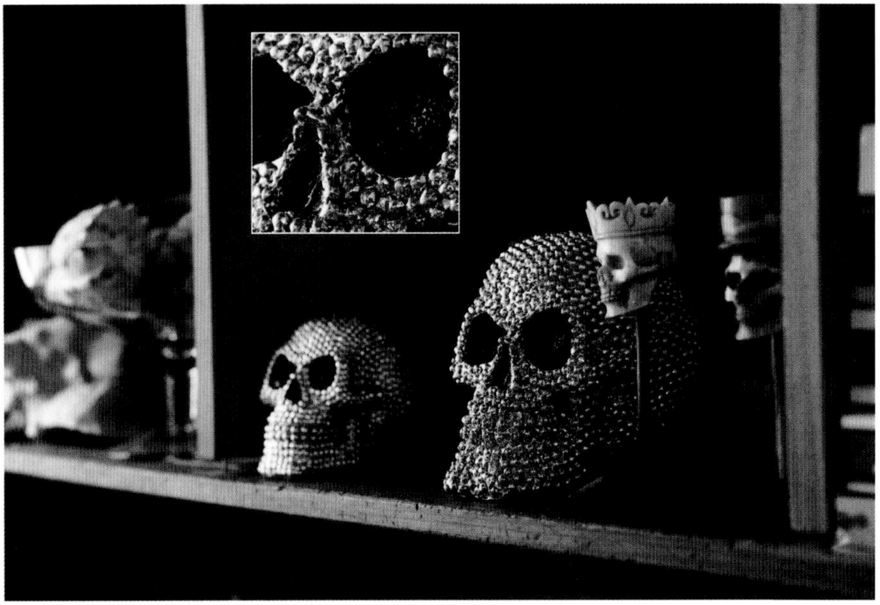

Fig. 143: Even at ISO 25600, the noise shaping of the **ACROS** film simulation delivers a natural-looking result with high resolution and fine details.

The best way to learn about film simulations is to experiment and compare the various options for yourself. The easiest way to do so is with the camera's internal RAW converter. Take one RAW file and process it with all available film simulations, and then import the JPEGs into your computer and compare the results on your monitor.

You can also use X RAW STUDIO [76] to conveniently remotely control your camera's built-in RAW converter from your Mac or your Windows PC.

Using the GRAIN EFFECT   TIP 106

Fujifilm is all about great film simulations with an organic look. For example, adding "analog film grain" to a digital image can be useful to achieve a more natural look with enhanced micro contrast.

GRAIN EFFECT offers three settings (OFF, WEAK, and STRONG) that can be combined with two grain sizes (SMALL and LARGE). It adds a layer of randomized, simulated film grain to the image and can be used with all film simulations.

Please note that I do *not* recommend using GRAIN EFFECT in concert with the ACROS film simulation—it would mix two different grain effects. After all, ACROS already brings its own noise-dependent grain to the table.

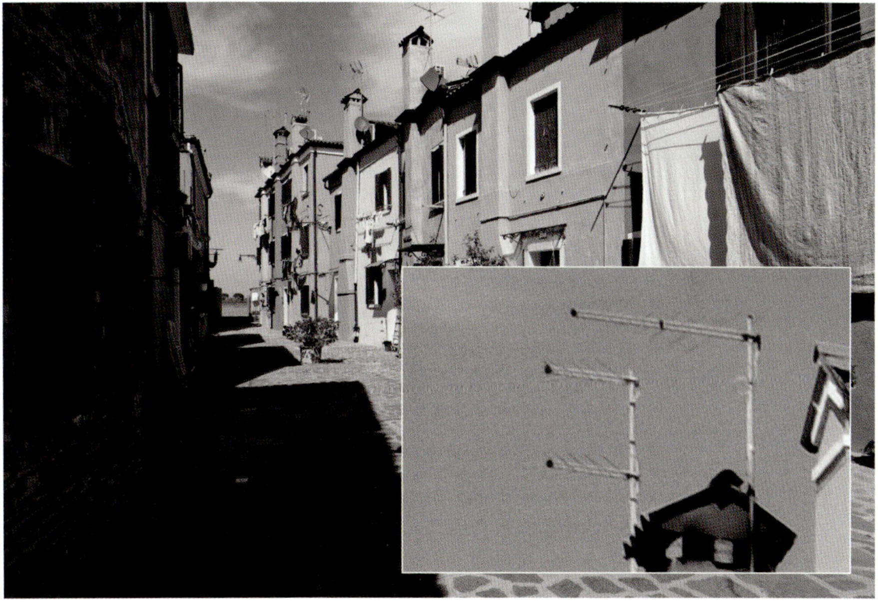

Fig. 144: At base ISO, using the ACROS film simulation in concert with minimal noise reduction (−4) results in a subtle grain effect that adds organic texture to the image.

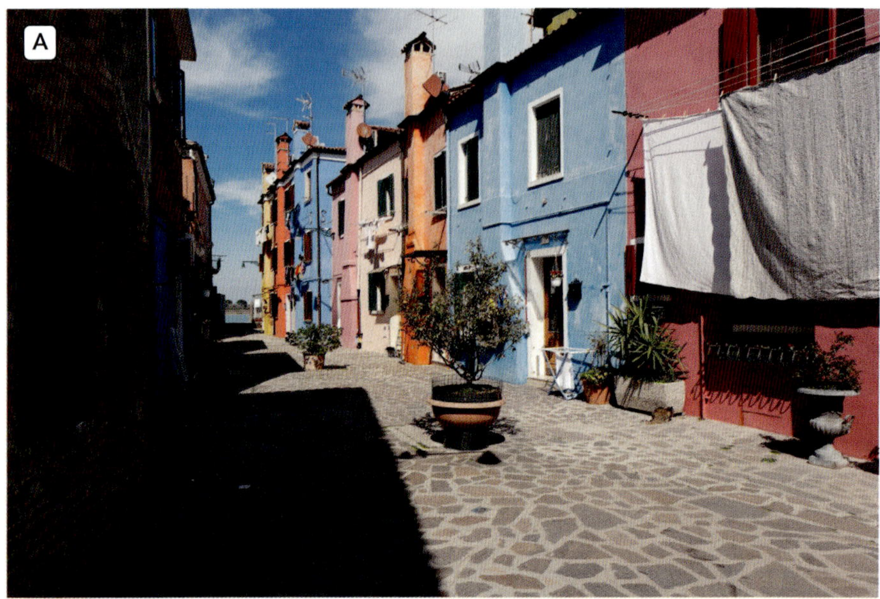

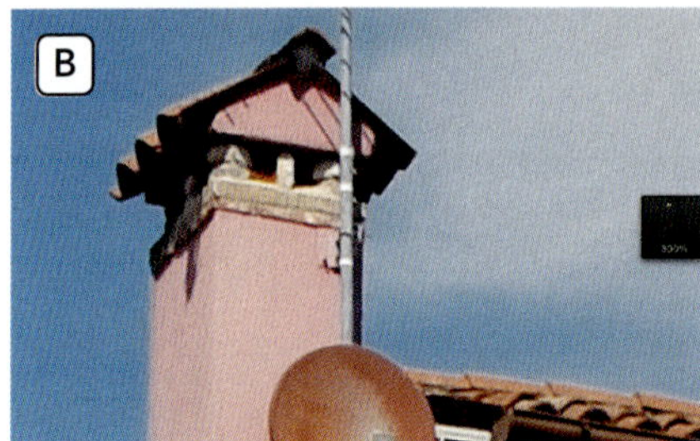
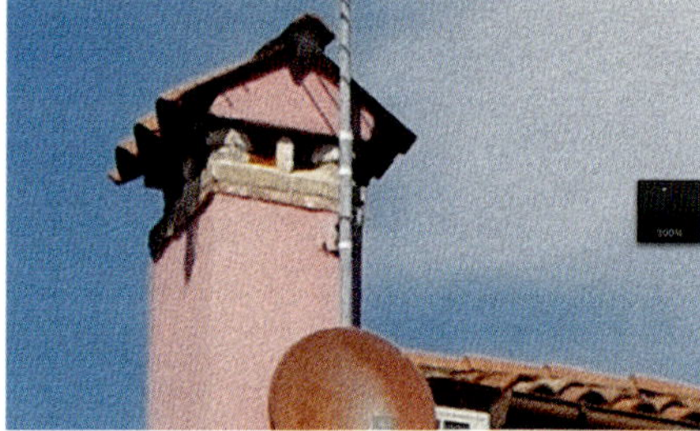
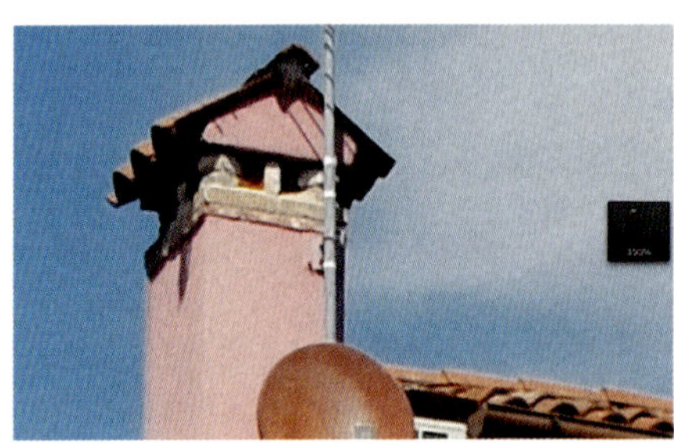
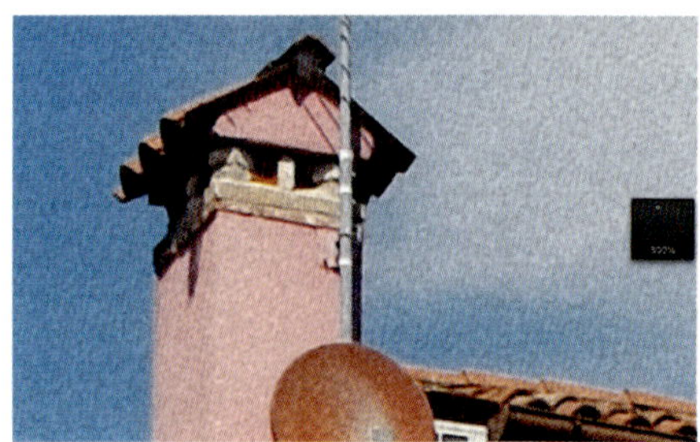

Fig. 145: Starting with the X-Pro3, Fujifilm has enhanced the GRAIN EFFECT with additional options. In addition to the Roughness setting (WEAK / STRONG), there's now also a Size setting to choose between SMALL and LARGE grain. This leaves us with four different combinations that are illustrated in this CLASSIC Neg. example. Image **A** shows the entire scene with a GRAIN EFFECT LARGE / STRONG setting. Image **B** displays four magnified crops. Upper left: SMALL / WEAK; upper right: SMALL / STRONG; lower left: LARGE /WEAK; lower right: LARGE / STRONG.

Adding artificial grain may not be necessary for shots that were taken with ISO settings of 800 or higher. Instead, you can reduce the NOISE REDUCTION setting to −4 to preserve as much noise (and detail) as possible.

Contrast settings: adjusting highlights and shadows	TIP 107

A useful feature of the X-T5 is its ability to independently set the contrast [77] for dark and bright parts of a JPEG image using the TONE CURVE (HIGHLIGHTS / SHADOWS) settings of the built-in RAW converter. This corresponds to the TONE CURVE setting (with options HIGHLIGHTS and SHADOWS) in the IMAGE QUALITY SETTING menu. These settings can also be used to extend a JPEG's dynamic range by lifting dark shadows or darkening bright highlights. To increase the overall contrast of a shot, you can increase both parameters in tandem by choosing a setting on the plus side. To reduce the overall contrast, pick a negative setting for both parameters.

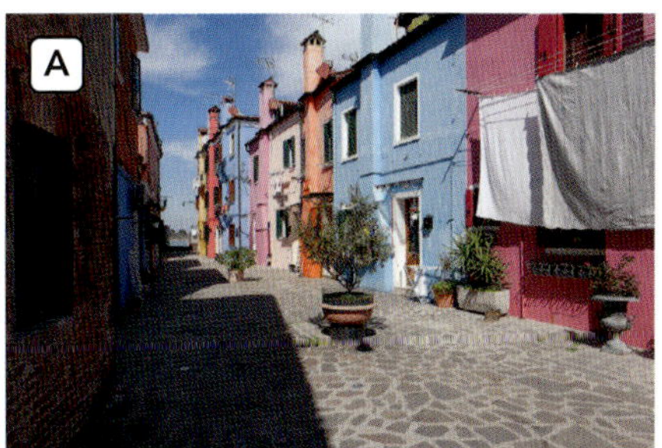

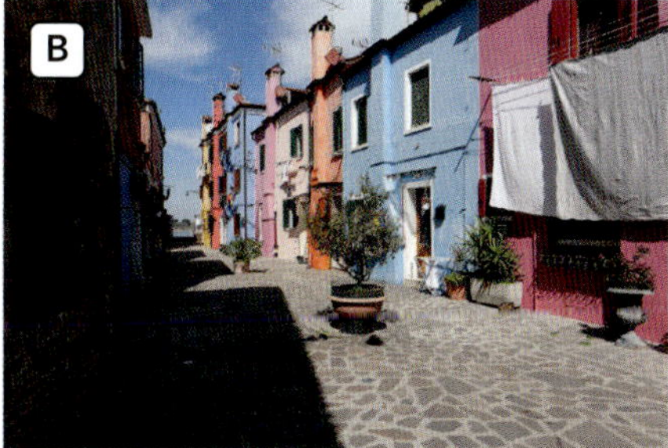

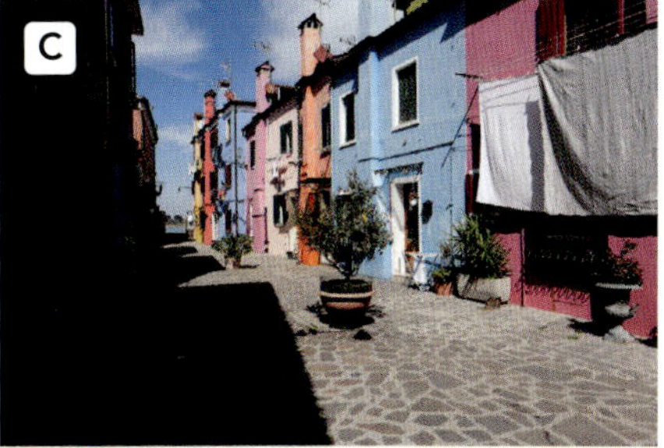

Fig. 146: Comparing **Tone Curve (Shadows)** settings: Image **A** shows a SHADOW TONE −2 version; image **B** shows a neutral 0 setting, and image **C** displays the RAW file processed with SHADOW TONE +2. Shadows and dark midtones were lifted by the reduction of the JPEG's shadow contrast, while the highlights remained untouched.

It's worth mentioning that increased contrast also enhances the impression of image sharpness and color saturation. This demonstrates that JPEG parameters always work in concert with each other.

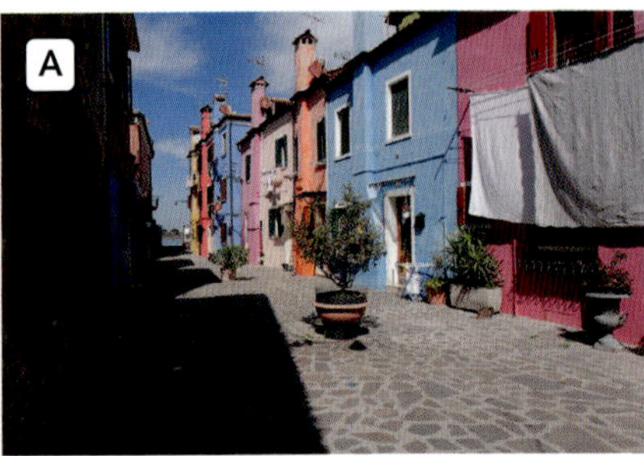

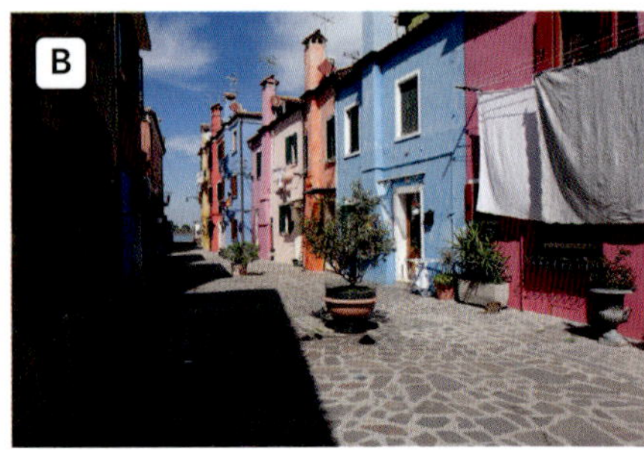

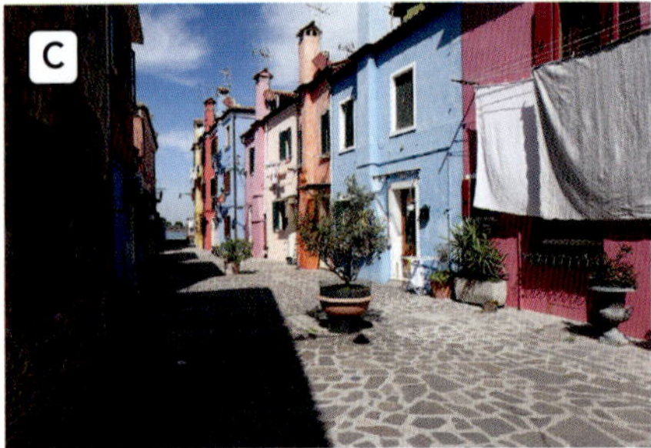

Fig. 147: Comparing **Tone Curve (Highlights)** settings: Image **A** shows the HIGHLIGHT TONE −2 version of a shot; image **B** shows the same RAW file processed with a neutral 0 setting, and image **C** displays the image with HIGHLIGHT TONE +2. Increasing the highlight contrast leaves the shadows and darker midtones untouched.

TIP 108	Color saturation

After picking a suitable film simulation mode, you still might want to change the color saturation [78] of an image. You can do so with the COLOR setting.

Too much color saturation can obscure texture and details. For example, VELVIA is a very saturated film mode that may sometimes require a reduction in color saturation.

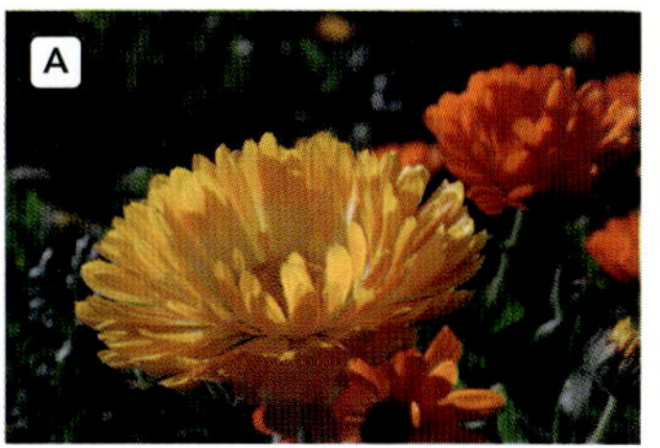 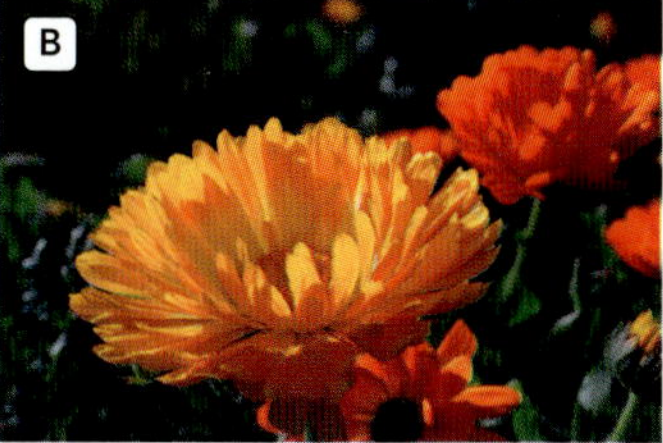

Fig. 148: Color saturation: Image **A** shows a PROVIA version with COLOR −4; image **B** shows the same RAW file processed with COLOR +4.

The COLOR CHROME EFFECT	TIP 109

Color Chrome Effect is a calculation-heavy process that adds depth to saturated colors in an image. I don't recommend using this setting in shooting mode. Instead, apply it as needed after the fact with your camera's built-in RAW converter.

COLOR CHROME EFFECT offers three settings: OFF, WEAK, and STRONG. It can be applied in concert with any film simulation and only affects the red and green channel components of the image.

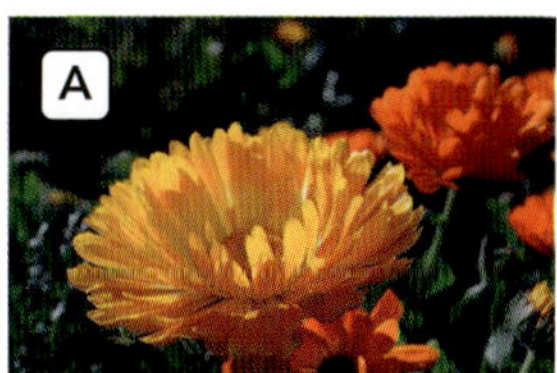 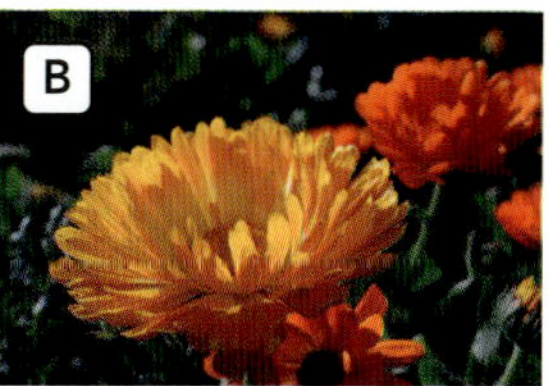 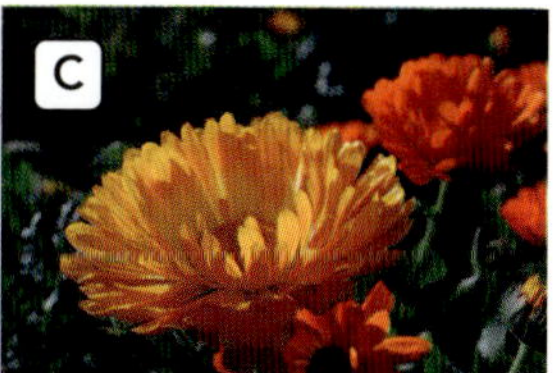

Fig. 149: This example illustrates how a regular Provia image (**A**) is changed by adding a COLOR CHROME EFFECT > WEAK (**B**), and STRIONG (**C**) setting.

COLOR CHROME FX BLUE works just like COLOR CHROME EFFECT but only affects the blue parts of your image. For example, you can use it to emphasize a blue sky.

To affect all colors in your image, you can apply both Color Chrome Effect options to an image.

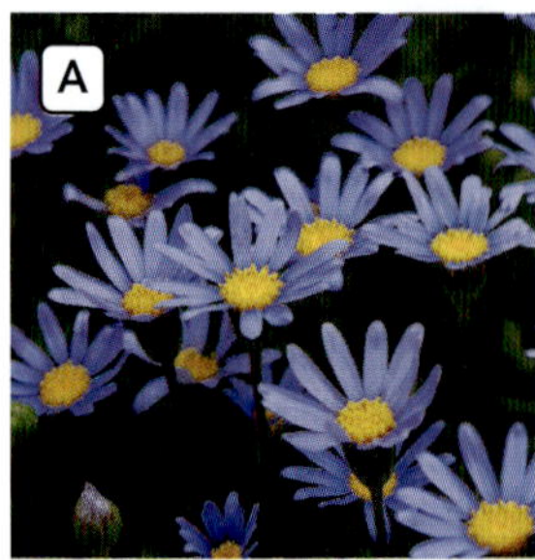
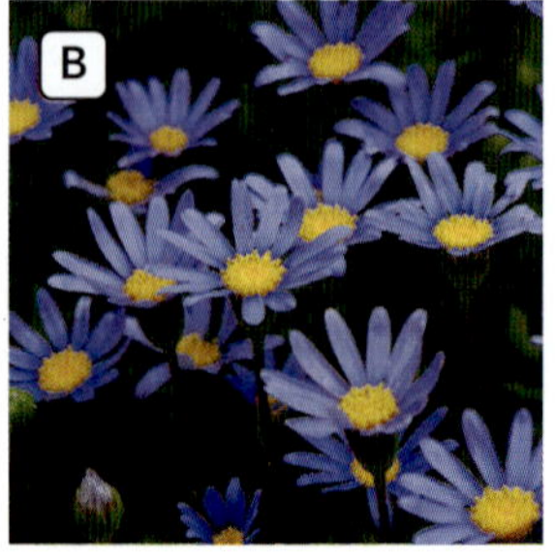
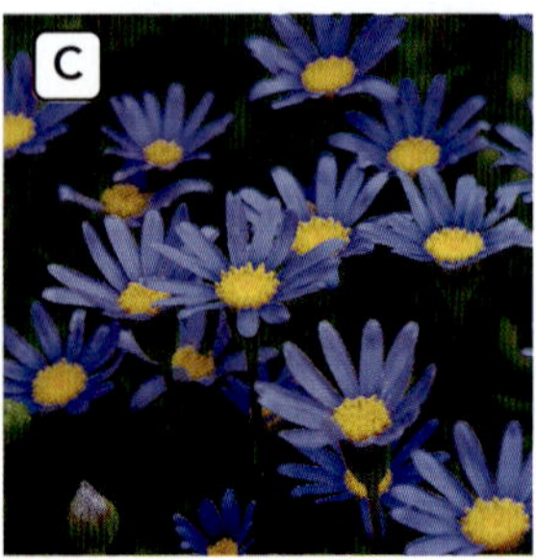

Fig. 150: This example shows JPEGs with COLOR CHROME FX BLUE > OFF (**A**), WEAK (**B**), and STRONG (**C**).

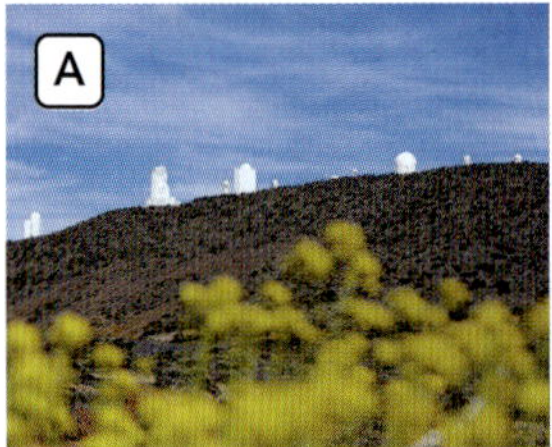
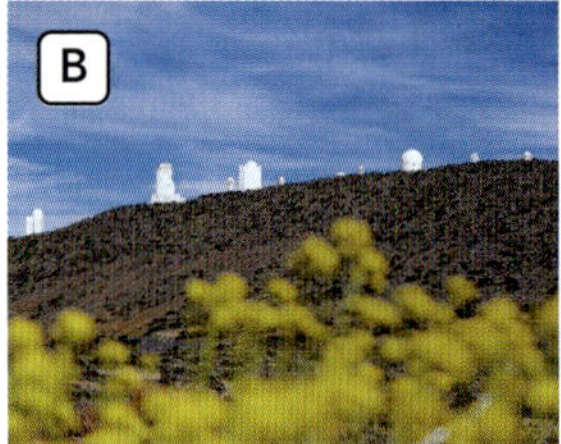
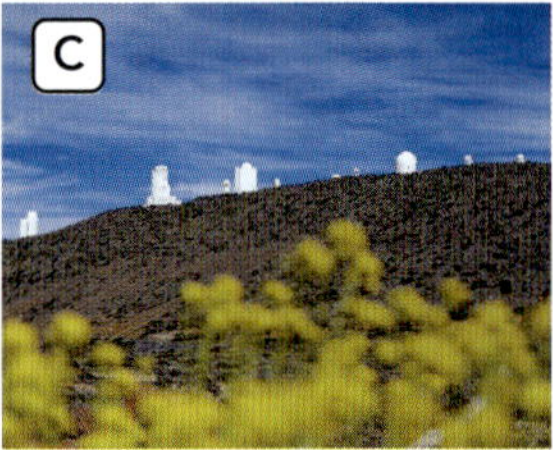

Fig. 151: A popular application of COLOR CHROME FX BLUE is adding contrast to a blue sky with clouds, like in this example with COLOR CHROME FX BLUE > OFF (**A**), WEAK (**B**), and STRONG (**C**).

TIP 110	MONOCHROMATIC COLOR: adding color tints to mono-chrome images

In many cases, printed black-and-white photos aren't just black and white, but they contain a warm or cool color tint. Even in photographic books, it's a common printing practice to add at least one color to monochrome pictures to increase the range of tones that can be realized during the printing process.

The X-T5 lets you add a warm or cold color tint to ACROS and MONOCHROME images. With the MONOCHROMATIC COLOR setting, you can change the neutral look of black-and-white images with a Warm/Cool adjustment on the vertical axis and a Magenta/Green adjustment on the horizontal axis.

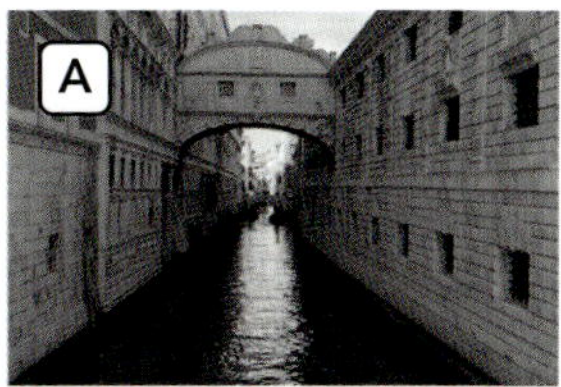 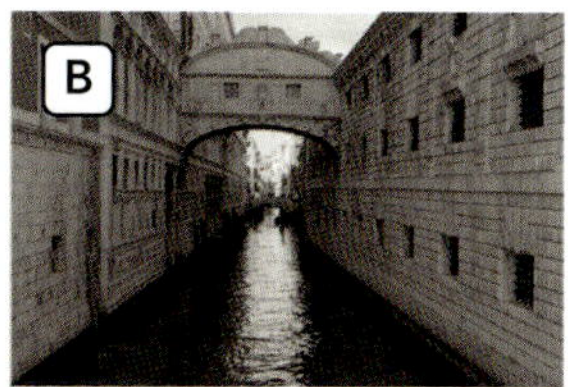 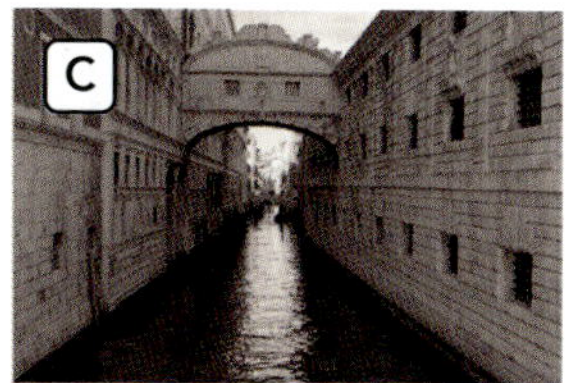

Fig. 152: This example illustrates the effect of the MONOCHRO-MATIC COLOR setting on black-and-white shots: Image **A** shows an ACROS image with a neutral setting of 0. Image **B** is the same shot, but with Warm/Cool set to +5. Image **C** adds a Magenta/Green −4 setting to the mix.

Using the SMOOTH SKIN EFFECT — TIP 111

High-resolution cameras like the X-T5 or GFX can some-times reveal "too much" detail, particularly when it comes to human skin in portrait shots. Of course, you can always get rid of blemishes in your external RAW conversion soft-ware or with programs like Photoshop. However, there's an easy way to get smoother skin in-camera: use the SMOOTH SKIN EFFECT.

This function is available in two strengths: WEAK and STRONG. Personally, I recommend only using the WEAK option because STRONG can lead to "plastic skin." That said, it's certainly a matter of taste, and there are also significant cultural differences.

Please note that SMOOTH SKIN EFFECT doesn't just affect human faces and skin tones but your entire image, so it's possible that other fine details are smoothened, too.

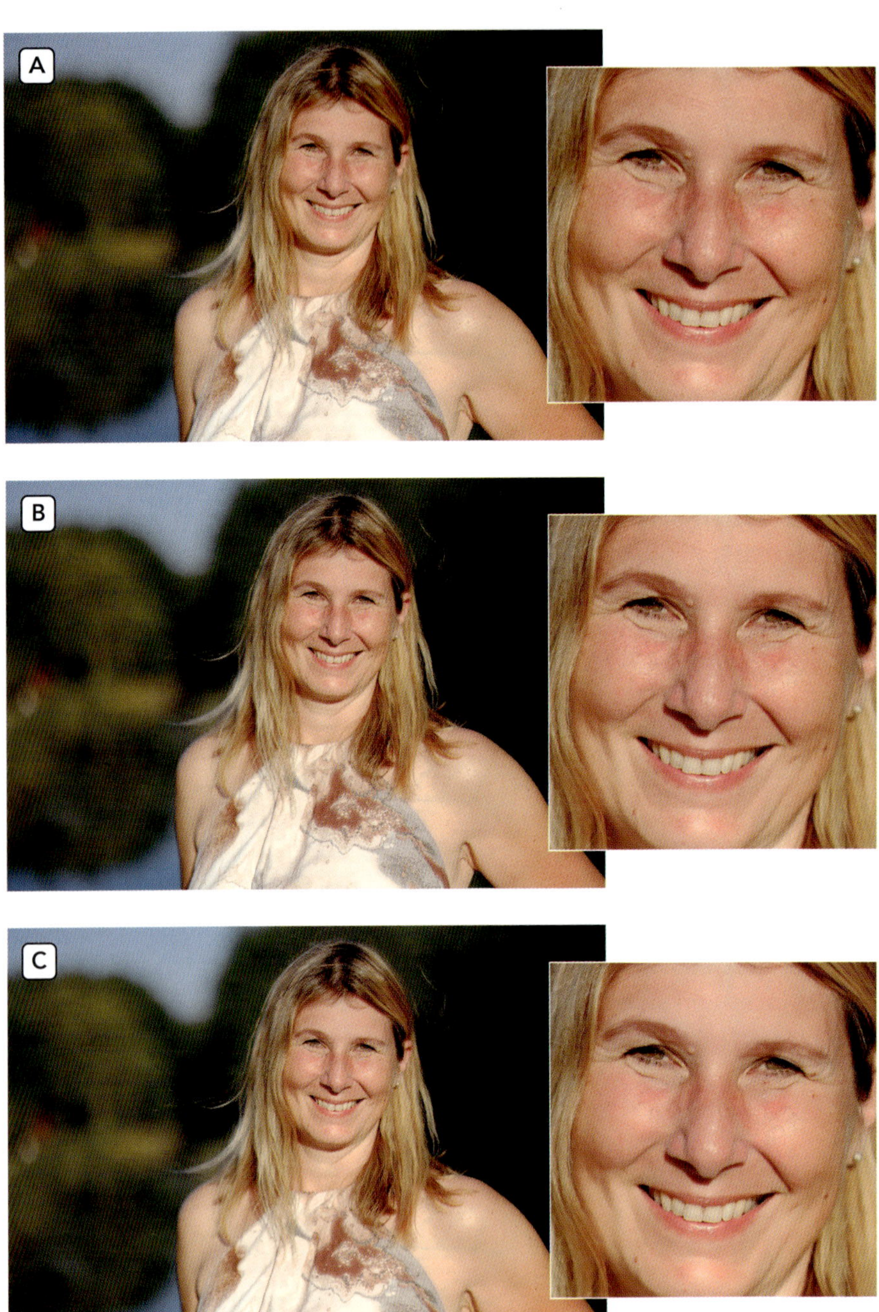

Fig. 153: This example shows the same portrait in three different versions: SMOOTH SKIN EFFECT OFF (**A**), WEAK (**B**), and STRONG (**C**).

<table><tr><td>Be careful with CLARITY!</td><td>TIP 112</td></tr></table>

CLARITY is a JPEG setting that you should only use after-the-fact with the built-in RAW converter, not during your actual shooting. In other words: CLARITY should always be set to 0 (zero) in the IMAGE QUALITY SETTING menu.

The reason: CLARITY significantly slows down your camera in a way that it may take up to two seconds to process and save a single image. Consequently, CLARITY is not available in concert with burst mode and bracketing modes. Using any of these modes will automatically reset CLARITY to zero. To save you all this trouble, it's better to apply clarity after the fact, for example with X RAW STUDIO, where you can also try out different strength settings and see their effect.

So, what does it do? CLARITY enhances or reduces the micro-contrast in your image. Basically, micro-contrast is the contrast (brightness difference) between neighboring pixels. More micro-contrast adds more grit and perceived sharpness (like a dehazing effect); reducing micro-contrast makes the image look softer and dreamier. The X-T5 lets you adjust the micro-contrast in 11 steps (−5 to +5), with 0 being the neutral default setting.

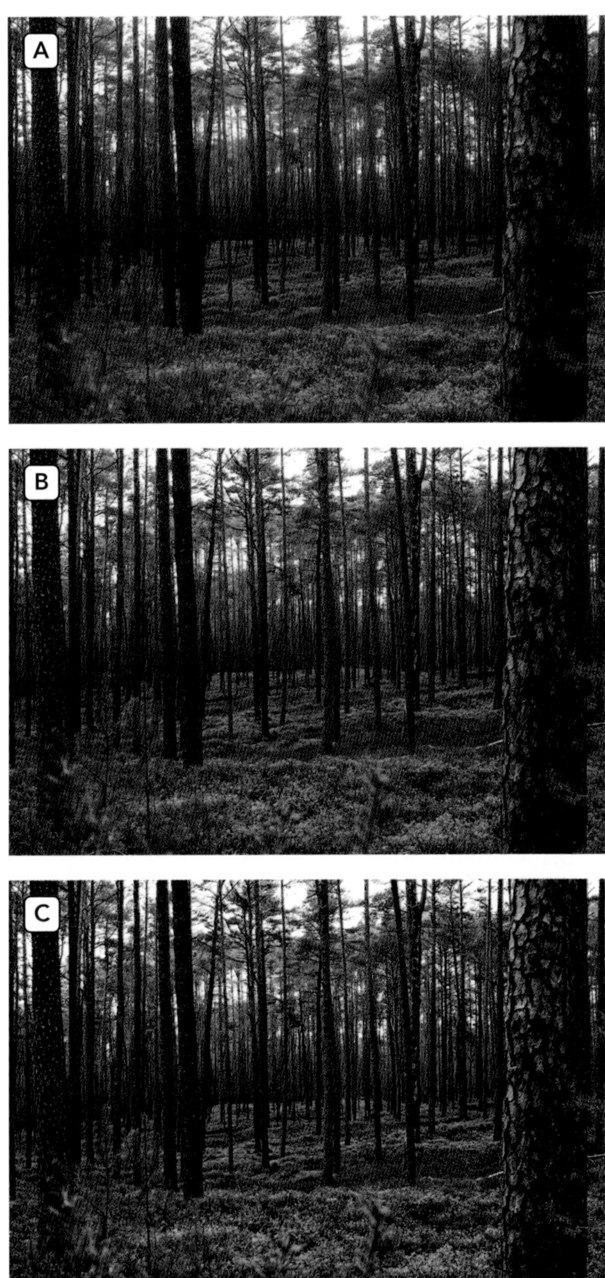

Fig. 154: This example shows the same image with CLARITY set to −5 (**A**), neutral 0 (**B**), and +5 (**C**).

<table><tr><td>Color space: sRGB or Adobe RGB?</td><td>TIP 113</td></tr></table>

A color space [79] is a way of organizing available colors. The X-T5 offers two options: sRGB [80] and Adobe RGB [81]. Both color spaces contain the same *number* of colors, but not the *same* colors—their gamuts [82] are different.

Adobe RGB covers a larger gamut than sRGB because its colors are optimized for CMYK printing. On the other hand, sRGB is optimized for computer monitors and all kinds of high-resolution displays, such as HD and UHD TVs, smartphones, and tablets. Since Adobe RGB encompasses a wider gamut than sRGB, the gaps between neighboring colors and tones are wider because both color spaces contain the same number of colors. Adobe RGB must spread out this number over its larger gamut. This larger gamut (compared to standard sRGB) is why Adobe RGB is also known as an extended color space.

Users often misunderstand and assume that "extended" means "better." It does not. The additional colors in Adobe RGB are only useful if you intend to print your JPEG or TIFF files with a commercial CMYK printer. This requires a calibrated workflow and a wide-gamut monitor that can display the entire Adobe RGB gamut. However, most computer monitors can only display the sRGB gamut. Using Adobe RGB on such a monitor would be like working with half-closed eyes because you wouldn't be able to see many of the colors you are using.

For most users (including me), sRGB is the best choice of color space. Images rendered in this color space can be viewed, processed, and printed on a wide variety of devices without unpleasant surprises. In any case, you should calibrate your computer monitor with hardware like Datacolor's Spyder. Uncalibrated screens will not give you an accurate representation of the colors in your images.

Important: *The COLOR SPACE setting in your X-T5 only affects the JPEGs, HEIFs, and TIFFs that are created inside your camera. It also affects the live-view image—and since the LCD display and the EVF only support sRGB, it would be a bad idea to shoot with Adobe RGB. The result would be a mismatch between what you see and what you get. WYSIWYG would be broken. Hence, always select sRGB in the IMAGE QUALITY SETTING menu!*

COLOR SPACE is a JPEG setting, so it doesn't affect RAW data. RAW files have no defined color space, yet. The color space is set when you export an image after processing the RAW. This also means that you can export the same image in different versions, including different color spaces.

TIP 114	Working with the built-in RAW converter

The RAW converter in your X-T5 serves two main purposes:

- You can create various versions of a shot; for example, a colorful Velvia version and a gritty black-and-white version of the same image. Not sure what's best or what you want? Quickly create multiple versions with different film simulations and varying JPEG settings, and then sort them out later on your computer screen.

- You can improve your images after the fact. Since it's hard (if not impossible) to guess and set the perfect JPEG settings for each shot in advance, it's more convenient to adjust these parameters later when you have time to look at your results. You can easily change parameters like white balance, color saturation, contrast settings, sharpness, or noise reduction. You can also adjust the exposure and try different film simulations.

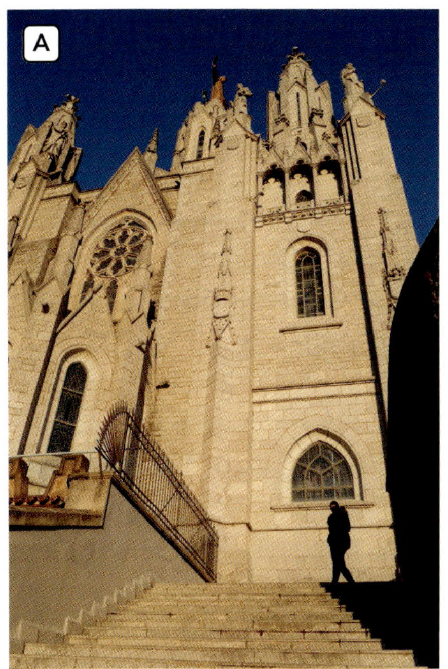
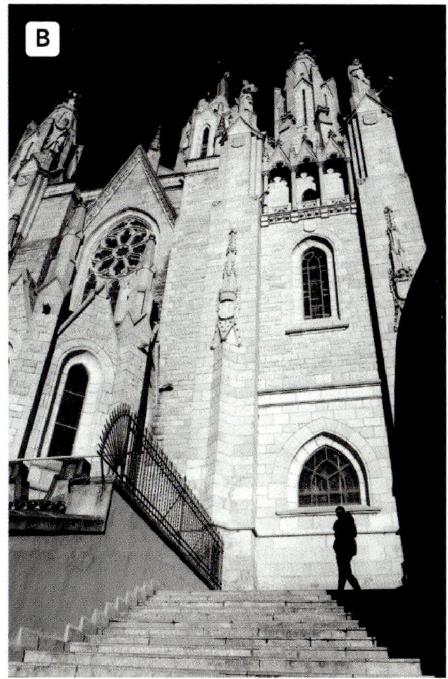

Fig. 155: Using the **built-in RAW converter** to change the look of a shot: image **A** shows the scene as it was recorded with the camera's default settings. Image **B** is the same shot processed with ACROS+Red Filter and maximum contrast (TONE CURVE (SHADOWS) +4 and TONE CURVE (HIGHLIGHTS) +4).

Here are a few things you can accomplish with the built-in RAW converter:

- Use PUSH/PULL processing to brighten (*push*) underexposed shots or darken (*pull*) overexposed images.

- Use the contrast settings (TONE CURVE) to selectively adjust the contrast of dark or bright parts of your image. It's perfectly adequate to combine these functions with PUSH/PULL processing. To generate JPEGs with maximum dynamic range for further post-processing on your computer, it may be useful to set both contrast parameters (shadows and highlights) to −2 and use a neutral film simulation like PRO NEG. STD or ETERNA.

- Adjust the color saturation of your JPEGs with the COLOR parameter. Reducing the color saturation can recover texture when one or more of the color channels appear oversaturated.

- Use SHARPNESS and NOISE REDUCTION in opposition with each other: increase sharpness while diminishing noise reduction to preserve more texture in high-ISO shots.

- Add or remove micro-contrast with CLARITY, beautify skin with the SMOOTH SKIN EFFECT, deepen colors with a COLOR CHROME EFFECT, add film grain with the GRAIN EFFECT, or tint black-and-white images with MONO-CHROMATIC COLOR.

- Adjust the white balance using one of the presets or a Kelvin value to make your shot look warmer or cooler. Use WB SHIFT to correct or introduce a color tint.

- Curious what the Lens Modulation Optimizer (LMO) is doing? Take a RAW sample and process JPEGs with and without LMO in the internal RAW converter. Then, compare the results on a computer screen. Happy pixel peeping!

- Picked the wrong color space? No problem! Just reprocess the shot with the correct color space.

- You can always *reduce* DYNAMIC RANGE, D RANGE PRIORITY, or an HDR setting. You can also *remove* a previously set DIGITAL TELECONVERTER, and you can *change* the IMAGE SIZE and aspect ratio, the IMAGE QUALITY (NORMAL or FINE), or the exported FILE TYPE (JPEG, HEIF, TIFF 8-bit, and TIFF 16-bit). Please note that TIFF 16-bit is actually a 10-bit file, and so is HEIF.

To process RAW files that have already been transferred to a computer, you can use the free X RAW STUDIO application as a remote control interface for your camera's built-in RAW converter.

By the way: Your X-T5 cannot process RAW files from other X-series models. For example, the built-in RAW converter of your camera cannot process RAW files that were taken with an X-H2. However, you can process RAW files that were shot with a different X-T5 camera.

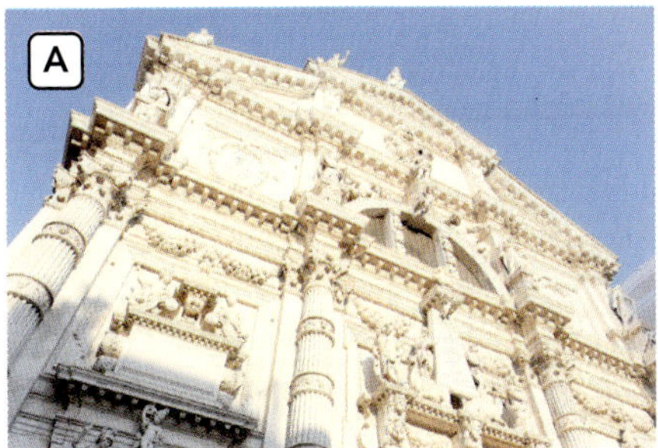

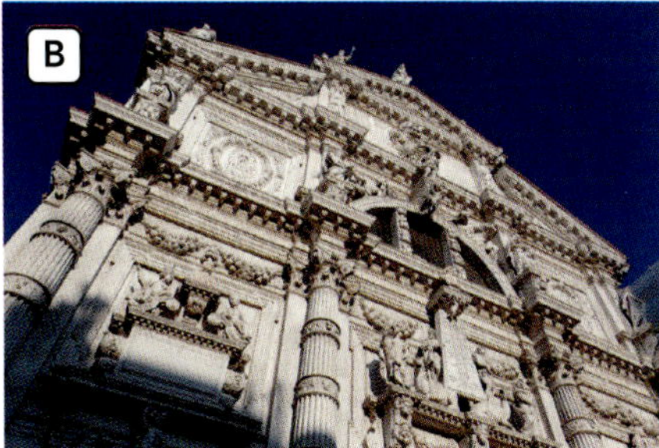

Fig. 156: You can also use the **built-in RAW converter** to correct a shot. Image **A** shows an overexposed sample shot that was recorded with PROVIA default settings and DR400%. Image **B** is the same shot reprocessed in-camera with a PULL of −2 EV, CLASSIC CHROME, DR200%, COLOR CHROME FX BLUE STRONG, AUTO WB WHITE PRIORITY, WB SHIFT R:−2, B:+4, TONE CURVE (HIGHLIGHTS) −1, TONE CURVE (SHADOWS) −2, COLOR +4, SHARPENING +2, HIGH ISO NOISE REDUCTION −4, CLARITY +2.

Working with X RAW STUDIO	TIP 115

The built-in RAW converter is a practical tool for on-the-fly RAW conversions while you are in the field. You can use your camera's LCD or EVF display (I recommend the latter) to create new and improved JPEGs from RAW files that are saved on the memory card in your camera.

But what if your RAW files have already been transferred to a computer? Instead of copying them back to a card and processing them in-camera, there's a better and more comfortable way: FUJIFILM X RAW STUDIO.

X RAW STUDIO is a free download for Windows and macOS [83]. Don't confuse it with a stand-alone RAW converter, though. Basically, X RAW STUDIO is a PC/Mac-based remote-control and user interface for the built-in RAW converter of your X-T5. This means that X RAW STUDIO cannot function without your camera, which must be tethered to your Mac or PC via USB.

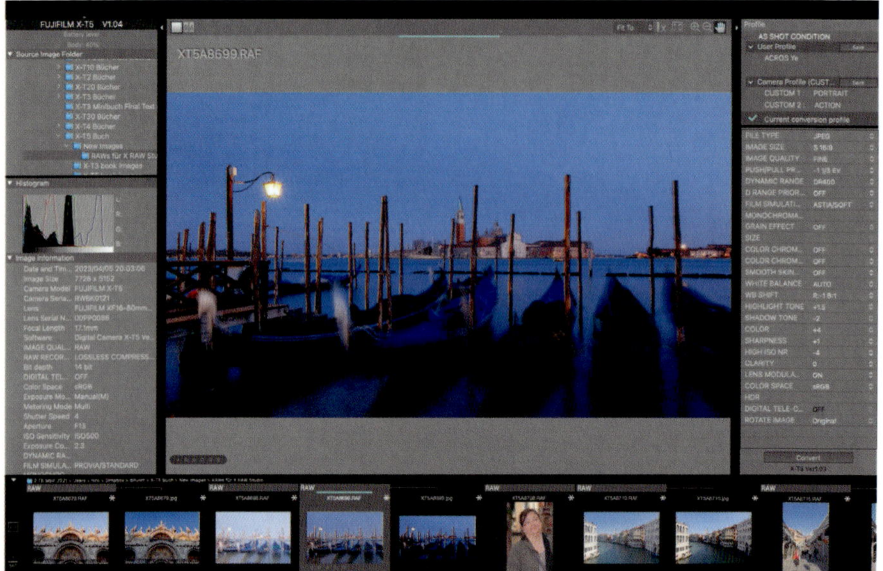

Fig. 157: FUJIFILM X RAW STUDIO is a simple way to remotely control the built-in RAW converter of your camera and use it to process RAW files that are stored on your Windows PC or Mac. The free app sends RAW files from your computer to the camera via a USB-C connection, where they are processed to "in-camera JPEGs" that are immediately returned to your PC. You get the best of both worlds: the ease of use of a computer interface (with a large display and convenient storage for all your images) is combined with the processing power and image quality of your camera's internal RAW converter.

Set-up your camera to work with X RAW STUDIO by selecting NETWORK/USB SETTING > CONNECTION MODE > USB RAW CONV./BACKUP RESTORE, and then connect it to your Mac or PC via USB while X RAW STUDIO is running. Operating the software is mostly self-explanatory, but feel free to consult Fuji's online manual [84].

Since it runs on a computer, X RAW STUDIO offers a more comprehensive user interface than the stand-alone converter in your camera. You can copy and paste development settings from one image to others, and you can set-up and save development presets (film simulation recipes) for later use. Batch processing of multiple RAW images is also no problem.

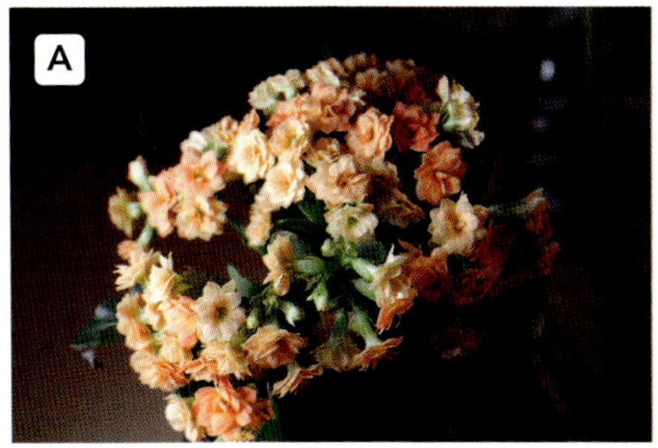
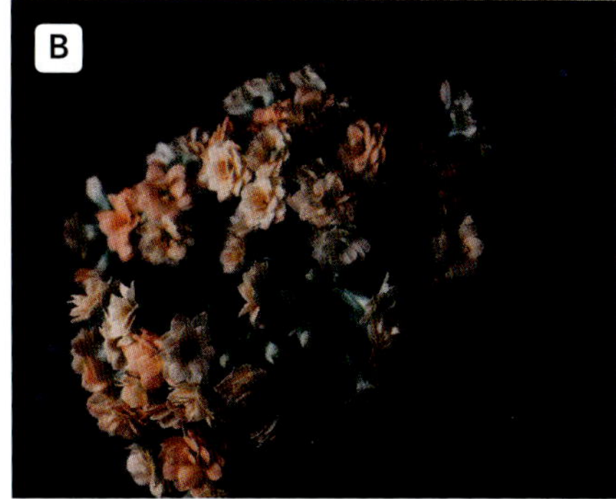
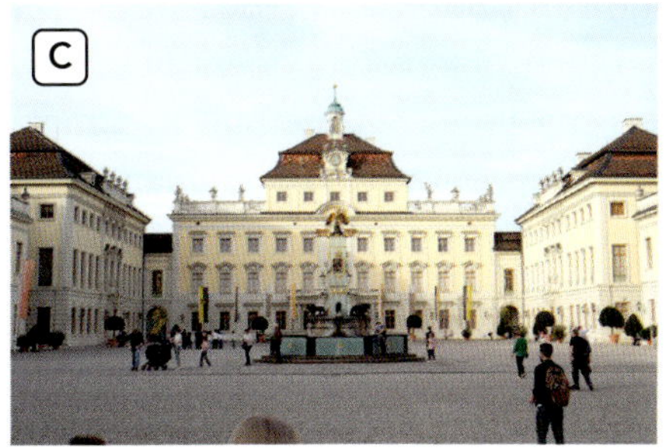
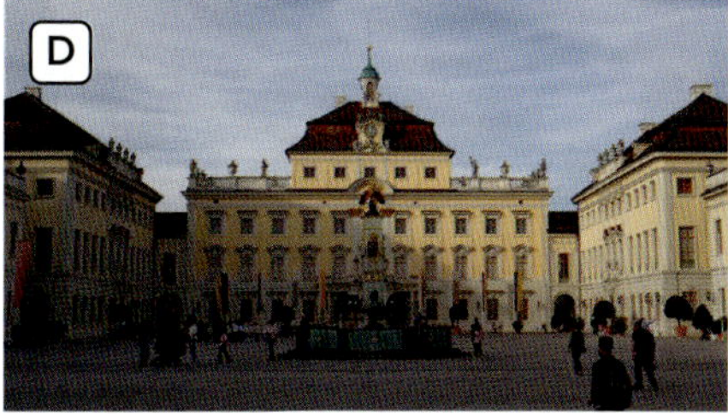

Fig. 158: X RAW STUDIO offers a straightforward workflow. After connecting the X-T5 to your Mac or PC, you begin with selecting a RAW image from your computer's hard drive, then apply various JPEG setting changes. You can also adjust the exposure with PUSH/PULL PROCESSING, decrease DR, DR-P, HDR, and teleconverter settings and change the aspect ratio and output size of the result.

Image **A** shows an unspectacular macro shot with PROVIA default camera settings at ISO 125. Image **B** is the same shot with a few JPEG setting changes: IMAGE SIZE 5:4, PUSH/PULL PROCESSING −1.66 EV, CLASSIC Neg., WHITE BALANCE AUTO WHITE PRIORITY, WB SHIFT R:+2, B:+2, HIGHLIGHT TONE −2, SHADOW TONE +2, HIGH ISO NR −4, CLARITY −5.

Image **C** shows a JPEG that was exposed for the highlights at Base ISO 125 with PROVIA default camera settings and AUTO WB. It looks rather bland. Image **D** is the same shot with the following adjustments: IMAGE SIZE 16:9, PUSH/PULL PROCESSING −1.66 EV, PRO Neg. Hi, COLOR CHROME EFFECT STRONG, COLOR CHROME FX BLUE STRONG, HIGHLIGHT TONE +2, SHADOW TONE −2, COLOR +4, SHARPENING +1, HIGH ISO NR −4, CLARITY +2.

2.6 FLASH PHOTOGRAPHY

Flash photography means taking a double exposure. The lighting in a flash shot always consists of two components: **ambient light** and **flash light**.

- The **ambient-light** component is metered like a regular exposure. Your camera is metering the scene with multi, average, center-weighted, or spot metering, while the auto exposure mode (**P**, **A**, or **S**) automatically selects suitable exposure parameters based on your adjustment of the exposure compensation dial. As usual, the live view and live histogram are your friends. You can also set the exposure of the ambient-light component manually in mode **M**, which is my preferred method in almost all situations. Basically, exposing for the ambient-light component works exactly like exposing a scene without flash.

- The **flash-light** component can be automatically metered and adjusted by the camera to match the overall exposure. To accomplish this, the camera employs a so-called TTL metering system [85]. TTL stands for Through The Lens. It means the flash light is entering the camera through the lens before it's metered with the image sensor. This happens with the help of a weaker pre-flash that is emitted solely for metering purposes. You can bias the strength of the automatic flash-light component either on the FLASH FUNCTION SETTING page, or directly on external Fujifilm TTL flash units like the EF-X500. Please note that while the live view and live histogram provide a preview of the ambient-light component, they completely ignore the flash-light component that will be added to the final image.

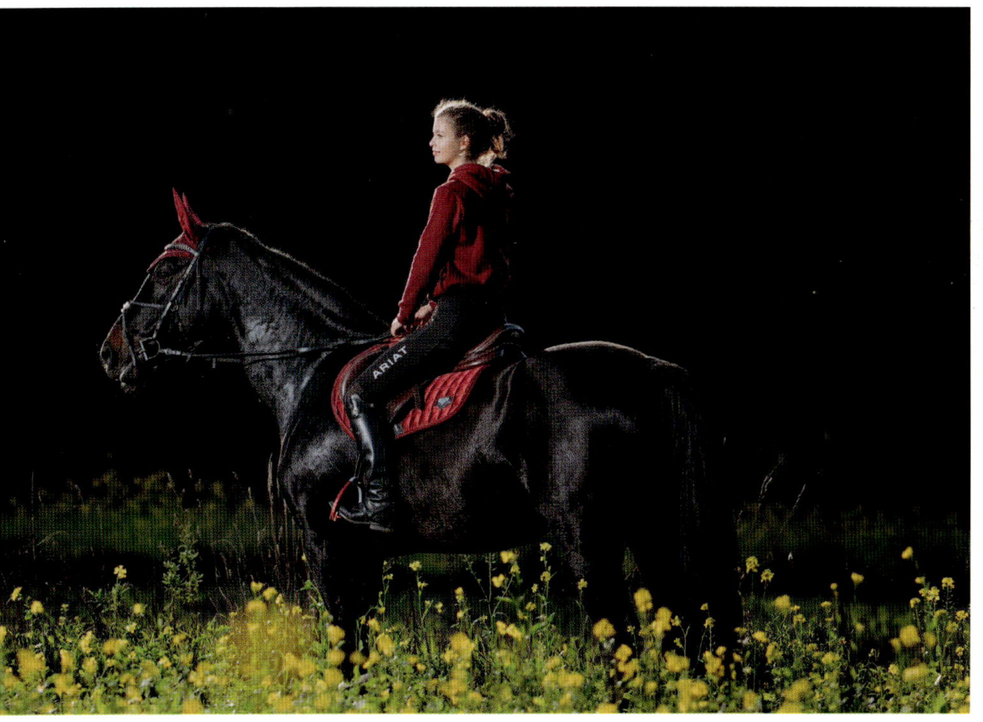

Fig. 159: In many cases, **flash photography** is about balancing the natural ambient light and the artificially added flash light.

In addition to Fujifilm-branded or Fujifilm-compatible TTL flash units, you can use generic third-party flash units. Pretty much everything that will fit onto the hot shoe will work. Using generic third-party flash units means that TTL flash metering is no longer available, so you must manually set the flash's power output. You can also use automatic flash units that use their own built-in light sensors to automatically measure and adjust the flash output independently from the camera.

<table>
<tr><td>TIP 116</td><td>Understanding flash modes</td></tr>
</table>

The TTL flash logic in your X-T5 supports several flash modes that can be selected in the Quick menu or on the FLASH SETTING > FLASH FUNCTION SETTING page.

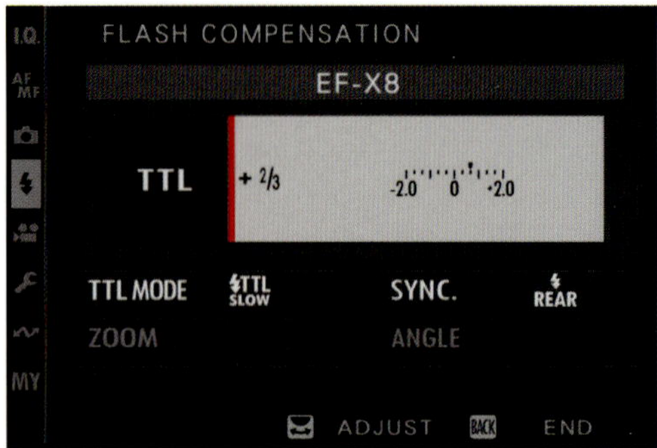

Fig. 160: The FLASH FUNCTION SETTING page lets you control flash parameters such as flash mode, sync. mode, and flash exposure compensation.

- TTL FLASH AUTO is available only in auto exposure mode P. It automatically fires an available flash unit if the camera decides it's necessary. It's a silly mode, since you probably know better than your camera whether you want to use a flash. When the flash is firing, it works just like regular TTL, which is our next mode.

- TTL STANDARD always fires an active flash unit. This setting is available in all four exposure modes (P, A, S, and M). In modes P and A (where the camera's auto exposure determines the shutter speed), the slowest available shutter speed is 1/60 sec., meaning parts of the scene that cannot be illuminated by the flash-light component may be underexposed.

- TTL SLOW SYNC. works like standard TTL but allows slower shutter speeds than 1/60 sec. to better capture the ambient-light component. This can be helpful when the light is poor, and you still want to capture more of the background. This setting is only available in exposure modes **P** and **A**. However, in concert with AUTO-ISO, this mode will only go slower than 1/60 sec. if AUTO-ISO has reached the ISO ceiling set with MAX. SENSITIVITY *and* the AE-determined shutter speed is slower than the MIN. SHUTTER SPEED setting. Hence, I recommend *not* using AUTO-ISO in concert with TTL SLOW SYNC. flash photography.

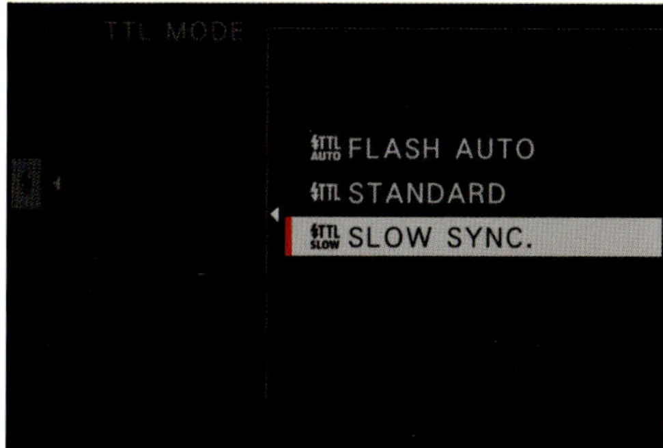

Fig. 161: If you insist on using the AE modes **P** or **A** to automatically expose the ambient-light component of your flash image, selecting TTL SLOW SYNC. will reduce the minimum shutter speed the camera can use to sync with the flash. However, I recommend exposing the ambient-light component in mode **M**. The main reason is maintaining full control over the look of the picture and the balance between ambient light and flash light.

- MANUAL FLASH works like TTL SLOW SYNC. but allows you to manually specify the light flash emission power. This setting is available in all four exposure modes (**P**, **A**, **S**, and **M**).

- OFF makes sure no flash is fired, even when the flash is switched on and connected to the camera.

- In the FLASH FUNCTION SETTING page, there is also an option to specify whether the flash is supposed to fire on the FRONT (1st CURTAIN) or REAR (2nd CURTAIN). This option is available in all flash modes, and it is relevant for shooting moving subjects at slow shutter speeds.

Since flash photography is a double exposure, it makes a difference whether the flash is fired at the beginning or at the end of a longer ambient-light exposure. With higher-end flashguns like the EF-X500, there's also an option called FP, which stands for Focal Plane. This is Fuji's version of High-Speed Synchronization (HSS), which allows firing the flash at all mechanical shutter speeds up to 1/8000 sec.

TIP 117 Controlling the ambient-light component

When you are metering a scene with your X-T5, you will quickly realize it makes no difference whether the flash function is turned on or off while doing so. The metering result will always be the same. In other words, the camera is metering the ambient-light component always in the same way, with or without flash. In case you choose to use a flash, the flash-light component will simply be *added* to the ambient-light component.

This is important because it tells us we don't have to fear some camera voodoo that may or may not influence the metering of the ambient light as soon as we switch on a flash. Instead, we can be certain the camera's metering will always deliver consistent results. This also means it's *our* job to balance both light components; for example, we can reduce the ambient-light component to make room for more flash light in the composite exposure.

If you want to use the TTL flash as a fill light to brighten a dark foreground (such as a backlit person), the flash-light component will brighten the foreground by filling in the light that's missing. However, if you use the flash on a scene that's already fully exposed by natural light, the camera's TTL flash metering will probably conclude that no additional light is needed. A forced flash would still fire, but with minimal output; it would probably be almost invisible in the resulting shot. To emphasize the flash-light component, you must reduce the exposure of the ambient-light component.

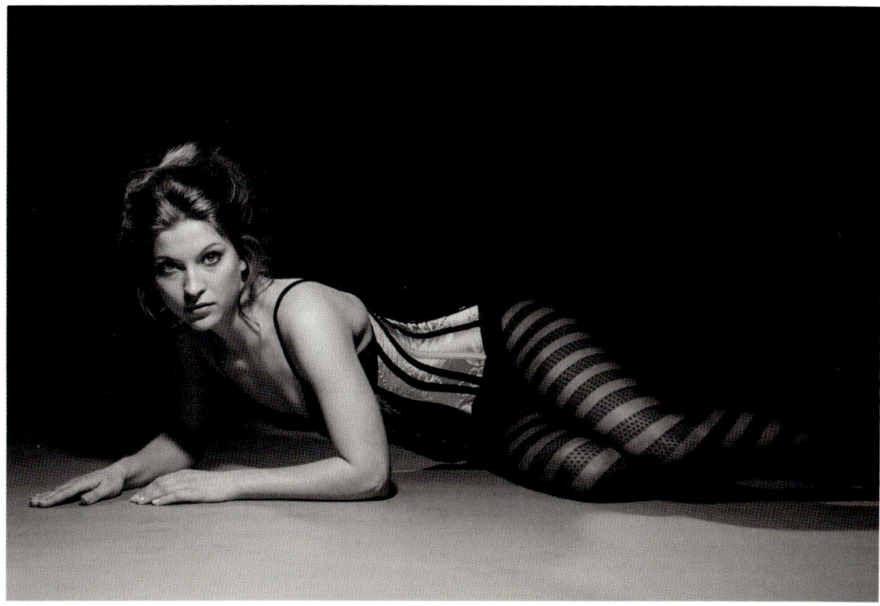

Fig. 162: Reducing the ambient-light component to darken the background leaves more room for the flash-light component. This is particularly easy in a studio, where you have full control over the intensity of both light components.

Here's how it works:

- You can control the exposure of the ambient-light component either with the exposure compensation dial or by setting an appropriate manual exposure (ISO, aperture, shutter speed). Less ambient light will prompt the TTL flash metering to add a stronger flash-light component, since the TTL flash system will always try to deliver balanced results. Changing the exposure compensation dial has no effect on the flash component of the shot; it only affects the exposure of the ambient-light component.

- To control the ambient-light component in manual mode **M** using the live view and the live histogram, make sure the exposure preview in manual mode is enabled by selecting SET UP > SCREEN SET-UP > PREVIEW EXP./WB IN MANUAL MODE > PREVIEW EXP./WB.

- In a studio setting, you often want to minimize the ambient-light component and illuminate your subject entirely with flash light. In such cases, I recommend smaller aperture settings (larger aperture numbers), base ISO 125, and a fast shutter speed. The fastest *official* flash synchronization speed of the X-T5 is 1/250 sec. To compose a studio scene with very little ambient light in mode **M**, make sure the exposure preview in manual mode is disabled by selecting SET UP > SCREEN SET-UP > PREVIEW EXP./ WB IN MANUAL MODE > OFF. Otherwise, it will be hard for you to see anything in the viewfinder other than a dark or black image.

- Sometimes the fastest available flash sync speed will still overexpose the ambient-light component, even at base ISO. Yes, you could stop down the aperture, but this might negate the purpose of achieving a nice subject-to-background separation with a shallow depth of field. In such a case, it's useful to attach a neutral density filter [86] to the lens to reduce the amount of light that hits the sensor by 3 to 6 stops. Alternatively, you can use a Fuji-compatible flash that supports high-speed sync (HSS).

- Like the DR function, flash light is often used to reduce the contrast between a darker foreground-subject and a brighter background. You can combine both features (flash and the DR function), which may be useful if the background—when viewed isolated from the foreground—still contains so much contrast that DR expansion is required. Think of a night scene with city lights, street lamps, and bright billboards in the background. In such a scenario, a flashgun could illuminate a person standing in the foreground, while the DR function (DR400%) would help capture the bright colors and textures of the city lights. DR400% is also useful when you are illuminating scenes with subjects that expand deep into space and don't have an equal distance to the camera. In such cases, DR400% will give subjects that are closer to the flash light an additional overexposure protection of 2 EV, which can be retrieved during external RAW conversion of your shot.

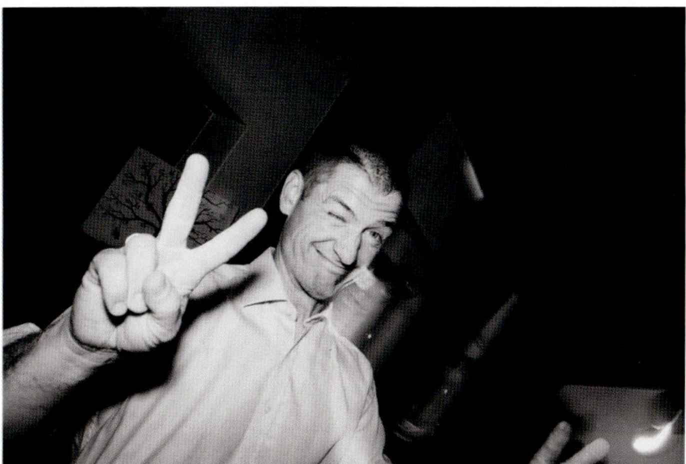

Fig. 163: Shooting close-ups with **a hot-shoe flash and a wide-angle lens** can make things tricky. For this snapshot, I used a XF16mmF1.4 lens at f/6.4, 1/6 sec., and ISO 800/DR400% in exposure mode **M**. The hand of the party guest happens to be much closer to the camera (and hence to the TTL flash) than his face, so with every "normal" camera, the hand would either be overexposed, or the face would be underexposed by the flash light. Not with Fujifilm, though. The DR function comes to the rescue. By manually setting DR400%, the guest's hand can be overexposed up to 2 EV by the TTL flash—and we can still fully recover it during external RAW conversion. In this case, I used Lightroom.

■ The previously discussed 1/60 sec. limit for the minimum shutter speed in modes **P** and **A** can lead to an underexposed ambient-light component. However, this limit can be somewhat useful because it prevents blurred backgrounds in hand-held shots. This isn't an issue when using a tripod, so you could circumvent the limit by selecting TTL SLOW or by manually setting a slow shutter speed in **S** or **M** mode. I personally recommend using **M** mode.

- Ambient light and flash light frequently exhibit different color temperatures, which makes it difficult to find a white balance setting that suits all parts of the image. Luckily, some RAW converters (like Lightroom) allow selective white balance editing in an image. Another method is to use a gel filter in front of the flash unit to warm or cool the flash light to better match the ambient light.

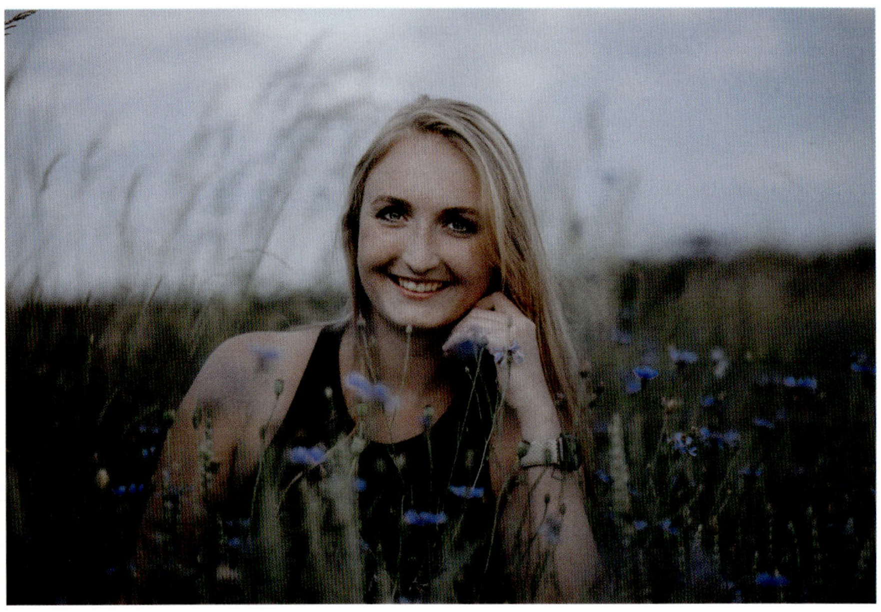

Fig. 164: With plenty of **ambient light**, the flash-light component takes a backseat. In this example, it simply added a spark to the eyes. The best flash shots are often those that are hard to identify as flash photography.

TIP 118	Controlling the flash-light component

If the flash-light component of your image turns out too bright or dark, you can bias the camera's TTL flash system:

- To bias the flash-light component of your shot, you can adjust the flash exposure compensation in the camera on the FLASH SETTING > FLASH FUNCTION SETTING page or directly on many external TTL flash units. Combining the in-camera flash compensation with an additional compensation setting on the flash unit itself can sometimes add-up both corrections, depending on the flash unit you are using.

- You will often get nicer-looking results by bouncing the flash off the ceiling, as this softens the harsh flash light. Of course, bouncing the flash light requires more power, so you may need a stronger flash. It's also worth noting that bouncing the flash from a colored surface will tint the light accordingly.

- To add a tint or to change the color temperature of your flash light, you can attach colored gel filters in front of your reflector. The color temperature of unfiltered flash light usually corresponds to regular daylight.

- The range of your flash unit depends on the set aperture, the ISO setting, and (of course) the power setting. In TTL mode, the camera is automatically adjusting the light output of your flash, but many flash units can also be set to manual. This way, you are the one setting the power output of the flash. In manual mode **M**, changing the shutter speed doesn't affect the brightness of the flash-light component of your shot if you remain at or below the official maximum sync speed of 1/250 sec. Hence, changing the shutter speed is a quick way to adjust the exposure of the ambient-light component without messing with your carefully balanced manual flash-light setup.

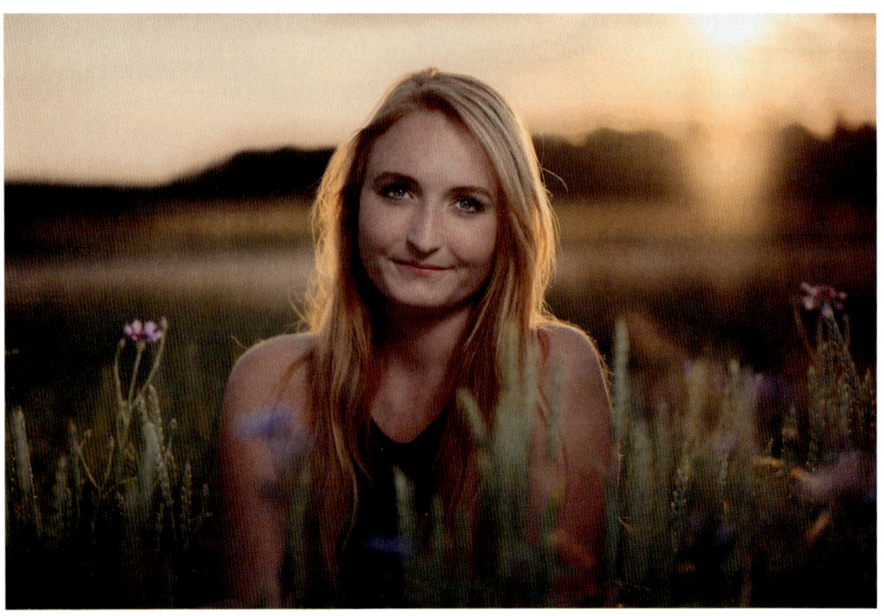

Fig. 165: Having **full manual control over both light components** is my preferred and recommended way of merging flash light and ambient light—as long as there's enough time to make the necessary adjustments.

- Don't forget that when using an on-camera hot-shoe flash, large lenses and lens hoods might block parts of the flash light, resulting in unpleasant shadows. It's better to remove the lens hood or to use an off-camera flash.

- Some wide-angle lenses cover a larger angle of view than the reflector of your flash can handle. This results in vignetting. In such cases, bouncing the flash light off the ceiling can be helpful. Alternatively, you can attach a diffusor to the flash reflector. Many flash units feature built-in diffusors—just don't forget to flip them on.

Front-curtain vs. rear-curtain flash synchronization	TIP 119

Flash photographs are double exposures consisting of ambient light and flash light. When you shoot the ambient light with a slow shutter speed, there is the question of when the flash (with its much faster speed) should fire. Normally, the flash is fired at the *beginning* of an exposure with the shutter opening its FRONT (or 1st) curtain. However, if the REAR (or 2nd) curtain has been selected, the flash fires at the *end* of the exposure when the rear shutter curtain closes.

Naturally, moving objects change their position during the exposure of a shot. Synchronizing the flash with the rear curtain ensures that moving objects are frozen where they are located at the end of the exposure as opposed to at the beginning. This often results in the moving object appearing more natural in the image.

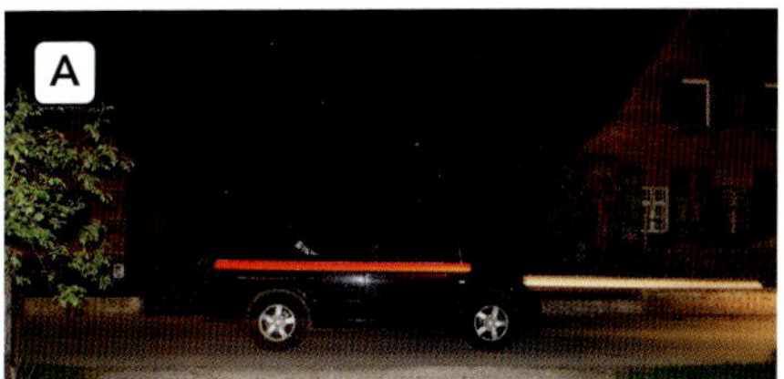
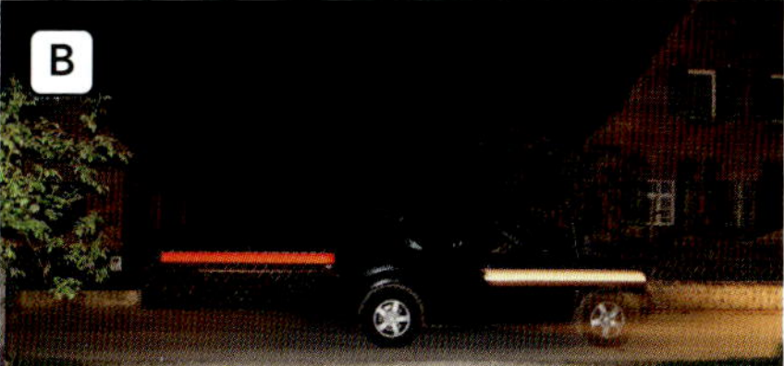

Fig. 166: Front- versus rear-curtain sync: This example shows the same scene photographed with front-curtain sync (**A**) and rear-curtain sync (**B**). Image A shows how the flash freezes the moving vehicle at the beginning of the exposure, while image B shows it being frozen at the end of the exposure. The rear-curtain version looks more natural and avoids the false impression of the car moving backward. This is also a good example to examine the nature of flash photographs as double exposures. You can see how the slow shutter speed captures the moving vehicle as a blurry trail of light, while the fast flash instantly freezes parts of it.

TIP 120 | Flash synchronization: what's the limit?

The maximum official flash sync [87] speed of the X-T5 is 1/250 sec.

- In exposure modes **P** and **A**, the camera will never offer a shutter speed faster than the official maximum sync speed. If this is too slow for the current light conditions, the ambient-light component will be overexposed. In this case, the shutter speed will be displayed in red. To avoid overexposure, stop down the lens, reduce ISO (but never below base ISO 125), or use a neutral density (ND) filter [88] in front of the lens.

- In exposure modes **S** and **M**, you can select shutter speeds faster than the maximum sync speed. Your camera will honor these settings in flash mode, but there is a price to pay: the resulting images may display some partial shadowing of the flash. That said, it's often possible to use shutter speeds that are a little bit faster than the official maximum sync speed without visible negative effects—it depends on the type of flash you are using. Its power setting plays a role, as well. Proceed at your own risk!

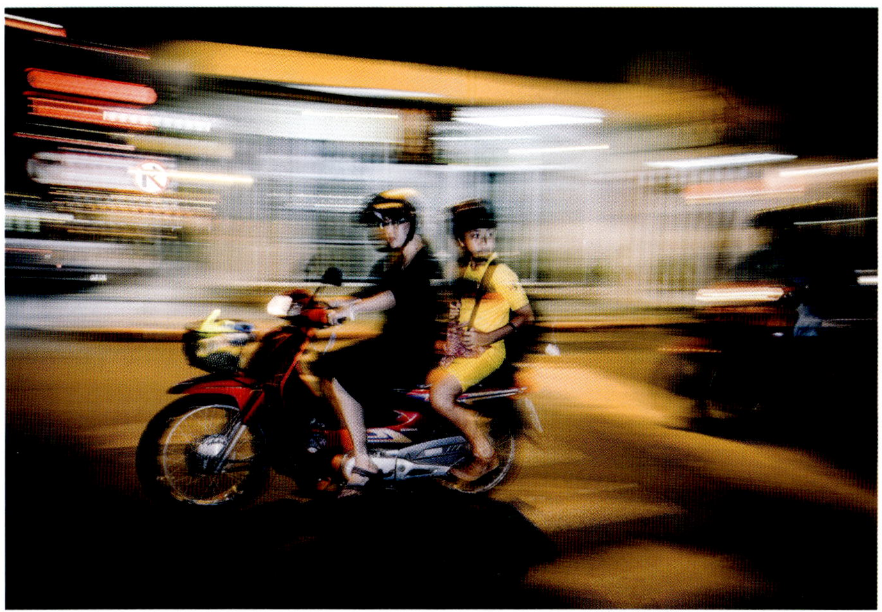

Fig. 167: Many photographers wish to use a **flash sync speed** faster than the maximum sync speed of their camera. However, it's also possible to deliberately use very slow synch speeds to create a blurry background behind a more contoured flash-lit foreground. This shot was taken with an EF-X500.

- High-speed synchronization (HSS, also known as FP mode) up to 1/8000 sec. is officially supported by the X-T5. To use it, your flash device must support HSS and Fujifilm's flash system.

- HSS/FP consumes more flash power, so you may need a more powerful flash device to compensate HSS-related losses. Depending on the brand and type of your flash, the effective power reduction that occurs at the transition point between normal sync and high-speed sync can vary.

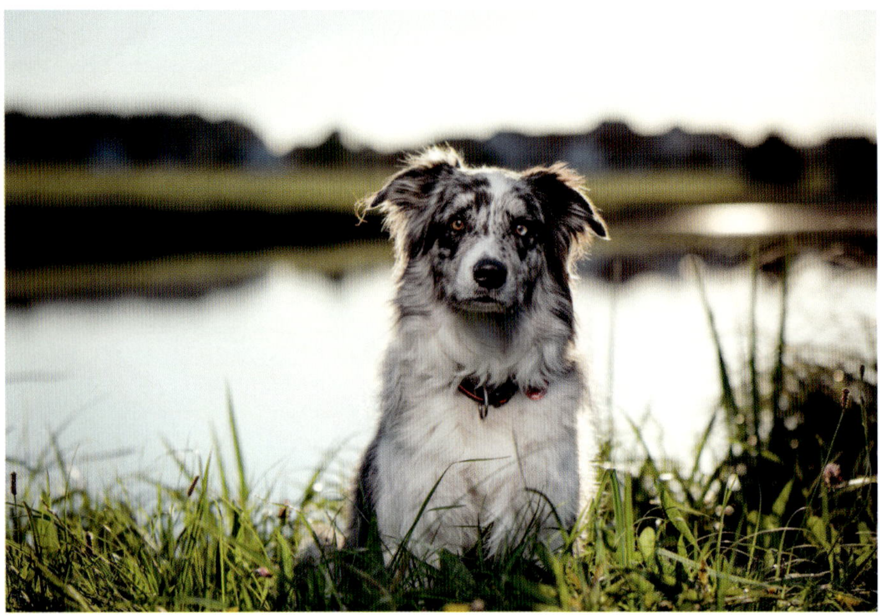

Fig. 168: This manually controlled **HSS** shot was taken at a shutter speed of 1/8000 sec.

TIP 121	Red-eye removal

If the flash and your subject share almost the same optical axis (a frequent occurrence with a hot-shoe flash), it can lead to the red-eye effect [89]: an unpleasant red reflection in the eyes.

If you pull up FLASH SETTING > RED EYE REMOVAL and then FLASH, the camera will emit a pre-flash prior to each shot that forces your subject's pupils to contract, thus reducing or eliminating the red-eye effect.

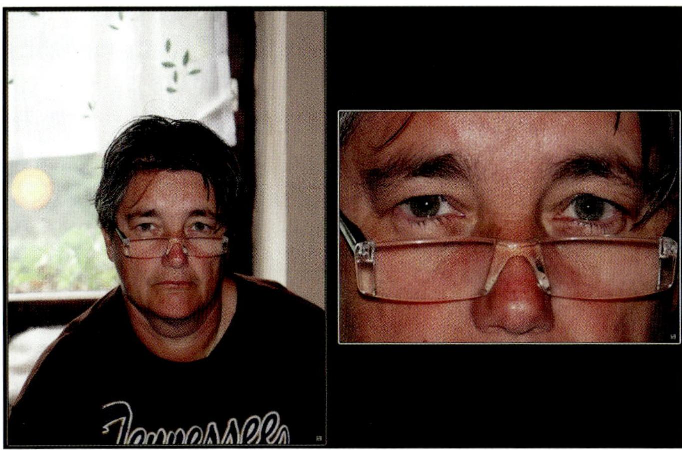

Fig. 169: The **red-eye removal** function emits a pre-flash that is bright enough to prompt your subject's pupils to contract.

Using TTL-Lock	TIP 122

TTL-Lock works like AE-Lock. Where AE-Lock locks the exposure of the ambient-light component, TTL-Lock locks the exposure of the flash-light component. To use TTL-Lock, you must first assign it to one of your camera's Fn buttons. To do so, press and hold the DISP/BACK button until the Fn configuration screen appears.

TTL-Lock can work in one of two ways:

- Keep and lock the exposure of the most recent flash exposure when you press the TTL-Lock button (FLASH SETTING > TTL-LOCK MODE > LOCK WITH LAST FLASH).

- Meter the flash exposure with a metering flash when you press the TTL-Lock button and immediately lock the metered result (FLASH SETTING > TTL-LOCK MODE > LOCK WITH METERING FLASH).

TTL-Lock is practical in situations where you want to take more than one picture of the same scene and maintain a consistent flash output for the entire series. A typical method involves setting the LOCK WITH LAST FLASH option, and then taking a few test shots of the scene and applying flash exposure compensation until the result looks great. Now press TTL-Lock to lock and maintain this "perfect" flash exposure while you take additional pictures of the scene.

TTL-Lock also allows higher frame rates in burst mode. In this scenario, you will probably prefer the LOCK WITH METERING FLASH setting. Pressing TTL-Lock will then meter scene and store the calculated flash exposure. As you then take images in burst mode, the frame rate will be faster because the camera doesn't have to emit and analyze a new metering flash before each frame.

TIP 123	Grand master: the Fujifilm EF-X500

The EF-X500 is Fuji's version of a professional hot-shoe-mounted flashgun, with wireless TTL control of several flash devices (organized in up to three independent groups) and stroboscope flash. It has a secondary LED reflector that can be used as a catch light [90], a more powerful AF assist lamp, or a video lamp. It also features FP high-speed sync to support shutter speeds of up to 1/8000 sec.

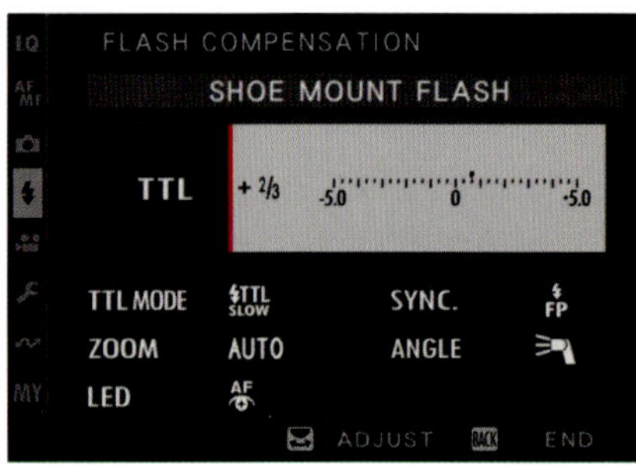

Fig. 170: With the fully featured **EF-X500** attached, the FLASH FUNCTION SETTING page adds several new items, including high-speed sync (FP), zoom settings, a reflector angle control, and control of the secondary LED, which can be used as an AF assist lamp and/or a catch light.

You can use the EF-X500 as a single clip-on flashgun or as a master/slave in setups with multiple wireless flash units. Communication between master and slave units is light based.

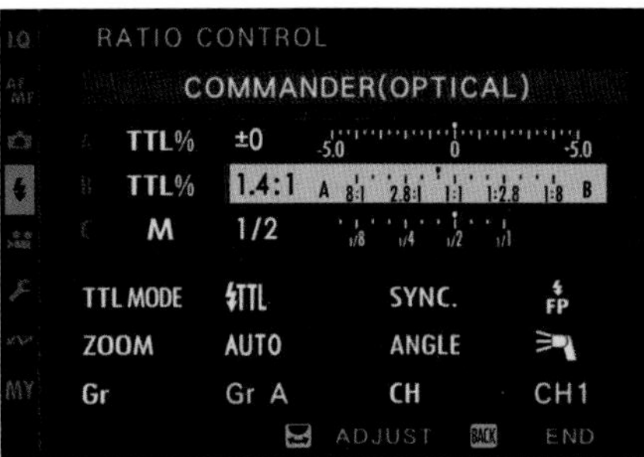

Fig. 171: In **TTL master mode**, one EF-X500 can control several compatible flashguns in three independent groups (A, B, C) via a light communication protocol. Each group can be controlled via direct TTL or as a ratio of another TTL group, or it can be manually controlled.

While the EF-X500 has many great features and delivers good quality, there are also a few negative aspects to it:

- The flash is quite large, heavy, and expensive.

- Wireless TTL control is realized with outdated light signals instead of state-of-the-art radio transmission.

- Users must purchase and attach a heavy and expensive EF-X500 as a wireless master controller. The small EF-X8 cannot be used as a master control flash.

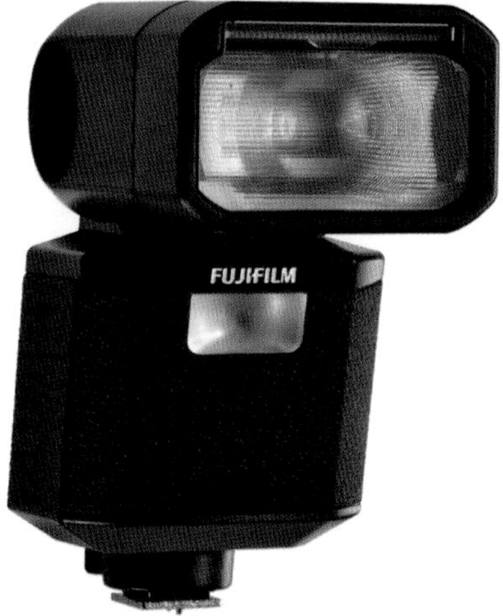

Fig. 172: The **EF-X500** is Fujifilm's pro speedlight. It leans a bit to the large, heavy, and expensive side. At this level, one would expect wireless TTL based on radio transmission instead of the outdated light signals it still uses.

<table>
<tr><td>TIP 124</td><td>Generic third-party flash units</td></tr>
</table>

Basically, you can use any modern flashgun from any vendor with your X-T5 if you are prepared to set its power manually. You can connect third-party flash units directly to the camera's hot shoe or use a cable or a wireless (radio) triggering device.

The camera's TTL modes are not available when you are using generic third-party flashes because the camera isn't *metering* the flash light, it's only *triggering* the flash. There's also no HSS support.

This makes using generic flash equipment possible but inconvenient. Luckily, major flash brands like Broncolor, Profoto, and Elinchom are now supporting Fujifilm with dedicated transmitters for the Fujifilm X-series. They also support HSS.

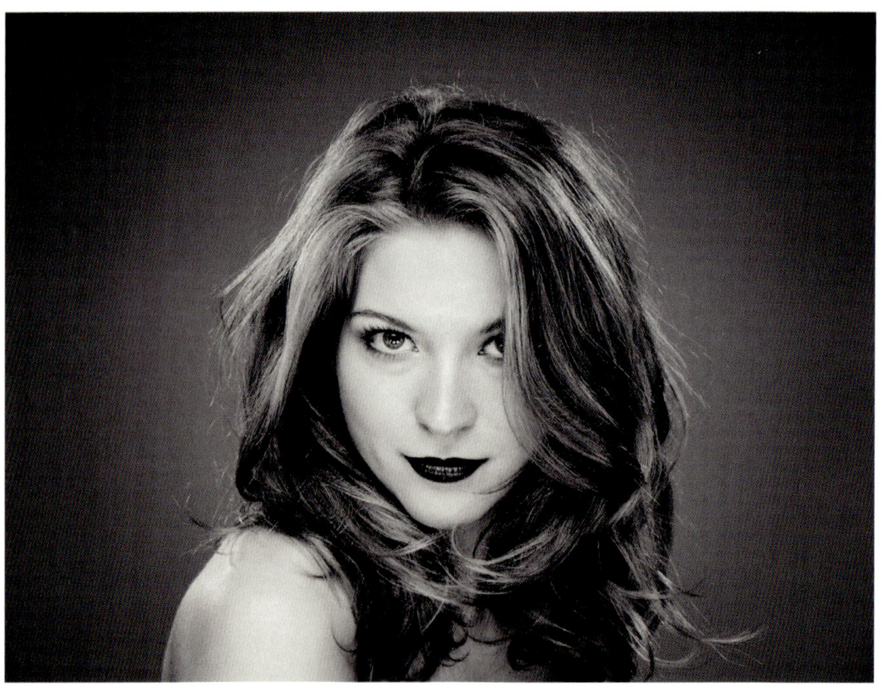

Fig. 173: A manually controlled **studio flash shot**.

2.7 USING ADAPTED LENSES

Thanks to its short flange-back distance, the X-mount system can host many full-frame, medium format, cinema (Super 35 and larger), or APS-C lenses. All you need is an appropriate adapter ring. This means that in addition to more than two-dozen native lenses, you have access to hundreds of additional modern and legacy lenses.

Finding the right lens adapter	TIP 125

X-mount lens adapters are available for many old and current lens mounts. Here are a few tips to help you find the right adapter for your third-party lens:

- Adapters are available at a wide range of price and quality levels, and, as usual, you get what you pay for. Don't try to skimp too much or you may end up buying twice. The German manufacturer Novoflex has set the benchmark here, but even their simple, mechanical adapters could cost more than the lens you are adapting. Manufacturers like Kipon or Metabones enjoy good reputations and they offer adapters for a wide variety of lens mounts.

- With mechanical adapters, third-party lenses can only be used as manual focus lenses with manual mechanical aperture control. Smart electronic adapters can translate between Fuji's AF protocol and the AF protocols of popular brands like Canon or Nikon, and they can also control the aperture of the lens. Some even support the OIS of the third-party lens.

- With mechanical adapters, adapted lenses always operate with a manually set working aperture. This means that when you are stopping down the lens, the live view and live histogram of your camera must contend with the smaller aperture's reduced amount of light. It also means that mechanically adapted lenses can only be used in exposure modes **A** or **M**. With smart adapters, all exposure modes should be available.

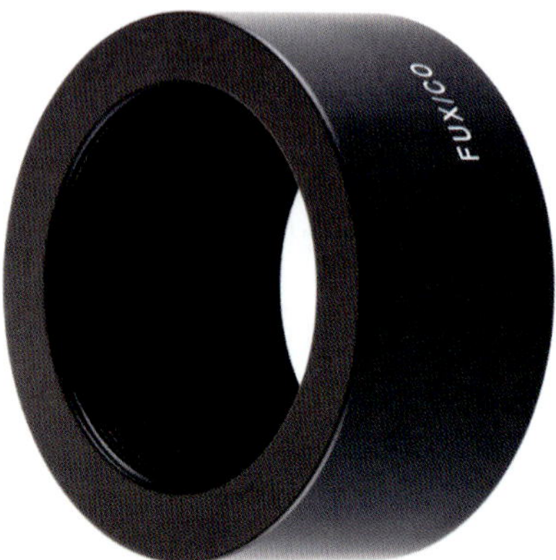

Fig. 174: Mechanical **M42 adapters** like this high-end model from Novoflex allow you to connect legacy M42 screw-mount lenses to X-mount cameras.

- Many modern third-party lenses that don't feature a manual aperture ring can still be mechanically adapted to your camera, but you can't change their apertures while they are connected via a mechanical adapter. This is why some of these adapters feature a mechanical replacement aperture; nevertheless, the results produced by these devices will differ from the results created by the original lens. If available, use a smart adapter for such lenses.

- Modern electronic features like optical image stabilization (OIS) aren't supported by mechanical adapters since there is no communication or power transfer between the camera and the adapted lens. In fact, the camera believes that there's no lens attached at all. Some smart adapters do offer OIS support, though.

- *Speed Booster Ultra* from Metabones offers the fascinating possibility to attach full-frame legacy lenses from several systems to X-mount cameras without changing their original angle of view or cropping the image on your camera's smaller APS-C sensor. With Speed Booster, your APS-C camera sees what a full-frame (35 mm format) camera would see. Speed Booster is a focal reducer—basically the opposite of a teleconverter [91]. It reduces the focal length of the adapted lens by a factor of 0.71. At the same time, the brightness (speed) of the lens is increased by about one stop. At $400 to $600 apiece, Speed Booster adapters aren't cheap. However, they offer better quality than knock-off products like the Lens Turbo II by Zhongyi Mitakon.

- Fujifilm offers its own X-mount adapter for Leica M-type full-frame lenses. This is a regular adapter (no Speed Booster), but it features electronic contacts, so your camera will recognize the adapter when it's mounted. It also features an Fn button that provides direct access to the camera's MOUNT ADAPTOR SETTING menu. With all other mechanical adapters, to take a picture you must set SET UP > BUTTON/DIAL SETTING > SHOOT WITHOUT LENS > ON.

- Be careful with cheap macro lens adapters with electronic contacts. These knock off adapters are designed to serve as macro spacer rings for native X-mount lenses. They promise full AF functionality thanks to their electronic contacts, but sometimes, these adapter rings can be a poor fit and can damage your camera and lenses. Instead, I recommend using Fujifilm's original electronic macro extension tubes.

- If possible, don't combine more than one adapter. Stacking adapters leads to a measurable and visible loss in quality. Instead, get the right adapter for your lens.

TIP 126	Adapting third-party lenses

When you connect third-party lenses to your camera via a mechanical adapter, the camera won't notice this due to the lack of electronic contacts. It will think there is no lens.

- To make the camera work with mechanically adapted lenses, select SET UP > BUTTON/DIAL SETTING > SHOOT WITHOUT LENS > ON.

- Enter the focal length of your adapted lens in the SHOOTING SETTING > MOUNT ADAPTOR SETTING menu. You can enter the focal lengths of up to six different lenses. Always enter the actual focal length of the adapted lens (the value that is printed on the lens), not its full-frame equivalent. This not only ensures that the EXIF data will display the correct focal length, but it is also a requirement for the built-in image stabilization (IBIS) to work correctly.

- If you are using an optical adapter that *changes* the focal length of the adapted lens, such as a Metabones Speed Booster, you must enter the *adjusted* focal length. For example, if the crop factor of your Speed Booster is 0.71x, you must multiply the focal length of your adapted lens with this value and enter the result. For example, using a 180 mm lens would result in a focal length of 180 × 0.71 = 127.8, so you'd have to enter 128 mm in the MOUNT ADAPTOR SETTING menu.

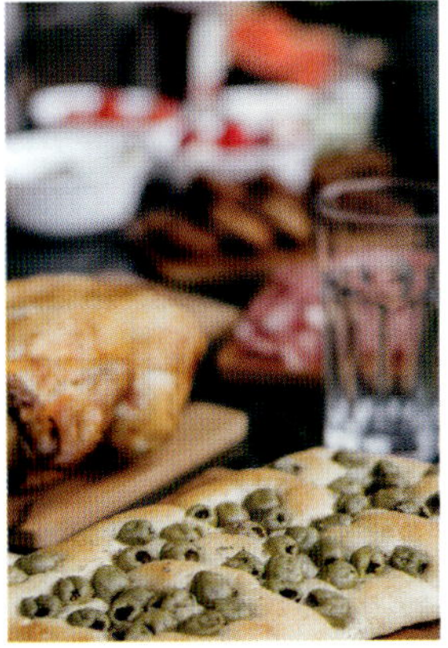 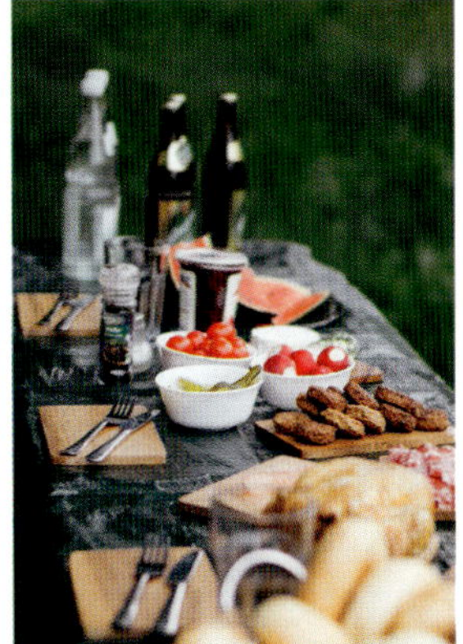 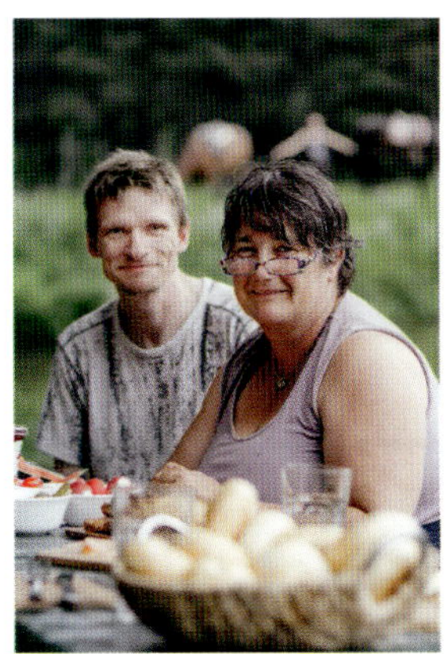

Fig. 175: Third-party lenses with "character" can help you achieve images with a distinctive look and bokeh. For this series, I attached a Voigtländer Heliar 75mmF1.8 M-mount lens and shot it wide-open at f/1.8.

Exposing with mechanically adapted lenses	TIP 127

Mechanically adapted lenses can be used in exposure modes **A** (aperture priority) and **M** (manual mode). There are also a few notable differences between exposing with native lenses and adapted lenses:

- Native lenses close to the working aperture when the shutter is half-pressed or when the shot is taken. Mechanically adapted lenses always operate with the aperture set by the user. As soon as you stop down an adapted lens, less light reaches the sensor and the camera's exposure metering. Stopping down adapted lenses increases the depth of field in the viewfinder.

- Since less light reaches the sensor when the lens is stopped down, the camera must increase the live view image amplification to display an accurate WYSIWYG simulation of the scene. This decreases the quality of the live view image and can also negatively affect the live view's frame rate.

- Since the camera thinks that there's no lens attached at all, the aperture is always displayed as F0 in the viewfinder (and f/1 in the EXIF data). There's no way for the camera to know which aperture has been set on a mechanically adapted lens.

- Shooting in poor light with mechanically adapted lenses can be tricky when you stop down the aperture. It's possible to reach the live view's amplification limit. Once this limit is reached, the live view and live histogram cannot display the actual brightness of the scene, so it appears darker than the image that will be exposed. However, exposure metering will still work correctly, and in aperture priority mode, the camera will display the correct shutter speed.

- Since the electronic live view cannot control the aperture of a mechanically adapted lens, it takes longer for the camera to adjust to abrupt brightness changes. The camera may need a few seconds for the live view to adapt to the changing brightness levels.

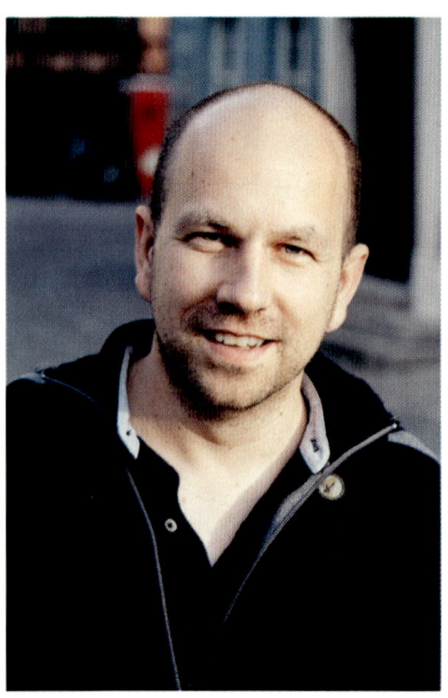

Fig. 176: With mechanical adapters, **exposing with adapted lenses** is limited to modes A and M, and metering always takes place at the set working aperture. No matter which aperture you set, EXIF data will always show f/1. For this street portrait, I attached a Helios 44M-4 lens to my camera using a Novoflex M42 adapter.

<table>
<tr><td>Focusing with mechanically adapted lenses</td><td>TIP 128</td></tr>
</table>

Mechanically adapted lenses can only be focused manually. Here are a few tips to make things easier for you:

- Set your camera to manual focus. This makes sure that MF assistants such as Focus Check, focus peaking, and digital split image are available.

- The electronic distance and depth-of-field (DOF) scale of your camera is useless in concert with mechanically adapted lenses. Instead, you must rely on analog scales and markers that may be engraved in the barrel of your adapted lens. Remember that the DOF scale on your lens is probably less conservative than what you're used to from the electronic scale in your camera. The analog scale doesn't guarantee pixel-sharp results at 100% image magnification. Instead, it will more likely resemble the FILM FORMAT BASIS option of the electronic DOF scale.

- The most important tool for focusing with adapted lenses is the magnifier tool. You can usually activate it by pressing the rear command dial (if you didn't change its default Fn button assignment). Turn the rear command dial to cycle between the available magnifications. Don't forget: instead of focusing and recomposing, it's better to select a focus frame position that covers the part of the image you want to be in focus.

- Use focus peaking or another MF assistant. You can cycle between these MF assistants and the standard view by pressing and holding the rear command dial. The magnifier tool can be combined with focus peaking, digital split image, and digital microprism. However, in concert with digital split image and digital microprism, only one magnification level is available.

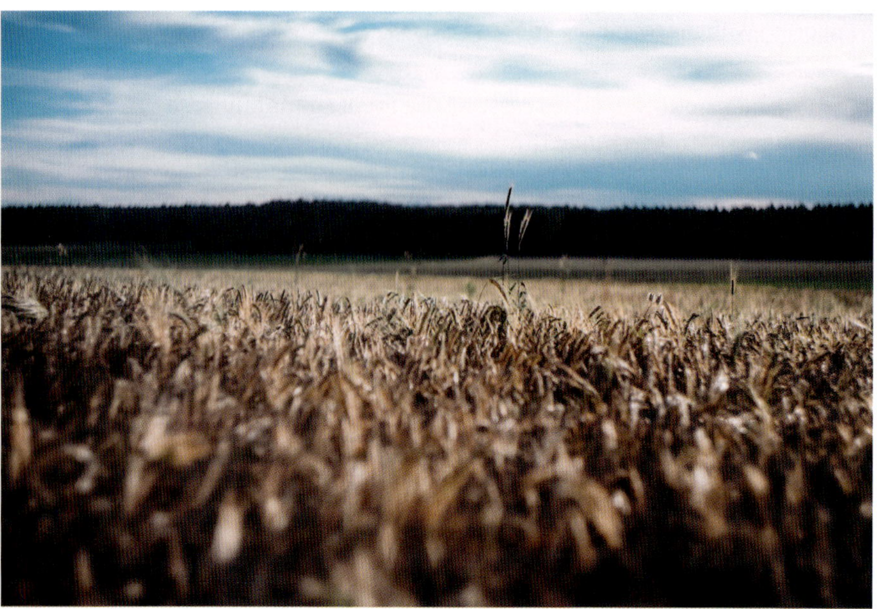

Fig. 177: Focusing mechanically adapted lenses can be tricky. My preferred method for obtaining manual pinpoint focus is to use focus peaking in concert with the magnifier tool. This example was shot with a Helios 44M-4 lens that was adapted using a Lens Turbo II focal reducer.

- The magnifier tool and MF assistants work best with the aperture wide open, when the DOF is as shallow as possible. However, some lenses exhibit focus shift, meaning the focus plane shifts when the lens is stopped down. The increased DOF from stopping down the lens may not be sufficient to compensate for the focus shift, so your carefully focused shot will end up out of focus when the aperture is closed. If you are using a lens with pronounced focus shift, it's better to focus with the actual working aperture instead of the wide-open aperture. Please note that focus shift isn't a matter of price—even a few high-end lenses from Leica and Zeiss exhibit it quite prominently.

<table><tr><td>Using the Fujifilm M-mount adapter</td><td>TIP 129</td></tr></table>

Fuji's own Leica M-mount adapter is a little bit different from conventional adapters:

- The adapter features electronic lens contacts to identify itself to the camera. However, there's no transmission of lens data since the adapter doesn't know which M-type lens has been attached or what distance and aperture has been set. Sadly, the electronic contacts also make the inner adapter tube thinner than normal, so not all M-type lenses are physically compatible with it. To be certain, you can review a list of compatible and incompatible lenses [92]. Fuji also encloses a template with its M adapter that you can use to find out if your M lens measures up with the adapter.

- Pressing the function button on the adapter directly opens the camera's adapter menu.

- The camera's adapter menu offers a few additional functions when a Fuji M-mount adapter is attached. In addition to entering the focal length, you can also enter correction values for lens distortion, color shading, and vignetting. Those corrections affect the JPEGs during RAW conversion with the built-in or external RAW converters. As usual, the corrections are burned into the RAW file metadata where they can be interpreted by RAW conversion software. However, color-shade data is currently only processed by the camera's built-in converter. For each adapted lens, you must find out the right correction values for yourself before you can enter them. There aren't any reference lists you can use that I know of.

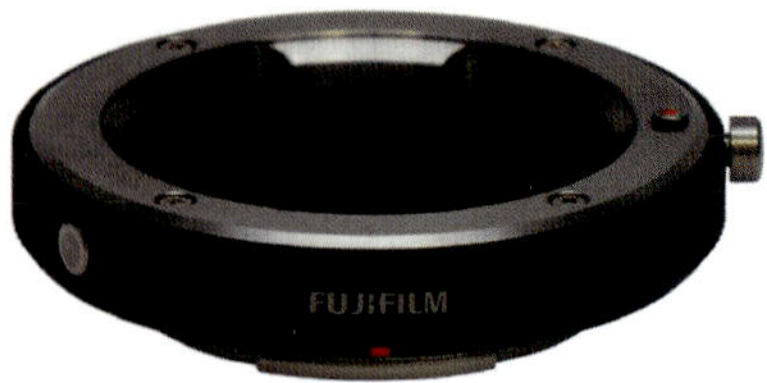

Fig. 178: Fujifilm's own **M-mount adapter** features electronic contacts and a function button that opens the camera's adapter menu.

| TIP 130 | Electronic smart adapters |

Electronic smart adapters have been designed for modern third-party lenses like the Canon EF system. These lenses have electronic contacts and they communicate with the camera body to offer functions such as autofocus, electronic aperture control, and optical image stabilization (OIS). They also get their power from the camera body.

Connecting modern EF lenses on the X-T5 with a simple mechanical adapter turns out to be a frustrating experience. You cannot change the aperture while the lens is attached to the Fuji camera, there's no autofocus, the OIS doesn't work, and there is no EXIF data transmission to the camera.

The solution: use an electronic smart adapter. Most smart adapters are designed to adapt Canon EF (and other EF-compatible) lenses, and there are also adapters for Nikon DSLR lenses.

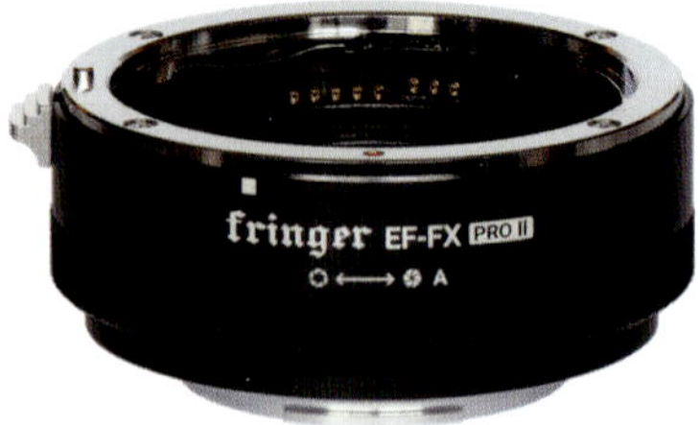

Fig. 179: The **Fringer EF-FX** was one of the first EF-to-XF smart adapters. You can also get the EF-FX Pro version (pictured here) with an integrated electronic aperture ring.

An ideal smart adapter should include the following features:

- Full electronic aperture control.

- Autofocus support (PDAF/CDAF, AF-S, AF-C, face detection, video, etc.).

- Support for built-in optical image stabilizers (OIS) in adapted lenses.

- Support for IBIS with adapted lenses that don't have built-in OIS.

- EXIF data transmission and recording (focal length, aperture, adapted lens model, serial number, etc.).

- Digital lens correction data transmission and conversion (chromatic aberrations, distortion, vignetting).

- Compatible with most or all lenses of the adapted system, including popular third-party offerings like Sigma or Tamron EF lenses.

- Frequent firmware updates to improve and maintain compatibility. New firmware updates should be easy to install from macOS and Windows computers. Alternatively, there should be support for adapter firmware upgrades via the lens firmware upgrade procedure of X-series cameras.

Smart adapters are available from several vendors. Some even offer built-in focal length reducers (like the Speed Booster) to project the full image circle of the adapted full-frame lens on the smaller APS-C sensor of the X-mount camera.

2.8 WIRELESS REMOTE CONTROL AND TETHERING

Fuji's Camera Remote app and the new XApp work with wireless iOS and Android devices, and they allow you to remotely control your camera by providing a live view image and a touch-screen interface to set the focus point, change exposure parameters, and release the shutter.

TIP 131	Using XApp or the Camera Remote app

You can control the X-T5 from an Android or iOS device running Fuji's Camera Remote app or the newer XApp. To use one of these free apps, you must first download and install them on your smartphone or tablet. You can find download links, instructions, and additional information online [93].

Here's how these apps work with iOS devices (it shouldn't be much different for Android users):

- Pair your camera to your smartphone or tablet via Bluetooth (NETWORK/USB SETTING > Bluetooth/SMART-PHONE SETTINGS > PAIRING REGISTRATION) and make sure that Bluetooth is switched on in your device. This allows your smart device to automatically connect to your camera's Wi-Fi network.

- Open the app, make sure your X-T5 is selected, and establish a Wi-Fi connection with the camera. Using the new XApp, this is done by selecting "Image Acquisition / Photography" in the app. The mobile device can now assume control over the camera and display a live view image along with options to adjust shutter speed, aperture, and exposure compensation. There's also a virtual shutter button and a basic shooting menu that allows you to adjust parameters like ISO, film simulation, white balance, macro, flash mode, or self-timer.

- To autofocus on a specific part of the live view image, double-tap on it with your finger. Focus will be confirmed with a green rectangle. If no focus lock can be established, the rectangle will appear in red.

- Adjust your exposure parameters as required. The brightness of the live view will change accordingly. Please note there's no live histogram.

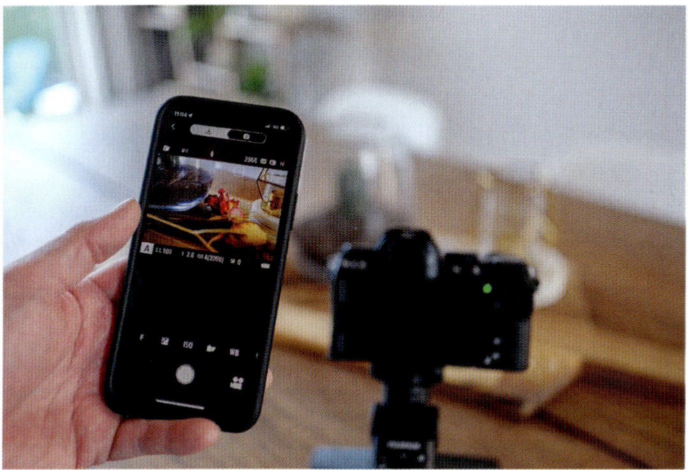

Fig. 180: **Camera Remote** and the newer **XApp** offer a simple interface to control your camera with a smartphone or tablet. To autofocus, double tap on a specific part of the WYSIWYG live view and wait for the green confirmation rectangle to appear. Sadly, there is no live histogram, and you can't magnify the live view. There is a rudimentary shooting menu and a virtual shutter button. You can also review images and transfer JPEGs to your mobile device.

Thanks to Bluetooth, location data and the current date and time can automatically be synchronized from your smartphone or tablet. There is also the benefit of a simple Bluetooth-based remote shutter release function, and there's the possibility to automatically obtain and install camera firmware updates. You can find more information on the new XApp online [94].

<table>
<tr><td>TIP 132</td><td>Streaming the live view via HDMI</td></tr>
</table>

The X-T5 offers HDMI live streaming, meaning that the contents of the live view (electronic viewfinder or LCD) can be transmitted to a monitor, TV, or projector via the camera's HDMI output. All you must do is connect the camera's Micro-HDMI jack to a suitable monitor with a digital input (HDMI, DVI, etc.). Real-time streaming will start automatically once the connection is established.

This is a useful feature for workshops, product demonstrations, or professional productions, where customers can watch on a monitor what the photographer is seeing in the live view.

You can also use the HDMI live view output to connect the camera to an HD frame-grabber, which is then connected to your computer. With this setup, you can make videos and screenshots of the live view.

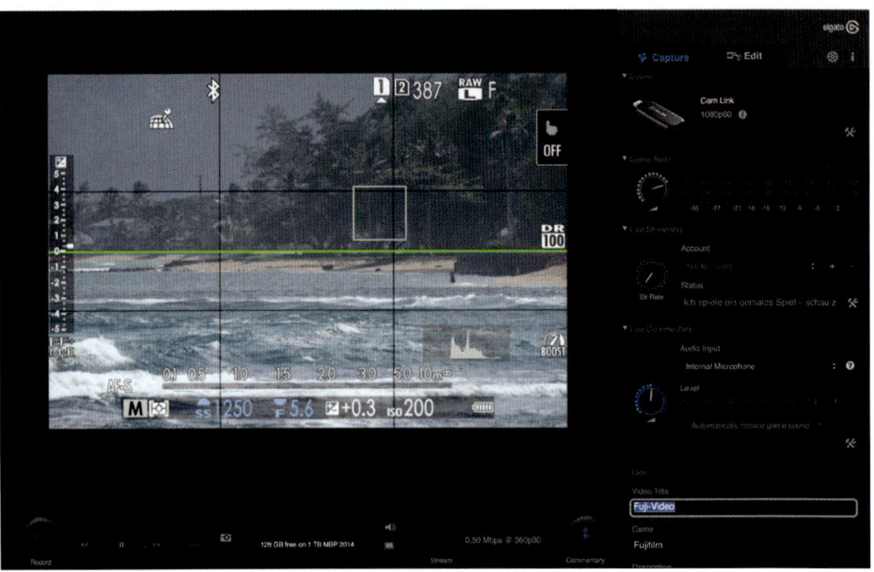

Fig. 181: The camera screenshots in this book were created by streaming the live view's HDMI output to my MacBook Pro, where I used **Elgato Cam Link** [95] to capture screenshots. You can also use this hardware and software to create 60 fps HD video recordings of your camera's live view.

Personally, I also use HDMI and Cam Link for video conferencing. However, there's an alternative way to use the USB port for this: Selecting USB WEBCAM in the NETWORK/USB SETTING > CONNECTION MODE menu allows you to stream video via the USB port to video conferencing software (like Zoom) on your computer.

Tethered shooting via USB or Wi-Fi	TIP 133

Tethered shooting involves controlling the camera via a computer that is connected (tethered) to the camera via a USB cable or a Wi-Fi connection.

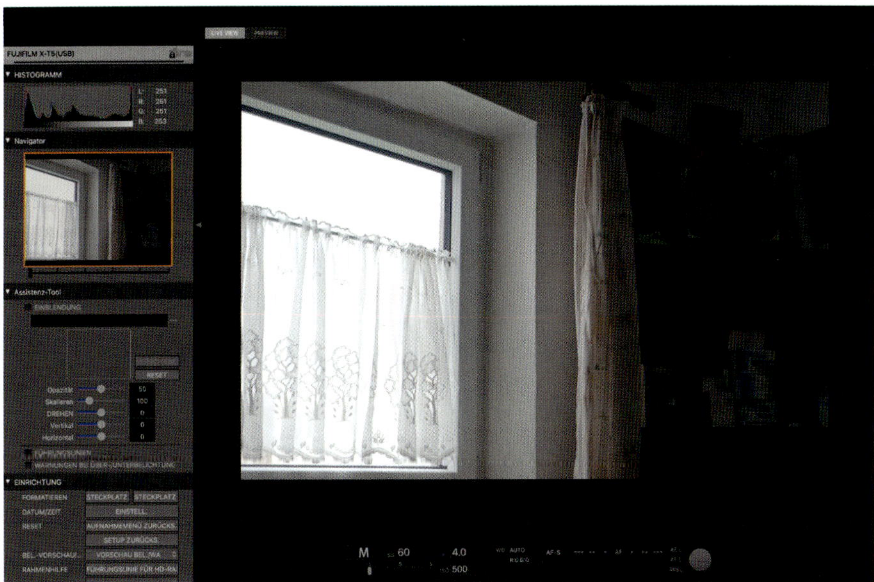

Fig. 182: The **Tether Shooting Plug-in Pro for Adobe Lightroom** includes a live-view image and comprehensive control over the camera. Features include color histograms, focus stacking, expanded bracketing, and the possibility to enter copyright information. You can also save and load full camera configurations.

To use USB tethering, you must select either USB TETHER SHOOTING AUTO or USB TETHER SHOOTING FIXED in the NETWORK/USB SETTING > CONNECTION MODE menu. This way, the camera is either recognizing (AUTO) or even forcing (FIXED) a computer connection via USB, yielding control to compatible tethering software on the computer. For Wi-Fi tethering [96], select WIRELESS TETHER SHOOTING FIXED.

Fujifilm X Acquire [97] is a simple freebie app for macOS and Windows that saves images to a hot folder from which other apps can obtain them. It also allows you to backup and restore full camera settings on your Mac or PC.

The **Fujifilm Tether Shooting Plug-in** [98] and **Tether Shooting Plug-in Pro** [99] are plug-ins for Lightroom/ACR. The Pro version offers shooting with a remote live view and remote control over most of the camera's settings.

In addition to that, **Capture One Pro** [100] also adds direct tethering support thanks to the partnership between Fujifilm and PhaseOne that was revealed in 2018.

2.9 ANYTHING ELSE?

Hopefully, this book has answered many of your questions that went beyond the user manual of your camera. However, this isn't the end: you can read my old X-Pert Corner blog, participate in Fuji X forums, join a virtual Fuji X Secrets workshop or book personal 1:1 training via Zoom.

<table>
<tr><td>Forums, blogs, magazines, and workshops</td><td>TIP 134</td></tr>
</table>

- High-resolution versions of some images in this book are available on Flickr [101].

- At Fuji X Secrets [102], you will find articles and reviews covering specific features, firmware, and products for X-series cameras.

- My X-Pert Corner blog [103] covers a variety of topics about the Fujifilm X series. You will find everything from service articles that go beyond this book to "First Look" previews of cameras and lenses.

- There are two online forums that focus on Fujifilm's X series: The Original Fuji X Forum [104] and The Ultimate Fuji X Forum [105].

- I am a regular contributor of gear-related articles in FUJI-LOVE [106], a dedicated monthly online magazine for all things Fuji X.

- Books, blogs, and forums are great, but what about a more personal touch? You can book a personal 1:1 training session that can answer your Fujifilm X-related questions. Thanks to my virtual Zoom setup with two screens, live-view streaming and 3.3K screen sharing with pixel-peeping quality, we can cover all topics, from gear via ISO-less exposure and focusing to RAW processing. Anything goes.

ONLINE REFERENCES

Websites are not run by Rocky Nook and are subject to change without our knowledge.

If necessary, we will update these references. For an updated version of this reference list, please download the available document at:

http://www.rockynook.com/fuji-x-t5-online-references/

[1]   https://fujifilm-dsc.com/en/manual/x-t5/
[2]   https://fujifilm-x.com/global/support/download/
[3]   https://fujifilm-x.com/global/support/download/procedure-x-interchangeable-ver2/
[4]   https://www.youtube.com/watch?v=xMJwqcll-fg
[5]   https://digitalcamera-support-en.fujifilm.com/digitalcameraeng pcdetail?aid=000003848&_ga=2.49993830.1779550970.167786 3511-1749972570.1672392523
[6]   https://digitalcamera-support-en.fujifilm.com/digitalcameraeng pcdetail?aid=000003852&_ga=2.23844730.1779550970.167786 3511-1749972570.1672392523
[7]   https://app.fujifilm-dsc.com/en/manual/camera_remote/
[8]   https://app.fujifilm-dsc.com/en/camera_remote/fw_update.html
[9]   https://fujifilm-x.com/en-us/support/compatibility/cameras/x-t5/
[10]   https://en.wikipedia.org/wiki/Crop_factor
[11]   https://en.wikipedia.org/wiki/Image_stabilization
[12]   https://en.wikipedia.org/wiki/Motion_blur
[13]   https://en.wikipedia.org/wiki/Panning_(camera)
[14]   https://en.wikipedia.org/wiki/Depth_of_field
[15]   https://en.wikipedia.org/wiki/Circle_of_confusion
[16]   https://www.cambridgeincolour.com/tutorials/diffraction-photography.htm
[17]   https://en.wikipedia.org/wiki/Vignetting
[18]   https://en.wikipedia.org/wiki/Distortion_(optics)
[19]   https://en.wikipedia.org/wiki/Chromatic_aberration
[20]   https://en.wikipedia.org/wiki/Exif
[21]   https://app.fujifilm-dsc.com/en/manual/camera_remote/usage/remote_release/index.html
[22]   https://app.fujifilm-dsc.com/en/manual/camera_remote/
[23]   https://app.fujifilm-dsc.com/en/manual/camera_remote/usage/live_view/
[24]   https://en.wikipedia.org/wiki/Exif
[25]   https://en.wikipedia.org/wiki/Dark-frame_subtraction
[26]   https://fujifilm-x.com/en-us/support/download/software/x-acquire/

[27] https://en.wikipedia.org/wiki/Raw_image_format
[28] https://en.wikipedia.org/wiki/JPEG
[29] https://fujifilm-x.com/global/support/download/software/raw-file-converter-ex-powered-by-silkypix/
[30] https://en.wikipedia.org/wiki/WYSIWYG
[31] https://en.wikipedia.org/wiki/Live_preview
[32] https://en.wikipedia.org/wiki/Zone_System
[33] https://www.cambridgeincolour.com/tutorials/histograms1.htm
[34] https://www.cambridgeincolour.com/tutorials/histograms2.htm
[35] https://en.wikipedia.org/wiki/Depth_of_field
[36] https://en.wikipedia.org/wiki/Motion_blur
[37] https://en.wikipedia.org/wiki/Aperture_priority
[38] https://en.wikipedia.org/wiki/Aperture
[39] https://en.wikipedia.org/wiki/Depth_of_field
[40] https://www.cambridgeincolour.com/tutorials/diffraction-photography.htm
[41] https://en.wikipedia.org/wiki/Shutter_priority
[42] https://en.wikipedia.org/wiki/Shutter_speed
[43] https://en.wikipedia.org/wiki/Motion_blur
[44] https://en.wikipedia.org/wiki/Panning_(camera)
[45] https://en.wikipedia.org/wiki/Long-exposure_photography
[46] https://www.cambridgeincolour.com/tutorials/camera-shake.htm
[47] https://en.wikipedia.org/wiki/Image_stabilization
[48] https://en.wikipedia.org/wiki/Crop_factor
[49] https://en.wikipedia.org/wiki/Bracketing
[50] https://en.wikipedia.org/wiki/Dark-frame_subtraction
[51] https://en.wikipedia.org/wiki/Neutral-density_filter
[52] https://en.wikipedia.org/wiki/Film_speed#Digital_camera_ISO_speed_and_exposure_index
[53] https://www.flickr.com/photos/ricopfirstinger/sets/72177720306684079/
[54] https://www.iridientdigital.com/products/xtransformer.html
[55] https://fujifilm-x.com/en-us/products/software/x-raw-studio/
[56] https://en.wikipedia.org/wiki/Multi-exposure_HDR_capture
[57] https://fujifilm-x.com/en-us/products/software/x-raw-studio/
[58] https://en.wikipedia.org/wiki/Rolling_shutter
[59] https://fujifilm-x.com/global/support/download/software/pixel-shift-combiner/
[60] https://digital-photography-school.com/the-problem-with-the-focus-recompose-method/
[61] https://en.wikipedia.org/wiki/Hyperfocal_distance
[62] https://en.wikipedia.org/wiki/Circle_of_confusion
[63] https://www.youtube.com/watch?v=1z-rq4RM2go
[64] https://www.youtube.com/watch?v=rnkib7FZ8S8
[65] https://www.cambridgeincolour.com/tutorials/hyperfocal-distance.htm
[66] https://dl.fujifilm-x.com/global/products/accessories/mcex/pdf/macro-extension-x-global.pdf
[67] https://en.wikipedia.org/wiki/Depth_of_field

[68] https://www.cambridgeincolour.com/tutorials/diffraction-photography.htm

[69] https://photography.tutsplus.com/tutorials/how-to-calculate-the-sharpest-aperture-for-any-lens--cms-25153

[70] https://en.wikipedia.org/wiki/Focus_stacking

[71] https://www.heliconsoft.com/heliconsoft-products/helicon-focus/

[72] https://en.wikipedia.org/wiki/Panning_(camera)

[73] https://www.cambridgeincolour.com/tutorials/white-balance.htm

[74] https://en.wikipedia.org/wiki/Exif

[75] https://en.wikipedia.org/wiki/Gray_card

[76] https://fujifilm-x.com/global/support/download/software/x-raw-studio/

[77] https://en.wikipedia.org/wiki/Contrast_(vision)

[78] https://en.wikipedia.org/wiki/Colorfulness

[79] https://en.wikipedia.org/wiki/Color_space

[80] https://en.wikipedia.org/wiki/SRGB

[81] https://en.wikipedia.org/wiki/Adobe_RGB_color_space

[82] https://en.wikipedia.org/wiki/Gamut

[83] https://fujifilm-x.com/global/support/download/software/

[84] https://fujifilm-x.com/en-us/stories/fujifilm-x-raw-studio-features-users-guide/

[85] https://en.wikipedia.org/wiki/Through-the-lens_metering#Through_the_lens_flash_metering

[86] https://en.wikipedia.org/wiki/Neutral-density_filter

[87] https://en.wikipedia.org/wiki/Flash_synchronization

[88] https://en.wikipedia.org/wiki/Neutral-density_filter

[89] https://en.wikipedia.org/wiki/Red-eye_effect

[90] https://en.wikipedia.org/wiki/Catch_light

[91] https://en.wikipedia.org/wiki/Teleconverter

[92] https://fujifilm-x.com/global/support/compatibility/accessories/list-of-compatible-m-mount-lenses/

[93] https://app.fujifilm-dsc.com/en/manual/camera_remote/

[94] https://fujifilm-x.com/global/products/software/xapp/

[95] https://www.elgato.com/us/en/p/cam-link-4k

[96] https://app.fujifilm-dsc.com/en/tether/tether_wireless.html

[97] https://fujifilm-x.com/en-gb/stories/fujifilm-x-acquire-features-users-guide/

[98] https://fujifilm-x.com/en-us/products/software/adobe-photoshop-lightroom-tether-plugin/

[99] https://fujifilm-x.com/global/stories/fujifilm-tether-plug-in-pro-features/

[100] https://www.captureone.com/en

[101] https://www.flickr.com/photos/ricopfirstinger/sets/72177720306684079/

[102] https://fuji-x-secrets.net

[103] https://www.fujirumors.com/category/x-pert/

[104] https://www.fujix-forum.com

[105] https://www.fuji-x-forum.com

[106] https://fujilove.com

INDEX

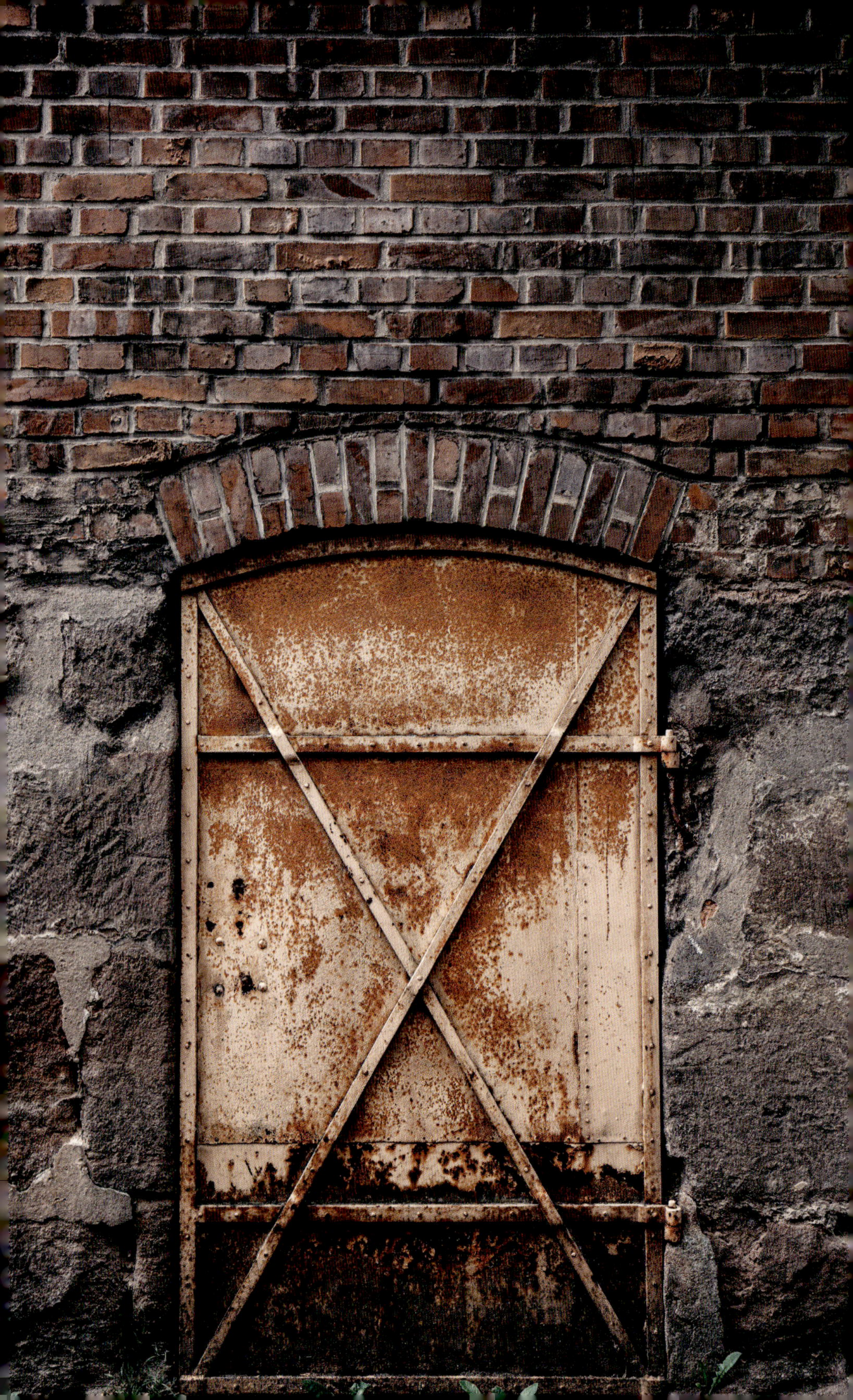